Designing and Interfaces with Figma
Second Edition

Elevate your design craft with UX/UI principles and create interactive prototypes

Fabio Staiano

‹packt›

BIRMINGHAM—MUMBAI

Designing and Prototyping Interfaces with Figma
Second Edition

Copyright © 2023 Packt Publishing

All rights reserved. No part of this book may be reproduced, stored in a retrieval system, or transmitted in any form or by any means, without the prior written permission of the publisher, except in the case of brief quotations embedded in critical articles or reviews.

Every effort has been made in the preparation of this book to ensure the accuracy of the information presented. However, the information contained in this book is sold without warranty, either express or implied. Neither the author, nor Packt Publishing or its dealers and distributors, will be held liable for any damages caused or alleged to have been caused directly or indirectly by this book.

Packt Publishing has endeavored to provide trademark information about all of the companies and products mentioned in this book by the appropriate use of capitals. However, Packt Publishing cannot guarantee the accuracy of this information.

Senior Publishing Product Manager: Larissa Pinto
Acquisition Editor – Peer Reviews: Jane D'Souza
Project Editor: Namrata Katare
Content Development Editor: Soham Amburle
Copy Editor: Safis Editing
Technical Editor: Karan Sonawane
Proofreader: Safis Editing
Indexer: Pratik Shirodkar
Presentation Designer: Rajesh Shirsath
Developer Relations Marketing Executive: Sohini Ghosh

First published: March 2022

Second edition: December 2023

Production reference: 1211223

Published by Packt Publishing Ltd.
Grosvenor House
11 St Paul's Square
Birmingham
B3 1RB, UK.

ISBN 978-1-83546-460-1

www.packt.com

Contributors

About the author

Fabio Staiano is an experienced Interface Designer and Figma Community Advocate from Italy. After having been part of the Italian creative agency Geko for several years, he later became a company partner, creating digital products for well-known brands and running local events for the creative community. He then began his career in Education in 2016, at *The Guru Lab*, teaching students about user interface and web design. In 2019, eager to embrace new horizons, he honed his development skills at the *Apple Developer Academy*, specializing in frontend development while launching various apps and boilerplate projects. Now, as a consultant for IT projects, he provides tailored solutions, and continues to educate at design academies. His journey embodies a fusion of design, education, and advocacy, showcasing his enduring commitment to his craft and the wider design community.

To my family, to whom I owe everything.

Special thanks to Gerel Burgustina, Fabio Di Corleto, and Alessia Saviano, for their precious contribution to the project.

About the reviewer

Reony Tonneyck has been a designer for 15 years in various domains, such as Cybersecurity, Education, and Data Analytics. Most recently, he led design systems at *Khan Academy*. Apart from that, he has also led design system efforts at multiple start-ups, alongside leading product design and contributing to front-end development.

Figma is where he found a new home within the design community. Eventually, he co-founded Figma's DC area community group for his "passion project" and proudly became an official Figma Community Advocate.

I couldn't have contributed to this book without my wife putting my son to bed each night. Thank you, Adalia.

Learn more on Discord

To join the Discord community for this book – where you can share feedback, ask questions to the author, and learn about new releases – follow the QR code below:

```
https://packt.link/figma
```

Table of Contents

Preface	xvii

Part 1: Introduction to Figma and FigJam — 1

Chapter 1: Exploring Figma and Transitioning from Other Tools — 3

What is Figma? 4
- Why Figma? • 5
- Creating an account • 6
- Choosing the right plan • 6

Desktop app vs web app 8
- Setting up Font Installer • 9

Transitioning to Figma from Sketch and Adobe XD 9
- Coming from Sketch • 9
- How difficult is it to go from Sketch to Figma? • 10
- Coming from Adobe XD • 11
- A quick final thought • 13

Exploring the welcome screen 13
- Recents • 14
- Drafts • 14
- Community • 14
- Teams and projects • 14

Figma and FigJam files • 17

Account and notifications • 18

Summary 19

Chapter 2: Structuring Moodboards, Personas, and User Flows within FigJam — 21

Exploring ideas and collaborating in FigJam 22

Exploring FigJam • 22

　A – Select and Hand tool • 23

　B – Marker • 24

　C – Sticky Notes • 24

　D – Shapes and Connectors • 25

　E – Text • 25

　F – Sections • 25

　G – Tables • 26

　H – Stamps and Reactions • 26

　I – Widgets, Stickers, Templates, and more • 27

Brainstorming with others • 28

Moving to the next step • 31

Creating moodboards and personas in FigJam 33

Research phase • 33

Conducting competitive analysis • 34

Starting a moodboard • 35

Creating user personas • 36

Building user flow in FigJam 38

The golden path • 39

Be the user • 44

Summary 44

Chapter 3: Getting to Know Your Design Environment — 47

Starting a new design project 48

Design files • 48

Frames and groups • 50

Interface overview • 52

Getting used to the toolbar 54

Main tools • 54

A – Menu • 54

B – Move • 55

C – Scale • 55

D – Frame • 56

E – Section/Slice • 56

F, G, H, I, J, and K – Shapes • 57

L – Place image/video… • 57

M – Pen • 58

N – Pencil • 58

O – Text • 59

P – Resources • 59

Q – Hand • 59

R – Comment • 60

Settings and more • 60

S – File title • 60

T – active users • 62

U – Share • 62

V – Dev mode • 62

W – Present • 63

X – Zoom/view • 63

Quick shortcuts • 63

Exploring the left panel 65

Layers and Pages • 65

Assets • 66

Exploring the right panel 67

Design • 67

Prototype • 69

Inactive state • 70

With an Active selection • 71

Help Center • 72

Summary 72

Chapter 4: Wireframing a Mobile-First Experience Using Vector Shapes   75

Evolving the idea to a Wireframe 76

What is a wireframe? • 76

Why mobile-first? • 77

Playing with Shapes in Figma 78

Basic shapes • 78

Combining shapes • 82

Advanced vectors with the Pen tool 86

What are vector graphics? • 86

Discovering the Pen tool • 87

Vector networks • 90

Developing the app structure 92

Flow to skeleton • 92

Shaping the interface • 95

What's next? 100

Summary 101

Part 2: Exploring Components, Styles, and Variants　103

Chapter 5: Designing Consistently Using Grids, Colors, and Typography　105

Getting started with Grids 106

Grids are everywhere • 106

Guides and layout grids • 108

Working with Typography, Colors, and Effects 112

Typography matters • 112

Choosing a Palette • 118

A – Color modes • 119

B – Blend modes • 121

C – Color palette • 122

G – Eyedropper tool • 122

H – Color models • 122

I – Color styles • 122

Creating effects • 123

Introducing Styles 125

Preparing your file • 125

Creating and managing grid styles • 126

Creating and managing text styles • 130

Creating and managing color and effect styles • 134

Summary 138

Chapter 6: Creating a Responsive Mobile Interface Using Auto Layout　141

Introducing auto layout 142

What is auto layout? • 142

A – Direction • 144

B – Gap • 144

      C – Padding • 145

      D – Alignment • 146

    Adding, removing, and rearranging elements • 147

    Nesting auto layout • 149

Resizing and constraints 150

    Resizing elements • 150

    Differences with constraints • 154

Applying auto layout to our interface 156

    Shaping a button • 156

    Completing the view • 167

Summary 174

Chapter 7: Building Components and Variants in a Collaborative Workspace   177

Creating and organizing components 178

    What are components? • 178

    Building a view using components • 182

      A – top navigation menu • 184

      B – main carousel • 187

      C – content cards • 191

      D – repeated rows • 194

Extending components with variants 198

    Why use variants? • 199

    Setting up our Content Detail view • 199

    Implementing variants • 203

Multiplayer mode, libraries, and version control 211

    Working with multiplayer features • 211

    Managing libraries • 213

    Preserving your work with version history • 217

Summary 220

Chapter 8: User Interface Design on Tablet, Desktop, and the Web — 223

Discovering responsive design 224

   Design to code with fluid layouts • 224

   Mobile first • 226

Adjusting the interface for tablets 234

   Introducing breakpoints • 235

      Login view • 238

      Sign Up view • 239

      Home view • 239

      Content Detail view • 242

Adjusting the interface for the web and desktop 244

   Scaling up to the web and desktop • 245

   Polishing details • 253

Summary 256

Part 3: Prototyping and Sharing — 259

Chapter 9: Prototyping with Transitions, Smart Animate, and Interactive Components — 261

Mastering transitions and triggers 262

   Moving between frames with transitions • 263

   Exploring triggers • 271

      On click/On tap • 272

      On drag • 272

      While hovering • 273

      While pressing • 273

      Key/Gamepad • 273

      Mouse enter/Mouse leave • 273

      Mouse down/Mouse up • 273

      After delay • 274

Animating with smart animate 274

What is smart animate? • 274

Getting advanced with smart animate • 276

Structuring interactive components 279

What are interactive components? • 280

Creating interactive components • 281

Creating interactive overflows and overlays 288

Making our view scrollable with overflows • 289

Creating interface overlays • 292

Summary 295

Chapter 10: Testing and Sharing Your Prototype in Browsers and Real Devices   297

Viewing your interactive prototype 298

Running prototypes on desktop/web • 298

Using the inline preview • 305

Running the prototype on a smartphone/tablet • 305

Sharing your prototype with others 309

Linking the prototype and managing permissions • 309

Embedding the prototype • 311

Working with feedback and reviews 313

Viewers and comments • 314

Structuring flows • 316

Advanced user testing • 319

Summary 321

Chapter 11: Exporting Assets and Managing the Handover Process   323

Exporting from Figma 324

What formats are supported? • 324

Single- and multiple-asset export • 325

Exploring Dev Mode 329

Table of Contents   xv

Switching to Dev Mode 331
Overviewing the file 333
    Design to code • 334
    Extending Dev Mode • 337
Handing over the project for development 338
    What's next? • 339
    Documenting, reiterating, and improving • 340
Summary 342

Chapter 12: Discovering Resources, Plugins, and Widgets in the Figma Community   345

Exploring the Figma Community 346
    Accessing and publishing to the Figma Community • 347
    Starting off with FigJam and templates • 350
Finding useful resources 351
    UI kits and design systems • 351
    More design resources • 354
Extending Figma with plugins 357
    Running and managing plugins • 357
Suggested plugins 362
    Iconify • 362
        Content Reel • 363
        Clay Mockups 3D • 364
        Contrast • 365
    LottieFiles • 366
    Speeding up your flow with AI • 366
    FigGPT • 368
    Figma Autoname • 369
    Wireframe Designer • 370
    Magician • 371
    Using widgets in Figma and FigJam • 373

Understanding the difference between widgets and plugins • 373

Suggested widgets • 375

Checklist (Figma/FigJam) • 375

Jira/Asana (Figma/FigJam) • 376

Giphy Stickers (Figma/FigJam) • 377

Jambot (FigJam) • 378

Summary 379

Chapter 13: Going Advanced with Variables and Conditional Prototyping   381

Understanding variables 382

When to use variables • 382

Variables, collections, and modes • 384

Going responsive and multilingual with variables • 397

Pushing further with conditional prototyping 409

The logic behind conditional prototyping • 409

Advanced prototyping with variables and conditionals • 411

Summary 422

Other Books You May Enjoy   427

Index   433

Preface

Being a driving force in the design tools market, Figma makes everything easier by bringing unique innovations and opening up real-time collaboration possibilities, so it comes as no surprise that so many designers have decided to switch from other tools to Figma.

In this book, you will be challenged to design a user interface for a responsive mobile application by researching and understanding user needs, and mastering all this in a step-by-step fashion by exploring the theory first and gradually moving on to practice. Your learning journey will cover the basics of user experience research with FigJam and the process of creating a complete design using Figma tools and features such as components, variants, auto layout, and much more. You will also learn how to prototype your design and expand your possibilities with Figma Community resources such as templates and plugins. As you progress, an advanced chapter will introduce you to using variables and conditional prototyping to add a higher level of interactivity and functionality to your designs.

By the end of this book, you will have a solid understanding of the user interface workflow, be able to manage the essential Figma tools, and know how to properly organize your workflow in Figma.

Who this book is for

This book is tailored for aspiring UI/UX designers eager to dive into Figma, as well as established designers aiming to transition to Figma from other design tools. It will guide you through the comprehensive process of creating a robust prototype for a responsive interface, harnessing all the tools and features that Figma has to offer. Hence, this book is ideal for UX and UI designers, product and graphic designers, and anyone looking to thoroughly understand the complete design process from the outset.

What this book covers

Chapter 1, Exploring Figma and Transitioning from Other Tools, serves as an introduction to Figma and its mission, explains the main differences between its desktop and web apps, explores the Figma welcome screen interface, and provides guidance on how to migrate to Figma from Sketch and Adobe XD.

Chapter 2, Structuring Moodboards, Personas, and User Flows within FigJam, is about how to work in FigJam, an additional tool implemented in Figma, using it to collect and analyze data in the early stages of design work.

Chapter 3, Getting to Know Your Design Environment, provides an overview of Figma tools in the toolbar, left and right panel functionalities, and instructions on how to start a new project from scratch.

Chapter 4, Wireframing a Mobile-First Experience Using Vector Shapes, focuses on defining the structure of the application and building its wireframe using Figma's shape and vector tools.

Chapter 5, Designing Consistently Using Grids, Colors, and Typography, dives into styles, a powerful feature that makes it easy to manage and reuse grids, typography, colors, and effects throughout a design project.

Chapter 6, Creating a Responsive Mobile Interface Using Auto Layout, introduces auto layout, one of Figma's advanced features, and provides guidance on how to best apply it using resizing and constraints.

Chapter 7, Building Components and Variants in a Collaborative Workspace, focuses on creating components and variants, both of which are crucial functions in Figma, as well as exploring other tools such as multiplayer, libraries, and version control.

Chapter 8, User Interface Design on Tablet, Desktop, and the Web, explores the basic principles of responsive design and focuses on how to adjust the interface design for different devices and screen resolutions.

Chapter 9, Prototyping with Transitions, Smart Animate, and Interactive Components, explores various prototyping possibilities and functions in Figma, from basic to more advanced.

Chapter 10, Testing and Sharing Your Prototype in Browsers and Real Devices, covers all the ways to view and test an interactive prototype, as well as how to share it with others and work with feedback.

Chapter 11, Exporting Assets and Managing the Handover Process, focuses on preparing design project assets for further development, along with providing an overview of the Dev Mode.

Chapter 12, Discovering Resources, Plugins, and Widgets in the Figma Community, covers the Figma Community and how to navigate it to locate the right files, widgets, and plugins that can improve your design workflow, side by side with AI-based add-ons.

Chapter 13, Going Advanced with Variables and Conditional Prototyping, introduces you to variables and conditional prototyping in Figma, aiming to add more interactivity to your designs, and making your prototypes more dynamic and functional.

To get the most out of this book

You will need any modern browser to use the web version of Figma, or alternatively, you can install the Figma desktop app on your computer. The book provides a step-by-step guide to designing an application interface, as well as recommendations for self-practice. To get the most out of the book, it is recommended that you follow the hands-on steps in the following chapters and devote some time to practicing your skills in Figma on your own.

To follow along with this book, you will need one of the following Figma apps:

- Figma – Web app (Chrome, Firefox, Safari, Edge) or desktop app (Windows, macOS)
- Figma – Mobile app (iOS, Android)
- FigJam – Included within Figma or iPad (standalone app)

In *Chapter 10, Testing and Sharing Your Prototype in Browsers and Real Devices*, you will be asked to test your design on devices with smaller screens, and to do so, you will need to download the Figma app (available for iOS and Android) on your smartphone and/or tablet.

Download the color images

We also provide a PDF file that has color images of the screenshots/diagrams used in this book. You can download it here: https://packt.link/gbp/9781835464601.

Conventions used

There are a number of text conventions used throughout this book.

Code in text: Indicates code words in text, database table names, folder names, filenames, file extensions, pathnames, dummy URLs, user input, and Twitter handles. Here is an example: "Create a new text layer in auto-width mode (with a simple click) anywhere inside the **Login** frame and enter Login."

Bold: Indicates a new term, an important word, or words that you see onscreen. For instance, words in menus or dialog boxes appear in **bold**. Here is an example: "In the **Design** panel, you may have noticed a section not yet mentioned, namely, **Effects**."

> **Important** notes appear like this

Get in touch

Feedback from our readers is always welcome.

General feedback: Email feedback@packtpub.com and mention the book's title in the subject of your message. If you have questions about any aspect of this book, please email us at questions@packtpub.com.

Errata: Although we have taken every care to ensure the accuracy of our content, mistakes do happen. If you have found a mistake in this book, we would be grateful if you reported this to us. Please visit http://www.packtpub.com/submit-errata, click **Submit Errata**, and fill in the form.

Piracy: If you come across any illegal copies of our works in any form on the internet, we would be grateful if you would provide us with the location address or website name. Please contact us at copyright@packtpub.com with a link to the material.

If you are interested in becoming an author: If there is a topic that you have expertise in and you are interested in either writing or contributing to a book, please visit http://authors.packtpub.com.

Share your thoughts

Once you've read *Designing and Prototyping Interfaces with Figma*, we'd love to hear your thoughts! Scan the QR code below to go straight to the Amazon review page for this book and share your feedback.

https://packt.link/r/1835464602

Your review is important to us and the tech community and will help us make sure we're delivering excellent quality content.

Download a free PDF copy of this book

Thanks for purchasing this book!

Do you like to read on the go but are unable to carry your print books everywhere? Is your eBook purchase not compatible with the device of your choice?

Don't worry, now with every Packt book you get a DRM-free PDF version of that book at no cost.

Read anywhere, any place, on any device. Search, copy, and paste code from your favorite technical books directly into your application.

The perks don't stop there, you can get exclusive access to discounts, newsletters, and great free content in your inbox daily

Follow these simple steps to get the benefits:

1. Scan the QR code or visit the link below

https://packt.link/free-ebook/9781835464601

2. Submit your proof of purchase
3. That's it! We'll send your free PDF and other benefits to your email directly

Part 1
Introduction to Figma and FigJam

In this part, we'll introduce you to Figma and take the first step in using it by building your first wireframe. Also, we will be exploring FigJam, which is a collaborative space where you can run a whole design process.

This part comprises the following chapters:

- *Chapter 1, Exploring Figma and Transitioning from Other Tools*
- *Chapter 2, Structuring Moodboards, Personas, and User Flows within FigJam*
- *Chapter 3, Getting to Know Your Design Environment*
- *Chapter 4, Wireframing a Mobile-First Experience Using Vector Shapes*

1

Exploring Figma and Transitioning from Other Tools

Whether you are taking your first steps in design or already have some experience in the field, the tool you choose significantly influences your design process and creative expression. It's not just about knowing all the functions for professional use; it's also about aligning with the tool's philosophy, recognizing the benefits it offers, and ensuring it supports your growth as a professional. Here's where Figma shines. A standout feature of Figma is its multiplayer functionality, which allows real-time collaboration and fosters a seamless workflow between designers. This aspect, among others, sets it apart in the competitive landscape of design tools, aligning well with the professional growth and collaborative spirit inherent in the design community.

Figma is one of the most advanced design tools available, continually introducing new features and enhancements. This commitment to advancement has transformed Figma into more than just a tool—it's an indispensable assistant for numerous designers. In this chapter, you will learn how Figma manages to consistently push the envelope and why it has become the favorite tool for many in the design community.

Figma is open to everyone and very flexible in many ways, allowing for personalized usage and adaptability to various design needs. It offers a variety of plans, including a free one, which is perfect for beginners in design and with no huge limits. Figma also has web and desktop applications, each of which has its own benefits. This chapter contains detailed information about all of these and will help you to make your own choices. Here, you will also learn how to switch to Figma from other tools, namely Sketch and Adobe XD.

After that, we will look at how Figma presents you with a welcome screen, where you will explore all the buttons, toolbars, and areas, such as drafts, teams, projects, and Community. It may seem overwhelming at first, but don't worry; we'll go over all the topics step by step. So, by the end of this chapter, you'll be ready to start putting Figma into practice!

In this chapter, we are going to cover the following main topics:

- Introducing Figma and its mission
- The difference between the desktop and web apps
- Transitioning to Figma from Sketch and Adobe XD
- Everything about the welcome screen

What is Figma?

You may have already heard about Figma, a powerful real-time collaborative tool known for its versatility in the design community. If you're new to this tool, get ready to learn what Figma is and what you need to know before using it.

Figure 1.1: Figma's icon

One of the most remarkable advantages of Figma lies in its accessibility. With the starter plan, you can use the majority of the tool's features without incurring any costs; all you need to do is go to `figma.com` and create a personal account.

You can download the Figma desktop app on your computer, but it also runs just as well in a modern web browser, allowing you to use it on any operating system: Windows, Mac, Linux, or even ChromeOS. Since Figma is cloud-based, you need to be connected to the internet to keep the auto-saved changes in your file. However, if you lose your internet connection and continue working, Figma will store every edit in your local cache. So, once you are back online, all the changes in your file will be synced immediately.

Why Figma?

There are many design apps available on the market right now that can be used to solve any kind of creative challenge, but Figma is surely the most popular at the moment. There are many good reasons for this. Let's talk about some of them:

- First, Figma allows designers and other teammates to work simultaneously in real time, which takes the collaborative workflow to a whole new level. This powerful feature makes Figma stand out among other tools because it improves not only design work but also the team collaboration process itself. "Collaboration is hard. We make it easier" is one of Figma's fundamental principles.
- Second, Figma has succeeded in bringing together a whole suite of design tools to provide an all-in-one solution. Figma covers just about everything you need to create a complex interface, from brainstorming and wireframing to prototyping and sharing assets. In addition to this, Figma goes beyond the design side of building a product and generates CSS, iOS, and Android code for developers to use.
- Finally, Figma is not only a design app but also a community platform for sharing ideas and solutions. Designers from all over the world use Figma, not only for interfaces but also for creating vector illustrations, graphic design for digital media, and team-building activities. You can even play board games in Figma; how crazy is that?! Yes, the Figma Community can definitely inspire you with tons of creative design projects, but it can also help you simplify your workflow by providing plugins and widgets created by other community members. You can even develop your own resources and share them with others!

Now you can see why Figma is a great tool, built for designers who want to stick to an effective and efficient workflow. However, keep in mind that neither Figma nor other tools will magically turn you into a good designer. Mastering a tool is not part of design, but it can save you time that you can reinvest into research and UX problem-solving.

Excited? Time to dive in and see it in action!

Creating an account

The first thing you need to do before using Figma is to sign up at `figma.com`. On the home page of the site, click the **Sign up** button and create an account with your email address and a password of your choice, or simply register using your Google account. That's it.

Figure 1.2: The Welcome popup

After registration, a few pop-up messages might appear with suggestions for creating a team. We will talk about teams later, but for now, just skip it and go straight to the **Welcome** screen.

Choosing the right plan

As mentioned earlier, you can use almost all of Figma's features while staying on the free Starter plan. This plan allows you to have unlimited cloud storage to keep your Figma and FigJam drafts, with unlimited pages and viewers, plus some additional advanced features, such as one team with three files, unlimited editors, and 30-day version history. This is more than enough if you are just making your first steps in UX/UI design or working on your own. You can be sure that there will be no hidden fees and you won't be forced to sign up for an expensive premium service.

If a **Starter** plan is not enough for you, Figma offers a few upgrade options: **Professional**, **Organization**, and **Enterprise**.

Chapter 1   7

Starter **Free** forever	**Professional** **$12 per editor/month** Billed annually or $15 month-to-month
Organization **$45 per editor/month** Annual billing only	**Enterprise** **$75 per editor/month** Annual billing only

Figure 1.3: Plans chart

- The **Professional** plan is perfect for small to medium-sized teams and allows you to have unlimited team projects, unlimited version history, shareable team libraries, Dev Mode, and custom file permissions. It can be billed monthly or annually – your choice.
- The **Organization** plan is suitable for larger or multiple teams and, in addition to all the benefits of Professional, provides file branching, advanced security, private plugins, shared fonts, and design system analytics. This plan is billed annually only.
- Lastly, Figma offers the **Enterprise** plan, tailored for sizable corporations with specific production and security requirements.

> **Note:**
> If you are a student or an educator, you can apply for a free Figma Professional license here: `figma.com/education`.

Once you've created your account, you can immediately start using Figma from any web browser you have. Google Chrome, Firefox, Safari, or Microsoft Edge—all of those work great with Figma. So, you can continue to use it on the web or download the desktop app if your computer is running on Windows or macOS.

Head over to figma.com/downloads if you prefer to have the desktop app (which has no exclusive features but better tab management and native support for local fonts). We'll see more about the differences between the two in the next section.

Desktop app vs web app

In fact, there are no technical differences between Figma's desktop and web applications—both give you almost the same experience. Figma won't open when you're offline whether you're using a desktop app or a web app. So, what's the point of downloading the application instead of using it in your favorite browser?

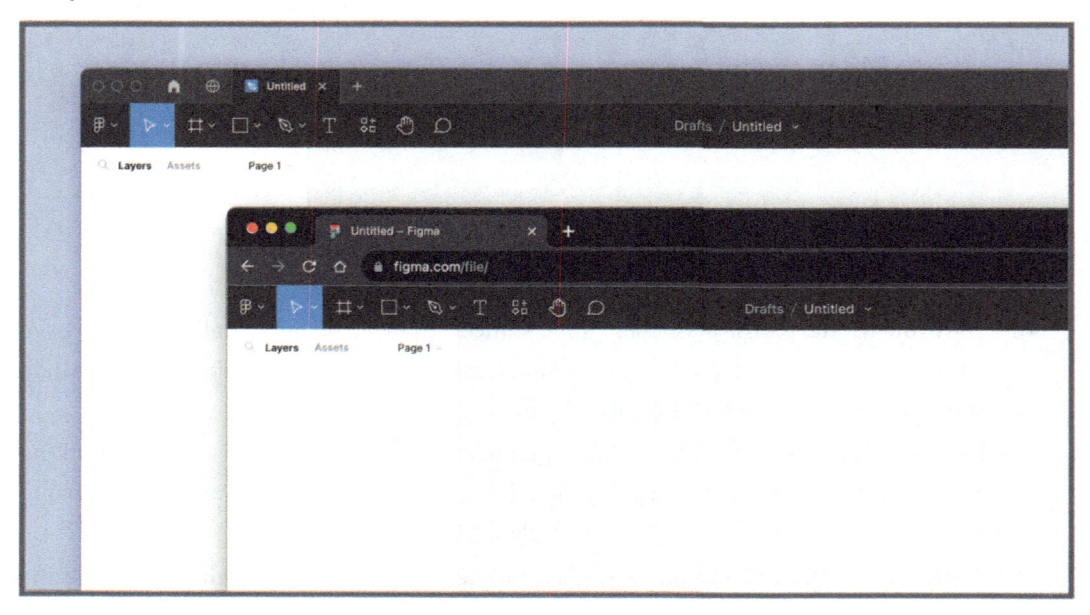

Figure 1.4: Web app and desktop app

If you prefer to minimize distractions in the environment while working on projects, you can go for the Figma desktop app. In addition to the clean interface of the app, you don't have to worry about all the other open tabs you might have in your browser, which could cause some crashes or slowdowns. Plus, with an actual native app, you can access the features of your operating system, such as setting up custom shortcuts or, on a Mac, quickly switching between apps using *Cmd* + *Tab*, or *Alt* + *Tab* for Windows. If you have an Apple silicon CPU, there are some performance advantages to using it as well.

One key difference between the web and desktop apps is the access to local fonts. In the desktop app, once installed, you can use all of your local fonts. However, in the web app, you only get access to Google Fonts (also available in the desktop app through the **Preferences** menu), and your local fonts won't appear in the list.

Setting up Font Installer

Fortunately, there's a workaround for accessing local fonts in the web app. Go to `figma.com/downloads` and download and install the macOS or Windows version of **Font Installer**. This quick step enables you to use all your favorite local fonts in the web app too. After installing the app on your computer, you can still access the Figma web app through your account and work with your files there. Figma will automatically save and sync all your changes across both versions, allowing you to work on your files even outside of your personal computer.

Whether you've chosen the web browser or the desktop app, it's time to give it a try, which you'll do very soon. If you have design files in other tools and wish to transfer them to Figma, you can follow the instructions in the next section.

Transitioning to Figma from Sketch and Adobe XD

This part of the chapter will be useful if you are not new to design, and you are thinking about switching to Figma from other tools. Switching to a new tool can be tricky and stressful, even if the transition seems smooth or your previous tool looks similar to the new one. Nobody likes to sacrifice an already-established and familiar routine for the sake of something risky and unfamiliar, something that will have to be explored and mastered all over again. But being a digital designer means adjusting to new technologies, tools, and specifications every day. In this part, you will find detailed instructions on how to switch from Adobe XD and Sketch to Figma as painlessly and quickly as possible. So, let's start without any hesitation.

Coming from Sketch

Sketch was a revolutionary tool that completely changed how we design today. It managed to combine everything that designers needed to create a UI in a simple and fast way. Designers used whatever tools they installed to create the UI, such as Corel, Illustrator, and Photoshop. Sketch was completely focused on the UX/UI-creating process, getting rid of everything unnecessary and providing a clean, simple, and ultra-fast tool.

Figma has taken this a step further by offering real-time collaboration and speeding up just about any challenge a designer might face. Be assured that you are making a great choice having decided to give it a try!

How difficult is it to go from Sketch to Figma?

The good news is that you don't have to worry about seeing a completely unfamiliar experience in Figma. Once you first open Figma, you can easily identify most of its features. Of course, there are still major differences between Sketch and Figma. Some of them will be completely new to you, but you will learn everything step by step in this book.

So, let's say you have a ton of projects created in Sketch. How do you transfer all the data from one tool to another? Unfortunately, Sketch doesn't have a magic button that says "Export to Figma"—no one wants users to leave their ecosystem. But don't worry, you have an import function in Figma, right on the first screen!

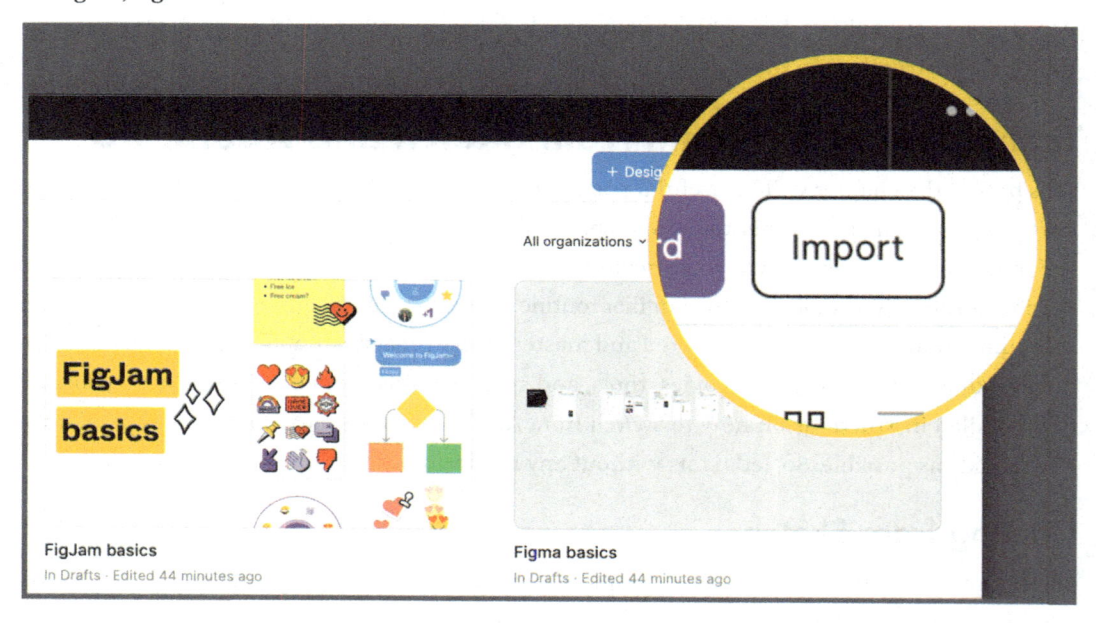

Figure 1.5: Import function

Just click on **Import**, select a `.sketch` file on your computer, and you're done. Alternatively, if you've already opened a new design file, access the menu bar at the top left, by clicking the Figma logo, then click **File | New from Sketch File**.

The loading time estimate will change depending on the size and complexity of the file. But after this simple operation, you will end up with a converted, fully working Figma file with all your Sketch pages, components, and layers. Nevertheless, no software automation is error-free, so the results of this transition may not be perfect.

If you convert simple shapes, vectors, and texts, you'll find everything as it should be in Figma. But if your source file contains a complex interface, or even a complete design system, it can take some time to create a satisfying Figma file. Sketch symbols will be converted into Figma components without any additional manipulation. But you will need to recreate styles and then apply them to your components to restore the original library. It is also better to double-check the entire file, clean up, reorganize layers, and so on.

Note:
Copy-pasting individual layers or artboards also works if you prefer to migrate manually, or you just need a few elements from the source file.

Coming from Adobe XD

After Sketch's revolution in the process of creating UIs, similar design tools began to come up in the market. Adobe upgraded Photoshop with artboards and additional interface design tools, but that still didn't help it gain popularity among interface designers. Therefore, the company released Adobe XD, an essential and simple tool built specifically for UX/UI. In fact, XD's standout line was its commitment to experience design.

The competition between Sketch and XD was quite intense from the beginning. Adobe XD did not have the same wide range of features as Sketch. But it was constantly updated and, most importantly, was included in the Creative Cloud subscription. It has also been integrated with other Creative Cloud software, such as Illustrator and Photoshop, making working with vectors and images easier than ever before.

When Figma was released, it managed to simplify everything from the ground up and speed up the workflow with collaboration features, variants, advanced prototyping, and auto layout. Now Figma is a driving force among design tools; it sets trends and introduces new ones.

So, now you may be wondering how easy it is to migrate all your files from the entire Adobe ecosystem to Figma. Well, this can be tricky since Figma doesn't have an import function for your .xd files like there is for Sketch.

The complexity of the transition from XD to Figma really depends on the content of the source file. If you don't need to transfer components, styles, or even raster images (JPEG, PNG, and so on), the fastest way is to copy and paste artboards individually from XD to Figma, or export elements in SVG format to import them into Figma.

The end result of these manipulations will be visually similar to the content from the original file, but the functionality from one tool to another will not be transferred. In most cases, this is not enough, and you will have to spend additional time manually rebuilding the base, renaming and organizing layers, creating components and styles, and prototyping your interface.

If you can't just let your old projects go, or you don't have time to rebuild the file to make it correct for use in Figma, there is an unofficial workaround. Go to `magicul.io` and select the from **Adobe XD** to **Figma** option in the converter.

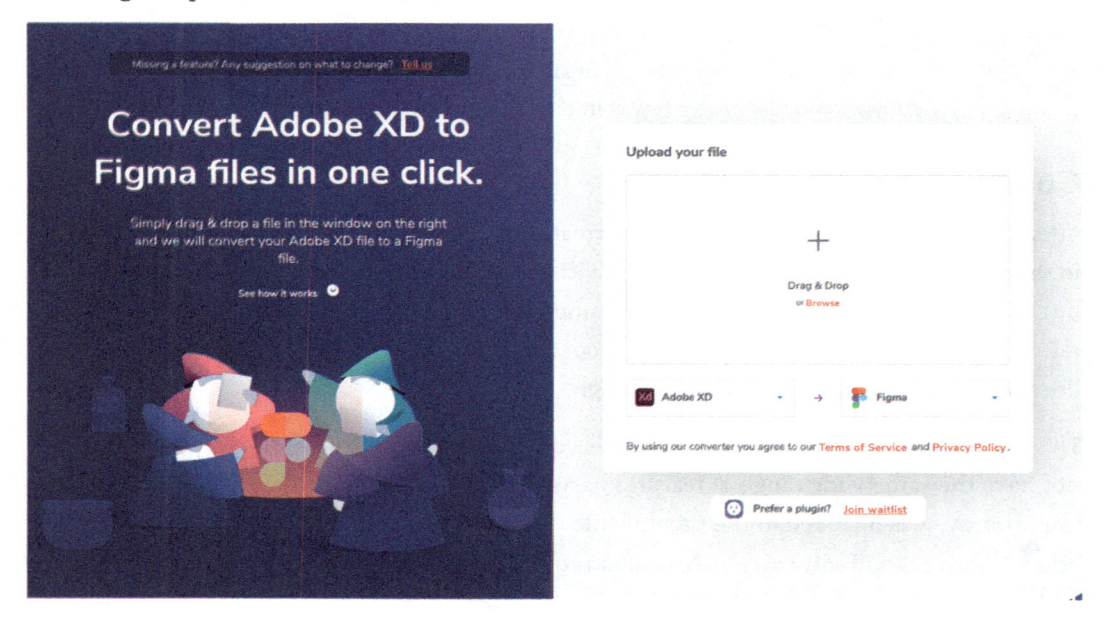

Figure 1.6: XD to Figma converter

After uploading the `.xd` file to the website, you will have a working `.fig` file with styles and components, ready to be imported into Figma. Sounds cool, but the service is not free. You will have to pay for each file you want to convert. Is it worth it? Up to you, but it surely is a time-saving solution.

A quick final thought

Transferring your designs to Figma may not always be easy, but with the right amount of time and patience, it is certainly doable. On a long-term project, you won't regret your transition because Figma helps recover any time lost, improving your daily tasks with more unique features available.

However, migration is not always the only and most convenient solution. Switching to a new tool does not mean transferring everything that you have done until today.

You don't have to say goodbye to Sketch and Adobe XD forever. Instead, you can keep them beside Figma, ready to open your old projects for quick changes if needed.

Now that the tricky transition is done, it's time to focus your attention on Figma and take a closer look at it!

Exploring the welcome screen

Whenever you open Figma, the first thing you see is the file browser. This is your personal hub with a huge amount of information and functions. It may take some time to learn everything that is presented on this screen, but at the end of this section, you'll know all about its functionalities.

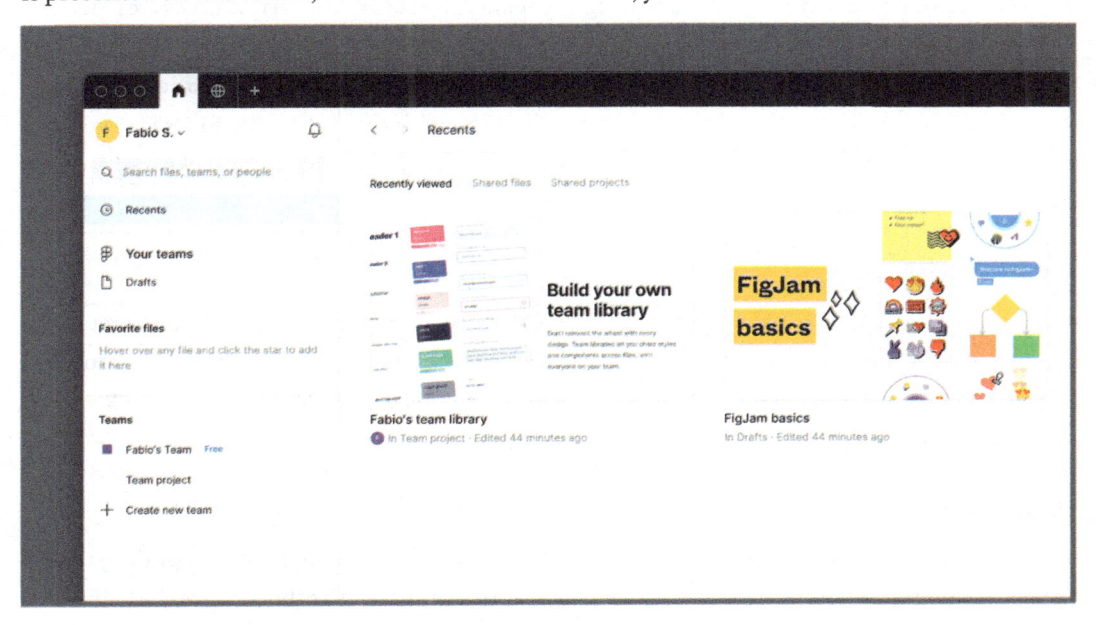

Figure 1.7: Welcome screen

Recents

If you have already used Figma before or you have just transferred some files from another tool, you'll see all of your most recent Figma and FigJam files. If you are just starting Figma for the first time, you may be confused by some files already appearing there. Don't worry, no one hacked your account; those are simply some pre-existing example files provided by Figma itself.

As a rule of thumb, **Recents** in the left sidebar shows you all the files and prototypes that you've recently opened or edited. This area includes files and prototypes from your drafts, teams, and any files you opened. You can only see recent files from the account you are currently using, not ones from other Figma accounts, if you have more than one.

Drafts

Let's now take a look at **Drafts**. Despite the obvious title, this page is more than just a collection of all your preliminary files. According to the pricing plans, there is no draft limit, not even on the Starter plan. This way, you can create as many files in Drafts as you like and keep all of them in the cloud.

The main difference between Drafts and a regular team project (like a folder) is access restrictions. This means that no one can view your draft files unless you share a personal link with them. As your personal space, Drafts lets you play with Figma, draw mock-ups, and test ideas without worrying about others seeing them. When you're done with the design file in Drafts, you can immediately move the draft file to a team project at any time. This action unlocks multi-editor capabilities for your file.

Community

Figma's Community feature is a place for all creators to share their design files, widgets, and plugins with others. It's a big topic that I'll help you dive into more. I know it sounds exciting, but it's better to stick to the basics for now. We'll get back to this in *Chapter 12, Discovering Resources, Plugins, and Widgets in the Figma Community*, for a close look.

Teams and projects

Figma wouldn't be Figma without its collaborative core. It succeeded in understanding the designer's struggle and came up with a brand-new way of working with others. Since the beginning, its focus has been to simplify this experience, making teamwork as easy as being in the same room, editing the same file.

Chapter 1 15

As stated earlier, **Drafts** is a safe place where you can freely follow your inspiration and test your ideas. But when that folder starts to get messy, which happens very soon, it's time to move on to teams, where you can better organize your design files. Moreover, **Teams**, unlike **Drafts**, are about collaboration. You can invite an unlimited number of viewers to your file in Drafts, but not editors (if you try to do this, you'll be prompted to move it to a team). Once you create or move your file to a team, you can add as many editors as you want, and you can all work on the same file in real time.

As you create your Figma account, you'll be prompted with your own personal team, ready to host up to one project, three Design files and three FigJam boards. Here's a simple breakdown: a team is your collaborative space; a project, just like a shared folder, helps organize your files within a team; and files are your actual design and FigJam documents. Each design file can contain one or more pages (up to three for a Starter plan).

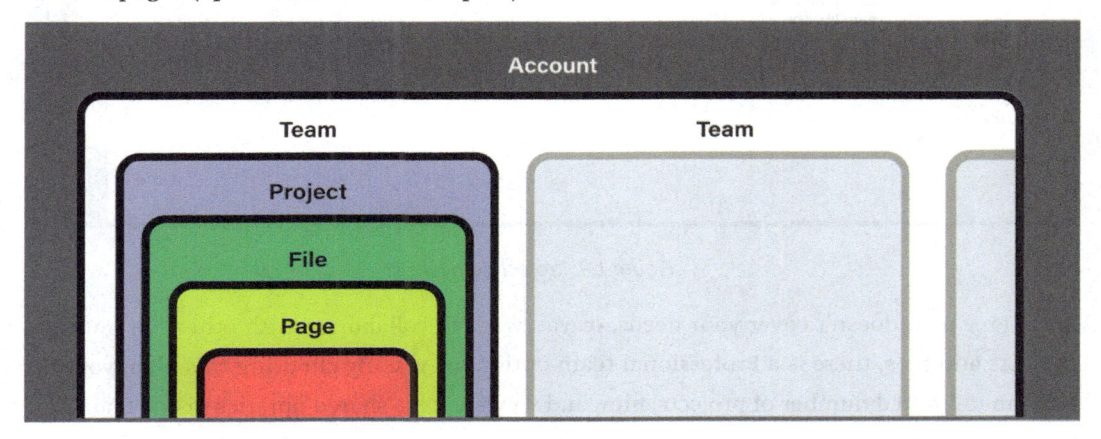

Figure 1.8: Visual structure of your account

We'll use the preset personal team soon as a playground for our step-by-step project, so you don't have to add anything new. But if you need to create a new team at a later point, follow these steps:

1. In the left column, click on **Create new team**.
2. Select a name for your team and click **Create team**.
3. You'll be asked to add collaborators to the team by entering their email addresses. Collaborators can instantly view, open, or edit any new file you create within this team. They can also create new files themselves unless you manually change the permissions. You can skip this part and add people to your team whenever you want.
4. The final step is choosing a plan. The free starter plan won't be available if you already have one.

Once your team is set up, you should see it on the left sidebar of the welcome screen, ready to be used. Clicking on it will take you to your team's private space and selecting an individual project will lead you to explore files within it and view a quick recap of it, plus contributors and used files.

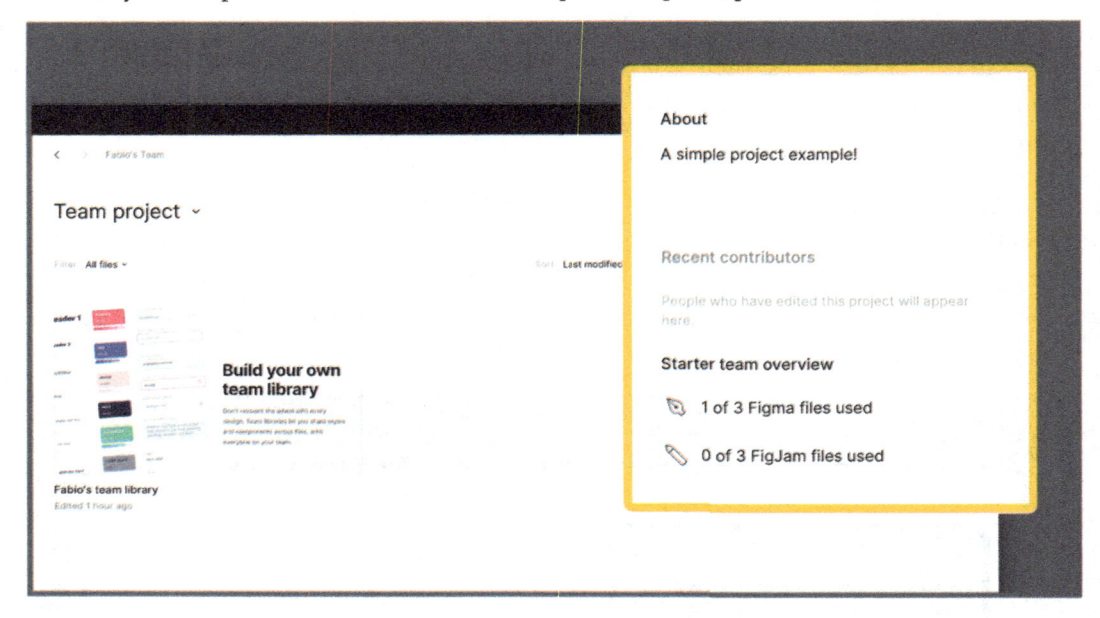

Figure 1.9: Project details

If the Free plan doesn't cover your needs, or you want to collaborate with others on multiple projects and files, there is a Professional team option for you. By choosing this plan, you can have an unlimited number of projects, files, and viewers, plus shared libraries in one team. But be careful; each editor in a Professional team needs to pay for access, even if they already pay for a different Professional team on their own.

Figma also has options for large companies that have multiple products offering Organization and Enterprise plans. Every Org/Enterprise team has access to Professional teams' functionality, as well as an unlimited number of teams and shared libraries across all these teams. Companies on those plans will have their Figma account linked to the organization's email address. Every file, including drafts created by members of this team, will be owned by the organization. Moreover, they get access to other extra, advanced features, such as branching and merging files, private widgets and plugins, shared fonts, improved security, and library analytics.

Figma and FigJam files

In this section, you will learn about two types of files that you can create right from the welcome screen in Figma: Design files and FigJam boards. FigJam is a whiteboarding tool that you can use with your team to brainstorm, build flows, organize your ideas, and even play activities! It's a very helpful tool, especially for working on the early phases of a project.

Figure 1.10: New file options

Before the release of FigJam, many professionals relied on dedicated tools designed for digital whiteboards and diagrams. Some attempted to use Figma itself for these functions but found it challenging for such tasks. Since Figma already managed to get us to ditch a lot of tools by bundling everything into a single solution, the introduction of FigJam seemed like the right way to fill the last gap. FigJam became a different space with a completely unique interface and new features.

Plus, it is still a part of Figma, and this makes it very easy to switch from one to another as if they were a unified experience.

Figure 1.11: FigJam file

We'll briefly introduce FigJam and you'll learn more about it in the next chapter. For now, let's take a look at one more thing on the welcome screen.

Account and notifications

It seems that every function placed on the top toolbar of the welcome screen is easy to understand. However, there is still something to clarify before moving on to practice.

Starting from the top-left search bar, Figma's search functionality is very powerful, as it can search through your personal and shared files, even within file content, as well as Community templates, widgets, and plugins.

There is a bell icon right next to your account name. This is where you will see all your personal notifications about invitations to shared files and so on. It's important to always keep an eye on this. Finally, by clicking on your name or avatar, you can access all settings, add accounts, log out, and more.

Chapter 1   19

Figure 1.12: Search, notifications, and account

Now, can you say that you are familiar with the welcome screen? If so, you're finally ready to sail!

Summary

As you can see, Figma is a revolutionary design tool that allows creators to take their workflows to the next level. It covers every need a designer could ever have. Therefore, it is equally perfect for individual workers as well as teams of small and large companies. Through this approach, Figma is gaining popularity among designers all over the world. Now you can become a part of this community, exchange experiences, and contribute to its growth. No other tool has achieved this level of user loyalty!

In this chapter, we learned about the ideology of Figma and its benefits over other tools. You also created an account and found out about Figma's plans and the difference between its desktop and web applications. Perhaps you even managed to switch from another tool! We also explored Figma's welcome screen, so now you know about some primary elements and sections, and what stands behind those.

In the next chapter, our journey will become even more exciting! We'll learn how to use FigJam in practice by structuring personas and creating user flows for your first file in Figma!

Learn more on Discord

To join the Discord community for this book – where you can share feedback, ask questions to the author, and learn about new releases – follow the QR code below:

`https://packt.link/figma`

2
Structuring Moodboards, Personas, and User Flows within FigJam

Now that you have an understanding of Figma as a design tool, and you know about some of its basic functionality, you are ready to dive into learning it by starting to do it. This is a reasonable and logical next step, since the best way to learn is to practice as much as possible. As mentioned in the previous chapter, Figma now consists of two types of files – design files and FigJam boards. You will start your practice with the second one, although it is a recently released brand-new feature. You might think that FigJam is Figma's complementary tool, but let's take a look at the reasons why you should start with it and not vice versa.

First, FigJam is much easier to use; consider it as a warm-up before you start practicing with more complex tools in Figma. Its functionality doesn't even come close to what the "design editor" has, since it was created for a different purpose, which we will talk about later. Second, it's important to study all stages of the design process, many or even most of which are not related to the creation of screens or even a wireframe. Before doing this, you must go through several brainstorming sessions with your team, collect and analyze data, get to know your user, and so on. In this chapter, you'll learn about these foundational activities, collectively referred to as "pre-design research." This encompasses all the preliminary work that informs your design decisions, and you'll practice each of these stages using FigJam within Figma.

This chapter may seem tricky and confusing to you because it's filled with a lot of information, and of course, it can be overwhelming, especially if you are new to design. Just know that the deeper and better you understand the basic principles of research and analytics in design, the easier it will be for you to get started with the user interface. So, there is no doubt that this chapter deserves your attention, and by the end, you will have a clear idea of what to consider when working with a real prototype.

In this chapter, we are going to cover the following main topics:

- Gathering and analyzing data in a collaborative environment
- Creating a moodboard and designing user personas in FigJam
- Defining a functional flow with FigJam tools

Exploring ideas and collaborating in FigJam

You were briefly introduced to FigJam in the previous chapter, but now it's time to learn how to use it and for what purposes. You will be guided through a complete workflow of collecting, analyzing, and processing data. This is a necessary part of a designer's work before building any prototype. All designers, freelancers, and those who work in agencies or in-house should devote a significant amount of their working time to the research stage. It will be a very challenging but interesting journey, and FigJam will be our main tool, with our aim being to learn it successfully. Before gathering any data, let's start with an overview of the FigJam interface.

Exploring FigJam

As you already know, FigJam is completely different from Figma's design file, although it is still implemented in Figma itself, so we don't need to install anything or create another account to start using it. It's a very easy-to-use tool that is as simple as using pen and paper while also allowing collaboration. Before diving into FigJam together, try to explore it yourself, and feel free to play with it in different ways to find your own unique approach, as if you were working on a personal notepad.

When you launch your first FigJam file – by clicking on the **FigJam** Board right on the welcome screen – you'll already have an idea of what this tool really does. Basically, it's a full-screen whiteboard that can be filled with ideas, notes, rich hyperlinks, images, even video, and so on. It's that simple.

The entire interface of FigJam is intuitive and simple. You can immediately see all the available tools in its toolbar at the bottom of the screen, as shown in the below image.

Each tool offers specific properties for customizing the output, but you will soon find out that FigJam doesn't have many options for colors, styles, and fonts. This is a conscious decision made by the Figma team because they don't want you to waste time choosing the right typeface instead of thinking about the underlying idea. The point is that FigJam is not a tool for designing, and this is the main reason behind its simplicity. Anyone in a team can take part in the initial stage of the project, participate in brainstorming, and show a different way of thinking, which certainly helps to conduct more effective research.

Let's now take a look at what each of these tools actually does:

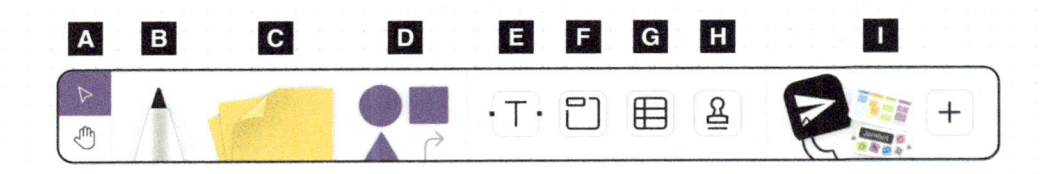

Figure 2.1: FigJam's toolbar

A — Select and Hand tool

Streamline your design workflow with the intuitive Select tool in FigJam. Activate it with a simple click, and you can effortlessly click and drag to select one or several elements, moving them freely within your workspace. For smooth navigation without altering element positions, switch to the pan (Hand) tool by clicking the hand icon in the toolbar. This feature allows you to glide across different areas of your design, ensuring a comprehensive view of your work.

An efficient alternative for quick canvas navigation is holding down the spacebar, which temporarily activates the pan tool. You can then click and drag to move around. Releasing the spacebar will revert you to the previously used tool, allowing for a seamless transition in your design process.

Keyboard shortcuts:

Press *V* to activate the Selection tool, press H for the Hand tool, or hold down the spacebar for quick panning across the board.

⬆ B — Marker

The Marker tool in FigJam offers a selection of colors and two thickness options for freehand drawing on the canvas. It's ideal for expressing ideas visually in your workspace. Additionally, under the marker tool, you'll find other useful tools (highlighters, tapes, and more), enhancing your ability to annotate, design, and collaborate within FigJam.

Keyboard shortcut:

Press *M* to select the marker tool.

C — Sticky Notes

Stick these anywhere on the canvas, as if you were doing it on a whiteboard, to quickly add notes or comment on something.

Figure 2.2: A shape and sticky note comparison

It's common to wonder about the differences between shapes and sticky notes in FigJam, especially since both can contain text. Here's a breakdown to clarify their differences:

Sticky notes:

- Predefined width options: Choose from a range of fixed widths.
- Adaptive height: Height adjusts automatically to fit the text length.
- Author identification: Displays the author's name, which can be toggled off.
- Flexible text alignment: Offers various text alignment options within the note.

Shapes:

- Customizable dimensions: Users can adjust both the width and height manually
- Diverse applications: Suitable for a wide range of design purposes
- Vertical text centering: Text within shapes is centrally aligned vertically

D — Shapes and Connectors

Effortlessly populate your canvas with the selected shape, or click on the right arrow to switch to a different shape, such as circles, rectangles, or triangles, along with more complex options. Every shape is easily resizable; simply drag its corners or sides to adjust its dimensions to your liking. In the same drawer, you'll find **connectors**, which you can use to create connections between any objects on your canvas. Whether you're linking text, shapes, notes, or components, this tool is versatile enough to link any element. Its magnetic feature ensures that it stays attached to an object's side and follows it around the canvas. It has everything you need to create flow charts and mind maps in seconds.

E — Text

Add any text to your canvas using this tool. It is perfect for creating titles, paragraphs, and even clickable links.

Keyboard shortcut:

Press *T* to activate the text tool.

F — Sections

This tool allows you to easily create colored sections on your canvas by simply dragging a selection over any area. It's an effective way to group various elements, greatly aiding in organizing your workspace.

Keyboard shortcut:

Press *Shift + S* to select the Section tool.

🖽 G – Tables

This tool is simple, as you may expect, and it lets you create tables by dragging to define an area on the canvas.

🖼 H – Stamps and Reactions

After clicking on this tool or pressing *E* on your keyboard, a selection wheel will pop up with two options in the center:

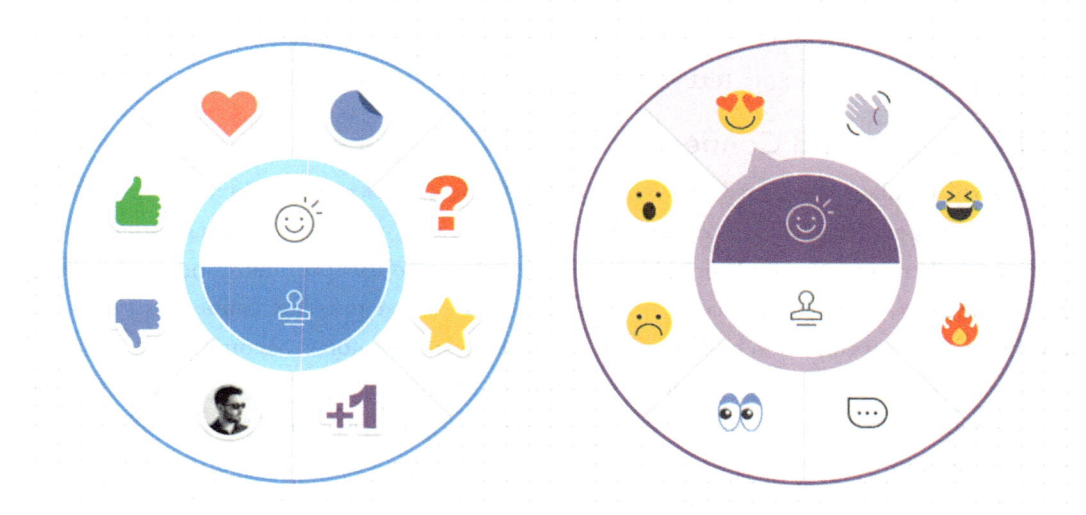

Figure 2.3: The stamp and emote wheels

The bottom one, stamps, contains all kinds of stickers that let you visualize your reaction and provide feedback, for example, with permanently sticking upvotes, downvotes, and more. If you switch to the top one, emotes, you will see a set of icons that will help you to express your live reaction. Select an emote, click on the canvas, and share your feelings in real time. Keep it pressed to trigger a flood of emotes. All those emotes appear temporarily and stay on the canvas only for a few seconds. You can also switch between emotes and stamps by hitting your *E* key repeatedly.

Among the emotes, there is one that is truly special – the chat bubble icon. This is not a simple temporary reaction but a fully functional live chat in FigJam, called **cursor chat**. By clicking on this icon, or using the / key (on non-US keyboards, this shortcut may differ), you can activate cursor chat mode; you will recognize it by the empty bubble attached to your cursor on the screen.

You can simply start typing your message and, without having to click anything to confirm sending, your text will be displayed in real time to all the users of the FigJam file at that time. After you finish typing, your message will stay for a few seconds and then disappear without leaving any trace, just like the other emotes. If you want your message to be visible for longer, or want to communicate with someone who is offline at that time, the best choice is the **comment** function. We will talk about this later in the chapter:

Figure 2.4: Cursor chat

▣▤ l – Widgets, Stickers, Templates, and more

The "More" element opens up a world of extended features, acting like a drawer brimming with additional resources. This includes a variety of plugins, widgets, sticker packs, and even basic templates. With just a few clicks, you can access these resources, allowing you to enhance your workflow and achieve efficiency in seconds. We'll explore this potential in *Chapter 12, Discovering Resources, Plugins, and Widgets in the Figma Community*.

As you can see, FigJam offers you many ways to discuss ideas with your team, exchange reactions, and communicate as if you were all in the same room. All these tools are simpler than they may seem and soon you will learn how to use them in the best possible way to achieve a great project kick-off.

Note:

FigJam is a separate tool within Figma that offers a free starter option and has a separate pricing plan. But you'll be able to get the most out of it without having to upgrade your subscription. Check out the official website to discover more: `figma.com/figjam/`

Brainstorming with others

Just like Figma, FigJam was launched as a collaborative tool. The advantage of FigJam lies in its simplicity and the ease with which users can engage in teamwork. While FigJam is perfectly suitable for solo use, its true power is unleashed when employed collaboratively. Sharing your files with others is incredibly simple, with the entire top bar of the interface designed to facilitate this collaborative purpose.

Figure 2.5: FigJam's top bar

All you have to do is click the **Share** button in the upper-right corner (*Figure 2.5* - E) and insert one or more email addresses of your collaborators. Be sure to provide the right permissions by switching between **can view** and **can edit**, depending on your intentions.

Chapter 2 29

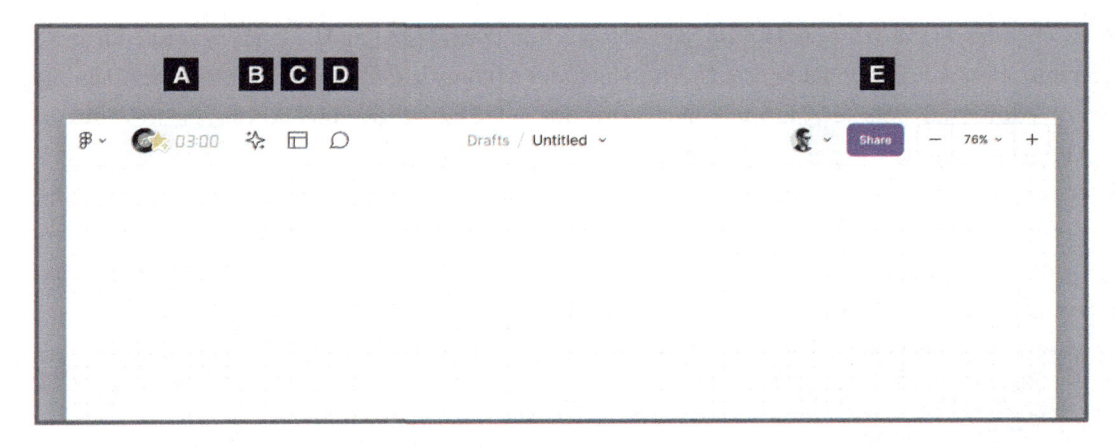

Figure 2.6: Sharing options

A less secure but easier way to do the same action is by clicking on **Copy link** and sending the link to your collaborators. Depending on what you choose under the **Anyone with the link** drop-down list, the recipient can edit your file or just view it. Be careful, because if your link goes public, you risk having unwanted guests in your file.

> **Note:**
> Until your collaborators accept the invitation or follow the link, their names will stay grayed out in the share dialog box. As soon as they open your file, you will see their avatars appear in the top-right panel and your guests' profile names become colored.

From now on, you and your colleagues will have the ability to see each other's cursors in real time while collaboratively working in the file. This opens up a world of incredible possibilities, such as brainstorming, design sprints, team building, workshops, and moodboards. Why not start with a convenient template? (*Figure 2.5 – C*). Additionally, AI can be utilized to generate ideas and more (*Figure 2.5 – B*), but this will be discussed in detail in *Chapter 12, Discovering Resources, Plugins, and Widgets in the Figma Community*. As remote communication becomes increasingly prevalent, workflows accelerate, and an agile approach becomes the norm, FigJam's role as an indispensable tool in our daily work becomes clear. We've already discovered the features of emotes, stamps, and reactions, but there are even more engaging and practical features to explore, particularly in the **Timer** menu located at the top left (*Figure 2.5 – A*).

By clicking on the **Timer** in FigJam, you access a hub of engaging tools, effectively transforming it into a multi-functional feature. This hub includes not only the standard timing capabilities but also additional tools such as music and voting options. The integration of these features enhances the collaborative experience, making it more dynamic and interactive. The Timer serves as a centralized control for managing various aspects of a group session, from keeping track of time during activities to setting the right ambiance with music, and even facilitating group decisions through the voting mechanism. This design ensures that all these tools are readily accessible, streamlining the collaborative process and enriching the overall user experience in FigJam.

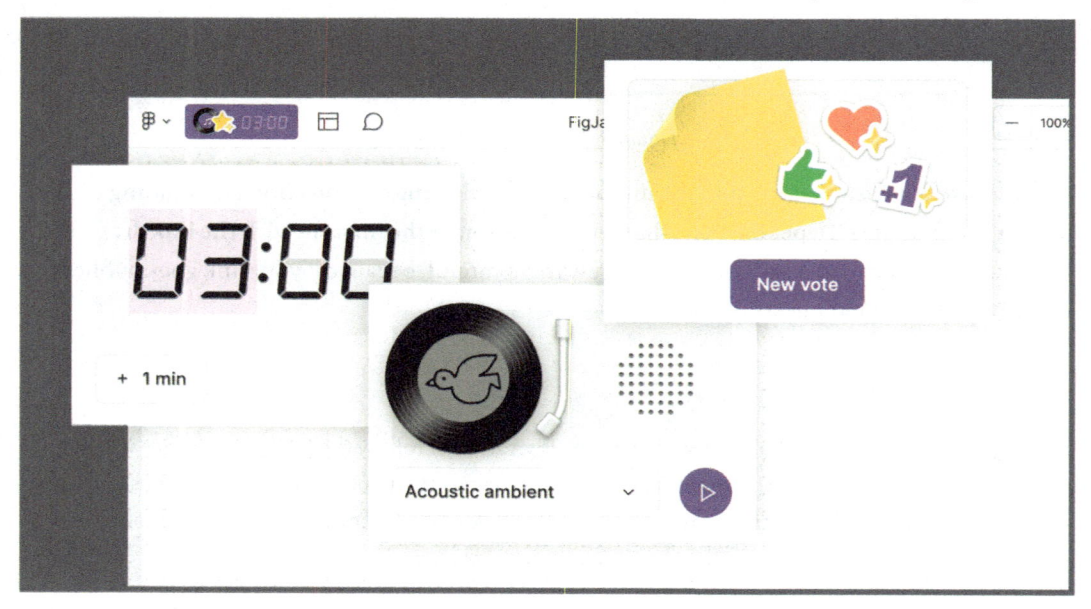

Figure 2.7: Timer, Music, and Voting

When working remotely with a team, real-time collaboration can sometimes be impractical. In such cases, FigJam's comment feature emerges as an essential one. It facilitates asynchronous communication, allowing team members to provide feedback, ask questions, or share ideas without altering the primary content on the whiteboard. This function is activated by clicking the comment icon (*Figure 2.5 – D*) or by pressing the *C* key, which changes the cursor into a chat bubble icon, enabling users to place comments anywhere on the board.

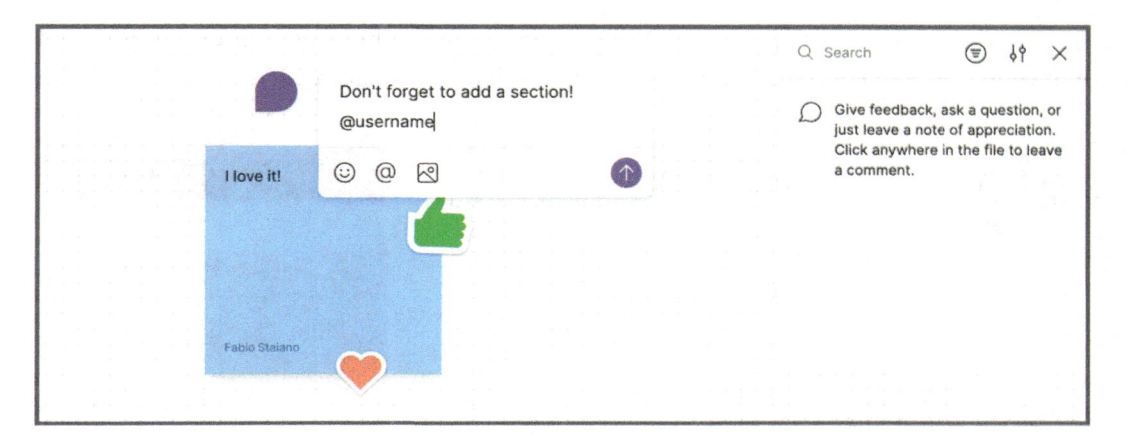

Figure 2.8: Leaving a comment

The comments feature is designed to keep team members informed and engaged. Those with access to the file can receive notifications about new comments both within the app and via email. For added efficiency, invited members are set by default to receive notifications only for threads in which they are mentioned. This ensures that they are alerted to relevant discussions without being overwhelmed by notifications. On the other hand, the file owner is automatically notified about all comments, ensuring they remain fully updated on every piece of feedback and discussion point. This thoughtful design of the comment function in FigJam greatly enhances collaborative work, especially in remote settings.

> **Note:**
> Currently, FigJam supports up to 500 participants (between viewers and editors) at the same time.

Moving to the next step

Now that you know about every FigJam feature, it's time to put together what you've learned and get some real work done. Let's say you just had a brainstorming session with your team. Generally, the result would be having a definition of the best idea, which then needs to be accepted by your potential client or your supervisor.

Once approved, it's time to get a general idea of the upcoming briefing, so take your time and write down all your concerns, which you can discuss later with stakeholders:

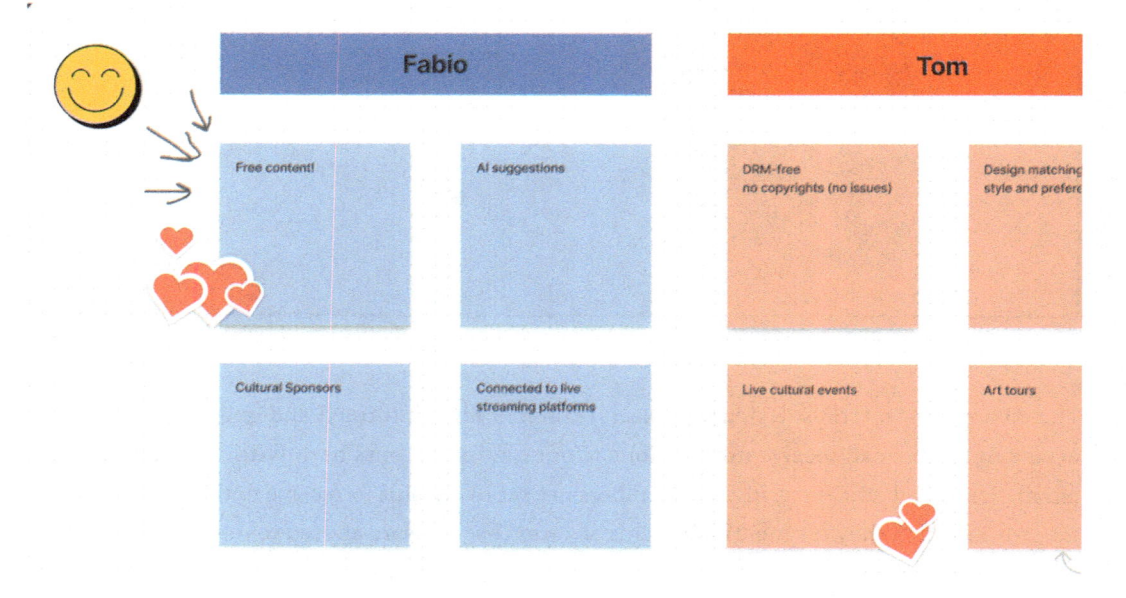

Figure 2.9: Brainstorming

Remember that every project is unique, and you can approach it completely differently each time. Of course, learning a standard flow can help you avoid missing important steps, but only with hands-on experience will you master the process. You should also keep in mind that the UX working process is very time-consuming and, consequently, needs the right budget. So, although it would be great to follow the best design path, you will not always have enough financial resources to cover all stages, and sometimes, you'll have to make some compromise between time and cost, while still achieving excellent results.

Let's keep it simple this time, starting a project with a brief that focuses on creating a brand-new streaming service filled with free documentaries and other cultural content, where you will be responsible for designing a fresh, modern, and intuitive interface for mobile, tablet, and desktop. This is your starting point.

So, once you have formed an idea, it's time to move forward and explore it from every angle. The next section teaches you how to do this as easily as possible.

Creating moodboards and personas in FigJam

Getting inspired isn't easy, especially when you're facing tight deadlines. But if you follow proven strategies and stick to the right design process, you will definitely achieve amazing results in a short period of time. This section will focus on defining some of the most common best practices.

Research phase

Whether you are creating a landing page, a complex website, or an entire ecosystem for a product, the research phase is very important for structuring a functional design solution. After analyzing the brief and understanding your stakeholders' vision, you need to set up a mission statement. This is a short and affirmative description of the project's purpose that highlights the problem your product is going to solve. In our first project, the mission statement could be as follows:

> **MISSION STATEMENT**
>
> An easy-to-use, modern streaming service that allows users to browse a collection of culturally interesting content, such as documentaries and movies for entertainment and educational purposes, for free.

Setting up a mission statement helps you and your team always keep the product's purpose in mind, reducing the risk of going off track.

Let's take a look at a few examples. Here are some of the big brands' mission statements.

- **Apple**: *"Apple strives to bring the best personal computing experience to students, educators, creative professionals, and consumers around the world through its innovative hardware, software, and internet offerings."*
- **Google**: *"Our mission is to organize the world's information and make it universally accessible and useful."*
- **Ikea**: *"To offer a wide range of well-designed, functional home furnishing products at prices so low that as many people as possible will be able to afford them."*

Once the mission statement is clearly formulated, the design process becomes much more integral. And now you can move on to the next stage – competitor research:

Figure 2.10: Competitor analysis

Conducting competitive analysis

Competitive analysis is important for many different reasons. When you deeply analyze the market, its participants, and how they present their products, you collect data on functionalities, design patterns, and conventions. Of course, you need to examine your competitors in order to understand all the positive aspects and then enter the market with at least a decent offer. But it is equally important to identify the negative sides of their products. This is perhaps even more useful because it allows you to create something that can fill a market gap or improve the user experience in a new way.

A study of competitors consists of exploring their products, taking screenshots, noting interesting solutions, and collecting your own notes and comments. FigJam is, of course, a perfect tool for this step. As you analyze your artifacts, try to figure out how they solve their users' problems by comparing all the results against your product's goal. Write down and mark everything, even small notions and concerns, which later on can stimulate your flow of ideas and analysis. All images, text, and comments can easily be gathered in FigJam. Plus, with its limited set of tools to choose from, you don't have to worry too much about styling.

Chapter 2   35

Before proceeding, try to create a FigJam board yourself by compiling the mobile, tablet, and desktop interfaces of the main competitors in the streaming services sector.

Starting a moodboard

If you've ever created a moodboard for any purpose, you will understand that it is more than just a bunch of images and text. As you work on analysis, research, and so on, you will inevitably find a lot of interesting content along the way, some of which can greatly inspire you for the next stages of design. And this is where the moodboard comes into play – a digital space with everything that may be useful in the future:

Figure 2.11: A moodboard example

(Photos by Mike Simon, Jeremy Yap, Karen Zhao, Mason Kimbarovsky, Rock Staar on Unsplash)

In general, a moodboard can be useful in two early stages. You can create it in a brainstorming session, alone or in a group, trying to put together content that can help you find inspiration. But also, most importantly, creating a moodboard is very helpful before building the flow and user interface. It's important to know that after you've created a moodboard, you can fill it out day after day by collecting anything that is currently getting your attention. You can find a lot of interesting and aesthetic content on resources made just for that purpose, such as Pinterest – a very special social network for creators. You might even discover something from your daily life and turn it into inspiration.

Take your time and feel free to update this collection of personally inspiring "items."

Try creating your personal moodboard in FigJam and start collecting anything that inspires you for the phases to come.

Creating user personas

Now that you've set a mission statement, analyzed your competitors, and created a moodboard, it's the perfect time to define a target. It's not enough to understand a problem and decide how to solve it; you also need to know who your product is for. The shortest way to collect the necessary data and figure out this unknown variable is to interview and/or poll a group of people of different ages, genders, and backgrounds. As a result, you can understand what their needs are and whether your product – whatever it may be – can somehow satisfy them or solve their pain points in any way. Social media and website analytics are also great sources of valuable information, but of course, that's something more suited to a restyling project than brand-new product ideation.

Once you have collected enough raw data to analyze, you can start creating a user persona – a fictional description of a person who represents your typical user. From now on, you will use it as a guideline for each subsequent phase of the project.

Creating a user persona is useful not only for designers but also for the entire team working on the project. One of the most common mistakes when designing something is forgetting who will be using your product, and you may end up following your personal preferences and tastes. Personas can also be used effectively by those who are keen to meet user needs, including stakeholders, marketers, and developers.

But how do we correctly create one or more user personas? There are no exact and strict rules but only general guidelines on what is useful to include and what is not. There is no doubt that when working on a persona, you should not trust your intuition or guesses but use an empirical method based on previously collected data. A careless and hasty user persona creation can lead to project failure, as well as undermine efforts made during the analysis and research phase:

Alyssa Gordon

"I don't have much free time, but I love theater and documentaries"

INFO
Age: 28
Status: Single
Occupation: Waiter
Location: San Francisco

She lives in a small apartment with Pongo, her dog. Works as a waiter for a famous restaurant but she wants to complete her studies to be a history teacher.

HABITS
- Works 8 hours per day
- Always reads a book before sleeping
- Wakes up early
- Travels twice per year

GOALS
- Finding new and interesting stories and documentaries
- Teaching history
- Visiting Louvre museum

FRUSTRATIONS
- Can't stand pop-ups
- Not having enough time for her studies
- Working during weekends

Figure 2.12: A user persona

Usually, to create a user persona template, you should fill in the following blocks of information:

- Name
- Photo
- Demographics (age, gender, relationship status, occupation, and location)
- A short biography
- Habits
- Goals, needs, and frustrations

Keep in mind that a persona should never, under any circumstances, represent people you know. Also, you should not use any personally identifiable information but rather rely on information from the general data collection. Obviously, if your data can identify different archetypes of typical users, it is highly recommended to create multiple user personas. Brainstorming various user profiles allows for a broader perspective and helps in designing a product that resonates with a wider audience.

Each persona should reflect a distinct segment of your target market, ensuring comprehensive coverage of user expectations and experiences. In addition, depending on the type of project you're working on, you might find it helpful to add other fields to your personas' templates, such as personality traits, commonly used applications, or even some more specific additional data, such as salary ranges.

For our sample project, it would be great if you could arrange an online survey – for example, using **Google Forms** – and send it to your group of friends. This way, you will learn how to best organize questions and collect data. This step may not be so easy the first time, since the survey needs to collect a lot of raw data to have any really effective results for analysis, so refer to our preceding user sample (*Figure 2.10*) if necessary.

Once you're done with your model, don't forget to share your user personas with anyone involved in the project to have a common reference when thinking about the product's target.

Note:

Tons of user persona templates are available within the community for both Figma and FigJam. We'll cover that in more detail in *Chapter 12, Discovering Resources, Plugins, and Widgets in the Figma Community*.

You have completed most of the research phase of your project, and now you know more about your target audience. Now, let's explore the actions a user can take in your product to learn how to provide them with a clear and intuitive interface on every page of the application. That's exactly what you will learn to master in the next section.

Building user flow in FigJam

You already know that analysis and research are important stages in the initial phase of the implementation of any project, even small ones. The tools and processes used so far are part of the so-called **User Experience (UX)** research. Often, in the most professional environments, the UX and UI are handled by different professionals. However, even if you are only responsible for the interface, it is better to know the basics of UX principles, as it may be the case that you have to figure it out yourself, such as if you do not receive very precise instructions from the UX department on how to design your product, what style to use, and where to place each element.

The profession of a UX designer is far from being creative and much closer to subjects such as marketing and psychology.

Both disciplines are essential in order to understand your users, analyze their behavior, and get a high-quality product as a result.

The golden path

You already know the preferences and goals of your target audience, so the next step is to determine the typical path that a user will take when using the product, and FigJam is again the perfect tool for this purpose.

You can create a new file or use a previously used one and dedicate a separate area for this. Feel free to choose your own way, depending on whether you prefer to collect the results of all stages of research and analysis separately or in a single file. However, with separate files, you can share each one with a different group of people – keep that in mind.

To build a navigation flow, you can use the classic flowchart. Select a rectangle from the shape tool and place it on the board. You can add others next to it just by repeating the operation; or, for a faster way, use the classic duplicate shortcut by holding the *Option* key (macOS) or the *Alt* key (Windows) and clicking and dragging an already existing shape. FigJam also makes duplication easier with the + button that appears on the sides of any shape on the canvas (**Figure 2.13 - A**). When you click it, the same shape will appear next to the existing element with a connector between the two (**Figure 2.13 - B**):

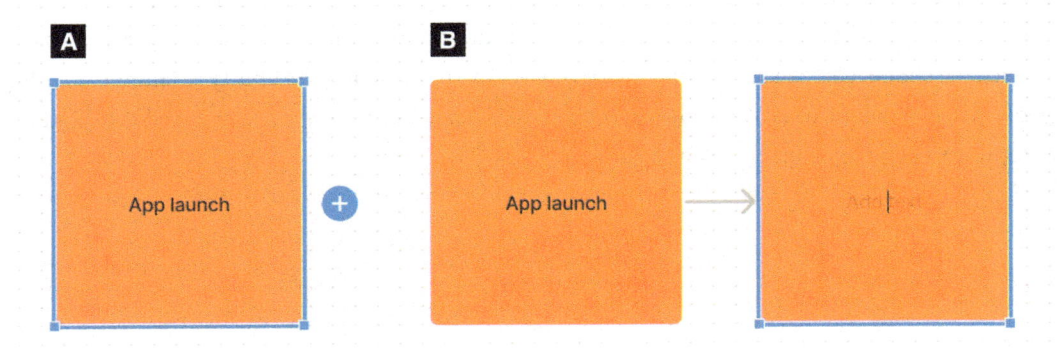

Figure 2.13: Shapes and connectors

This way, you can create a horizontal diagram for our mobile app, which is simple but essential, that represents the golden path that leads the user from the starting point to the final point of the digital product, generally defined by the conversion goal:

Figure 2.14: A basic flow

This is a good start, but now it is necessary to add all the paths that users can take, also considering any direct or indirect choices they encounter along the way. To do this, you can take full advantage of the various features that FigJam provides for creating diagrams. First, by selecting an existing shape, you can access its parameters at any time, having the ability to change its color, stroke, and the shape itself. This allows you to distinguish between various parts of the diagram to represent different types of elements:

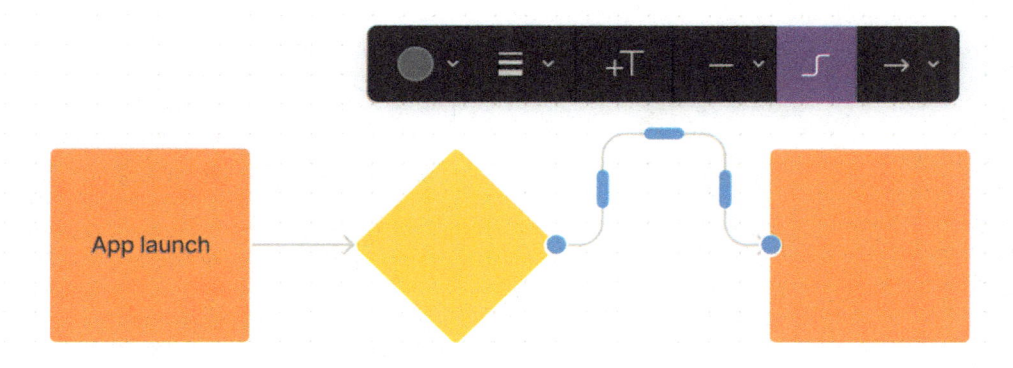

Figure 2.15: The connector's edit mode

Now, let's take a closer look at the connectors between shapes, which can be customized as well. When you hover over any connector, you will see blue handles on it that allow you to manually edit the shape of the path. You can also see that a connector has two blue dots; these are its start and end points. By clicking and dragging any of them, you can easily move and attach the connector to any other object on the canvas.

For now, you don't need to manually edit the lines – when you move items on the board, the connectors will automatically follow the ones they are attached to, but you still need to use the **Add Text** property, or just double-click on the center of the line, which allows you to add text in the middle of the selected connector.

This is a great feature for clarifying and making multiple paths more intuitive, as shown in the following example:

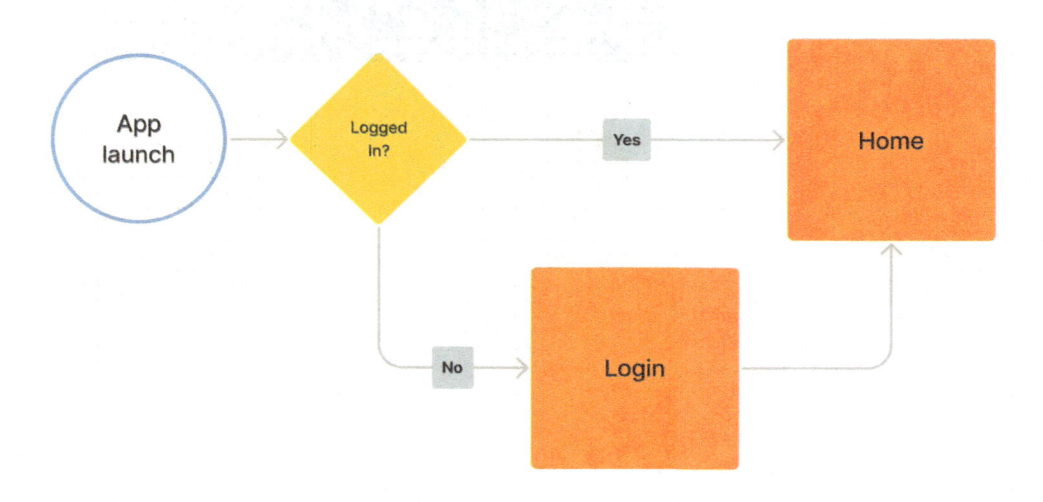

Figure 2.16: A flow with variables

Here, you can observe the initial iteration of our mobile app's login process. This diagram is composed of various shapes and colors, each designed to clearly signify different elements and steps within the process. Connectors are used to illustrate the flow and relationships between different components.

In the current scenario, we're considering that the user might have previously signed in. Thus, it is possible that the user will immediately enter the home page after opening the application. Your flow should include these two cases – the user either creates an account for the first time or opens the home page directly.

It takes a lot of effort to structure the entire flow because you have to anticipate all the possible actions the user can take in the application. It is very easy to miss essential features, such as login password recovery, so it is extremely important to test other real applications before working on your user flows. During testing, you need to break down and organize all the functionality into several paths and then make sure that your product does not miss anything.

This is one of the most important steps in the transition from the early stages to the UI, as it provides clear navigational guidance from the beginning and, as a result, saves you from compromising all the work in the advanced design stages:

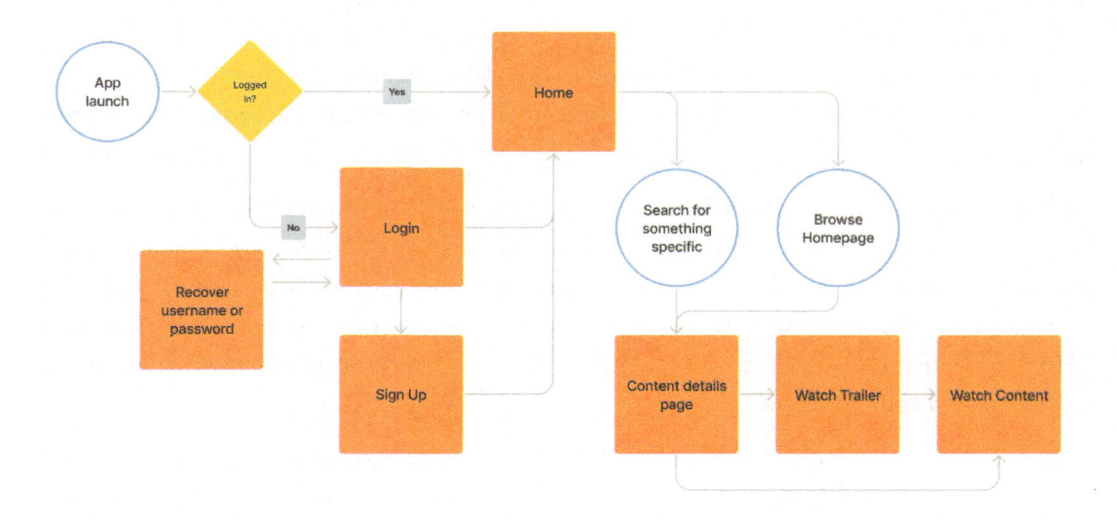

Figure 2.17: A complex flow example

This second iteration (*Figure 2.17*) represents a more complete example of what our app could be, even though secondary paths such as all the category pages, user profile pages, and settings are still missing. In this diagram, you can clearly distinguish between user steps (circle-shaped) and application pages (rectangular-shaped) triggered by user actions. This is a fundamental difference between a user flow and a more technical site map that only displays all the web or application pages.

> **Note:**
>
> FigJam provides a bunch of basic shapes, colors, and styles, but if you need even more customization, remember that it's incredibly simple to copy and paste any sort of asset from the Figma design files.

Be the user

It is impossible to cover all the information about the complete UX process in a few pages, but now at least you have learned the fundamental part that every designer should know. If you wish, you can find specialized sources about UX and study this topic deeper. But for now, you will explore the UI and related tools. However, it does not mean that the UX research is complete. Design should never be confused with drawing. A good designer always remembers the purpose of a product and whom it serves at every stage of the project, with no exceptions. Therefore, a user-centered interface based on qualitative analysis will certainly achieve its intended goals.

Before moving on to the product wireframe stage, make sure that you have your content arranged. Interfaces are nothing more than custom-made containers adapted to present intended content. The most common mistake designers make is starting to design an interface without even having a vague idea of the actual content that the product will contain, which ultimately leads to them artificially inventing it. The famous *Lorem ipsum*, most commonly used as placeholder text, can be both useful and dangerous.

To give a practical example, let's take our streaming service project and imagine that you start designing interfaces right now with what you have. You've collected user data and built the flow, but you still don't know anything about the actual content of the service. How are you going to work on a detail page for individual video content without having the slightest idea of what data to show to the user? Should you include information about the author, the director, and the duration? Of course, you can copy some content from competitors, but nothing guarantees that it will match the real data to be loaded onto the service. Therefore, without real content, there is always a risk of creating a beautiful container that is unsuitable for placing the final data in.

It is not always possible to obtain real and ready-made data at this stage due to the agreement with the stakeholders, but it is almost always possible to request a sample or demo information. In the case of a streaming service, you need at least one example of a detailed description to get started so that you know what data has to be presented on the interface.

Summary

It is clear that Figma tries to be more than just a design tool, providing everything you need at all stages of product design. FigJam is the perfect proof of this. Keeping all your artifacts in FigJam allows you to access them in two clicks without even leaving Figma. You can create and organize FigJam boards as you like, dedicating some for team activities and others for your own templates to reuse in further projects.

So feel free to experiment with this tool to see how many amazing things you can do with it!

In this chapter, we covered the basics of the UX part of the design process, such as collecting and analyzing data for your project, defining a persona, creating inspiring moodboards, and building effective user flows. You've also explored all of FigJam's functional tools and learned how to use them and for what purpose. Now, you have a great set of artifacts that will come in handy in the next stages of our project. It's important that you do not forget the concepts learned in this chapter when working on your next projects. Remember that only with practice and experience will you be able to complete these initial steps as successfully as possible, making your professional life much easier.

In the next chapter, you will explore more Figma tool basics and set up your first design project. Get ready to continue this amazing journey!

Learn more on Discord

To join the Discord community for this book – where you can share feedback, ask questions to the author, and learn about new releases – follow the QR code below:

```
https://packt.link/figma
```

3

Getting to Know Your Design Environment

In the previous chapter, you discovered the basic concepts of the UX process, like moodboarding, personas, and flows, which are without a doubt an essential part of any design project. As you work, it's best to keep all research results, analysis data, and other attributes nearby so you can always check if you're on your planned design path. Remember that the usability and clarity of your final user interface will directly depend on the quality of your UX work.

However, creating a user interface is also a tricky and time-consuming part of design work. You might have done some excellent research and collected enough relevant data, but your actual design work may not always be smooth and easy. In real life, anything can happen – maybe the chosen style will not be approved by the customer, or maybe your team will decide to add a tablet version of your product. This book cannot anticipate all the challenges a designer might face, but you will definitely learn how to make your user interface work faster and more efficiently.

One of the key components of optimizing your workflow is knowing as much as possible about the capabilities of your design tool so you can get the most out of it. What basic and advanced features can it provide? Where can you find all the possible operations with elements? How can you organize your layers and assets and get quick access to them? You are about to get all the answers right below.

In this chapter, we are going to cover the following main topics:

- Starting a new project from scratch
- Overview of the Figma toolbar

- Learning about the features of the left panel
- Exploring the right properties panel

Starting a new design project

In this chapter, you will temporarily step away from analysis and research work in FigJam files and instead discover Figma's essential tools and functions. You will find a lot of material to learn, and it's completely normal to feel overwhelmed by all this new information. But the good thing about this chapter is that you can refer to it from time to time when you're unsure of any of the basics of Figma. So don't worry about memorizing all the concepts of each function; you will see how everything works later in the book, and each tool and feature will be explained in a more practical way.

Design files

You already know that Figma has two types of files – FigJam and design. You've learned about FigJam boards in detail in the previous chapter. This time, you will go back to the file selection and make another choice, by creating a design file. To create a new blank design file, open the welcome screen and click on **Design file** right at the top.

To go to the welcome screen, if you still have FigJam open in your browser with the previously created files, click on the **Main menu** (the Figma logo in the upper-left corner) and select **Back to Files** from the drop-down menu. Then, just proceed as previously described. However, if you are using the Figma desktop app, you can skip returning to the welcome screen and immediately press the + button to the right of the current file's tab. Figma will prompt you to open a new file where you can choose the type of new file – FigJam or design. You can also hit *Command + T* (macOS) or *Ctrl + T* (Windows) to quickly open a new tab, like in your browser, and you will be given a choice for your desired file type:

Figure 3.1: A new file from the tab menu

Once you open a new design file, you can finally see Figma as it is, which is significantly different from what you had earlier with FigJam. It is a much more complex and robust working space that will allow you to create truly stunning masterpieces.

Note:

To easily distinguish between file types within your Figma projects, simply hover over a file, and you'll notice distinct icons and colors for design and FigJam files. Plus, you have the option to filter file types, allowing you to conceal those that are currently irrelevant to your needs.

Frames and groups

When you first launch a design file in Figma, you're greeted with a vast, empty gray space, which serves as your workspace. This space is neatly framed by functional panels on either side and a comprehensive toolbar at the top. At first glance, the assortment of areas, each with different functionalities, may appear complex and somewhat daunting. Such a reaction is normal, as this isn't just a simple canvas; it's the foundation where the entirety of your project's interface will take shape. Fear not, as you will gradually become familiar with all the tools Figma offers. Initially, your primary point of interaction in this empty file will be the top toolbar, which acts as your gateway into the world of design within Figma.

To start using Figma to its fullest, you need to create an artboard. You may be familiar with this concept from other design tools. However, Figma does not have standard artboards but rather something similar yet much more powerful – frames. While they share basic traits with artboards, frames differ in functionality. They can be nested, and also have auto layout, layout grids, and all prototyping functions set. You will learn more about this later, but for now, let's stop here.

What is a frame? Simply put, it's a container. You can use custom-sized frames or choose practical presets for the most common standards, such as mobile devices, tablets, desktop resolutions, and even social media.

So, it all starts with a single frame:

Figure 3.2: The Frame tool's presets

To create a frame, you can use the **Frame** tool from the top toolbar (using the *F* or *A* shortcuts) and proceed in three different ways:

- Click any blank area on your workspace to create a default 100 x 100 frame.
- Click and drag with your cursor to create a custom-sized frame.
- Click on any preset size on the right panel to automatically create a frame of the appropriate size.

As you can imagine, the third option is most useful for immediately starting your design without having to search the internet for screen sizes of various devices. For example, clicking **iPhone 13 mini** will immediately create a 375 x 812 frame. You can add more than one frame in your workspace, and no matter how many there are in your file, it is unlikely to slow down Figma.

But frames are not just artboards. They can act as containers as well, letting you nest as many elements or any other frame as you like. To quickly create a frame around one or more objects, simply select whatever you want to put together and press *Option + Command + G* (macOS) or *Ctrl + Alt + G* (Windows).

However, there is an alternative way to combine objects, and this method is called groups. Understanding the difference between frames and groups can be very confusing, as they share some basic functions, and you may think they are interchangeable, but this is mostly untrue. You will likely be using frames more often since they offer a bunch of extra features, but there may be situations where you don't really need their advanced capabilities. Instead, you will be satisfied with something simpler, such as a group, that just combines several objects into one layer without flattening them, allowing you to maintain a fixed relationship between inner elements when scaling. If you want to create a group of objects, just press *Command + G* (macOS) or *Ctrl + G* (Windows) after selecting the desired elements on the canvas. We can ungroup at any time by pressing *Shift + Command + G* (macOS) or *Shift + Ctrl + G* (Windows).

To visually understand frames and groups, combine two shapes into one frame and do the same with a group, and then try resizing the two containers. In the group, the shapes will be resized accordingly, while in the frame, what is scaled is only the frame itself, while the shapes retain their original size and position. Over time, as you progress through the chapters, you will fully understand the potential of frames, one of Figma's exclusive features, and this will lead you to have a clearer view of concepts that may now seem very complex.

Interface overview

You've added the first frame to your work area, and you may have noticed that the interface now provides you with a lot of new functions to explore. Now, it may seem similar to many other design tools you may have used. However, compared to Adobe Photoshop, for example, Figma still looks like a tool that offers a rather limited number of features, and this may undermine your belief that Figma is still the best choice.

Of course, as mentioned earlier, it is also possible to create interfaces using Photoshop, but you will inevitably run into limitations, such as poor smoothness with numerous artboards and, above all, a lack of tools dedicated to prototyping. If, for example, you want to apply a watercolor effect to an image in your design, Figma will not be suitable for such purposes. However, it's important to emphasize that Figma has the essentials, and in most cases, that's pretty much all you need to create a complete interface. As a flexible collaboration tool, Figma can easily convert anything you create in it into web or mobile app development code, which is the point:

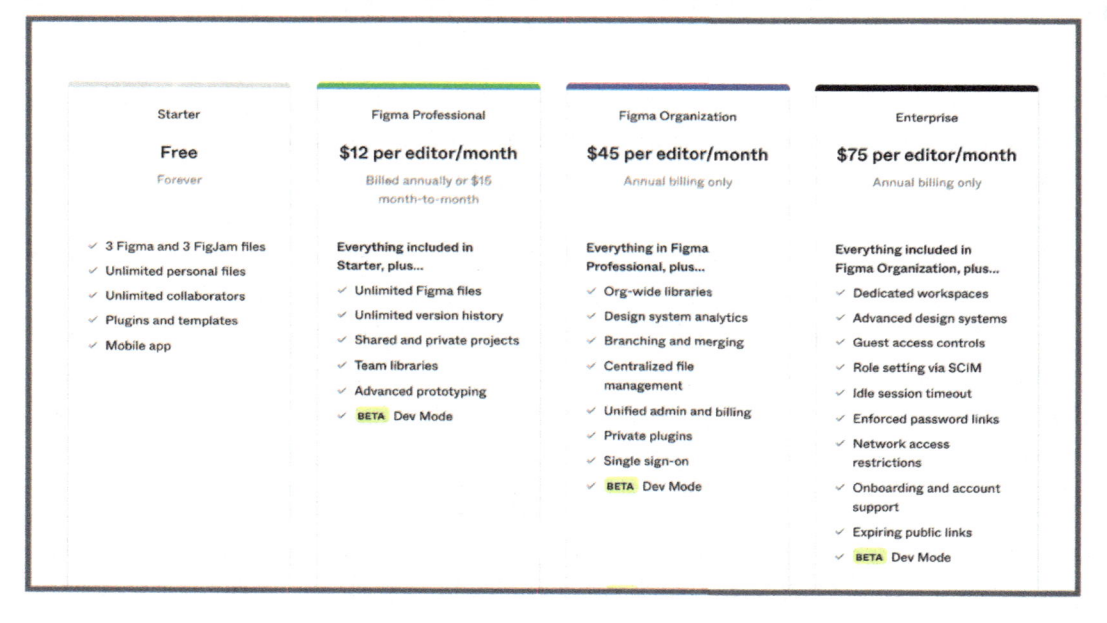

Starter	Figma Professional	Figma Organization	Enterprise
Free	**$12 per editor/month**	**$45 per editor/month**	**$75 per editor/month**
Forever	Billed annually or $15 month-to-month	Annual billing only	Annual billing only
✓ 3 Figma and 3 FigJam files	Everything included in Starter, plus...	Everything in Figma Professional, plus...	Everything included in Figma Organization, plus...
✓ Unlimited personal files	✓ Unlimited Figma files	✓ Org-wide libraries	✓ Dedicated workspaces
✓ Unlimited collaborators	✓ Unlimited version history	✓ Design system analytics	✓ Advanced design systems
✓ Plugins and templates	✓ Shared and private projects	✓ Branching and merging	✓ Guest access controls
✓ Mobile app	✓ Team libraries	✓ Centralized file management	✓ Role setting via SCIM
	✓ Advanced prototyping	✓ Unified admin and billing	✓ Idle session timeout
	✓ BETA Dev Mode	✓ Private plugins	✓ Enforced password links
		✓ Single sign-on	✓ Network access restrictions
		✓ BETA Dev Mode	✓ Onboarding and account support
			✓ Expiring public links
			✓ BETA Dev Mode

Figure 3.3: Figma effects versus CSS effects

For example, if Figma allows you to apply a blur effect to an image, it's only because that effect can be applied in the same way as a CSS rule in web development. A **Cascading Style Sheets (CSS)** rule is a set of instructions used in website design to control the appearance of elements on a web page, such as color, layout, and in this case, effects like blur.

However, there is no filter that can be applied with the code to apply the watercolor effect. This way, Figma guarantees that everything you design can be reproduced in code without much difficulty. Does this mean you can never apply a watercolor filter? Not at all. Without any problem, you can directly import an image that has been previously filtered into Figma. Adobe Photoshop and Adobe Illustrator are tools that can be perfectly combined with Figma to get more impressive results. However, using Figma as your main tool saves you from mistakes in design that can lead to problems in product development. As a result, you don't need to have any coding skills or worry about any technical constraints to create reliable layouts.

In addition, to make the experience even more user-friendly, Figma makes the most of a context-sensitive interface. This means that you will never see, for example, a left-align text icon unless you have selected text that can be aligned at that point. It is a method that more and more software has implemented in recent years, providing the user with the right tools and functions at the right time. Of course, for those of us new to this kind of UX, it can be difficult to find what they expect, but it really is only a matter of hours until you can no longer live without it:

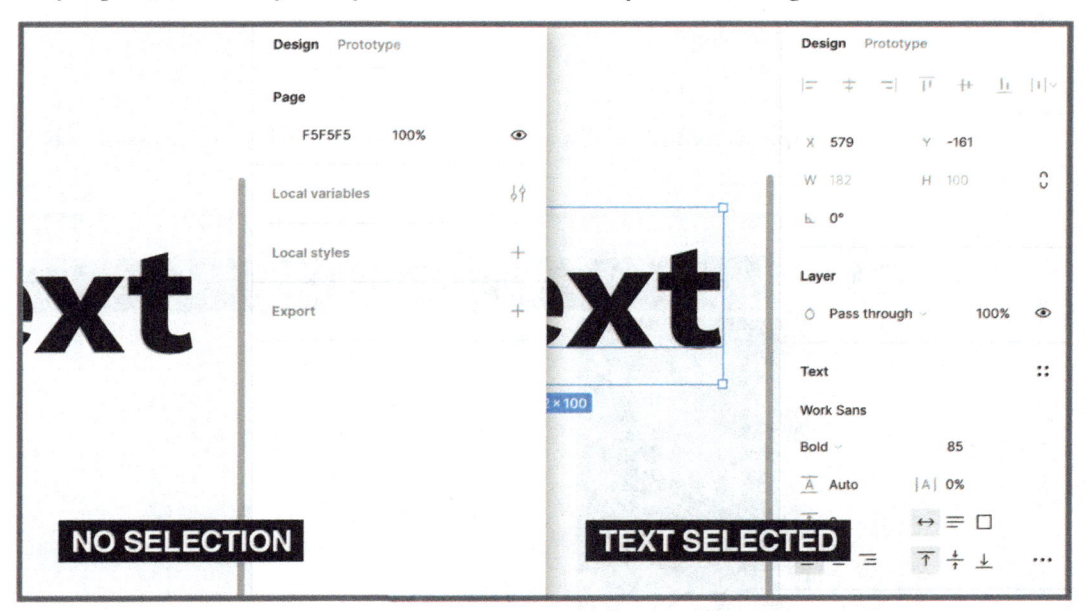

Figure 3.4: An example of context-sensitive options

So, if you can't find a specific feature, it probably isn't available to you at the moment, likely due to Figma's context-sensitive interface. This interface only displays tools and options relevant to your current selection or activity within the program. If a feature seems unavailable, first check if you've missed any steps in the process or if you've selected the wrong element.

To access certain features, you might need to make a specific selection, such as clicking on a textbox to see text editing tools. Once you're in the right context, everything becomes extremely simple and clear, with errors minimized as much as possible.

Now, let's get down to exploring the interface piece by piece to get an idea of the tools and functions that Figma provides.

Getting used to the toolbar

We'll start by exploring the top toolbar – this is where you'll find all of Figma's basic tools and settings. For the most commonly used basic tools, try to learn as many shortcuts as possible right from the beginning. It will greatly improve your workflow!

Main tools

Figma divides its core tools into several sections, all of which you can see in the top bar. You will get an overview of all the sections in order, from left to right, and start by exploring the main set of features.

A – Menu

The Figma logo in the upper-left corner hides a significant drop-down menu that opens when you click on it:

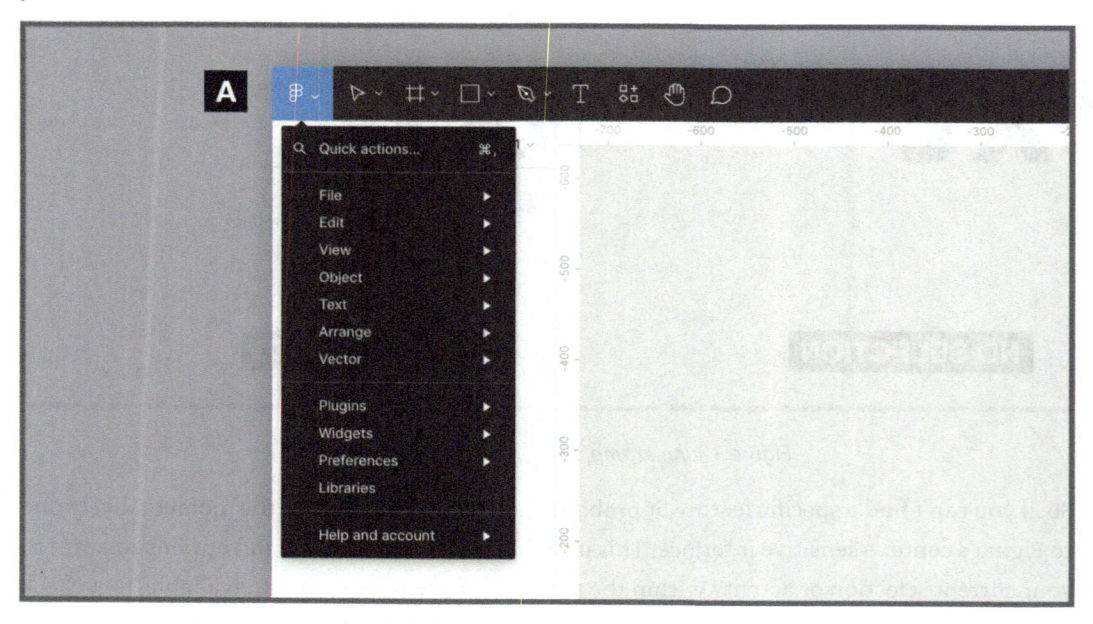

Figure 3.5: Figma's main menu

This is the main control center where you can find import, export, select, display, and many other functions. However, most of these features can be accessed in other ways. For example, anything on the **Text** menu is usually displayed in the context-sensitive panel (on the right) when any text is selected. It is not necessary to open each of the points contained here now, but you will try them in practice from time to time in the corresponding activities.

B – Move

This is the main tool that you will undoubtedly use the most. You can use it to select, move, resize, and rotate any element on the screen, including frames. By clicking and dragging, you can draw an area that will include and select all items inside it. The **Move** tool is quickly accessible with the *V* key on your keyboard, but you'll notice that Figma itself will automatically return you to this tool when you're done with any other tool:

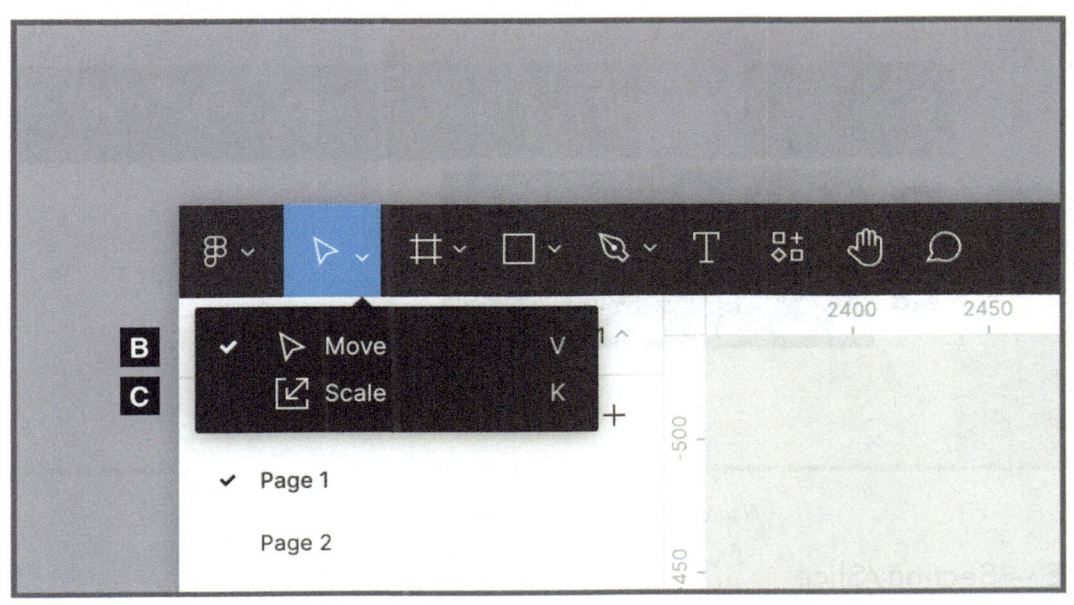

Figure 3.6: The Move and Scale tools

C – Scale

Like the **Move** tool, the **Scale** tool (to quickly switch to this function, use the *K* shortcut) is used to resize any element in your working area. But the **Scale** tool works differently – it resizes any object in proportion to its original dimensions or the frame in which it is nested. To understand this better, type some text by pressing the *T* key, and then select and enlarge it with the **Move** tool. You can see that only the textbox will be larger and not the text itself.

Instead, if you use the **Scale** tool, the font-size property will resize to fit the textbox.

D – Frame

As you know, with the **Frame** tool, you can create a container by choosing from the available presets or by drawing a custom size. Since this is one of Figma's core tools, you will be using it very often. Now you understand frames in Figma but you still have a lot more to learn about them, which you will do later in this book. For now, remember the useful keyboard shortcut for quickly adding a frame onto your canvas; there are two options – the *F* and *A* keys. Regardless of which one you choose, the result will be the same:

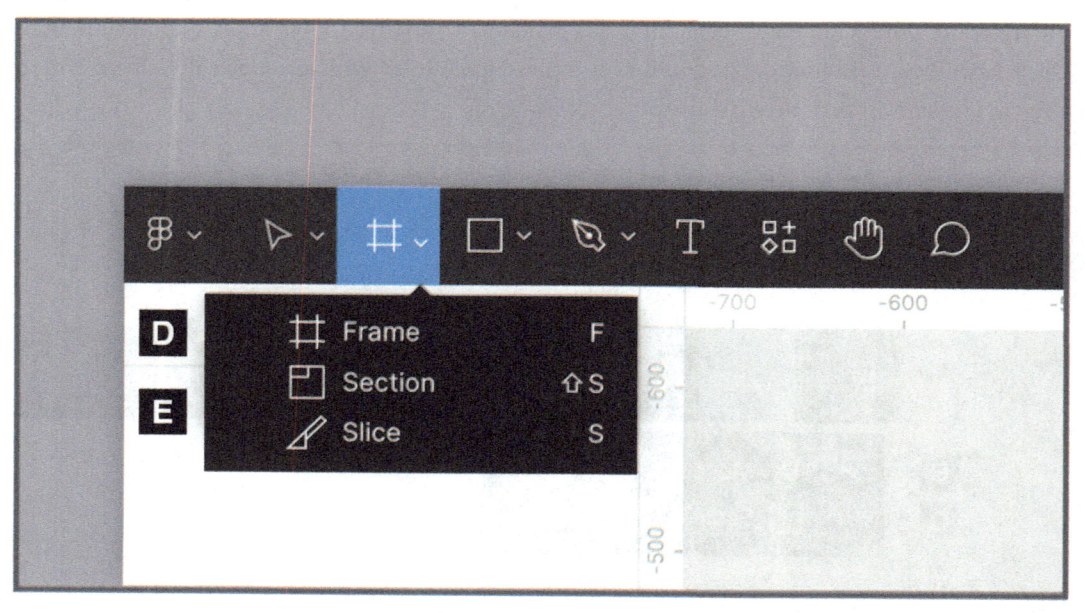

Figure 3.7: The Frame, Section, and Slice tools

E – Section/Slice

Do you remember the sections in FigJam? Well, everyone loves those, so they made their way into Figma. Just like in FigJam, you can use colored sections to visually group areas in your workspace. The **Slice** tool, instead, allows you to select and "cut" any areas in your workspace and export those areas with everything they visually contain. This tool comes from some old website design methods, so don't give it too much of your attention.

F, G, H, I, J, and K — Shapes

This is a set of tools useful for creating all kinds of shapes, from simple lines to star shapes. Each of them has its own specific editing properties. For example, a line can become an arrow by changing the appropriate option in the context-sensitive right panel. Also, you should keep in mind that all shapes created this way are vectors, so you can easily modify them manually any way you want. You will explore shapes in detail in the next chapter:

Figure 3.8: The shape tools

L — Place image/video...

If you need to quickly add an image or a video to your workspace, click the **Place image/video...** tool, and a dialog box will appear, where you can select a media element to import from your computer. Alternatively, you can directly drag and drop it from a folder on your computer to your workspace. It's important to note that while images will display statically, videos can only be played within the context of a Figma prototype. In Figma, a prototype is an interactive version of your design that simulates how it would function in a real-world application, and we'll explore this in depth in *Chapter 10, Testing and Sharing Your Prototype in Browsers and Real Devices*.

M – Pen

This one is as easy as it is powerful. With the **Pen** tool, you can draw any shape using so-called Bézier curves. Bézier curves are a mathematical way to describe smooth, scalable curves and shapes. They are created using points and control handles that allow you to adjust the curve's direction and steepness. From a simple line to the most abstract element, Bézier curves provide a high degree of control in shaping your designs. And all this will be strictly in the vector. While a traditional raster image is composed of a grid of pixels, a vector creates shapes using primitives and mathematical calculations. This allows you to draw simple or complex illustrations that can be scaled to any size without loss of resolution. The *P* keyboard shortcut for the **Pen** tool is undoubtedly worth remembering:

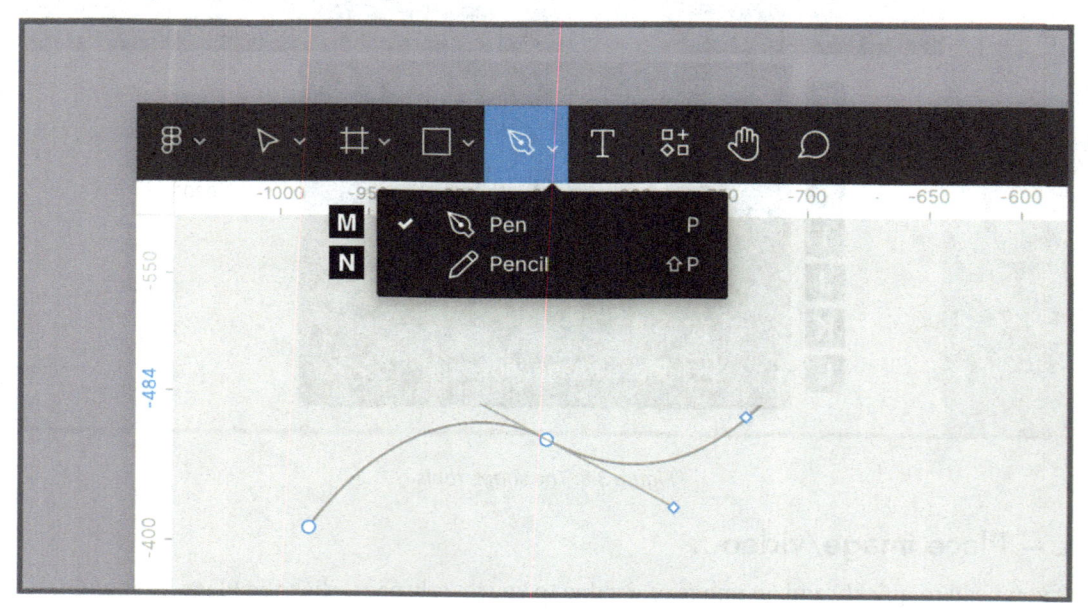

Figure 3.9: The Pen tool with an example Bézier curve

N – Pencil

This is a vector tool like the **Pen** tool, but it doesn't have a Bézier handle system for drawing curves. The **Pencil** tool is for freehand drawing but with the advantage that lines and curves are automatically enhanced and softened after you stop pressing the mouse button to finish drawing. This can be useful, especially if you want to use Figma as a digital whiteboard or take quick freehand notes.

Chapter 3
59

O – Text

The **Text** tool does exactly what you'd expect, allowing you to add text to your design. A shortcut for inserting any text is the *T* key on your keyboard, which you should definitely keep in mind. What's important to note about the **Text** tool is that there are two different methods for entering text. When you click anywhere on the canvas, you create a variable-width text. This text is contained within a "bounding box," which is an invisible, resizable box that adjusts its size automatically to fit the content. On the other hand, if you click and drag instead of just a single click, you create a fixed-width textbox. In this case, the text you enter will be confined to the predefined dimensions of the box and will not extend beyond this fixed space.

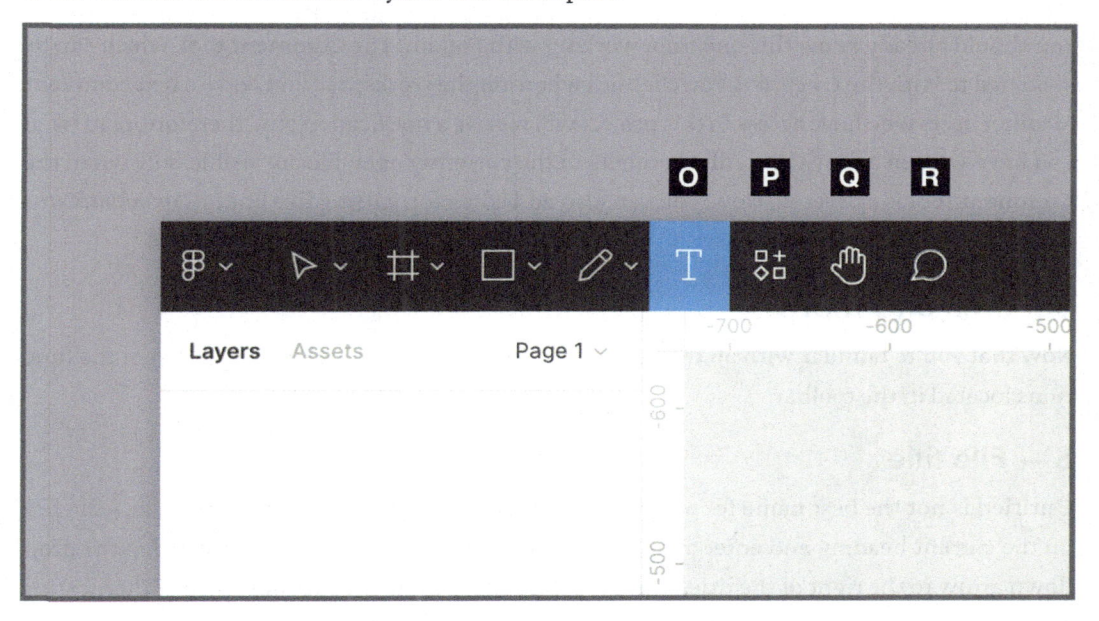

Figure 3.10: The Text, Resources, Hand, and Comment tools

P – Resources

From here, you can quickly access your libraries' components. Moreover, you may extend Figma's features by adding plugins and widgets to your workspace. We'll learn more about this later in the book.

Q – Hand

This tool allows you to pan around the workspace using your mouse or trackpad, preventing accidental selection, repositioning, or any other impact on objects on the canvas.

To activate the **Hand** tool, you can select it from the toolbar, but there's an easier and quicker way. You can press and hold the *spacebar* on your keyboard. This is a much more practical method that will save you time. Imagine that you are currently using the **Move** tool but, from time to time, you need to move around the board without affecting objects on the screen. In this case, you can simply hold down the *spacebar* to temporarily switch to the **Hand** tool. As soon as you release the key, you will automatically return to the **Move** tool. Also, if you are working on a trackpad, just swiping on it with two fingers will allow you to pan over your canvas. Lastly, if you are using a mouse, you can click + hold on the mouse wheel, then drag to pan around.

R – Comment

You should already know this one from working with FigJam. The **Comment** tool, which can be switched to with the *C* key, lets you click anywhere on the workspace and leave a text comment. All other users who have access to this project will receive a notification and, therefore, read what you have written at any time. All comments in the currently open file are visible only when the **Comment** tool is activated. Now, you can also add some formatting like bold (*Command/Ctrl + B*), italics (*Command/Ctrl + I*), lists, and even hyperlinks.

Settings and more

Now that you're familiar with all the basic tools, let's move on to looking at the rest of the functions located in the toolbar.

S – File title

Untitled is not the best name for a good organization of work, is it? To rename a file, just click on the current heading and enter a more appropriate and descriptive one. By clicking the dropdown arrow to the right of the title, you can access a few additional actions, such as duplicating and deleting a file, or moving it to another project, which allows you to convert the file from a draft to a team project.

Here, you will also find version control – that is, the ability to access all saved versions of the file created while you work and, if necessary, restore the old version. This feature saves up to 30 days of history when using the free starter plan, while there is no limit for the paid ones. Think of it like how Google Docs automatically saves your changes as you and others work on the document:

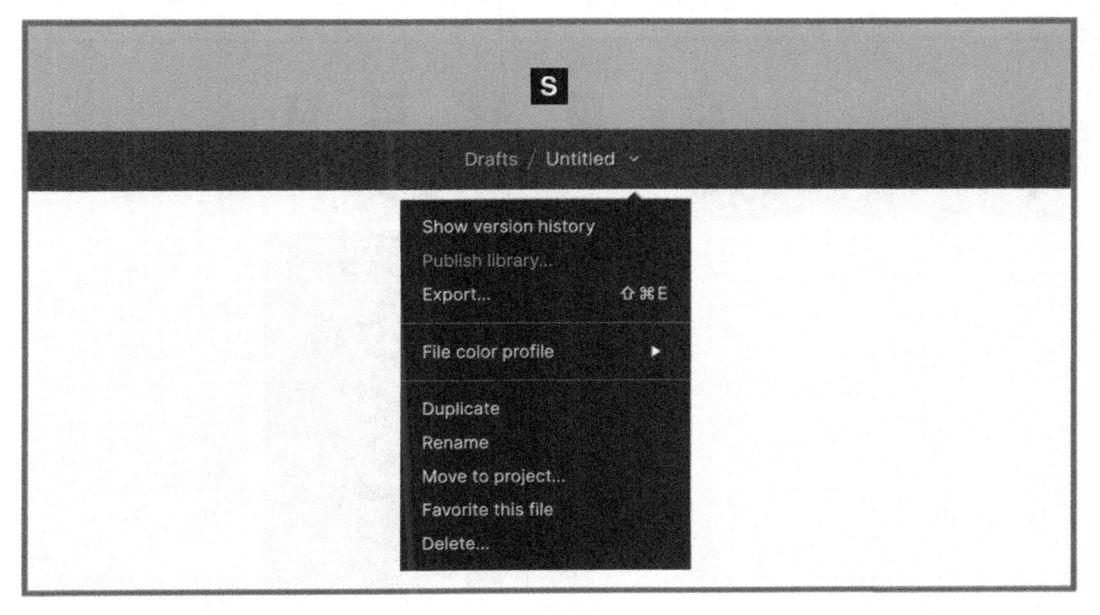

Figure 3.11: File settings

T — active users

Here, you will always have a real-time overview of the online users who are currently in this file. If you click the avatar of another active user, you activate **Observer** mode for yourself, in which you will see exactly what the selected user sees and does.

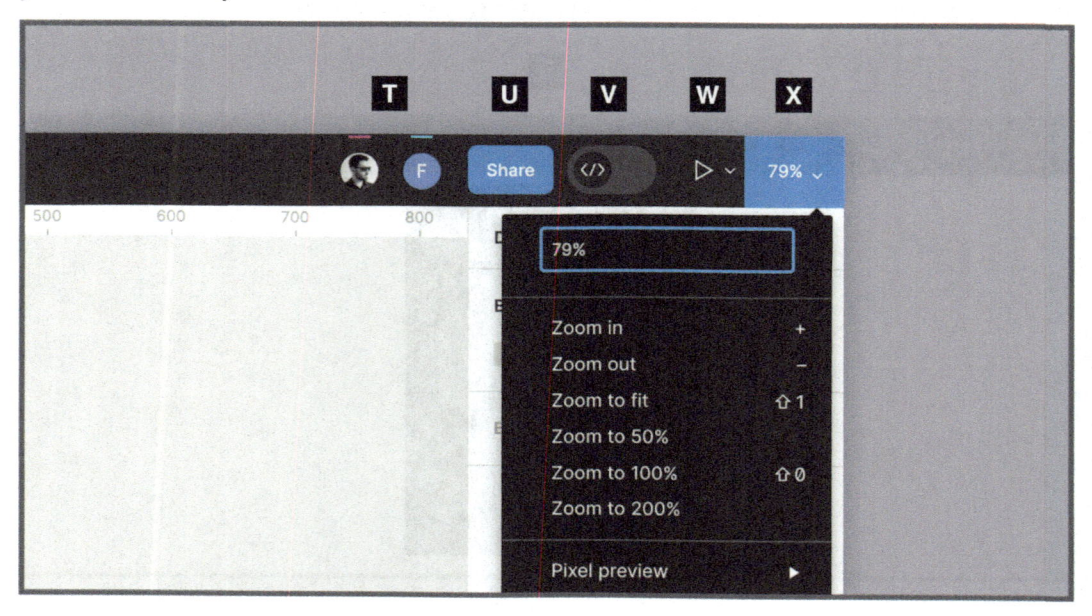

Figure 3.12: The Collaboration, Testing, and View tools

U — Share

This is a gateway to the many sharing opportunities that Figma offers. When you click on the **Share** button, a special dialog box will open where you can not only check the complete list of people who have access to this file and the permissions they have but also add new ones, or get a sharable link that allows you to invite anyone to the project. From here, you can also make your project publicly available to the Figma Community. You will explore this opportunity in the last chapter of the book.

V — Dev mode

By engaging the **Dev mode** switch in Figma, you enter a specialized view designed to bridge the gap between design and development. This mode functions similarly to a browser's Inspect tool. It provides a detailed, code-centric perspective of your design, offering insights into the underlying CSS, layout properties, and other technical specifications.

Essentially, Dev mode translates the visual elements of your design into a format that can be readily interpreted and used by developers. This is particularly useful for ensuring that the design's implementation in code accurately reflects the original design intent.

W — Present

Here, you can bring your design to life, allowing you to view both static previews of your chosen frames and complex interactive prototypes. The viewer opens in a separate tab and acts as a separate file, so you can share the preview with selected people or publicly while keeping the project source safe for yourself.

X — Zoom/view

What you see here numerically is the current zoom value set in your workspace, and it changes in real time as you zoom in/out with your mouse wheel, pinch and zoom on a trackpad, or with the + and - keys on your keyboard. Clicking on it opens a drop-down menu dedicated to zooming and display settings, where you can not only use predefined functions to change zoom values but also manually set them by entering a number. There are also several toggles for options, such as the ability to activate or deactivate rulers.

Quick shortcuts

As you can see, Figma's top toolbar is the source of its core tools, some of which help you add elements to your design; others are for working within your workspace. There is no doubt that you can call this area very "feature-rich." But the more you practice, the more you will understand how easy it is to find and switch from one tool to another. Your workflow will speed up even more if you implement the use of keyboard shortcuts in your daily work. Start with the easy ones and then, little by little, add more complex ones.

You can always check out all available keyboard shortcuts listed right in Figma, so you don't even need to consult the tutorials on the website or google anything. Just click the **?** button in the bottom-right corner and select **Keyboard shortcuts**, and you will see a hotkeys panel sorted by the functions they run.

Those filled with blue mean that you have already used them at least once; the gray shortcuts are those that you have not yet tested out:

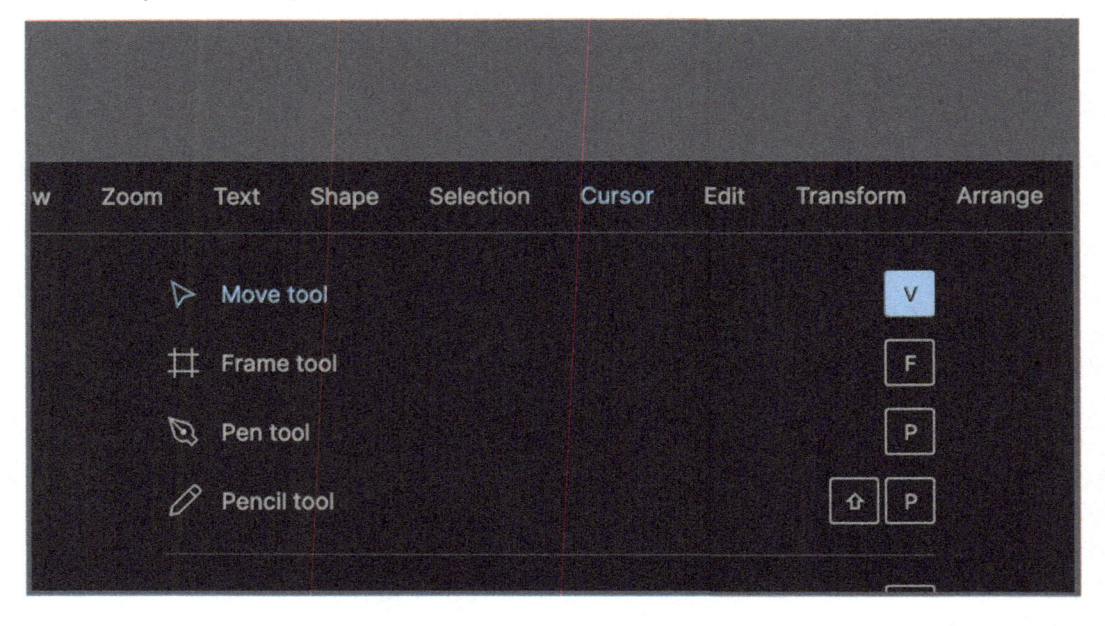

Figure 3.13: The shortcut helper panel

Note:

Figma defaults to a U.S. QWERTY keyboard layout for its shortcuts, which can pose conflicts or challenges for users with international keyboards. Fortunately, if it doesn't automatically detect your keyboard layout, you can easily change it by clicking on the question mark icon and selecting **Change keyboard layout...**. This option may provide you with simpler shortcuts in some cases.

So, now that you have a basic understanding of the general features of Figma and can add something to your workspace, it's time to see where you can access all the layers in your files.

Exploring the left panel

Learning about Figma's tool sets can be challenging, but it is important to have at least a basic understanding of the features so you can quickly get started using them. Don't worry if you still feel insecure every time you launch Figma. You will soon learn the concept of each tool in a real workflow. However, tools are just one part of everything to learn in Figma. It is equally important to know how to work with layers and assets in your project. All of these will be displayed in the left sidebar, so let's take a deeper look at its interface.

Layers and Pages

Every time you create a new text layer, shape, or any other element, its name is immediately displayed in the **Layers** panel. Likewise, when you delete an object from the work area (you can do this simply with the *Backspace* key on macOS or the *Delete* key on Windows), it will also be removed from the sidebar. So, think of the **Layers** panel as a container that collects everything in your project and helps you organize all the elements better:

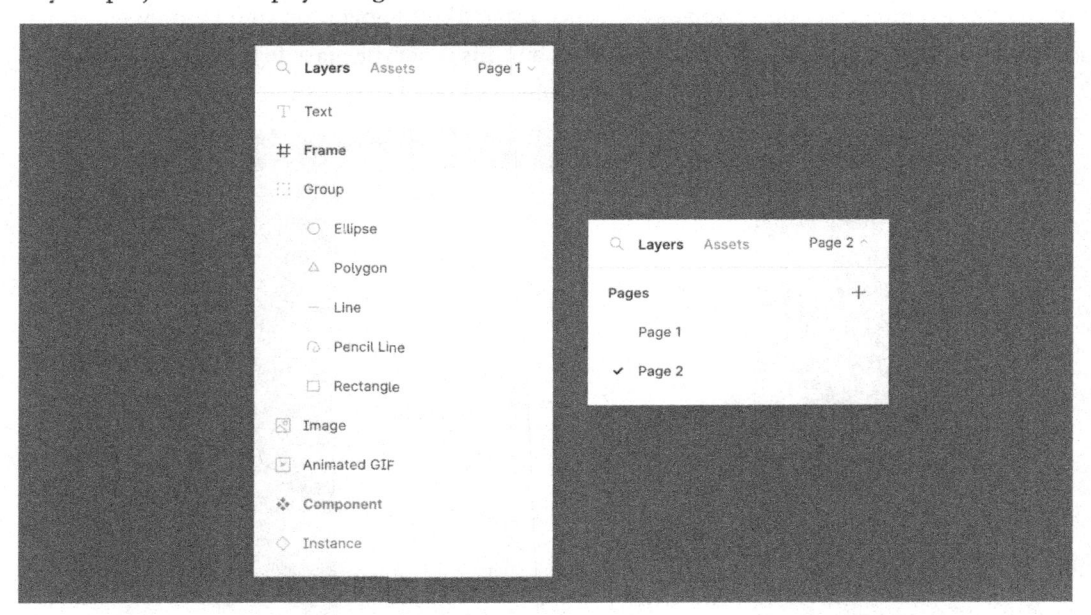

Figure 3.14: The Layers and Pages panels

First, pay attention to the visual meaning of the icons in the panel and how they differ depending on the type of layer you are creating. A shape layer, for example, has a thumbnail of the shape itself. Don't worry if some of the layer types are not familiar to you. You'll soon be working with all of them, and as a result, you'll remember every icon that appears in the panel.

The number of layers you have grows faster than you might imagine, so it's important to always keep them organized. It's very good practice to give each layer a suitable and meaningful name. This will also help anyone else you're collaborating with have more context into the purpose of the layers. However, be careful when moving the layers because the hierarchy present in the **Layers** panel also reflects their order of depth on the canvas.

When there are too many layers to organize properly, pages come into play. Essentially, pages are separate workspaces, almost like independent sections within the file, but in fact, if they are placed in the same file, they belong to the same ecosystem, so you can freely use styles, resources, and more on all the pages. They are very useful for organizing, for example, different design stages in the same file. You will soon see how to build this kind of page structure in a file in an effective manner.

Assets

The **Assets** panel is an indispensable tab on the left panel that is used to organize all the elements of your design project for reuse. You haven't encountered components on your journey yet, which is one of the most important concepts in Figma, but this is not the place to get to know them. For now, you should just keep in mind that this is where you will soon be able to find them:

Figure 3.15: The Assets panel

The more the **Assets** area begins to fill, the more difficult it becomes to visually search for the required components from the list. In this case, you should use the search bar at the top, which filters the results by the names assigned to the components. This is another good reason to choose the correct names for all of the elements – to make them easier to find.

Finally, in **Assets**, you can also find the **Team Libraries** (under the book-shaped icon), an incredible feature that lets you use styles and components from other files, either personal or from the Figma Community.

So, now you know that in the left sidebar in Figma, you can see and organize your layers, add new pages, and find your assets quickly. This is still just a general overview of this panel, and you will inevitably get to know it more deeply as you practice. Now, let's move on to the next section of this chapter, which will be devoted to the context-sensitive right panel.

Exploring the right panel

Last but not least, you will explore the right panel, commonly referred to as the **Properties** panel. This area is context-sensitive, so it changes every time you click on something in your design file. Depending on the selected object, you can see different options, functions, and parameters. Therefore, it is better to learn and remember the functionality of the right panel in practice, and this section is just a short guide for it, which will simplify your further work. As you can see, the right sidebar is split into two tabs: **Design** and **Prototype**. Let's start and proceed in order.

Design

This is the panel tab that Figma opens by default, which makes sense since you will no doubt use it the most. Whatever you're looking for about visual edits, you'll always find it in the **Design** panel. If nothing is selected in your workspace, the panel may seem empty.

But as soon as you click on any element on the canvas, you will see some functions appearing there:

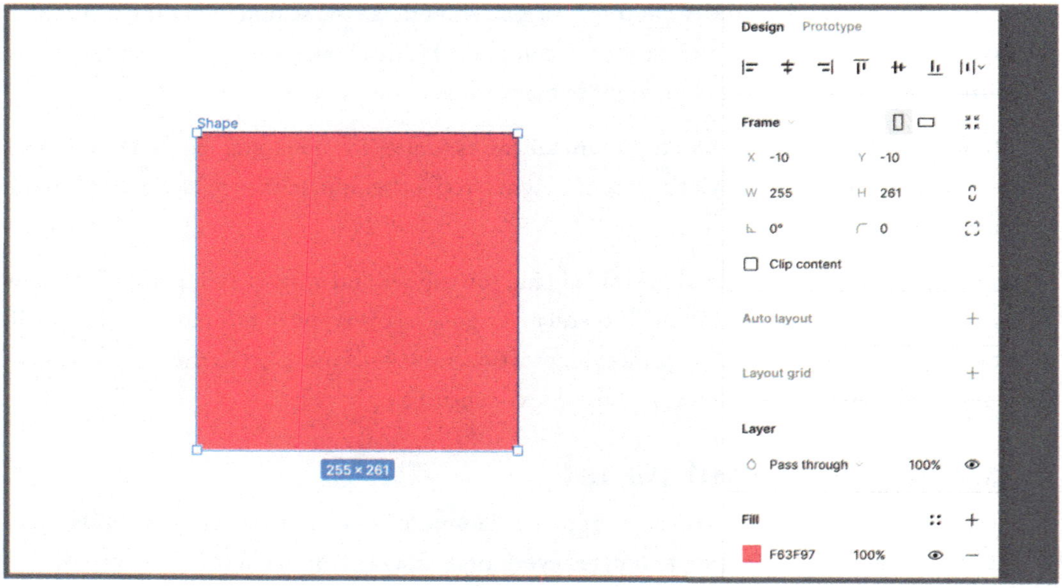

Figure 3.16: The context-sensitive options of a frame

At first glance, this may seem tricky. So, to get a better understanding of the concept, ask yourself this: would it be helpful to see the font size settings every time you work with a vector shape? Not at all. And therefore, in Figma, you will never see any function that is not needed or not usable at the moment.

Let's click on the frame you created at the beginning of this chapter, which represents the screen size of the iPhone 13 mini, and see what happens in the **Design** panel. Functions you've never seen before came out of nowhere. If you look closely, you can see that all the options are consistent with the functionality of the frames. This way, you can change its size (manually or using the usual list of presets), the background color, corner radius, and many other advanced features that you will discover later.

If you now try to deselect the frame by clicking anywhere outside the element, the **Design** panel will hide the display of all previous settings. You see that it is almost empty again and only offers you the option to change the background color of the workspace itself. You can do that if you ever need to increase the contrast between the design and the background.

It won't take you long to learn to appreciate the benefits of using context-sensitive features, and soon, you won't be able to imagine your workflow without them. But in case you're looking for a particular setting and can't find it, remember that most of the basic functionalities can also be accessed from the drop-down menu under the Figma icon in the upper-left corner, or by right-clicking on any object in your workspace.

Prototype

The **Prototype** panel is quite different from the **Design** panel, allowing you to add interactions to your elements and presenting everything dynamically:

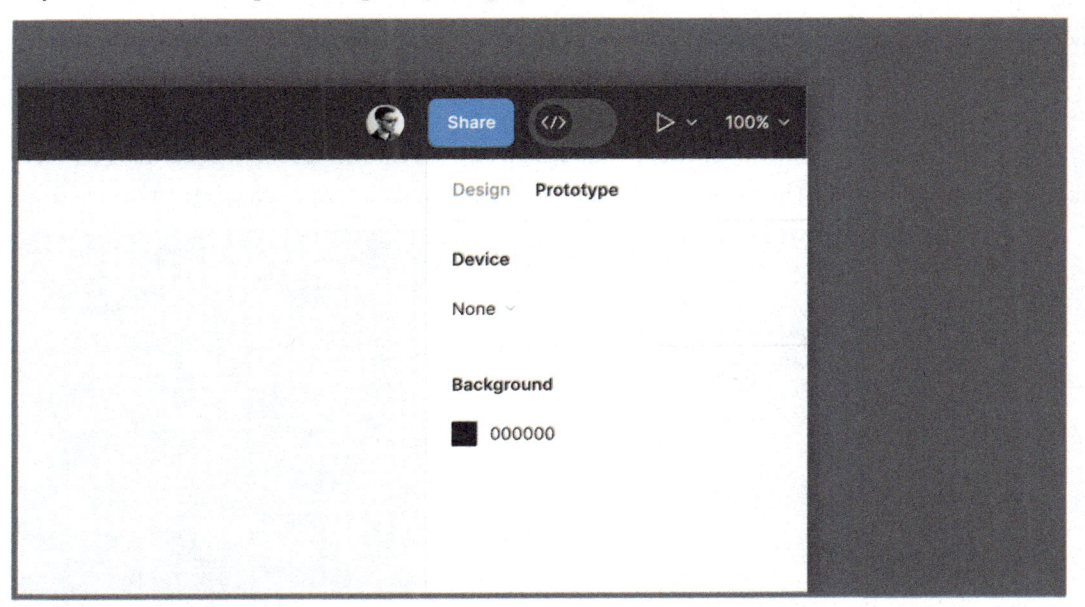

Figure 3.17: The Prototype panel

This panel is also context-sensitive, so the settings you find here are related to the currently selected item and will be exclusive to it. But in this case, however, not all elements really have functionality available upon selection. If you click on the text, for example, nothing will appear in the **Prototype** panel, just like clicking on a shape or image. This is because not all elements need to be made interactive.

Thus, the **Prototype** panel also has two states: inactive (after clicking anywhere outside of your elements in the workspace) and another state when frames or components are selected.

Inactive state

In the first state, as before, you are only allowed to change the background color of the canvas, plus you can see general **Prototype** settings that are associated with each page.

The first option presented in this panel is the **Device** section, which allows you to choose how the prototype will be displayed. If you open the drop-down list under the name of the section, you will see various presets for commonly used devices. You can choose any of the devices on the list, and for some models, there are even colors to choose from. As you remember, you previously selected the iPhone 13 mini to set the size of your frame, but this does not mean that you will see this device in presentation mode. To see your design on a specific device model, you need to select it in the **Device** section. This selection also allows you to test your frames on different device sizes:

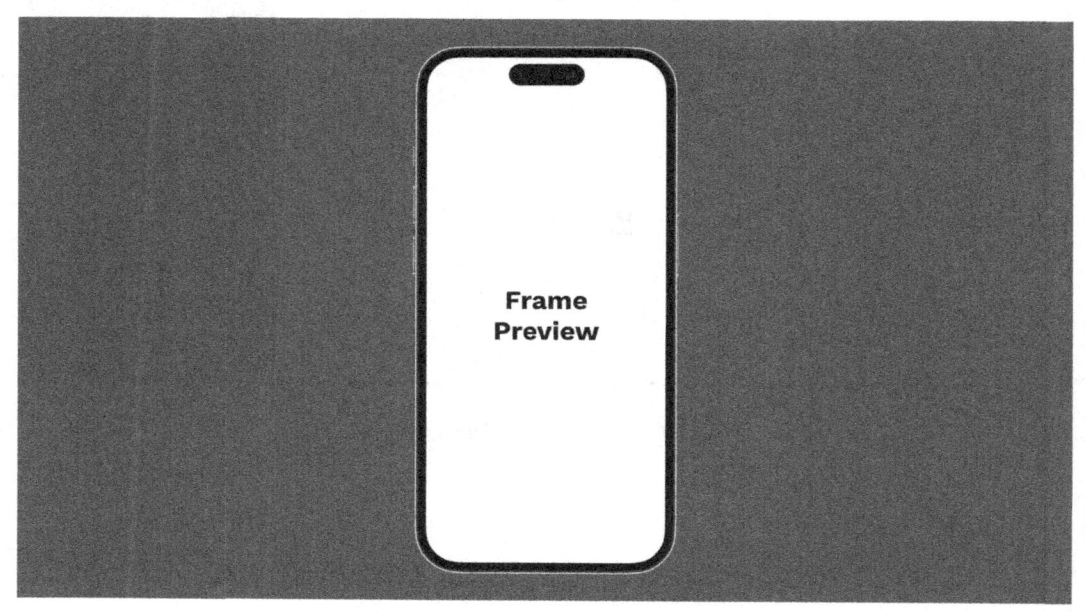

Figure 3.18: The Frame Preview window

Chapter 3

The next setting you'll notice is the background. Here, you can set the background color for the prototyping screen if you want to change the color behind the selected device. You can also change the orientation of your device from portrait to landscape, or vice versa.

With an Active selection

Like the **Design** panel, **Prototype** is also context-sensitive. Thus, after selecting any frame or component on the canvas, instead of the device and background settings, the panel will display other more advanced features. In this scenario, Figma doesn't prompt changes to your objects. Instead, it provides options for interacting with elements on-screen, like defining actions following a button press or setting a scrolling direction:

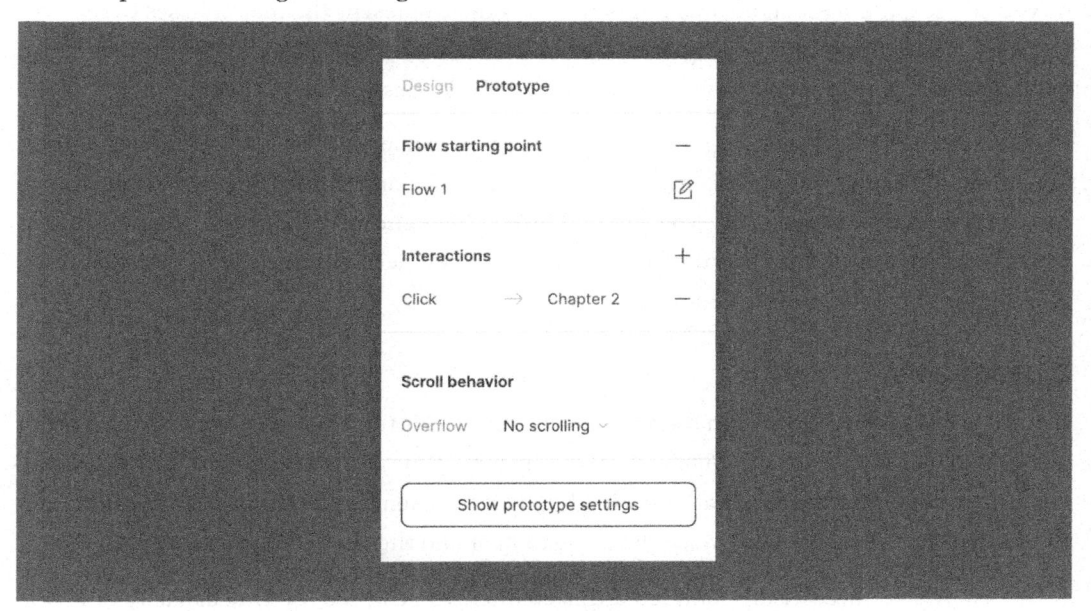

Figure 3.19: The Prototype panel with an active selection

At first glance, the **Prototype** section might not seem as equipped with various settings as the **Design** panel. But its simplification is justified by the fact that everything here is done extremely intuitively. The entire interaction system plays on the mechanics of "if this, then that," allowing you to select an element, assign it an action type (touch, click, hover, and so on), and determine the result that this action will produce – for example, moving to another page, or opening or closing an overlay.

One of the most recent additions to the **Prototype** panel is the **Flows** section, which was a very significant upgrade. This feature allows you to create more than one flow in the same project file to compare or test different realizations of the same scenario.

Are you curious to know more about all this? Don't worry – in *Chapter 9, Prototyping with Transitions, Smart Animate, and Interactive Components*, and *Chapter 10, Testing and Sharing Your Prototype in Browsers and Real Devices*, you will have the opportunity to explore in depth the amazing power of prototyping in Figma.

Help Center

As you can see, the right sidebar contains two tabs that represent the main phases of the user interface – design and prototyping. It is in this order that you will get more and more practice, and as a result, you will learn how to use each function in those panels.

If you have any difficulty finding information about any Figma tool or want to refer to official resources, you can always do this in the **Help Center** by clicking the floating circle button with ? in the lower-right corner. Here, you can find links to content from the official website, Figma YouTube videos, the support forum, and so on. So, all you need now is a bit of patience and a willingness to further explore Figma!

Summary

If you feel like all the new information you've just received is too much to remember, you're not alone. When getting started in Figma, it especially takes time to get used to its interface and become fluent with its features. That's why it is highly recommended to return to this chapter from time to time to refresh your memory about the toolbar and the left and right panels.

Now that you've successfully completed this chapter, you can see the true capacity of Figma and how powerful it can be in many ways. To help you create high-quality designs in the best possible way, Figma never stops working on introducing new or improved features. Stay tuned to the official Figma X (formerly Twitter) profile (`@figmadesign`) for new features and releases, and try testing them and incorporating them into your work routine so that Figma's tools will have nothing mysterious or unknown to you.

From now on, with each chapter, you will get more and more familiar with Figma! In the next chapter, you'll start working on your first wireframe, using shapes and other basic elements. Get ready for an exciting new challenge!

Learn more on Discord

To join the Discord community for this book – where you can share feedback, ask questions to the author, and learn about new releases – follow the QR code below:

`https://packt.link/figma`

4

Wireframing a Mobile-First Experience Using Vector Shapes

You've reached the point where you have essential knowledge of the UX process and Figma's interface. Now it's time to put it all together and get started with the user interface of our streaming service application. Keeping all artifacts from the UX phase within easy reach is crucial – this includes the mission statement, personas, user flows, and other collected data. This chapter marks an important transition from theoretical concepts and hypotheses to the practical task of creating an actual application structure. You'll achieve this through the wireframe method, a foundational step in bringing your design to life.

This is a very important part of product development, but there is nothing to worry about since this chapter will guide you through the entire process of this phase. However, before moving on to wireframing, you will need to have a basic understanding of what it is and why it is so helpful for all UX/UI designers, no matter how much experience they have. You will also learn about the tools you will need in this step and practice using them right on the canvas.

So, this time, the information will be quite varied, but by the end of the chapter, all the knowledge and skills that you have gained so far will turn into something directly related to your first prototype of a mobile application in Figma!

In this chapter, we are going to cover the following main topics:

- Evolving the idea to a wireframe
- Playing with shapes in Figma
- Advanced editing of vectors with the Pen tool
- Developing the app structure

Evolving the idea to a Wireframe

Since the analysis and research phases have been completed and the idea has been approved, you are ready to turn it into something real. This time, you'll learn how to create a skeleton for our previously introduced streaming service application, which is a wired structure for visualizing and experimenting with usability and product functionality. This is an important process called wireframing that takes place before you start designing the first prototype and allows you to choose the right product structure. There is some theoretical knowledge that you should have about this step, so in this section, you will learn some important concepts about the interface and the related navigation elements.

What is a wireframe?

If you are a beginner, you may not know what a wireframe is and what it is for. A wireframe is essentially the first draft of a UI, presented without any style, detail, or color. It's a crucial step in the design process, allowing you to lay out the basic structure of your product before delving into more detailed design elements.

Although you may be eager to work on a more detailed design, remember that wireframing is integral to creating a practical and useful product. It helps in identifying and solving design problems early, which is vital for a successful user experience. The first iteration of the wireframe can even be a simple sketch on paper, as shown in *Figure 4.1*, but you'll create it in Figma using the artifacts from your research, like the user persona and user flow.

Figure 4.1: A paper wireframe example (Photo by Halacious on Unsplash)

The wireframing itself does not take too long, and even a very raw draft can help identify problems during user testing. Thus, you can make any changes at an early stage and better work out the usability of a product based on the testers' feedback. If you skip the wireframe stage and jump straight to UI design, you run the risk of revealing all the problems in the near-final version of the product. As a result, you will inevitably spend a lot more time working because it will take a huge effort to make changes to an already polished prototype.

Don't worry if you still can't come up with a clear idea of a real wireframe that can be applied to our brief. You will soon learn how to structure it, and everything will become much clearer.

Why mobile-first?

Before proceeding directly with the creation of the wireframe, you need to select an initial product format. This will depend on what is planned to be developed. For example, if you are creating a product that will be used primarily on a computer, the desktop screen will be the starting frame. And since the mobile version is secondary to this product, you can get started with it later.

However, in most cases, you will usually choose the smallest initial format, which is the format of mobile devices. Is this just a set rule? Not really. The reason for this choice is based on the analysis of statistical data. For several years now, people have been using smartphones instead of desktops to browse the web and use apps for basic internet operations. So, because of this significant change in the behavior of people in the digital space, the design of user interfaces has become primarily focused on mobile devices.

But even when choosing a mobile device as the primary format, a new dilemma arises as to which screen resolution to go for, since it can vary from device to device. Except in special cases where there is exact data on which smartphone model will be used by many of the users, it is better to stick to a medium-resolution mobile device format. Then, you can gradually increase the size of screens to higher resolutions for smartphones, then tablets, and finally desktops and TVs.

We will not design for every Android device and all iPhone models. It would be useless, since the main goal is not to release a real product but to design a product that can become a detailed blueprint for developers.

So, let's set up our application for release on a mobile device, a tablet, and a computer. For the wireframe, the standard screen of the mobile device will be selected. At later stages of the work, an adaptive approach will be integrated to account for all other device sizes and to ensure that the product works well on all available devices, without leaving anything to chance.

Now you know what is behind the creation of the skeleton of the future application interface and what the initial screen size should be. But before you start drawing in Figma, you'll learn about and practice with some of the tools you need to create your first wireframe.

Playing with Shapes in Figma

You are already familiar with many of the basic tools in Figma, but so far, you have not tested them that much. This is not a problem, as you will actively try out every useful feature, which you will start doing right now. You don't have to worry about knowing any advanced tools to create a wireframe; all you need is simple geometric shapes.

Basic shapes

As you already know, the top toolbar has a set of **Shape** tools that allows you to add different geometric shapes that you can then edit on the canvas. Besides basic shapes such as ellipses and rectangles, you can use more complex ones. For example, the **Star** tool creates a classic five-pointed star by default, but the element can be edited after it is added to the canvas.

You can change the number of the star points, increasing or decreasing them by clicking the **Count** handle (*Figure 4.2*) and dragging the cursor up or down:

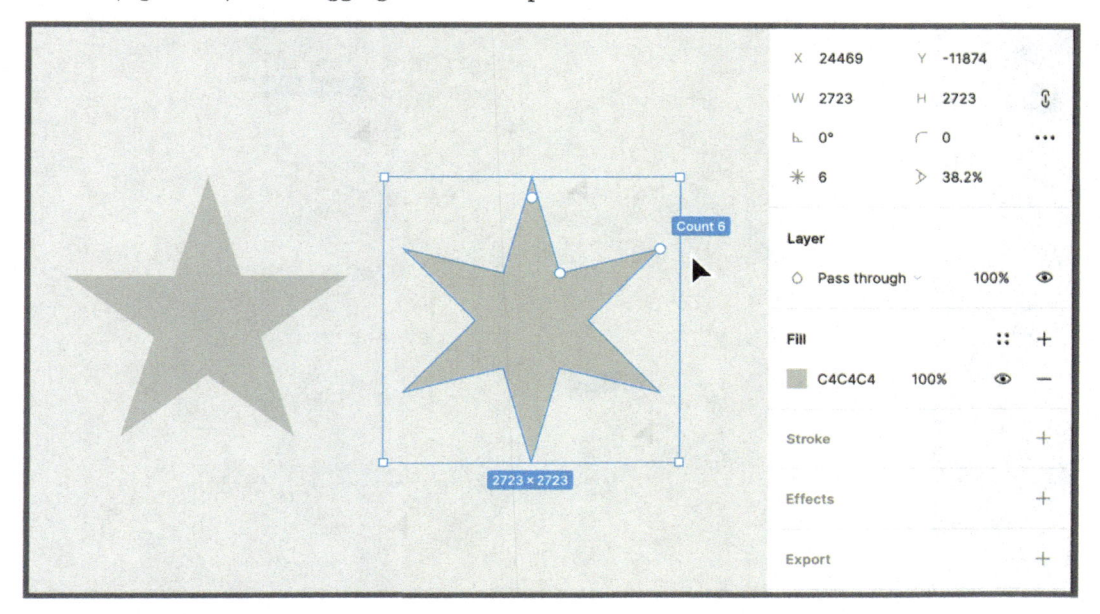

Figure 4.2: Editing a star

Likewise, with the **Polygon** tool, you can create a default triangular shape and then increase the number of sides, thus creating more complex shapes, such as pentagons and hexagons. The other shape-editing handle, **Radius**, allows you to quickly adjust the roundness of each shape.

The **Ellipse** tool seems simple because you would obviously expect it to create circles or ellipses. But with the **Ellipse** tool, you can also create pie charts very easily. How? Draw a circle on the canvas, select it, and hover over it so that an **Arc** handle appears. Dragging this marker inside the circle creates a gap that allows you to create pie charts. This action also brings up additional markers on your circle, each with a specific function:

- **Sweep**: This is the handle you initially used to create the gap in the circle.
- **Start**: This handle allows you to rotate the starting point of the gap, giving you control over where your pie chart begins.
- **Ratio**: Using this handle, you can transform the circle into a ring by moving it toward the center of the ellipse.

These features of the **Ellipse** tool enhance its versatility, enabling you to create more than just simple shapes but also effective visual data representations like pie charts and rings.

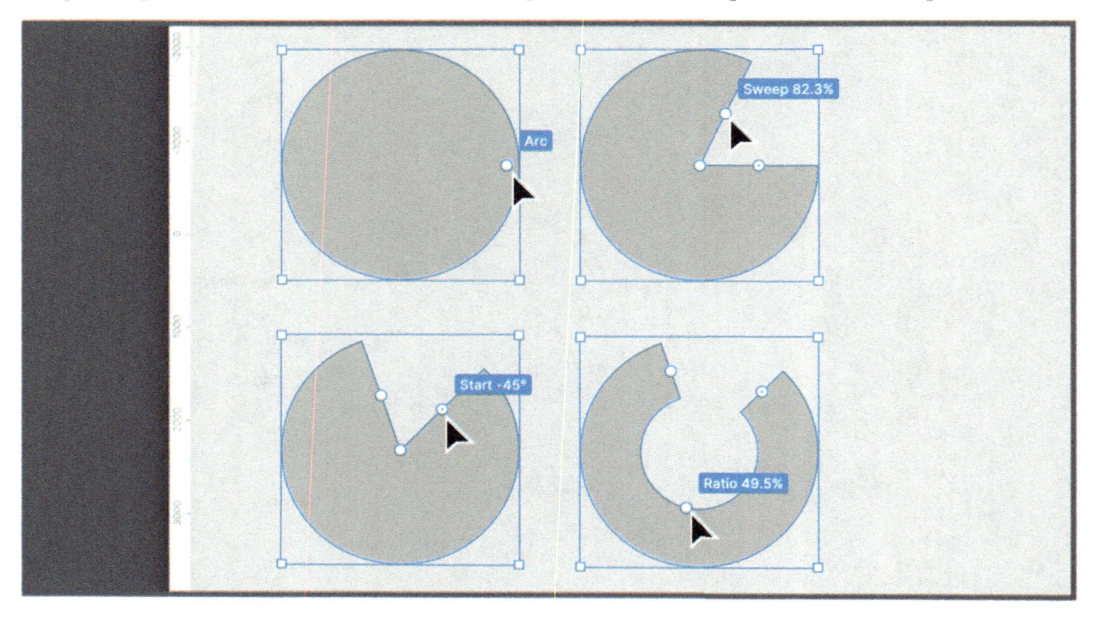

Figure 4.3: A circle's edit handles

> **Note:**
>
> By holding down the *Shift* key while resizing the shape, you can easily keep its proportions. If you instead press and hold the *Option* key (macOS) or *Alt* (Windows), the shape will be resized from its center. You can also use both keys together to resize the shape proportionally to its center. Feel free to experiment with these tricks on different shapes and elements!

You might have noticed that Figma automatically applies a default style to any shape added to the canvas, typically a gray background color. While this default is sufficient for creating your initial wireframe, even minor adjustments to this style can make the flow more intuitive and functional. For instance, you can use a stronger color to highlight elements representing a suggested user path, making it easier to visualize the actions leading to the intended outcome.

Chapter 4   81

Changing the style of a shape in Figma is straightforward. Simply select an element on your canvas, and the right sidebar will display various style options. Feel free to experiment with different colors and styles – you'll become more familiar with each as you progress.

It's important to remember that every shape added to the canvas is a vector, meaning it's fully editable to suit your design needs. To edit a shape, just click on it and press *Enter*, or double-click it, to enter edit mode:

Figure 4.4: The vector edit mode

While in edit mode, you can edit each point of the selected shape, or even add new points with the **Pen** tool. And that is not all. In edit mode, the usual Figma toolbar is replaced with some dedicated vector editing tools. With the **Bend** tool, for example, you can click and drag any vector point on a shape and convert it to a curve. When you are finished editing the shape, click **Done** on the toolbar to exit edit mode, or press the *Enter* or *Esc* key again.

Edit mode is incredibly powerful, and you will need to take some time to learn how it works. Don't worry – in the next section of this chapter, you will find detailed information on the vector graphics capabilities and the functionality of the **Pen** tool in Figma. This will be your starting point for practice on your own.

Combining shapes

You may have noticed that after you select any shape on the board, a new set of icons appears in the center of the top toolbar (*Figure 4.6*), where the file name is usually displayed. You can access even more features by selecting two or more items together. To do this, drag a selection on those elements by holding down the left mouse button, or click one of the shapes first, and then while holding down the *Shift* key, click the rest. Once selected, you will see three icons in the middle of the top toolbar; the last of them, which is the Boolean groups, can only be applied to a group of objects, not a single element.

Using this newly discovered set of functions, you can perform many different operations on a group of objects. If you choose two shapes, you can, for example, combine them in a special way. To understand this better, let's try to create a crescent using two circles:

1. Create the first circle by selecting an ellipse in the shapes or by pressing the *O* key on your keyboard. Remember to hold down the *Shift* key while drawing to get a perfectly even circle.
2. Change the default circle background color by selecting it and clicking the colored square below the **Fill** section in the right sidebar. A new window will appear with a color selector. Just pick any shade of yellow:

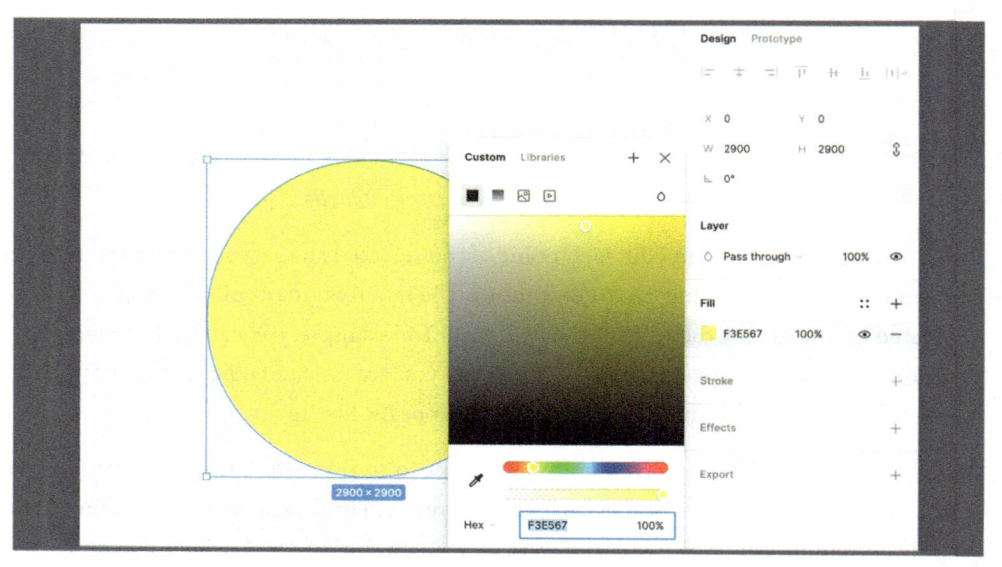

Figure 4.5: Selecting a color

Chapter 4 83

3. Duplicate the yellow circle by clicking and dragging it slightly to the right while holding down the *Option* (macOS) or *Alt* (Windows) key, or by using the *Command + D* (macOS) or *Ctrl + D* (Windows) keyboard shortcut. These shortcuts make it easy to duplicate any layer.
4. Select both shapes.
5. Click the drop-down arrow of the third icon in the center of the toolbar – the Boolean group – and choose **Subtract selection**. This will use the layer above to subtract from the layer below:

Figure 4.6: Subtract selection

The result will be a simple crescent.

Each of the functions in this drop-down menu allows you to get a different result, from combining individual shapes to excluding or intersecting selected shapes:

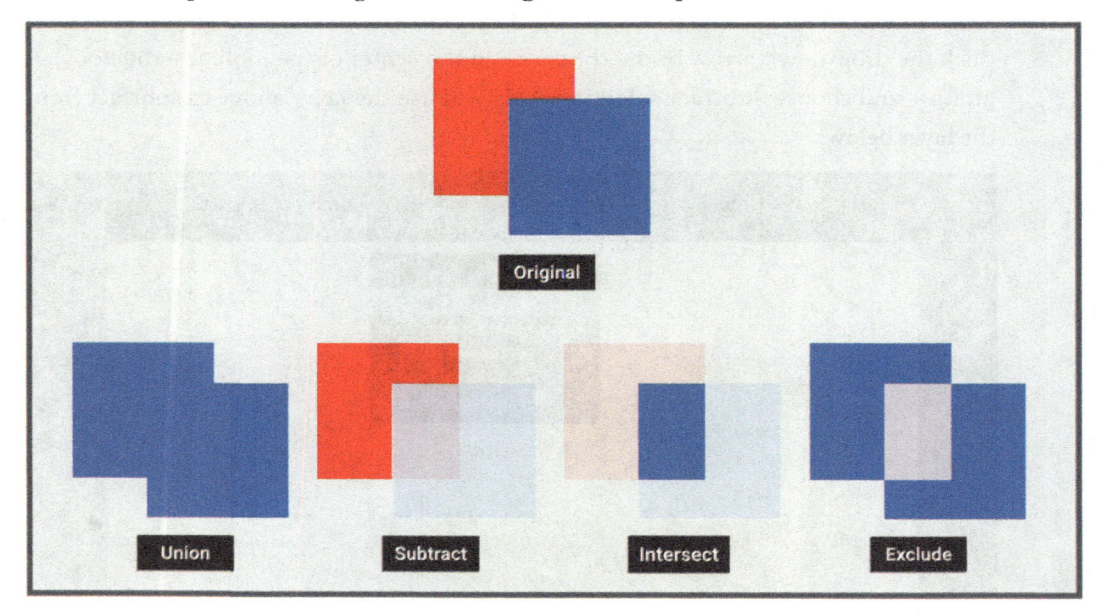

Figure 4.7: The vector's Boolean groups

Almost all of the functions in this menu are simple and clear, and you can test them by yourself on any two shapes you select. However, the **Flatten** function, which can also be run using the *Command + E* (macOS) or *Ctrl + E* (Windows) key combination, requires a few more details. Flatten selection allows you to combine multiple shapes into a single vector while still preserving each shape's outline (you can find a visual example of this in *Figure 4.8* as follows, showing you the difference between shapes combined with **Union** and **Flatten**). This is possible due to Figma's incredible "vector network" feature, which we'll explore in the next section of this chapter.

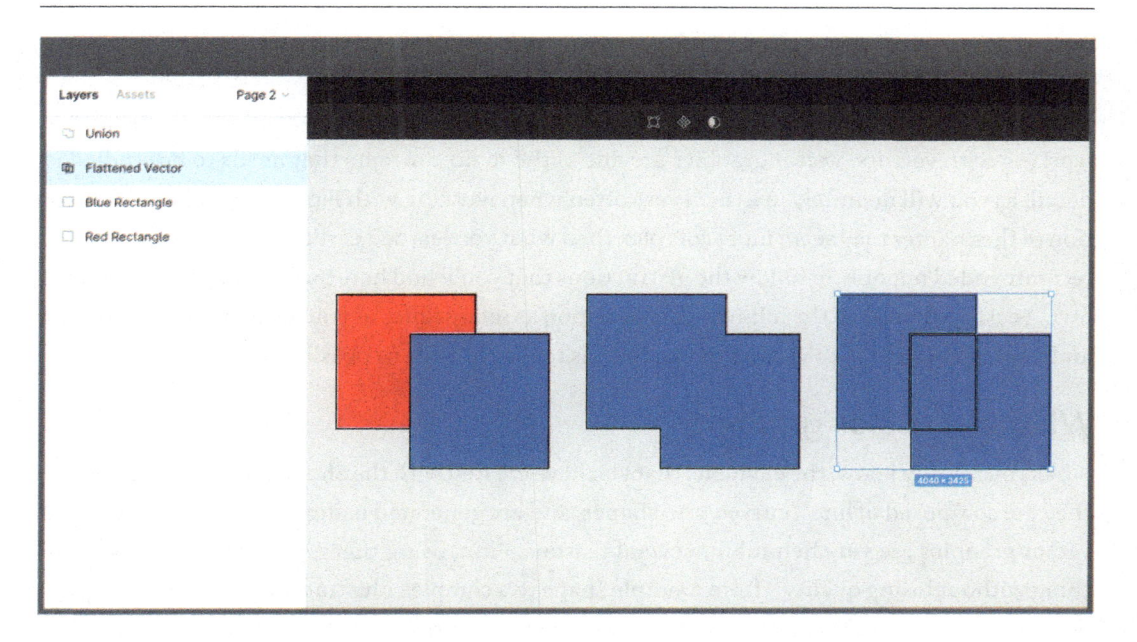

Figure 4.8: The differences between Normal, Union, and Flatten

Note:

In Figma, Boolean operations are non-destructive. This means that when you apply a "shape combine" operation, Figma creates a group containing your elements, allowing you to easily change the final result by editing the individual shapes at any point in time.

You've now learned about a whole bunch of new tools that will make it easy to get more complex shapes. The next topic in the chapter will be devoted to the more advanced features of Figma, and you will learn how to effectively work with vectors.

Advanced vectors with the Pen tool

Before you get some practice by implementing our brief, let's dive deeper into the principles of working with vectors. Vector graphics are one of the main concepts that needs to be studied in detail, as you will definitely use them very often when working with Figma. The topic of this section of the chapter may seem more complex than what you learned earlier. This is why it is highly recommended not only to follow the instructions that you'll find here but also to practice on your own. Feel free to refer to the following information as many times as you need; try experimenting and getting creative with vectors to master this tool as quickly as possible!

What are vector graphics?

So, as you already know, the elements that you have created with the **Shape** tool so far are vectors; they are composed of lines, curves, and shapes, and are generated using mathematical formulas. Vector graphics are very helpful for several reasons. First, using them, you can freely scale anything without losing quality – from a simple shape to a complex illustration. This magic happens because when you resize a vector shape, Figma recalculates the data that it is composed of, so the result of the resized shape or image will not be grainy. In contrast, raster (or bitmap) images – for example, a .jpeg photo imported into Figma – are composed of a finite amount of data, which is a grid of pixels of specific sizes, where each pixel is associated with an exact color. If you double the size of this bitmap image, there is not enough chromatic information at its disposal to cover this mesh, and you end up with a grainy, low-quality image that should be absolutely avoided in production:

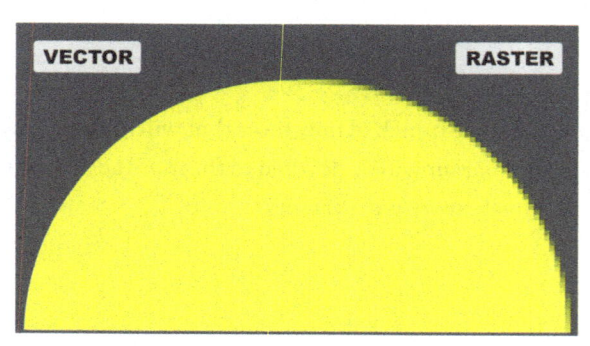

Figure 4.9: Vector versus Raster

Another advantage of a vector object is that it is very easy to edit and, more incredibly, it is very light in file size. But if vector graphics have so many advantages, why do you need bitmap at all? The point is that vector graphics are not suitable for all situations.

For example, a photograph cannot be vectorized, unless you want to accurately redraw it as an illustration. Complex details, light, and shadows cannot be reproduced with lines, curves, primitives, and intersecting shapes.

When it comes to logos, icons, and illustrations, it's always best to create them in vector format. But how do you know that you have a vector and not a raster object? Everything that is created in Figma is already a vector by default. But when you import an external element, you need to check the file extension – for example .jpeg or .png files can never be vectors. The most common format for vector content is **Scalable Vector Graphics (SVG)**, which has increased in use in recent years thanks to its support in modern browsers and operating systems. Because of the simplicity of vector editing, SVG has also become incredibly efficient for animation.

> **Note:**
> You can move vector shapes from Adobe Illustrator to Figma by simply copying and pasting them. If you want to do the opposite, right-click the shape in Figma and choose **Copy | Paste | Copy as SVG**. Go back to Illustrator and paste by pressing *Command + V* (macOS) or *Ctrl + V* (Windows).

There are also other file extensions that may contain vectors, such as **.AI (Adobe Illustrator)**, **.EPS (Encapsulated PostScript)**, and **.PDF (Portable Document Format)**. These are proprietary formats, and you need to convert them to SVG before importing them into Figma. However, you should be aware that the extension is still not enough to be sure that you are using vectors because any of these file formats can contain some bitmap objects as well. You can check this by simply resizing the object. A vector element will always have smooth and sharp edges, no matter how large you make it. Also, you can recognize elements by their layer's icon, since raster images have the classic icon that represents a picture while a vector is represented with a custom shape icon.

Now that you understand some of the key concepts of the vector format, let's see how to create more complex vector elements with the incredibly powerful **Pen** tool.

Discovering the Pen tool

If you already have some experience with design applications, you have probably heard about the **Pen** tool – a tool that lets you create vector points, lines, and curves to create complex shapes. In fact, this is not a Figma-exclusive feature, but a must-have in any design app.

This tool may seem very difficult to master at first, but once you understand its basic mechanics and then explore its powerful capabilities, it could become your favorite.

First, let's draw some simple lines and curves:

1. Select the **Pen** tool (*P*). You will see the cursor turning into a pen, ready to use.
2. Click anywhere on the canvas to place the first starting point. From now on, you will see the line following the cursor – consider this as a preview, showing you what your vector will look like if you click elsewhere again.
3. Let's create a straight horizontal line. Move the cursor slightly to the right of the first point, and when you are satisfied with the line shown in the preview, just click again. You will notice that it isn't hard to be precise because Figma helps you draw straight lines with magnetic sensitive guides active by default:

Figure 4.10: A straight line made with the Pen tool

From now on, you can create as many points and lines as you want to achieve the desired shape. This was just one way to use the **Pen** tool; let's now move on to drawing your first curved line:

4. Select the **Pen** tool (*P*) again.
5. Click anywhere on the canvas to place the starting point. Make sure you are creating a new shape; do not connect your point to the shape from the previous example.

6. Move the cursor slightly to the right of the first point, and this time, click and drag. You will see that your line will now be curved, and the more you drag, the more pronounced the curve will be:

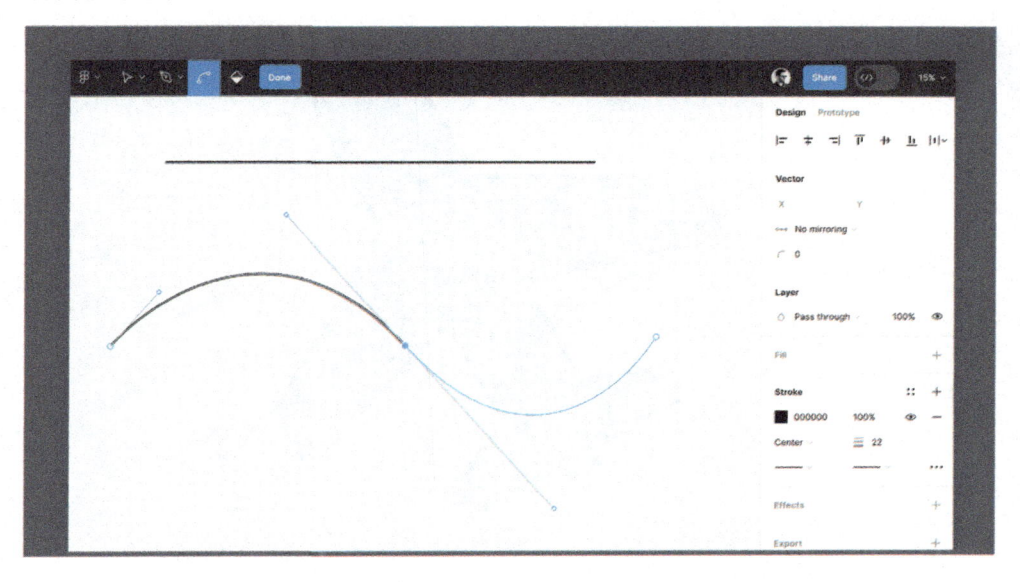

Figure 4.11: The Pen tool with a Bézier curve example

Great! You've just created your first Bézier curve. You now have more than just two points and a line; you also have new handles positioned before and after the curve point. The first handle adjusts the trajectory of the curve you've drawn, while the second shapes the direction, angle, and length of the next segment you're about to draw.

To further develop your skills with these curves, try playing the **Bézier Game** (bezier.method.ac). This interactive online resource guides you through a series of exercises, enhancing your ability to manipulate Bézier curves for different shapes.

Once you're comfortable, connect the last point you created with the starting point to form a closed shape. This can be customized in the **Design** panel, for instance, by adding a fill color. Start experimenting with creating more complex shapes using just a single line. Begin with basic shapes like triangles and rectangles, and then move on to more challenging ones like stars, hearts, or even a plane, as shown in the following screenshot.

These exercises not only improve your technique but also expand your creative possibilities in vector design.

Figure 4.12: A complex vector example

All the lines and shapes that you create with the **Pen** tool are consistent with the original default shapes that you have already encountered. This means that you can combine, for example, a rectangle and a complex custom shape to get a whole new bunch of shapes.

Likewise, you can modify any line or shape created with the **Pen** tool at any time by switching to edit mode (by selecting the shape and pressing *Enter* or double-clicking on it). In this mode, you can not only move points and add new ones but also change corner points, smoothing them using the **Bend** tool. You can also switch between a smooth and straight corner by holding *Command* (macOS) or *Ctrl* (Windows) and clicking the vector point you want to change.

Vector networks

In any other tool for vector graphics, the vector has very specific characteristics and is distinguished by open and closed paths. The path is defined as closed when the first point coincides with the last of a shape, thus generating a filled area. Figma, however, introduces a new concept – vector networks – a unique feature that allows you to push the boundaries of vectors even further.

Chapter 4   91

In traditional vector graphics, vectors are typically unidirectional, meaning they follow a path from one point to another in a specific sequence. This sequence usually starts at the first point and ends at the last, forming a closed path if these points meet, thus creating a filled shape. However, Figma introduces an innovative concept called **Vector networks**. Unlike standard vectors, those are multidirectional. They allow for the creation of complex shapes by connecting points in any order, not just from the first to the last. This flexibility enables designers to create more intricate vector shapes without the need to merge multiple shapes or create additional layers. One such example can be seen in the following screenshot:

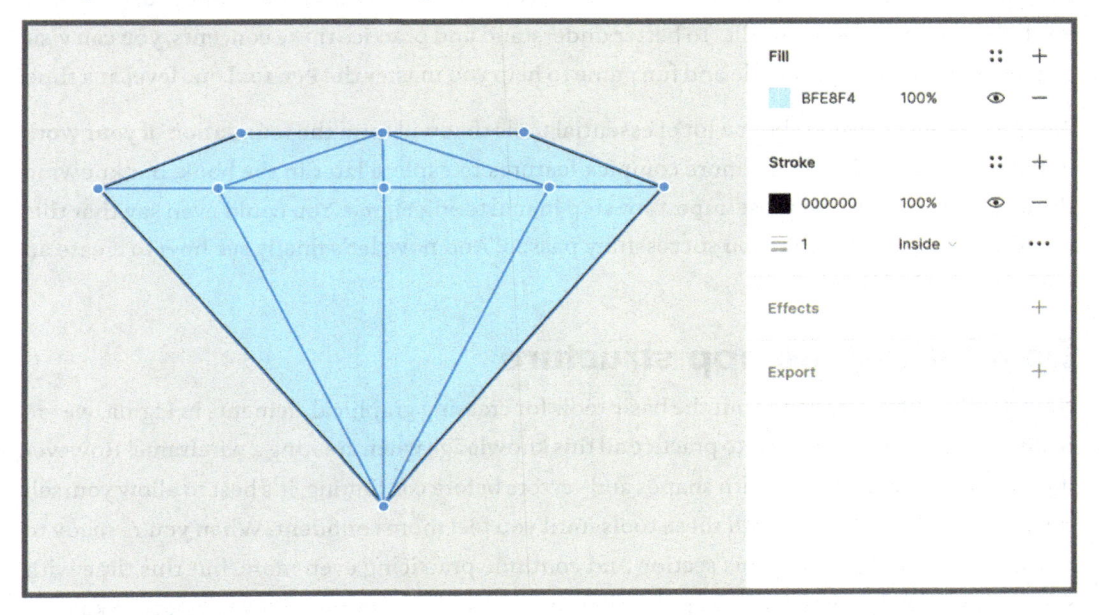

Figure 4.13: A vector network example

If you've never worked with vectors before, this feature might seem like behavior you would expect from the **Pen** tool, feeling like second nature. Otherwise, it will take some practice for those who are used to vectors in other applications. But exploring vector networks will open unique opportunities for you.

However, with incredible opportunities, you can also face some difficulties. The complex shape that you create in one single vector path can be difficult to color, but it can be done in a simple and quick way. Activate edit mode by selecting the shape and pressing *Enter*, and now you can add more points and lines inside the shape to divide it into separate areas. To apply color to individual sections of your shape, you will need to use the new **Paint Bucket** tool on the top toolbar in **Pen** tool mode.

After selecting the **Paint Bucket** tool (*B*), and then hovering and moving your mouse over the shape, you will notice that various separate parts are highlighted. By clicking on different sections, you can turn the fill color of that particular area on or off, and even use a new color for each section of the same vector shape.

Before moving on, try creating different shapes yourself and then editing them. This practice is especially important if you are new to using these tools. The **Pen** tool and, in particular, Bézier curves may seem difficult to master at first, but with a lot of practice, you can draw all sorts of complex shapes. Keep in mind that a well-made vector shape has a minimal number of points, so it is lightweight and easy to edit. To better understand and practice these concepts, you can visit bezier.method.ac for a simple and fun game to help you master the **Pen** tool one level at a time.

Well, you've just learned about a lot of essential tools that will form the foundation of your work in Figma. There will be many more complex features to explore later in the book, but knowing the basics is the first and most important step in mastering Figma. You could even say that this was the first milestone that you successfully passed! And now, let's finally see how to create an application wireframe.

Developing the app structure

Now that you have learned about the basic tools for creating graphical elements in Figma, we are ready to summarize and put into practice all this knowledge when creating a wireframe! However, if you need to practice more with shapes and vectors before continuing, it's best to allow yourself time to experiment a little with these tools until you feel more confident. When you're ready to move on, you can return to this section and continue practicing even more, but this time with something directly related to our application. We will start by learning how to create a skeleton for our streaming service and end up with our first functional wireframe.

Flow to skeleton

Do you remember the flow you built earlier (see *Chapter 2, Structuring Moodboards, Personas, and User Flows within FigJam*) in FigJam? By creating it, you defined the potential future structure of the application. However, the flow is something quite abstract, and it was mainly useful for understanding the project, while the wireframe is a primitive version of the product with its navigation elements indicated. So, it's time to brush up on the flow and use it as the basis for building your wireframe.

Let's start with a new blank file and define the screen resolution as a starting point. Since our hypothetical stakeholders are interested in using the mobile version of the application, this will be the mobile interface. First, you need to transform the flow into frames, so let's add them to the canvas. Use the **Frame** tool from the top toolbar (or press the *A* or *F* key on your keyboard) and select a preset from the **Phone** category to set the container to the appropriate size. We'll be using **iPhone 13 Mini**, but it's important to note that our interface design is not limited to iOS devices. At this stage, we are simply choosing a common screen size as a reference point. Additionally, we have opted not to use the latest or largest iOS device, as it may not be the most widely used among our target audience. Obviously, this time, you will need more than one single frame in the working area. It's important to know that the more frames you have, the more difficult it is to recognize them and to work with layers if you don't give them unique and meaningful names. You can rename a frame by simply double-clicking the label at the top of the frame itself, or, something that also works for any other element, double-clicking the name of the frame you want to rename in the **Layers** panel:

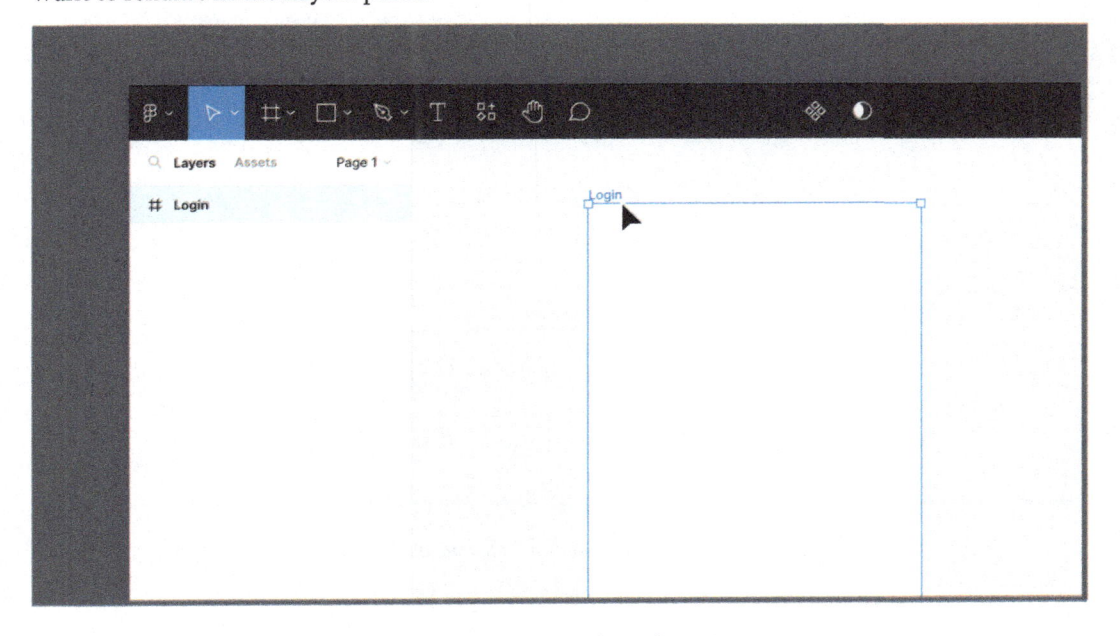

Figure 4.14: Renaming a frame

According to our flow, after launching the application for the first time, the user sees the login page, so it makes sense to use Login as the name of the first frame. After this frame has been renamed, it's time to add the rest.

You can do this again with the **Frame** tool, but it's much faster to just click and drag an existing frame while holding the *Option* key (macOS) or *Alt* (Windows). Then, you can add two more frames this way, or duplicate the last copy of the frame using the *Command + D* (macOS) or *Ctrl + D* (Windows) keyboard shortcut – this will automatically create a copy of the frame to the right of the duplicated one. Give each new frame an appropriate name, such as `Sign Up`, `Home`, and `Detail` page. Thus, you will have prepared the basis for a complete wireframe.

Renaming layers can seem unnecessary, especially for drafts like this, but it's best to always keep the layers organized correctly. A convenient and well-thought-out naming system and layer hierarchy significantly increases the efficiency of teamwork, saves time, and, in general, makes your workflow much easier and more enjoyable. You can give the frames any names you see fit, or just copy them from the following screenshot:

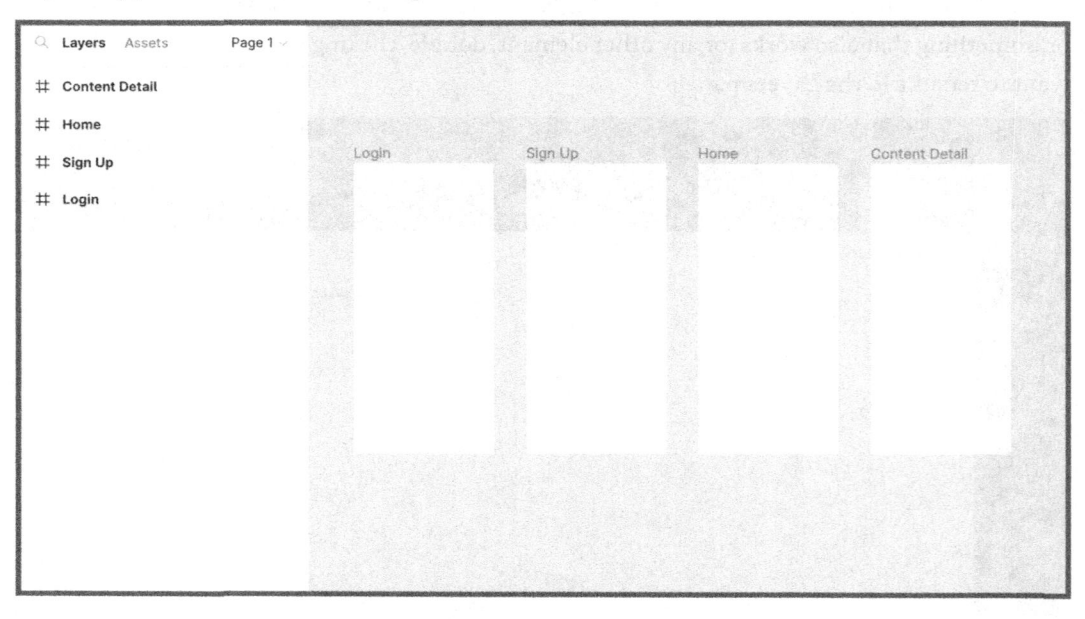

Figure 4.15: A blank structure

Once you are done adding all the frames and renaming them, you will see that the flow is now fully displayed as the skeleton of our application. Now, you have a new challenge – to think about what elements to add to all the screens to set the individual view of each of them.

Shaping the interface

So, you have created a skeleton, which is a general display of all the screens of the mobile application. Now, it's time to work on each screen individually and determine what content structure they can display. There is no need to use Figma's advanced features such as constraints and auto layout to do this; you will learn about them later when working on the actual UI. For a simple wireframe, it is more than enough to use the tools you just learned about.

At this stage, as before, it's best to stick to the order of your flow, so let's start with the first view of the application, which is the **Login** page. At this point, you will need to do some research again. It's important to think through and define the elements that typically make up the page you create to make sure that nothing is overlooked. So, what elements must the **Login** page contain? No doubt, it must include username and password text fields, a confirmation button, a password recovery function, and a link to the **Sign Up** page if your user doesn't have an account yet.

Now that you have a list of all the screen elements you need, all you have to do is place each one in the **Login** frame, leaving enough room for text fields, buttons, and other elements. Let's get started:

1. Select the **Rectangle** tool (*R*) and draw a 315 x 50 rectangular shape (while drawing the shape, you can check its size in real time underneath it). It is important to know that if a shape or any other object is originally drawn in the frame, it will be placed directly inside it. Try creating another shape temporarily out of frame, and you'll see that the two shapes are positioned differently in the **Layers** panel.

2. If you select a rectangle within the frame, you can see its dimensions (**W** = width and **H** = height) and its position (**X** = horizontal and **Y** = vertical) in the **Design** panel on the right. Since this shape is placed inside the login frame, its positioning values will be relative to the outer container, starting at the top-left corner. Place the rectangle at **30** on the **X** axis and **272** on the **Y** axis.

You can modify these values visually by moving the rectangle with the mouse or directly by manually changing the numerical values in the right panel:

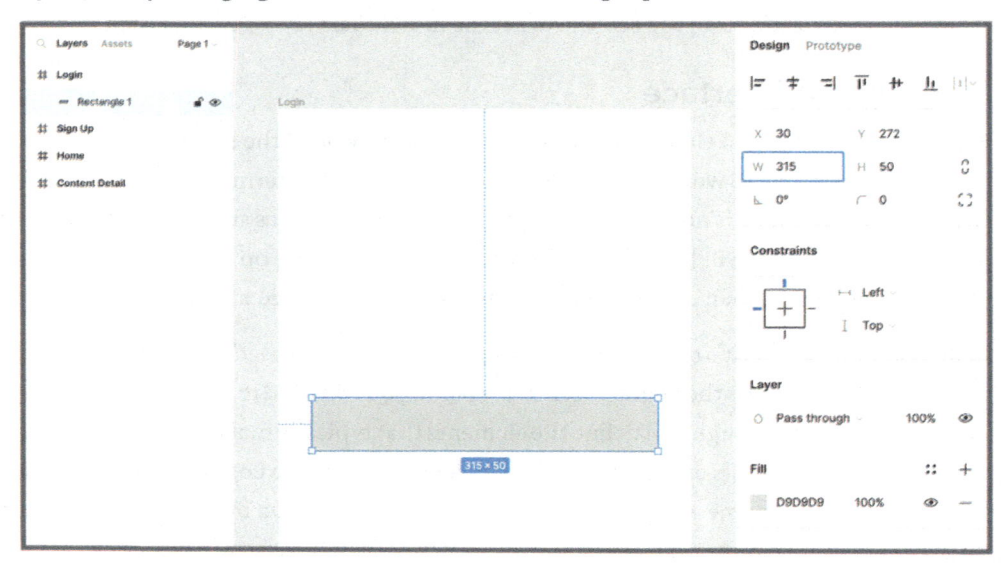

Figure 4.16: Positioning a shape

3. In the **Fill** section of the **Design** panel, click the color code and write `lightgray` (no spaces); or, if you prefer, enter the hex code `D3D3D3`. You will learn more about colors in the next chapter.

4. Then, select the **Text** tool (*T*) and click just above the upper-left corner of the rectangle. Enter `Username`. Make sure it is well aligned to the left. If you select the text and drag it, Figma will show you contextual guides to help you align that element with others nearby. Once this is done, your first text field with a corresponding indicative label is ready.

5. Next, select the label (text) and the text field (rectangle) together and duplicate everything as you did before by clicking and dragging the elements while holding the *Option* (macOS) or *Alt* (Windows) key, or using the *Command + C* (macOS) or *Ctrl + C* (Windows) classic keyboard shortcut to copy and *Command + C* (macOS) or *Ctrl + C* (Windows) to paste. In this case, you need to move the duplicated elements down by about 100 px:

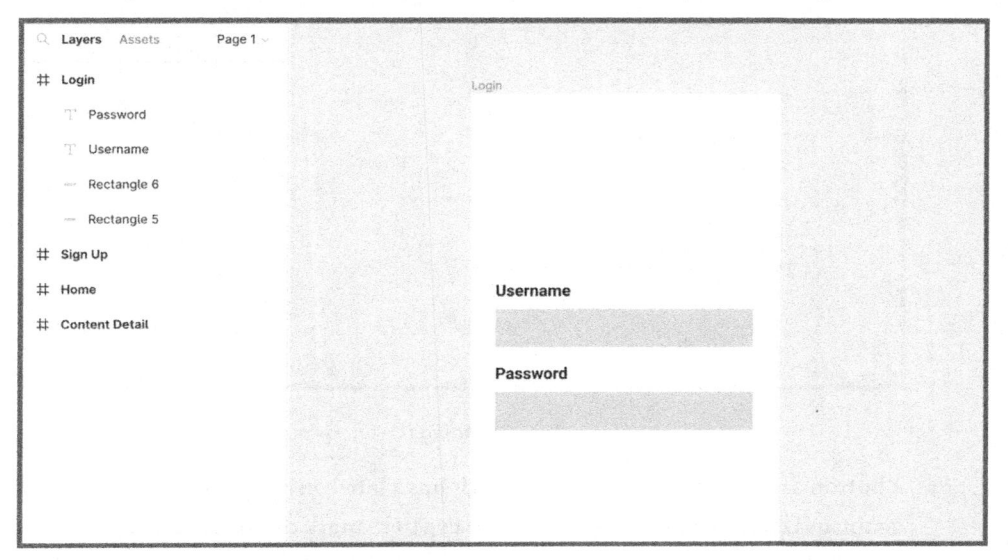

Figure 4.17: The Username and Password text fields

6. The rectangle you just duplicated will be the **Password** field. Therefore, change the duplicated label text from Username to Password by double-clicking it to enter edit mode.

7. Now, select the **Rectangle** tool (*R*) again and draw a 315 x 75 shape below the two fields. This time, it will be a confirmation button to submit the user's login credentials, so let's place it about 200 px below the **Password** field.

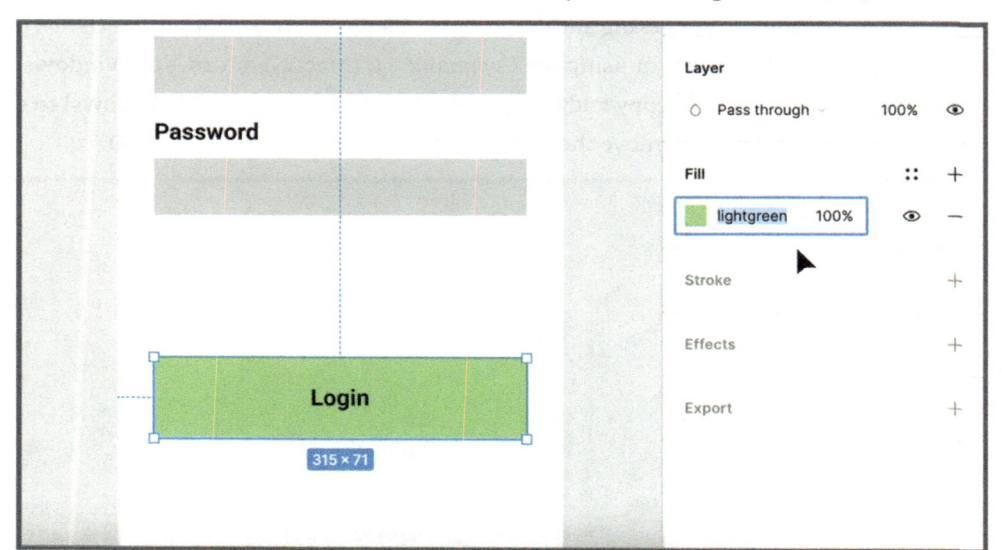

To make the button more accented, since this is a key action, let's give it a `lightgreen` color:

Figure 4.18: Changing the background color

8. A button cannot be fully identified until it has a label on it. So, let's select the **Text** tool (*T*) again and click inside our button. Enter `Login` to mark the action for the element. Try to position the label exactly in the center of the button using the mouse and sensitive guides.

9. The last elements you need to add are the **Signup** button (it's a secondary button, so it will not be highlighted) and a link to restore the user's password right under the password text field. Before moving on, look at the **Layers** panel, and you will see that your layers are getting messy. It would be bad practice to leave it this way. So, before you continue, spend a few minutes to renaming each layer so that they can be easily identified:

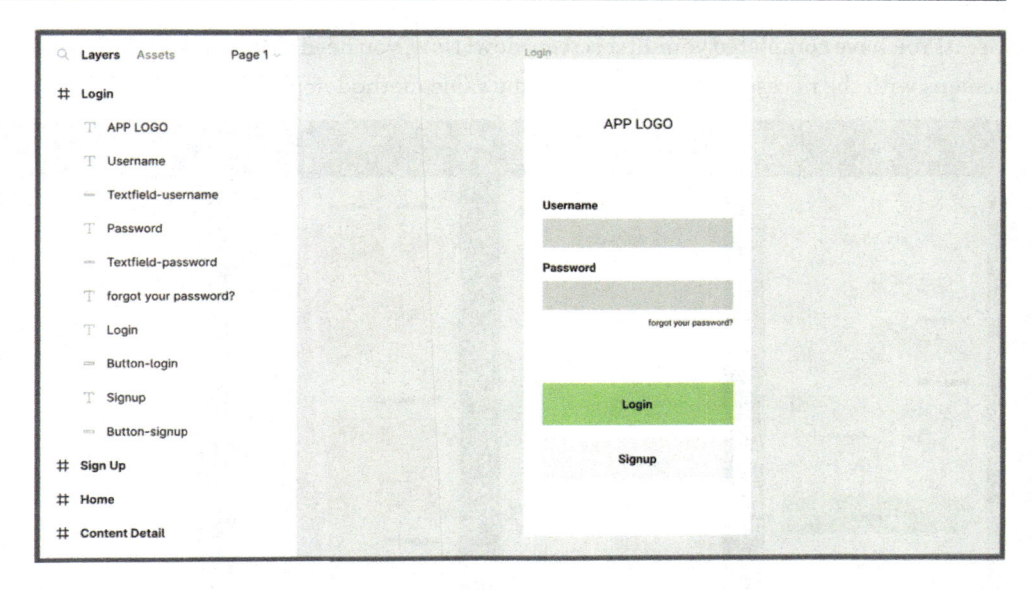

Figure 4.19: The polished wireframe of the Login view

To organize your layers even better, you can group the **Username** label with its text field by selecting them together and pressing *Command + G* (macOS) or *Ctrl + G* (Windows) on your keyboard. Try to group the password label and its text field in the same way and each button shape with its respective text label, and then give these new groups proper recognizable names in the **Layers** panel. Remember, since this is a wireframe, don't stress too much about the specific names you assign to these groups. This stage is more about structuring and basic organization. The names are just for temporary reference and will likely be refined as you continue to develop and enhance your design. Right now, the focus is on laying out the elements effectively; precise naming can be fine-tuned in subsequent stages.

Great! You have completed your first screen view! Now, you need to fill the rest of the application screens with the necessary elements using the same methodology:

Figure 4.20: The finished wireframe structures

You can see that once you are done with the wireframe, the structure of any application or website that you might work on in the future becomes much clearer. After this step, the next one is to test the flow by sending your wireframe to users in your target audience. Remember that with a well-made, tested, and approved framework, further design steps will be much more deliberate and enjoyable.

What's next?

As you can see, this chapter was full of all sorts of new information for you, but if you have reached this point, you can be proud of yourself. Now, you've got an idea of what a wireframe is and why it's worth spending enough time on it. However, the real purpose of the wireframe isn't just filling in the screen-sized frames with shapes that represent your future components. The essential meaning of this part is to make sure the flow you came up with during the UX design phase is the best one for your user. There is only one way to find out – to test this flow on a group of people belonging to the reference target. To do this, you need to make your wireframe live by prototyping it so that you can show and test the dynamic flow during user testing sessions.

The testing process is very important and must be taken very seriously; otherwise, you risk missing structural or usability issues. So, you should be prepared to review and modify your user flow and then the wireframe according to the test results, which will take more time, but it will still be much better than starting the implementation of the final product with uncertainty or doubt.

Since you are not yet familiar with Figma's prototyping function and the principles of user testing, we will keep our framework static. But when your journey of learning Figma is complete, you can come back to this chapter and build a prototype with this wireframe and then test it if you like. This would be great practice before you start doing it in your actual future design projects.

Summary

If you had any doubts about the importance of the UX part of your design workflow before, this chapter will have hopefully cleared them up. Once you've identified the optimal user flow, it's much easier to build a wireframe based on it, although it may well happen that you need to spend more time researching which elements to use and how to place them on screens, especially if you don't have a lot of design experience. Of course, it takes time to learn about the different types of buttons, menus, bars, and other components, but with experience, you will have no problem figuring out which elements are suitable to include on a particular screen. You can also help yourself by paying more attention to the details of your favorite apps in daily use as well as discovering new ones.

So, this chapter was your first milestone in learning how to create a user interface in Figma. You learned and tried out many new tools, and then used them to create the first wireframe of our application, which was a great way to put your fresh knowledge into practice! It's twice as helpful if you haven't just followed the practical instructions in this chapter but have also tried them out on your own, as it will speed up your learning curve in Figma!

In the next chapter, you'll discover a whole new pack of amazing features in Figma, specifically how to work with images, text, colors, grids, styles, and more!

Learn more on Discord

To join the Discord community for this book – where you can share feedback, ask questions to the author, and learn about new releases – follow the QR code below:

`https://packt.link/figma`

Part 2
Exploring Components, Styles, and Variants

In this part, you will be introduced to all the features of Figma, from the basics to the more advanced ones. By the end of this part, you will have designed a static user interface.

This part comprises the following chapters:

- Chapter 5, *Designing Consistently Using Grids, Colors, and Typography*
- Chapter 6, *Creating a Responsive Mobile Interface Using Auto Layout*
- Chapter 7, *Building Components and Variants in a Collaborative Workspace*
- Chapter 8, *User Interface Design on Tablet, Desktop, and the Web*

5

Designing Consistently Using Grids, Colors, and Typography

Well, you've done a great job learning the most basic Figma tools and even applying them to the wireframe of our application. In this chapter, you'll take a big step by getting started with the interface while discovering more advanced features. But before diving into the topic, you should know that when it comes to mastering any software or tool, it is essential that your learning process is not just about memorizing all the functions but also trying to understand what is behind each feature, what benefits it gives you, and how best to use it. After all, your main goal is not to apply as many functions as possible but to make them work well and efficiently.

The set of tools that you will learn in this chapter is fundamental, and you need to not only be able to use them but also to use them correctly since you will most likely need them in every future design project. In this chapter, you will also learn how to set up and apply these tools consistently across all your layouts. Excited? Let's get started!

In this chapter, we are going to cover the following main topics:

- Getting started with Grids
- Working with Typography, Colors, and Effects
- Introducing Styles

Getting started with Grids

At this stage, we understand that the design of any interface consists of technical and analytical solutions aimed at satisfying a user's needs. Remember that a good designer will never let personal taste affect a product. Therefore, the design of an interface, except for the initial stages of creating sketches and wireframes, must be done with precision for every detail. Figma has a whole bunch of dedicated tools to help you achieve this successfully.

Starting from this chapter, you will no longer have random frame sizes, colors, fonts, and other elements in your design files. From now on, you only need to move forward when you are confident in every step of creating the interface of your application. Therefore, you will need tools to help you minimize or eliminate possible errors. One of these is grids, and the first section of this chapter will be devoted to this fantastic function.

Grids are everywhere

Grids are a very old design tool, dating back to the 13th century. At that time, all books were handwritten and, therefore very expensive and valuable, and it took a lot of effort to create one book. Grids were invented to harmonize each page of a book by neatly positioning handwritten text on the paper and ensuring that content appeared evenly on each page. From then on, the grid system remained indispensable in publishing houses, as it was used to organize the layout of printed pages. Publishers, editors, and writers looked to grids for the perfect harmony of displaying content on pages. Grids are usually made up of columns and rows placed on a page, with a set spacing and padding from the page edges. Because the same grid was applied to all pages, text and images were consistent throughout the book or magazine. Thus, a reader was attracted to the visuals of the printed pages, but most importantly, it was easier to focus on the content. The following diagram shows an example of a layout grid:

Chapter 5

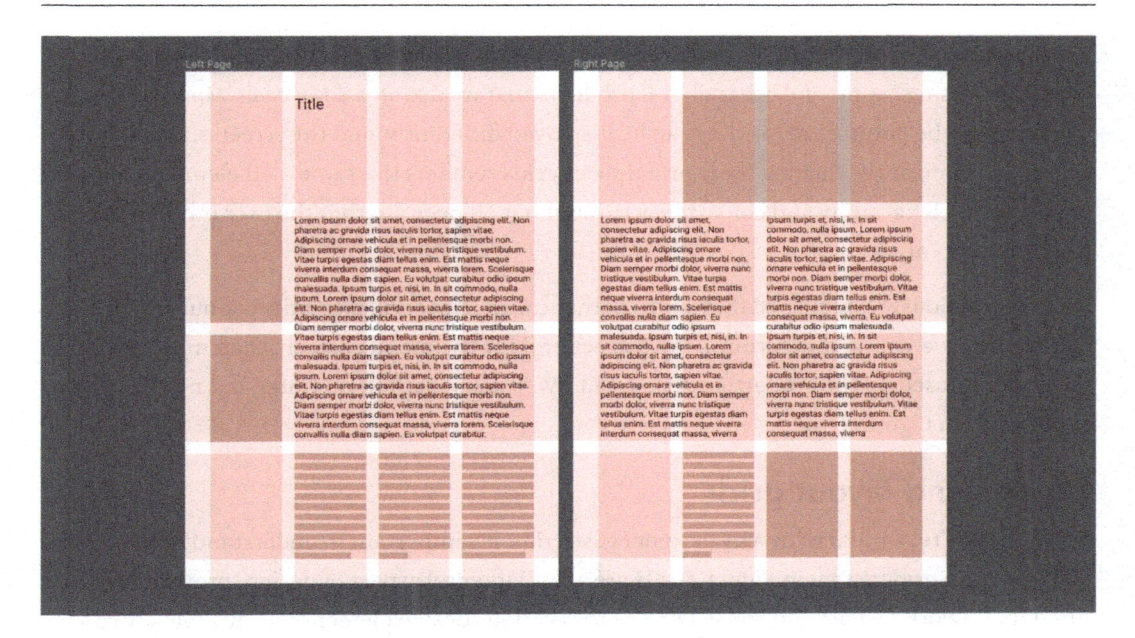

Figure 5.1 – An example of a book layout grid

The method of grids was then used in graphic design, and grids still form the basis of any simple or complex composition. Suppose you look at any artwork for the first time. In that case, you may not immediately notice that the elements are arranged according to some positioning rules. Still, grids are behind every self-respecting design project, from books to posters and even photoshoots.

Because virtual pages have a lot in common with printed pages, grids are also widely used in creating websites, apps, and other digital products that we use on a daily basis. However, digital pages cannot be permanent, as they can be displayed differently, and the screen sizes of devices can vary significantly. But the basic principle of grids remains the same – all elements must be organized with harmony and consistency throughout all pages so that the user is not distracted from the content.

Since we previously established that our hypothetical audience will primarily use our smartphone application, we will first determine the correct grid for the mobile screen, then move to higher resolutions based on the properties of this grid. We'll come back to this later, but now let's learn about grids in Figma.

Guides and layout grids

Now that you're familiar with why designers use grids, it's important to understand how to create and operate a grid system in Figma. Grids are a fundamental aspect of design, providing a structured framework to maintain consistency across various design elements. They typically consist of intersecting vertical and horizontal lines forming columns and rows. This structure helps in aligning elements systematically and ensures a harmonious, balanced layout. Before we dive deeper into grids, let's also understand **guides**, another versatile tool in Figma used for aligning elements within the same frame. Guides are simpler than grids and are used for more specific alignment tasks. They appear as thin horizontal and vertical lines and offer a quicker and easier way to move and reposition elements compared to the structured format of grids. Understanding how to use guides effectively is a vital step before fully embracing grid systems. To better grasp how guides work, let's try them out on the canvas:

1. First, you need to activate the rulers in your view. To do this, head to the Figma menu under **View** and select **Rulers**. You will see that two rulers appear at the top and left of your working area, as you can see in the following screenshot (*Figure 5.2*).

2. Create a frame of any size you like, which you'll delete right after using guides on your canvas.

3. To add a horizontal guide, click and drag the horizontal ruler. You will see a red line that you can drag toward your work area. Likewise, you need to click and drag a vertical ruler to have a vertical guide. Note that when a ruler is placed on a frame, it gets automatically cut to the frame's borders:

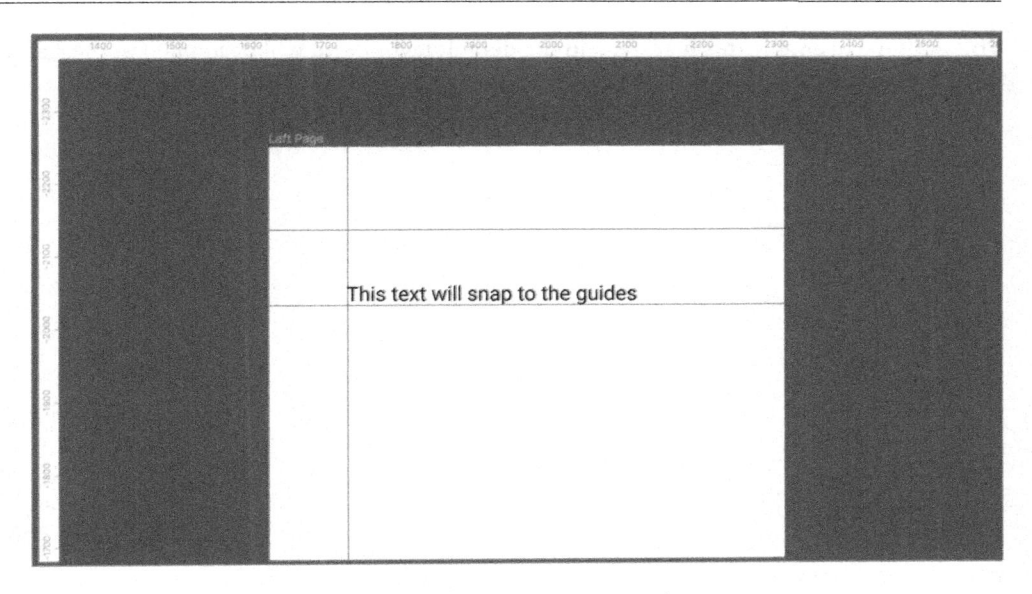

Figure 5.2 – Text snapping to guides

4. To remove the guide, drag it back to the ruler or use the *Delete* key after selecting it.

You can add as many guides as you like and move them manually anywhere on the canvas. This makes them a very versatile tool, but guides have limitations, as it is challenging to create a flexible, efficient grid just using guides alone. For this, Figma has layout grids.

> **Note:**
> With a single *Shift + R* keyboard shortcut, you can toggle the ruler on and off in your working area.

As a more complex function than guides, layout grids open new possibilities for designers to create consistent product designs across multiple platforms. First, you need to know that layout grids can only be applied on frames – and, therefore, on components – both main and nested. To apply a layout grid to a frame, select one on your canvas, and, with the selection active, click + next to **Layout grid** in the right sidebar.

This action will enable this feature, and the default layout grid will be applied to the frame:

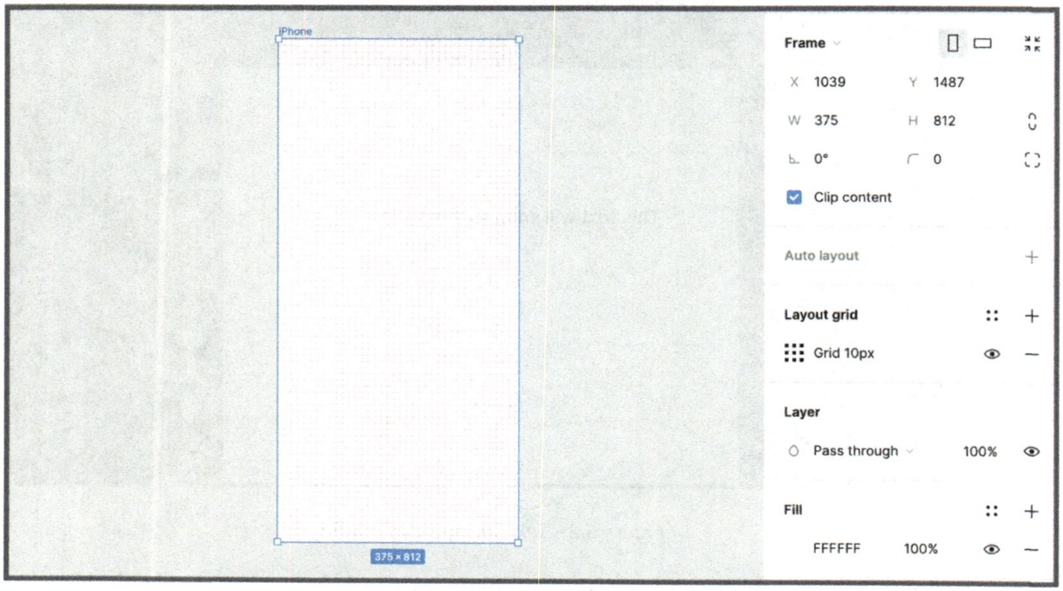

Figure 5.3 – The default layout grid

Before changing the grid settings, you need to understand what grid properties will fit the contents of this frame. The columns and rows of the grid must not be randomly arranged in the frame. You need to select the correct properties for them so that the grid becomes a practical design assistant when working on interfaces for different screen sizes. Many web development frameworks such as Bootstrap, Tailwind, and Materialize use 12-column grids to better organize content within them. Moreover, this structure allows you to change the layout depending on the device and its resolution with a little effort. Therefore, at this stage, it is essential to find out, based on the project's needs, which technologies will be used by the developers in your team. This can help you choose a grid system that can then be efficiently converted to code easily.

To change the settings for the layout grid and update its properties, click the **Grid** icon under **Layout grid** in the right sidebar when frame selection is active. Here, in the drop-down menu at the top, you can see three options of layout grids – a uniform square **Grid**, **Columns**, and **Rows**:

Chapter 5

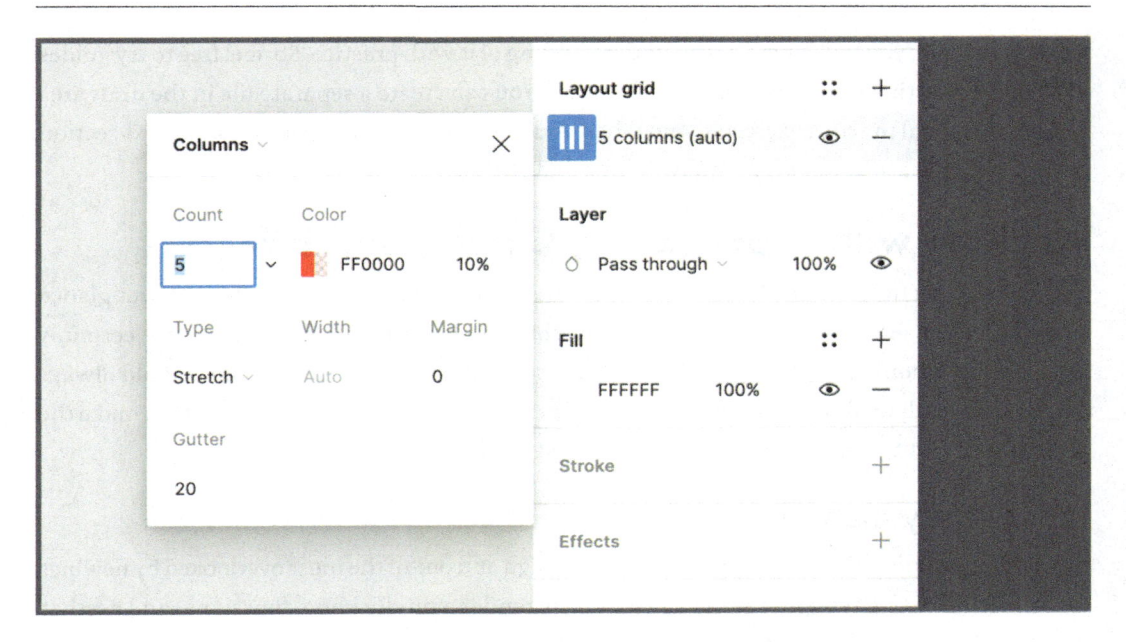

Figure 5.4 – The layout grid types

While the settings for a uniform grid are limited only by the size in pixels of each resulting cell and the grid color, columns and rows allow you to select, respectively, the column or row **Count** value you want to apply, as well as set **Margin**, **Gutter** (the distance between each row or column), and **Type**. With the grid type feature, you can align the grid **Right**, **Left**, or **Center**. But if you want the grid to adapt to the size of the frame, there is a **Stretch** option that automatically sets the column/row widths and makes your grid responsive.

It is important to know that the layout grid can be applied to the outer frame and the nested ones; thus, you can create inner grids that can be very useful – for example, when designing a small icon in your interface. Alternatively, you can add more than one layout grid for a frame, meaning you can apply a column-based layout grid and then add a row-based grid on top of it, having an even more customizable structure.

From the moment you apply the grid to any frame, it will always be visible on top of all other elements. While working, you will certainly need to turn off the grid visibility sometimes to reduce visual noise on your interface. You can do this with one click by selecting the frame to which the grid is applied and clicking the **Eye** icon in the layout grid section in the right panel, or by pressing *Ctrl + G* (macOS) / *Ctrl + Shift + 4* (Windows).

As with any tool, you will have a better understanding of it with practice. So, feel free to try guides and grids by setting different properties for them. You can create a separate file in the draft area for your personal practice exercises. And when you're ready, you can move on to the next section, where we will learn about typography, colors, and effects.

Working with Typography, Colors, and Effects

This chapter section will be dedicated to the fonts, colors, and effects in Figma. At first glance, these functions may seem more creative than what you have done before – and they certainly are – but you should never forget that every choice, including elements of style, should always be based on analytical conclusions. Therefore, you will need to refer to your artifacts to make the right choice, but for now, let's take a closer look at each tool.

Typography matters

Typography is one of the most critical aspects of design and one of the most overlooked by newbies. However, the wrong typography choices instantly render a product non-functional and aesthetically unpleasant. This is because choosing the right font is not easy, and only experience, study, and practice can help you master this aspect. To learn more about typography, it is recommended that you read *Just My Type: A Book About Fonts* by *Simon Garfield*, which will help you better understand the uniqueness of each font and, therefore, determine when it is appropriate to use them.

Several factors can dictate typographic choice. If, for example, you want to build an app exclusively for iOS, it might be a good choice to use a system font such as San Francisco (sans-serif) or New York (serif) in order for the product to comply with Apple's visual guidelines (which you can consult here: `developer.apple.com/design/human-interface-guidelines`). Likewise, when building an Android app, the Roboto font might be a safe choice. In the following figure, you can see a visual comparison of these famous fonts:

San Francisco
Sans-Serif typeface

Aa Qq Rr
Aa Qq Rr

New York
Serif typeface

Aa Qq Rr
Aa Qq Rr

Roboto
Sans-Serif typeface

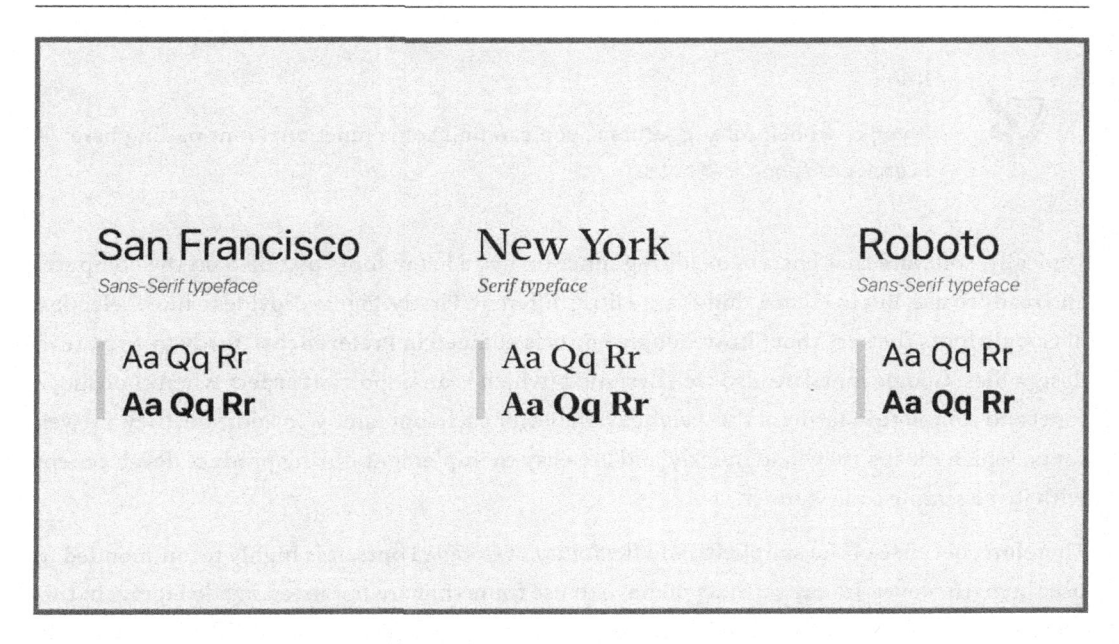

Aa Qq Rr
Aa Qq Rr

Figure 5.5 – The differences between serif and sans-serif typefaces

Another important factor is, of course, context. A font may be more appropriate for one use and less appropriate for another. In general, with sans-serif fonts being more readable by the human eye, they are suitable for menus, buttons, etc. If you need to display very long text content, a serif font may be more appropriate. It may also be that the brand you are working for already has its own brand guide with recommended fonts for digital use.

Sometimes, it is possible, or even necessary, to use more than one font in an interface. In this case, you should first check whether there are any technical limitations on the development side. Each integrated font has weight and can consequently slow down the loading of an application. After that, you need to ensure the selected fonts match well.

> **Note:**
> If you need helpful suggestions, you can find some functional font pairing here: figma.com/google-fonts.

Typically, software that has a text-editing function has a list of fonts installed on the computer and ready to use. But in Figma, things are a little different. Firstly, Figma provides a huge selection of Google fonts (be sure that **Show Google Fonts** is enabled in **Preferences**), ready to operate in design files. Google fonts are also well designed (which is an important aspect when choosing a font) and complete in terms of the weight available for each font family. In addition, they are web fonts, which means they load quickly and are easy to implement during product development with just a simple code snippet.

Therefore, because of the simplicity and flexibility of Google Fonts, it is highly recommended to use them. However, it may be that you have to use fonts that are not listed inside Figma. In this case, you should use the desktop version of Figma, where, in addition to Google fonts, you will have all the fonts installed on your computer at your disposal. Optionally, you can also access local fonts through the Figma web app, but this requires an extra step, namely installing the font service (available here at figma.com/downloads for both macOS and Windows).

Now that you know what fonts you have at your disposal, let's take a look at the **Text** tool. You have already used it before, but now you will find out all its possibilities. First, you need to know that the **Text** tool lets you insert two different types. If you select the **Text** tool (*T*) and then just click somewhere on the canvas and start typing, you will get text with an automatic width that isn't limited. This means that the width of the text container will grow indefinitely as you type until you start a new paragraph with the *Enter* key. The width of this container can then be reduced by clicking outside of it and manually using the cursor to adjust its size, both horizontally and vertically, within which the text will be contained. There is another way to place text on the canvas. Instead of just typing, you can draw a text container right after selecting the **Text** tool (*T*). This way, your container will keep the width you set earlier, and the text will not go beyond it and only change the height as you type. You can then modify the width of the container manually.

Regardless of your preferred method, both will have the same result, namely creating a new text layer in the **Layers** panel. If you select any text layer, the **Design** panel automatically adjusts to your selection and displays functionality exclusively for texts and paragraphs in the **Text** section.

Chapter 5   115

The following screenshot (*Figure. 5.6*) shows all the available options for working with text layers. Let's take a closer look at each of them:

Figure 5.6 – The text options

The first parameter (*Figure 5.6 - A*) is the already mentioned list of all available fonts. You can click the drop-down menu and see a great variety of different fonts for any occasion. To quickly check for a specific font that you might need, instead of scrolling through this long list, you can start typing the font name, and the autocomplete system will suggest the best search results for you.

> **Note:**
> If you use local fonts, make sure that the other people working on the same file also have these fonts installed on their computers; otherwise, Figma will show them a yellow alert with an **A?** symbol next to the missing font name.

In addition to a font family, you can choose a specific **Weight** (*Figure 5.6 - B*) for it (for example, **Light, Regular, Bold,** and **Extra bold**) and styles (for example, **Italic**) of the same font. Not all fonts have the same number of options for adjusting weight and styles, so it's best to consider this when choosing the primary font for your project.

It is recommended to use the one that has enough options to play with to be able to create a visual hierarchy of interface elements, highlight important text information, and so on. Different **Sizes** (*Figure 5.6 - C*) of the selected font are also used for similar purposes.

The following options for working with a text layer can be better understood by having a multi-line block of text on the canvas. **Line height** (*Figure 5.6 - D*), also called leading, is the spacing between each line of text in a paragraph. In the default mode of any selected font, the lines will not overlap, but you can manually change this value to improve the readability of the text. Here, you can enter a value in pixels or a percentage; in both cases, it is closely related to the font size. A standard paragraph with font size 18 has a line height of 21 (or 115%). **Paragraph spacing** (*Figure 5.6 - F*) works the same way as line height, with the difference that only complete paragraphs are separated, not individual lines of text.

Letter spacing (*Figure 5.6 - E*), or kerning, is used to separate individual characters in text from each other to make small optical adjustments. You can add or decrease the spacing between all letters in your block of text by simply selecting the entire layer and changing its letter-spacing value. But what's more, you can also separate any two single characters in a paragraph from each other by placing the text cursor between them and changing the spacing in the panel.

As you can see, Figma provides many options for working with the text layers. However, if you are a beginner, you should not overuse these functions, as the most famous fonts, made by experienced designers, are already worked out to the millimeter, and any careless modification can break this harmony. With time and experience, you will train your eyes to know when it is worth making any such modifications to the selected font.

Finally, there are three sets of toggle parameters, each of which only has one option. The first group of functions (*Figure 5.6 - G*), mentioned earlier, allows you to change the behavior of the text layer itself. If you are creating auto-width text (with a simple click after selecting the **Text** tool), for example, the first option will be active, then you can easily switch to a fixed size, and then the text area will have the specified size. The last option, automatic height, is a combination of the two. If you select it, the width of your text container will remain fixed and defined by you, but its height will automatically adapt based on the amount of text you enter. The second group (**H**) concerns the alignment of the text relative to the area in which it is contained. You can choose one of the following text alignment options: left, center, or right. The third group (**I**) is also for aligning the text relative to its area, but this time vertically, and you can choose between top, middle, and bottom alignment.

So, the changes you can make to the text are very numerous, but if that's not enough, you have a **...** button(*Figure 5.6 - J*). If you click on it, you will see many additional features, such as underling and strikethrough, numbered or bulleted lists, or converting an entire text box to uppercase, lowercase, etc. This expanded panel also has a practical preview window, the contents of which change depending on which options you hover over. The preview is shown to help you better understand all the features in this panel. In the following screenshot, you can see this panel with the preview and some additional functions:

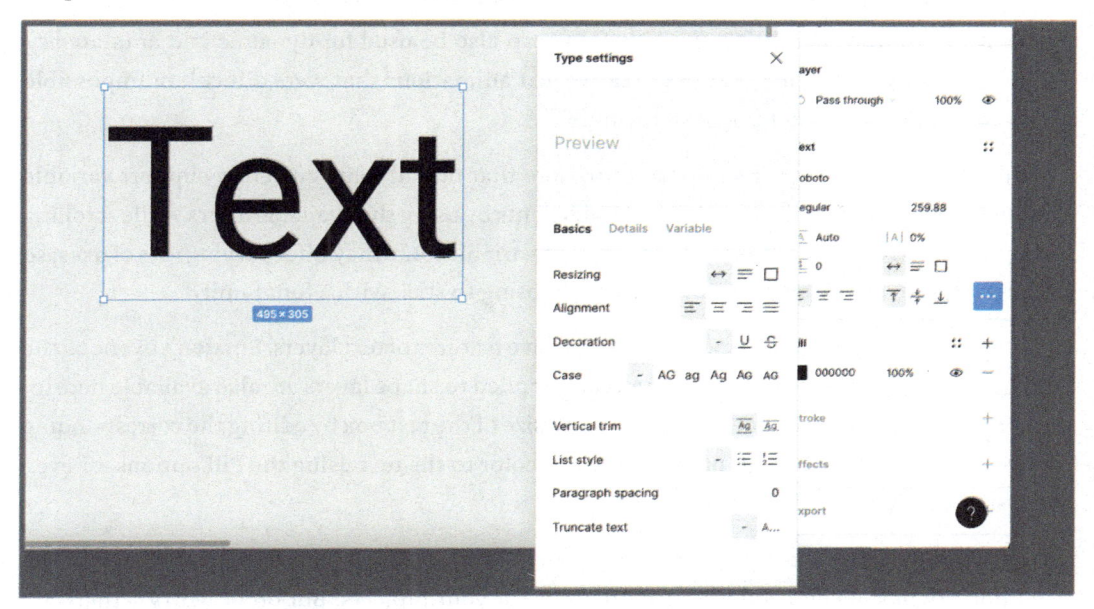

Figure 5.7 – Advanced text options

In here, you'll also find something new worth mentioning: variable fonts.

Variable fonts are a relatively new and exciting addition to the world of typography that have also been integrated into design tools like Figma, allowing for greater flexibility and creativity when working with text. Here's all the advantages:

- **Single-font file with multiple styles**: Unlike traditional fonts that come in separate files for each weight and style (e.g., regular, bold, italic), variable fonts contain all these in just one file. This leads to smaller file sizes, faster loading times, and greater efficiency.
- **Interactive font customization**: Designers can interactively adjust these variables to create custom font styles that suit their design needs. Instead of choosing from a limited set of predefined styles, you can fine-tune the typography to fit your design perfectly.

- **Consistency across platforms**: Variable fonts help maintain consistency across various devices and screen sizes. They can adapt and respond to different contexts, ensuring your typography looks good and remains legible on small mobile screens and large desktop monitors.
- **Improved accessibility**: Accessibility can be enhanced by providing more options for customizing text. Designers can adjust font attributes to improve readability for specific audiences or individuals with different visual needs.
- **Animation possibilities**: Variable fonts can also be used for dynamic and animated typography effects, allowing for creative text animations that were difficult or impossible to achieve with traditional static fonts.

Exciting, isn't it? However, it's important to note that not all fonts currently support variable axes. In Figma, you can quickly identify variable fonts by using the available filters while scrolling through the font list. Keep in mind that different variable fonts may offer varying sets of axes, so it's advisable to review their specifics before choosing to stick with a font family.

So far, we have explored all the specific and exclusive features of text layers. But don't overlook the fact that other common features we've already applied to shape layers are also available here for text. Therefore, you can change the position and size of the text box by editing the corresponding values at the top of the **Design** panel, apply any color to the text using the **Fill** options, or even add a stroke to it using the **Stroke** options.

As you can see, all the settings for working with text layers in Figma are pretty simple. But the real difficulty lies in choosing one or more fonts for your projects. But don't worry – there are tons of resources to help you learn this skill. Later in this chapter, we will choose a font that suits the content and functionality of our application, but first, we will learn about colors in Figma.

Choosing a Palette

Like typography, color is an important design aspect of any project and should never be overlooked. You can have a great user experience in your application, but the wrong choice of color palette can spoil the perception of this, and all your efforts will be wasted. Each color has its own message and has a particular impact on people, so you need to make sure that your product interacts properly with the user. Before starting the UI design, you should have a clear idea of which direction to go in terms of colors, or at least enough data to easily figure it out. We'll make color choices together later, but first, let's figure out how to work with colors in Figma.

Chapter 5   119

The most important tool for working with colors, as you can imagine, is the color picker, which we already tried out in *Chapter 4, Wireframing a Mobile-First Experience Using Vector Shapes*, while learning about shapes. Whether it's a background color, fill color, stroke color, or anything else, the **Design** panel will always display a preview of that color, so you can simply click on it to open a dedicated window:

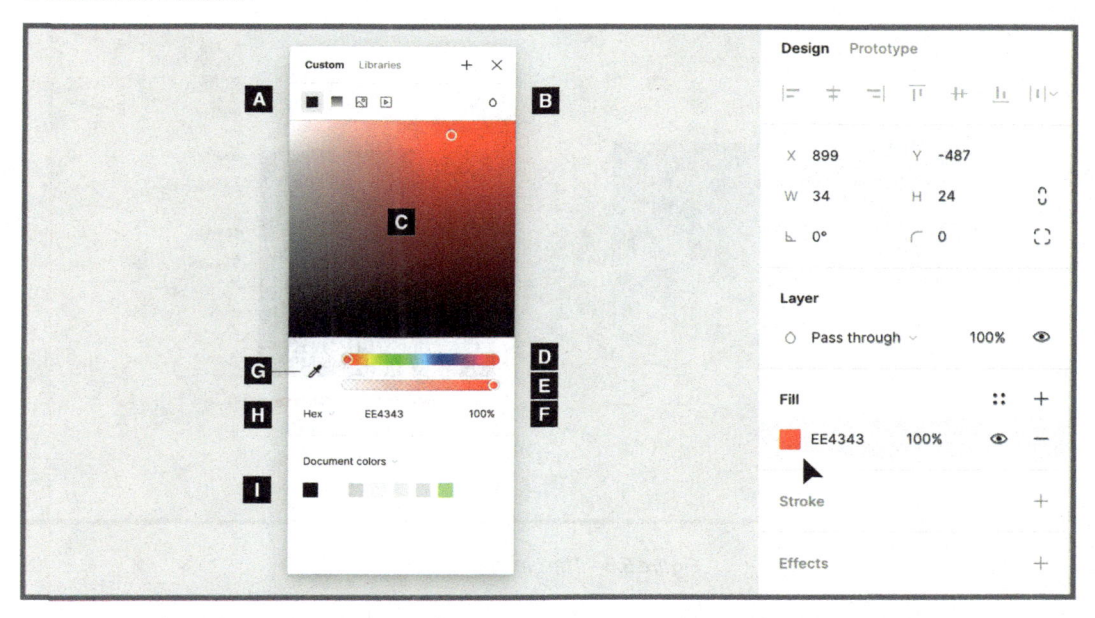

Figure 5.8 – The color picker

To learn more about each color picker option, select any element with a color on the canvas, create any shape, or add a fill or stroke to the created element. Then, just open the expanded window in the **Design** panel by clicking the square with the element's color.

A — Color modes

From this drop-down selector, you can choose between four different fill modes: **Solid**, **Gradient**, **Image**, and **Video**. The first category includes the default option, **Solid**, which allows you to select a solid color using the appropriate visual selector. The second category includes **Linear**, **Radial**, **Angular**, and **Diamond**, which are gradient options, each with a different diffusion. If you choose any of those gradient options, you will be prompted to choose not one but two or more colors, the combination of which will smoothly transition from one color to another. To change one of the colors, simply click on a color in the gradient bar and then use the classic color picker.

To apply any additional color to your gradient, click on any empty spot in the gradient bar, and a new colored square will appear. You can move the markers of individual colors to determine how smooth the color transition will be, as you can see in the following screenshot:

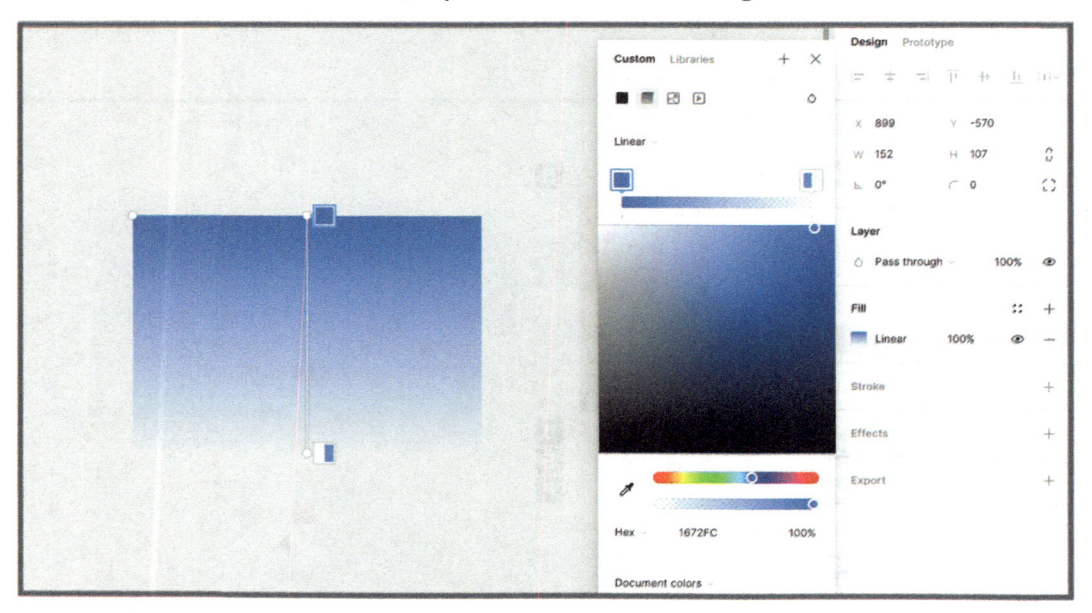

Figure 5.9 – The Linear gradient

You can also change a specific gradient trend by moving the gradient strip's start and end points that appear directly on the selected element on the workspace. Take time to experiment with gradients to see how any changes you make produce different results.

Finally, the last two **Image** and **Video** options allows you to import static or dynamic images in .gif format and short videos from your computer and use them as an element's **fill** property. To import a media element, click the **Select Image/Video** button while hovering over the preview field, or drag any content into this space:

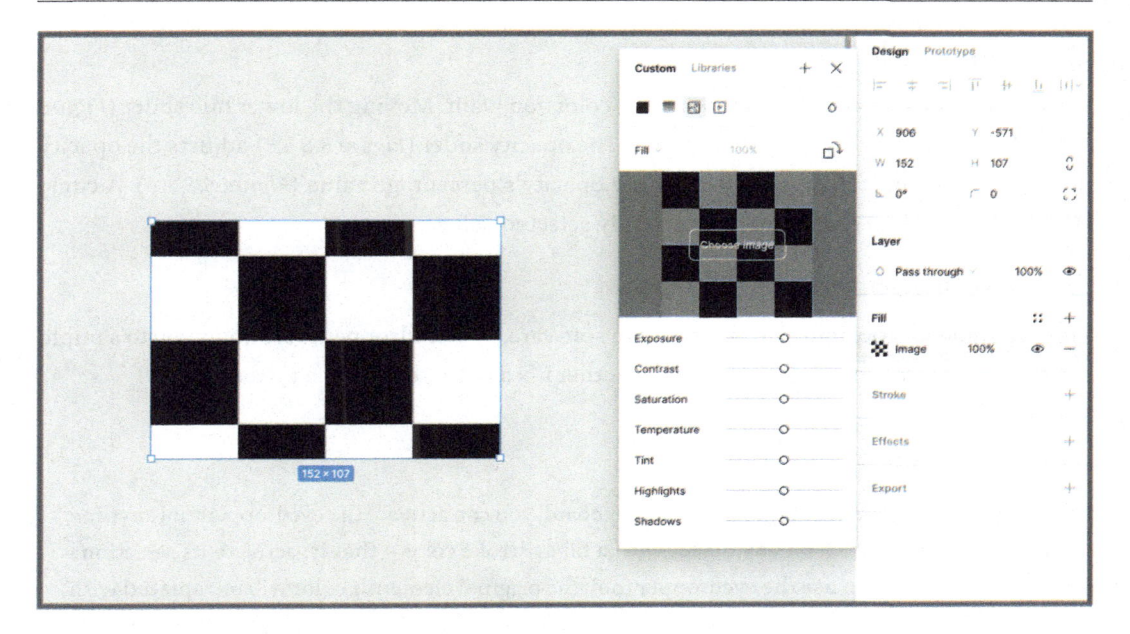

Figure 5.10 – Image fill

When working with images, this turns your panel into a small but functional image-editing center with the ability to retouch **Exposure**, **Contrast**, and so on. Keep in mind that the imported image is used to fill your element. This means that if you select a star shape and set an **Image** fill, it will be inserted into the shape, and above all, the layer will continue to be of the shape type. Thus, importing an image on the canvas and inserting an image fill are entirely different operations. For this reason, with the **Image** fill option, you will find various settings in the color picker – you can fill the space, adapt to it, crop the image, or repeat it in tiles.

B – Blend modes

With this function, you can blend the two layers in different ways. All the options are listed in the drop-down menu. Depending on the selected mode, the blending is calculated for each individual pixel of this layer and the layer below it.

C – Color palette

In this area, you can visually pick whatever color you want. Moving the lower hue slider (*Figure 5.8 - D*) changes the displayed color tones. The opacity slider (*Figure 5.8 - E*) adjusts the opacity of the color, or you can manually enter the opacity's percentage value (*Figure 5.8 - F*). A circle with a white outline represents the currently selected color.

G – Eyedropper tool

This is a standard tool found in every design software. The eyedropper tool allows you to sample a color from any element on the screen, whether it's a vector object or a raster image.

> **Note:**
>
> By pressing the *I* key on your keyboard, you can activate the eyedropper tool anytime. If you click on any object with a fill or stroke color – that is, activate its selection – and then use the eyedropper tool, the original element's color will be replaced with the sampled one. With no active selections, it is still a valid tool for displaying the color code of the color you hover over on the screen.

H – Color models

By default, the reference color model will be the **Hex** code, which is the hexadecimal alphanumeric representation of the color. This mode is most popular in digital design and is equally convenient for web developers. But if needed, you can switch modes in the dropdown and choose **RGB** or **CSS** (which is also RGB but formatted in a web-friendly way). RGB, which stands for red, green, and blue, allows you to assign a value from **0** to **255** to individual channels. Finally, there are **hue, saturation, brightness (HSB)** and **hue, saturation, luminance (HSL)**, which are very similar, as they generate color by changing their respective parameters.

I – Color styles

In **Document colors**, you can quickly access the entire color palette used in your current file. You can also access color from shared libraries using the drop-down menu. We will learn more about how libraries work later.

We have explored all the tools to help you work effectively with the colors. There's one more thing to clarify before moving on to the following tool. As you already know, the **Design** panel, being contextual, displays settings according to the selected element, and the color tools work the same way.

But what if you select more than one object at a time? If the fill or stroke of the selected elements matches in color, you will not notice anything unusual, as the unique value will be displayed in the panel as before. However, if the colors of the elements were different, a new section called **Selection Colors** will appear in the panel. In this section, you can see all the colors present on the selected objects, and you can change every property individually:

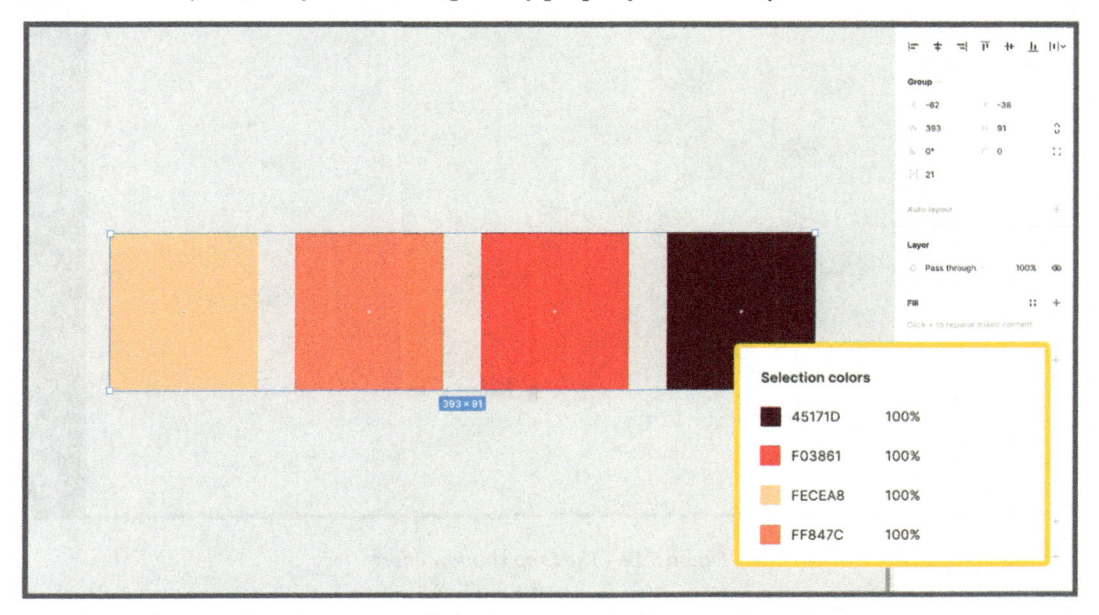

Figure 5.11 – Selection colors

Colors are a big topic to learn, but Figma makes them easy to, giving you a set of tools that are easy to master. Always remember that before adding any color to your design, you must ensure your choice is correct. We'll pick a color palette for our app later in this chapter, but now, feel free to play with colors in your drafts if you like.

Creating effects

In the **Design** panel, you may have noticed a section not yet mentioned, namely **Effects**. This is a tool that deserves an in-depth study, as you can apply various effects with it to elements, such as **Inner shadow**, **Drop shadow**, **Layer blur**, and **Background blur**.

Each of these effects has its own characteristic behavior. **Drop shadow**, for example, replicates the depth of Material Design (which is the official design system made by Google for its apps and services; you can check it out here: `material.io/design`) or cards in general, and **Background blur** simulates the iOS opaque glass effect.

To change the effect's settings, simply click the sun-shaped icon, and you will see all the properties that can be modified, such as positioning, **Spread** for outer/inner shadows, or **Blur** levels for blur effects:

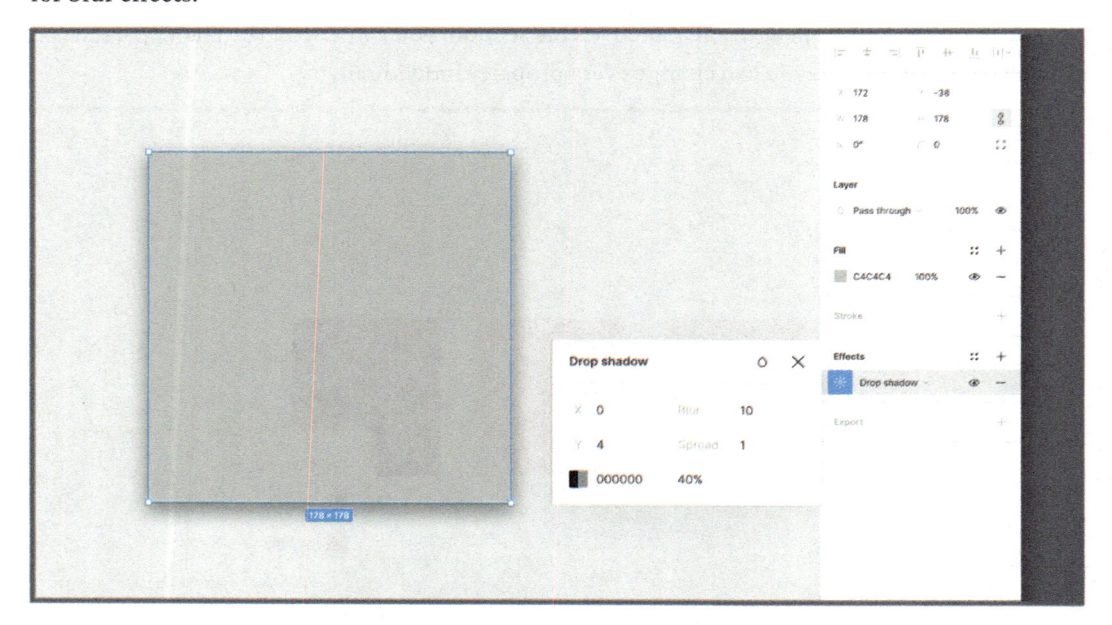

Figure 5.12 – The Drop shadow effect

As you can imagine, **Effects** has many properties, and describing each of them would take too many pages of this book, which is somewhat irrational, given that our main goal is to learn how to design a fully-fledged interface in Figma. So, try exploring the effects in more detail in your draft file, setting different effect properties and watching the results. But you should know that it is better not to overuse effects when working on real projects. The main purpose of this feature is to highlight elements to make them more visible to the user. Especially in your first steps in design, it's best to stick to the well-known guidelines for effect recommendations. As your experience grows, you can experiment and create your own effects, even mixing them up.

In this section, we have enriched our knowledge of Figma with three main functions, without which it would be difficult to imagine design. If you are concerned that you have not used any of these functions in our interface so far, don't worry, as in the next topic, we will learn how to do it in the simplest and smartest way.

Introducing Styles

Well, we've mastered the basics of grids, typography, colors, and effects, but now it's time to learn how to effectively manipulate these tools. And that is what we will practice in this section. As you can imagine, it would be incredibly irrational to apply our chosen font to every text layer in our design. In this hypothetical situation, you risk changing the fonts of all the text on all the screens in your application if you ever decide to replace the selected font with a different one. Figma provides a simple and flexible feature called Styles.

Styles in Figma is an incredibly powerful feature that allows you to save and reuse color palettes, fonts, and effect attributes in your design project. This means that you can apply the approved style properties to any element with a single click. And if you ever need to change any property, you can do it just as quickly in all layers of your file, or even across multiple files!

Preparing your file

So, let's see how to style our application in practice. This step is very important because it is the transition from a **Low-Fidelity (Lo-Fi)** wireframe to a **High-Fidelity (Hi-Fi)** final design, so you need to prepare your file in the best possible way:

1. In the upper-right corner of the **Layers** panel, there is a drop-down label that shows and hides all the pages in your file. At this point, you only have one page in your design file that contains the wireframe, which Figma has automatically named Page 1. Let's rename it Lo-Fi by double-clicking the page name.

2. Duplicate the page by right-clicking its name and choosing **Duplicate Page** from the drop-down menu. A second one with the same name will appear under the first page.

3. Rename the duplicate page to `Hi-Fi` – this is where we will be working on the actual UI of our application. Remember, a Starter plan can contain up to three pages in one team file. As a result, you should have a structure similar to the following:

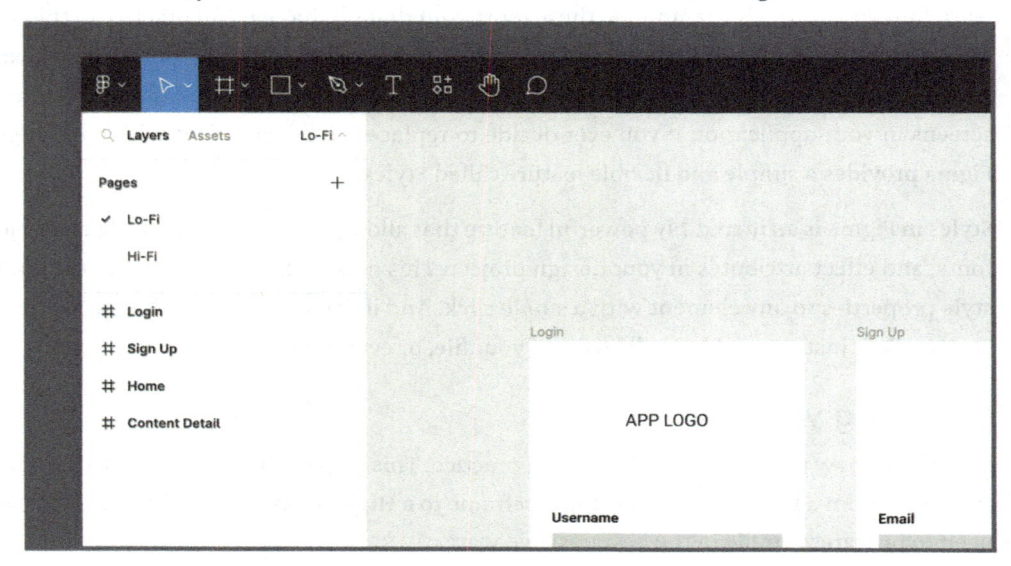

Figure 5.13 – Lo-Fi and Hi-Fi pages

As you have probably figured out, the first page of your file will only contain the wireframe you have already created, and the second will be dedicated to the actual design of our application.

Creating and managing grid styles

Duplicating any page means copying all its content, so you can see all the same wireframes created earlier on the Hi-Fi page. Let's not change the elements inside the frames for now but start by setting layout grids as a first style property. To do that, follow these steps:

1. Select the **Login** frame.
2. Add **Layout grid** from the right sidebar by clicking on the + icon.
3. By default, the uniform grid will be applied. Click on the grid icon and select **Columns** from the dropdown.

Chapter 5

4. From the grid settings, set the column **Count** value to 12, the **Type** value to **Stretch**, the **Margin** value to 16, and **Gutter** to 8:

Figure 5.14 – The grid settings

Obviously, the values that you have just entered for your grid cannot be random. In our case, as mentioned earlier, the 12-column structure is one of the most commonly used in well-known development frameworks. The **Gutter** value is set for a design with an 8-point system, in which everything will be a multiple of 8, starting with a **Margin** of 16px. This system of multiples makes it much easier to keep spacing consistent. This grid system is very simple and effective, but it is not the only one, right? So, feel free to experiment with new options when you feel more confident.

Since you applied the grid to the **Login** frame only, you must do the same for all other screens for consistency. But doing it manually for each frame is an inconvenient operation, especially if you have many more views than in our work area. To simplify, speed up, and optimize this process, let's save this grid as our first style:

1. Select the **Login** view with the layout grid you've just created.
2. Click the **Style** icon (see the following screenshot).
3. Create a new style by clicking on the + icon of the **Grid Styles** dialog.

4. Give a proper name to this grid style, such as `12-column-fluid`, which quickly makes it recognizable as a stretchy 12-column grid:

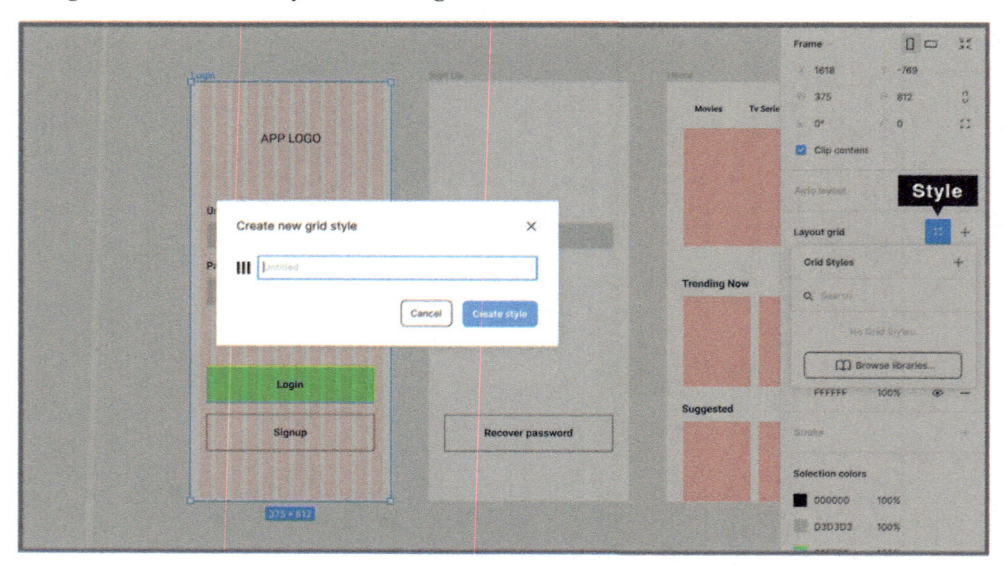

Figure 5.15 – A new grid style

Done! The layout grid you created has just been converted to a style, and you can see it in the right sidebar. Now, all that remains is to apply this grid style to all the other frames:

1. Select all the frames with no grids (**Sign Up**, **Home**, and **Content Detail**).
2. This time, instead of pressing **+**, click the **Styles** button, and you will see the grid style that you just created.
3. Select your grid style to apply it to all the views in your file with one click.

Now, you can see how easy it is to complete this operation with minimal effort. However, you should never forget that after applying the same style to multiple frames, you will no longer be able to change the layout grids of individual views, as they all relate to the same source of truth. If you want to change your grid style, you can do so in the **Styles** dialog box by selecting the style you want to edit and clicking the **Edit Style** icon:

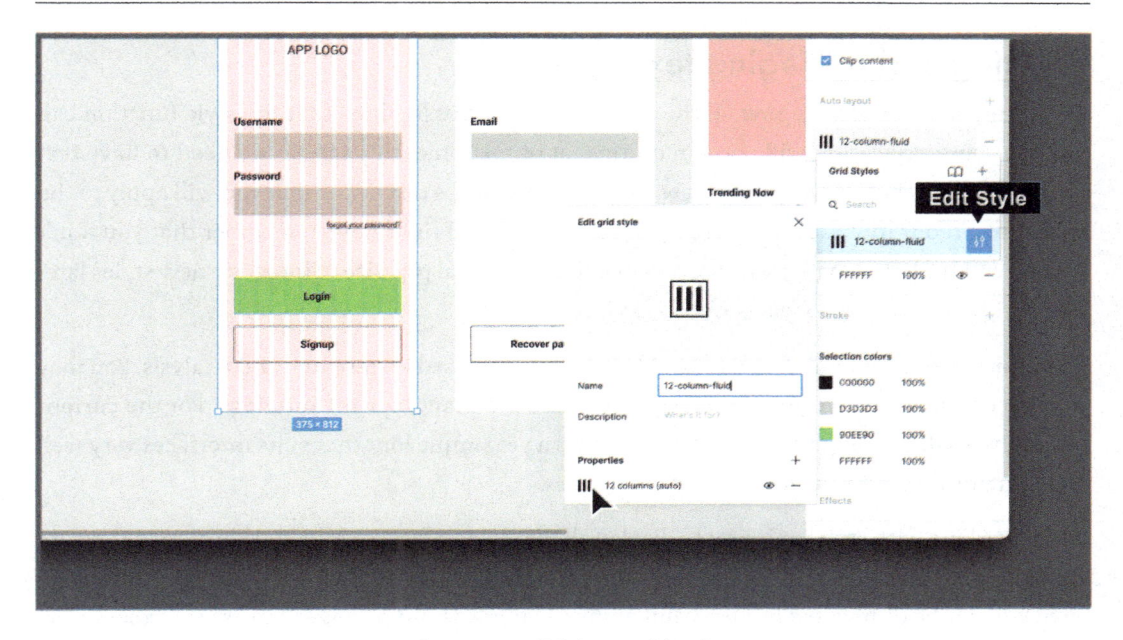

Figure 5.16 – Editing a grid style

After you have saved your changes, all the views to which the style was applied will undergo the same modification. See how easy it is, and again in a few clicks!

> **Note:**
>
> You can still change an individual grid. To do this, select the frame you need and click **Detach Style**, the broken chain icon next to the applied style. Beware that this will permanently unlink the selected frame's grid from the grid style unless you undo the change.

So you've just created your first style, which will be one of many – splendid work! Now, let's select a font for our project and convert it to a style as well.

Creating and managing text styles

In creating a grid style, we saw all the advantages and possibilities that the style function can provide. Our application will contain quite a lot of text on each page, so we need to have text styles as well. As before, you first create a foundation for the text styles that you will apply to the text layers in our interface. If you're feeling overwhelmed right now, remember that you don't need to create all the text styles simultaneously. It is normal practice to integrate new styles later if the original core of the style is well organized.

The choice of fonts for any project should, of course, be based on research and analysis. You may want to consider one or more fonts (try not to use too many) for the interface. For the current project, we will be using *Source Sans Pro*, a modern yet simple font that suits interfaces very well and remains incredibly legible even at small sizes.

When working with styles, it is best to display all the style properties outside the interface layouts. We can allocate one page for this. So, create the third (and final) page in the file. This time, the page will not be duplicated but new and empty. Rename this new page `Styles + Components` – here, you will collect all the reusable parts of the UI. On this new page, create a new frame with a preset desktop size (1440 x 1024) and rename it `Typography`. This frame will be the container for all the text styles you will add soon:

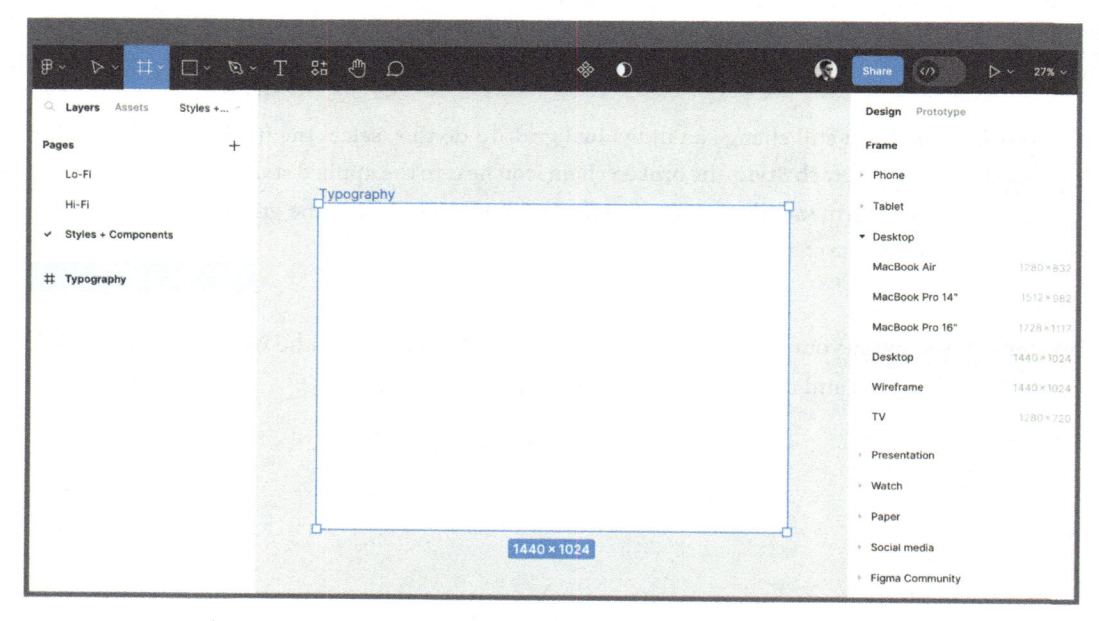

Figure 5.17 – The Typography page

Chapter 5   131

You don't need to add a lot of styles for this project, only the ones that you really need for the app layouts. As for the text style, we'll use multiples of eight and start with the body text (the one used for standard paragraphs). We'll then move on to other text styles in terms of their importance. Follow the next few steps to get it done easily:

1. On the **Styles + Components** page, create five new text layers. It is best to use a pangram as a sample text. A pangram is a sentence that holds all the letters of the alphabet. This way, you will always have a visual display of all the characters of the selected font. One of the most famous pangrams is **The quick brown fox jumps over the lazy dog**.
2. Place these text layers vertically one after the other.
3. Starting with the top text layer, assign the following parameters to each text layer:

    - **Source Sans Pro | 32px | Bold**
    - **Source Sans Pro | 24px | Bold**
    - **Source Sans Pro | 16px | Bold**
    - **Source Sans Pro | 16px | Regular**
    - **Source Sans Pro | 16px | Light**

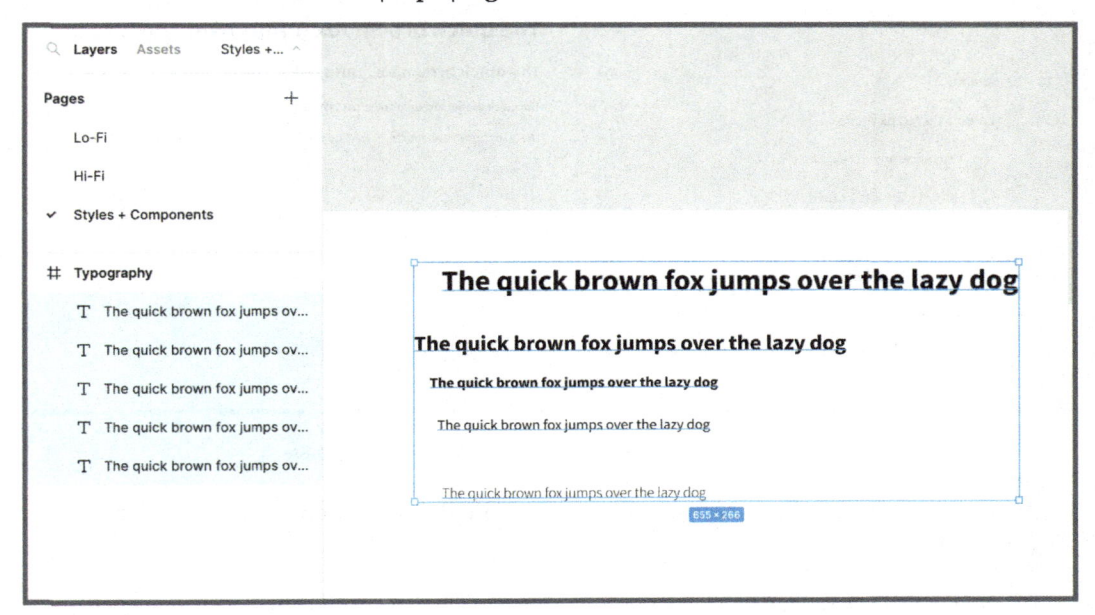

Figure 5.18 – Styled text layers

After you've finished formatting all the text layers, if the result looks messy, align them by using the alignment section in the **Design** panel.

Select all the text layers, click the **Align left** button, and then click **Distribute vertical spacing** in the right drop-down list with a few more options. After these two clicks, the frame's contents should be arranged perfectly.

> **Note:**
> If you want to select multiple elements from the **Layer** panel, you can hold the *Command* (macOS) or *Ctrl* (Windows) key.

To finish tidying up your text style container, you can add a label next to each sentence, which is a simple overview of the rules applied to each text layer. It's even better if you combine labels and related texts into groups:

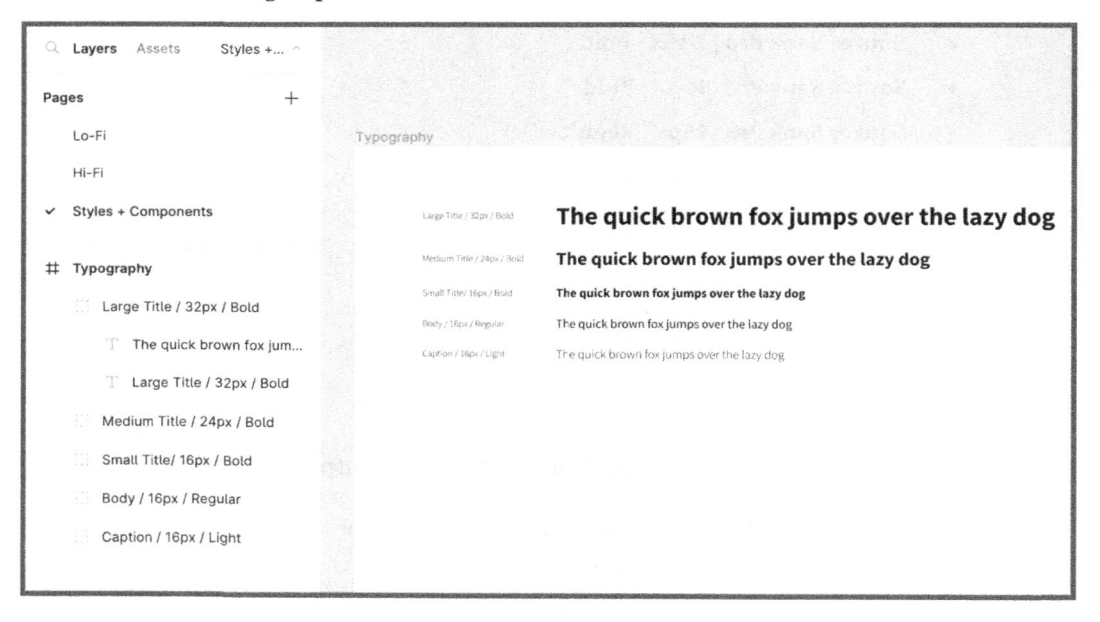

Figure 5.19 – Styled and ordered text layers with labels

It's time to create text styles based on this structure, finally, and it won't be much different from how you did it earlier with grids:

1. Select the top text layer.
2. Click on the **Style** button next to the **Text** section label in the right sidebar.
3. In the **Text styles** dialog, click the + button.

4. Give this first text style a name, such as `Title / Large`.
5. Repeat the process for every successive text layer in order, with the following names:
   - `Title / Medium`
   - `Title / Small`
   - `Body / Regular`
   - `Body / Light`

We are following a standard way of naming text styles to group them based on where they're used. Right now, we're keeping it simple, but as you come across more text styles, it's important to find a good way to organize them. Using slashes helps create folders in our library, making it easier to group similar styles together based on where they belong.

So, the text styles are set up and ready to be used in our app design. It is important to know that each text style can have a set of rules governing the font family, font weight and size, line height, letter spacing, text decoration, text transformation, and so on. But unlike other design tools, text styles do NOT include alignment and color. This feature makes text styles incredibly flexible, eliminating the need to create text styles for each alignment or color. In the following screenshot, you can check out our text styles in the right panel of Figma:

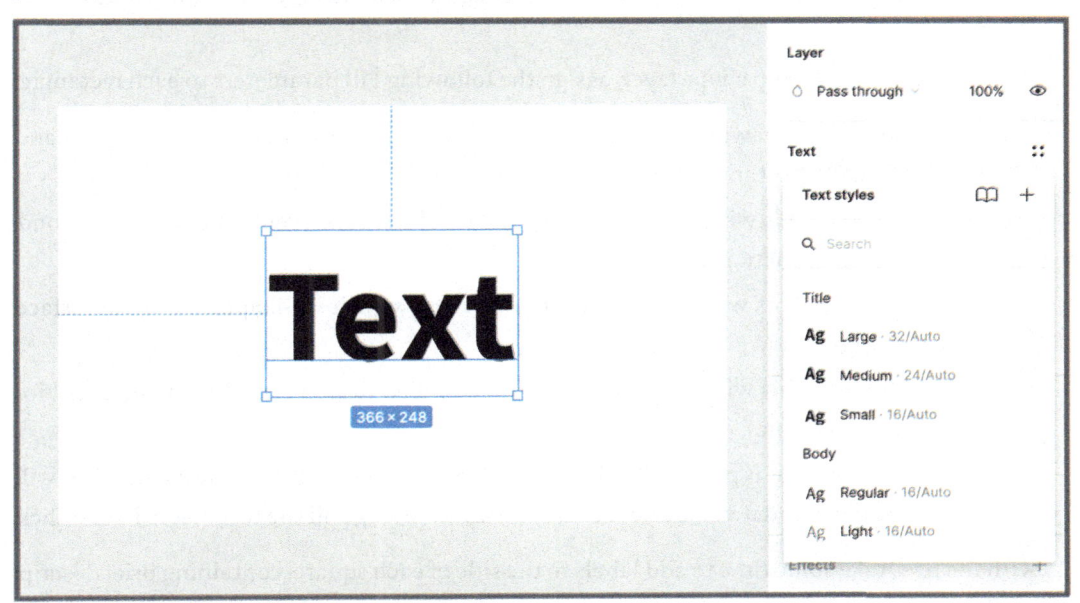

Figure 5.20 – Text styles

When you feel more confident about your design, you can experiment with creating a complete UI kit that includes styles for any need and can be reused as a basis for your future projects. The font scale's rhythm is a more complex subject than it might seem. To get the most harmonious scales, you can use ratios, but since not every creative is in love with math, here is a convenient site that can help you with that and take care of all the mathematical aspects: `type-scale.com`.

Creating and managing color and effect styles

Now, our project has styles that consist of a layout grid and typography, so it's time to add the third essential property – colors. Again, to make the right choice of color palette for any application or site you develop, it is important to refer to the artifacts you collected during your research and analysis, namely the moodboard in this case. You will see which colors suit our video streaming app project in a moment. But first, let's add a new **Desktop** frame to the `Styles + Components` page, next to the **Typography** frame, and rename the new frame `Colors`. Then, follow a few simple steps to create color styles:

1. Add five rectangle shapes of 130x130 px in the new **Colors** frame.
2. Place them vertically, at a short distance from each other. To arrange them neatly and apply equal vertical spacing between them, select them all and use Figma's auto-alignment feature.
3. Starting with the top shape layer, assign the following **Fill** parameters to each rectangle:

    - `FF5959`: This will be our accent color, which we will use for calls to action and other important operations.
    - `272B45`: This will be our secondary color, which we'll eventually use on a secondary user's actions.
    - `0F1022`: This will be our background color, which we'll apply to the interface background.
    - `8A8C99`: This will be our inactive color, applied to elements that are disabled for some reason.
    - `FFFFFF`: This is pure white. This one will be our text color since the background will be dark, and it will be needed if we want to change all the text colors in one click.

As with the text, take some time to add labels to the side of each square, containing brief descriptions of the color use cases.

Chapter 5

In addition, you can add a 1px-thin black stroke to all the colored squares to make the light colors stand out from the background easily:

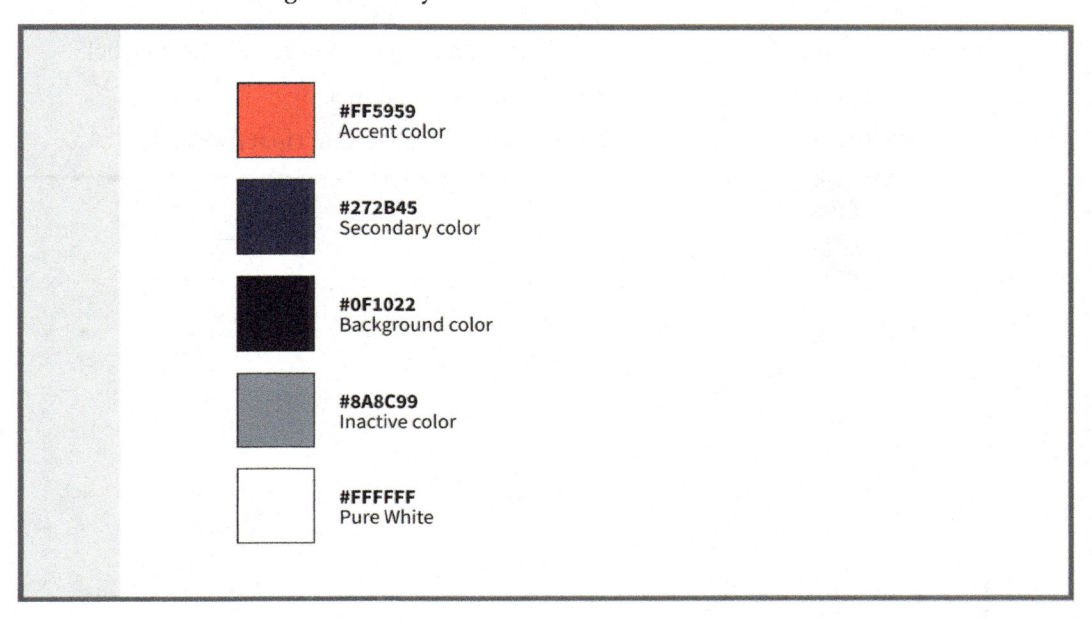

Figure 5.21 – The color palette

As you probably guessed, all the colors need to be converted to Styles. Therefore, you need to select colored squares individually and create a corresponding style for each. You can name each color style the same as its label (such as `Accent color`). Creating a style from the **Fill** section does not mean that this color can only be used for fill. If you ever want to apply it to a stroke or shadow, it can be done without a problem. As with fonts, you may need more colors than you chose at the beginning, so that you can include new color styles later. You can add new color styles at any time, if necessary, but it is especially important that all colors that are used in your file are always linked to styles, except for a few unique cases.

Choosing the right color palette is a skill that comes with experience. Once you have mastered the basics, you can learn more about colors. There are many resources that can explain the psychological meaning of colors, as well as their relationship to different cultures. It is also very important to study the subject of accessibility in depth, which also includes the use of sufficiently contrasting colors to a set of rules so that legibility is adequate, especially for people with visual impairments.

Finally, you need to style the effects, following the same pattern. Follow these steps:

1. Select the white square in the **Colors** frame.
2. Add an effect from the right sidebar by clicking the + button near the **Effects** label.
3. Click the sun icon to the left of the **Drop shadow** dropdown.
4. Set **X** to 0, **Blur** to 15, **Y** to 4, **Spread** to 5, **Color** to 82B2DE, and **Opacity** to 22%:

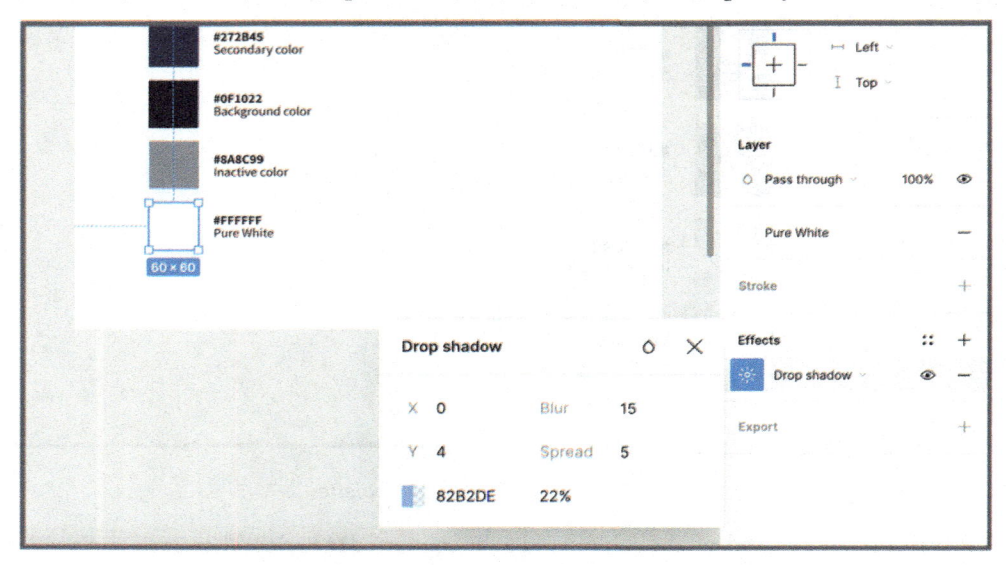

Figure 5.22 – The Drop shadow settings

5. Save this effect as a style and name it `Light Drop Shadow`.

6. Now, you can apply this effect style to each of the colored squares, removing the black stroke for a more polished look:

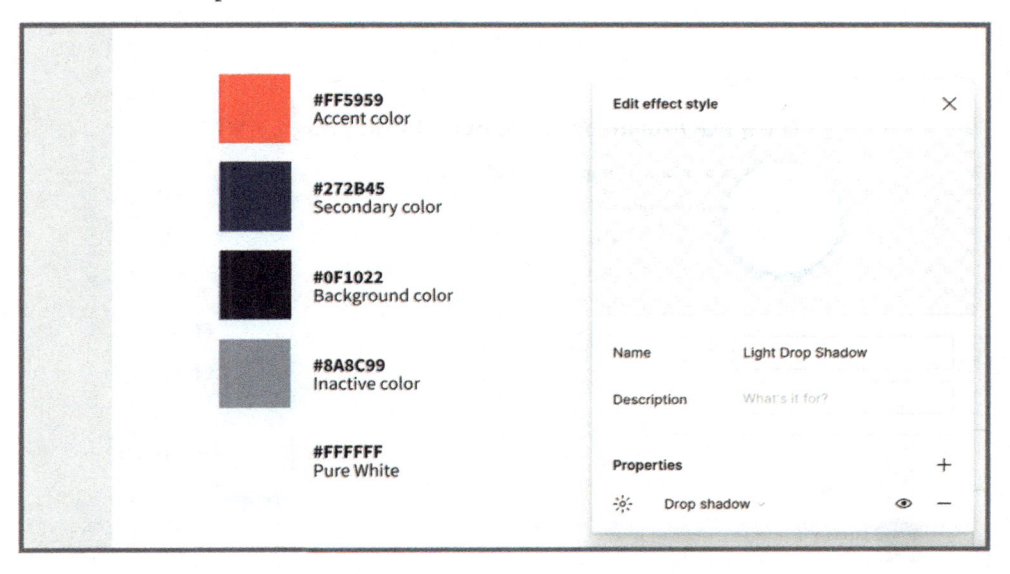

Figure 5.23 – The color palette with drop shadow

This effect can be applied to any layer you want.

Well, you have finally created all the sources of truth needed for our project. In the next chapter, you will learn how to make the best use of styles. Let's look at everything you've created so far. To do this, simply click on any empty space on the canvas of the page. When nothing is selected, you can see the list of styles in the **Design** panel, and from here, you can quickly edit any of them.

After making changes to a style, all elements to which it was applied undergo the exact same change:

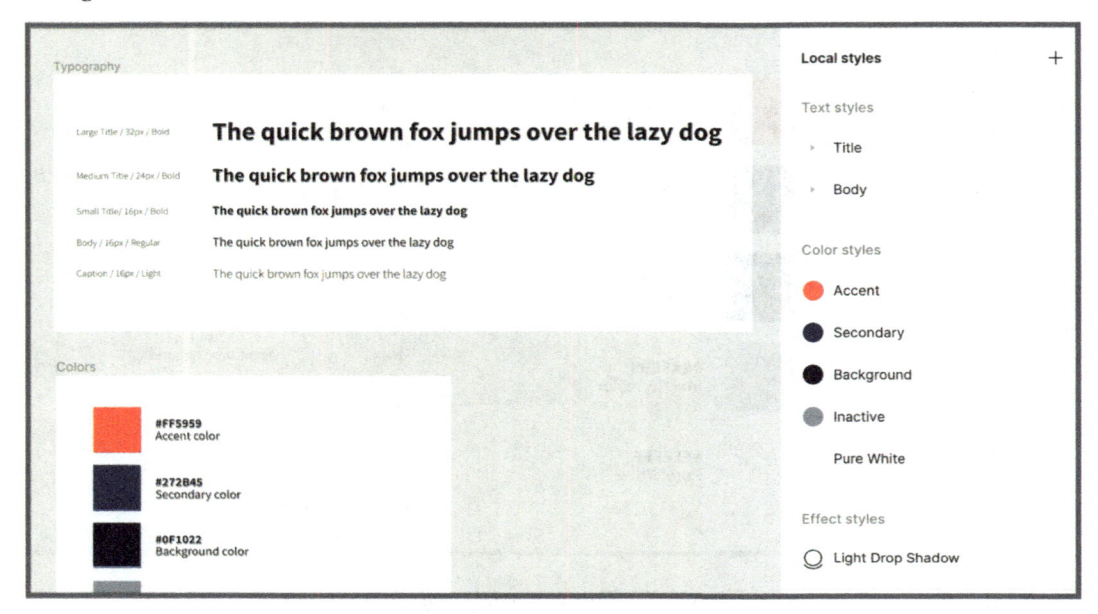

Figure 5.24 – Grid, color, text, and effect styles

So, your design file now contains three pages, one of which is completely dedicated to styles. Later, you will add other elements, such as reusable components. After working on the design of our application, you can even reuse this library of styles and components in other projects. You will learn about this and everything else as you travel along this exciting journey!

Summary

As stated earlier, the main goal of a UX/UI designer is not to be creative but to provide an interface in which every user will feel confident and nothing will distract them from the functionality of any digital product. Thus, you need to make sure your design is intuitive and inclusive. This means you have to be well aware of your user's needs and pains, and anticipate specific cases where your app or website might be used to keep your design consistent and accessible. As you learned in this chapter, you must follow these principles even when choosing typography, colors, and effects.

Aside from practicing these tools, we now know how to make the best use of them by converting them to styles. Styles are one of the most essential features in Figma, and you've done a great job learning them. From now on, you will discover and practice even more advanced features, and later, you will add other properties to your **Styles + Components** page, such as extra styles and reusable UI elements. Now that you feel more confident using Figma, you are ready to explore its unique and compelling features. One of them is Auto Layout, which you will learn about immediately in the next chapter!

Learn more on Discord

To join the Discord community for this book – where you can share feedback, ask questions to the author, and learn about new releases – follow the QR code below:

`https://packt.link/figma`

6

Creating a Responsive Mobile Interface Using Auto Layout

In the previous chapter, you already started the transition from lo-fi to hi-fi, which is the actual design of our video streaming app. It is important to know that this is the stage of the project where you need to be focused, precise, and clear, since your hi-fi files will be used by the developers. It may take you a while to achieve this, which is perfectly fine, but thanks to Figma's awesome tools, you can avoid inaccuracy as much as possible. In this chapter, you will discover one of those tools, namely auto layout.

The topic you are about to explore in this chapter can be defined as advanced. So, you will first start with the theory, and then smoothly move on to practicing on our project file. But this does not mean that you cannot complement the process of learning new principles in this chapter with your own practice in your draft files. It would be even better if you include in this practice some of the tools that you have already learned, especially those that you may not feel very confident with yet. The more you experiment, the faster you'll learn. So, open up your Figma and let's get started!

In this chapter, we are going to cover the following main topics:

- Introducing auto layout
- Resizing and constraints
- Applying auto layout to our interface

By the end of this chapter, you will have a good understanding of the auto layout, resizing, and constraint features in Figma and will be able to create responsive views using them.

Introducing auto layout

In this section, you'll start by discovering the powerful Figma auto layout feature. Its use covers many aspects of a designer's work, from improving the flow of your interface to speeding up your workflow. At first, auto layout may seem similar to the **grids** you explored in *Chapter 5, Designing Consistently Using Grids, Colors, and Typography*, as they are both used for precisely aligning elements in your designs. As you know, grids are incredibly useful for ensuring that all elements follow the same harmony and layout logic. However, relying solely on grids can be risky because they are inherently static. They don't adapt dynamically to content changes or varying screen sizes, which can lead to design issues in responsive or content-heavy interfaces. This is where the **auto layout** feature in Figma becomes invaluable. The word "auto" gives you a hint that once you set properties, you don't need to worry about checking whether everything is positioned correctly. With this feature, you can save yourself from making mistakes that are sometimes difficult to track down. But auto layout goes beyond that and does a lot more, and you'll soon find out about all its amazing capabilities.

Before diving into the massive topic of auto layout, let's take a look at where you are in your journey right now. At this point, you've already seen that the process of creating a good design is not as easy as expected. It is not enough to have an idea and then implement it by simply placing elements on the screen and styling them. So, after the research phase, you started working on the wireframe interface in *Chapter 4, Wireframing a Mobile-First Experience Using Vector Shapes*. Wireframes are made up of simple shapes and lines where you don't have to pay too much attention to detail and be too precise. Now that you have successfully completed that task, and started preparing the base with styles and grids for your layouts in the previous chapter, it's time to create a real design. So, let's finally take a look at what auto layout is and how it will help you in your future work on the interface.

What is auto layout?

Auto layout is one of the most significant features in Figma. Once you apply it to any frame, it will become dynamic, by shrinking or growing according to the size of its content. This means, for example, that if you have an auto layout frame containing a text layer and then you add another layer to it, that frame automatically resizes itself to easily fit both elements. Moreover, **Auto layout** is great for creating lists and menus, as any new element triggers the frame to adapt responsively, as you can see in the following figure:

Figure 6.1 – Auto layout affecting a list of items

Auto layout is a complex and challenging topic to explore, but once you learn how it works, it can greatly simplify your workflow and improve the quality of your design and workflow. You will discover more about this in the next section of this chapter, but for now, let's start with a general overview of this feature. All the auto layout settings are presented in the contextual right sidebar. But as you have already seen in other typical cases, it will only be shown and activated after the element with auto layout is selected. You can add auto layout to frames (whether empty or full), components (which you will explore in the next chapter), groups, and multiple-layer selections.

Note:
If you select a group and apply **Auto layout** (using the shortcut *Shift* + *A*), the group will automatically convert into a frame. This feature underscores that auto layout is specifically designed for frames in Figma.

From the moment auto layout is activated – by clicking the + buttons next to the **Auto layout** label on the right sidebar – the frame automatically resizes to fit the content inside it. If it has no elements inside it, it will be adjusted as soon as you add anything to this frame.

Activating auto layout opens a whole range of new properties in a dedicated section, as shown in the following figure:

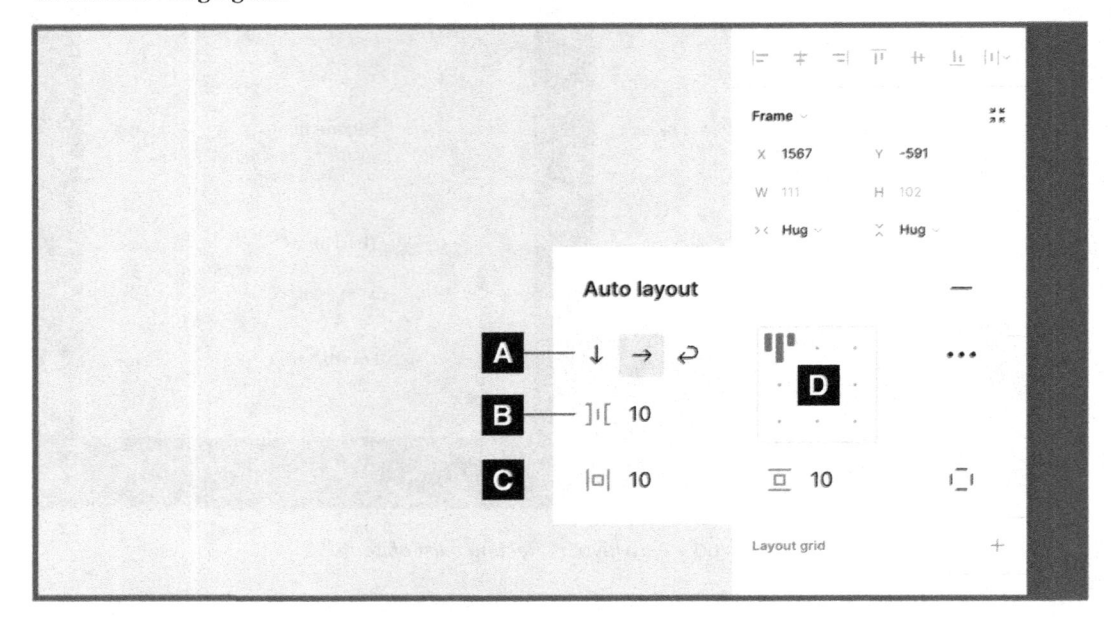

Figure 6.2 – The auto layout section

Let's take a closer look at each of these settings in the **Auto layout** section.

A — Direction

With this option, you can set the direction of your layout, namely, horizontal or vertical. Depending on the option selected, the layout will automatically align to a row or column, readapting all the elements contained in the frame. Additionally, the introduction of a third option – wrap – enables you to control how items are displayed when they overflow the available space along the main axis, allowing you to specify whether the flex items should wrap onto a new line or remain on the same line within the container.

B — Gap

When a frame with an active auto layout contains more than one element, whether horizontally or vertically, there will be equal spacing between each element. You can change the gap value as in the following image:

Chapter 6 145

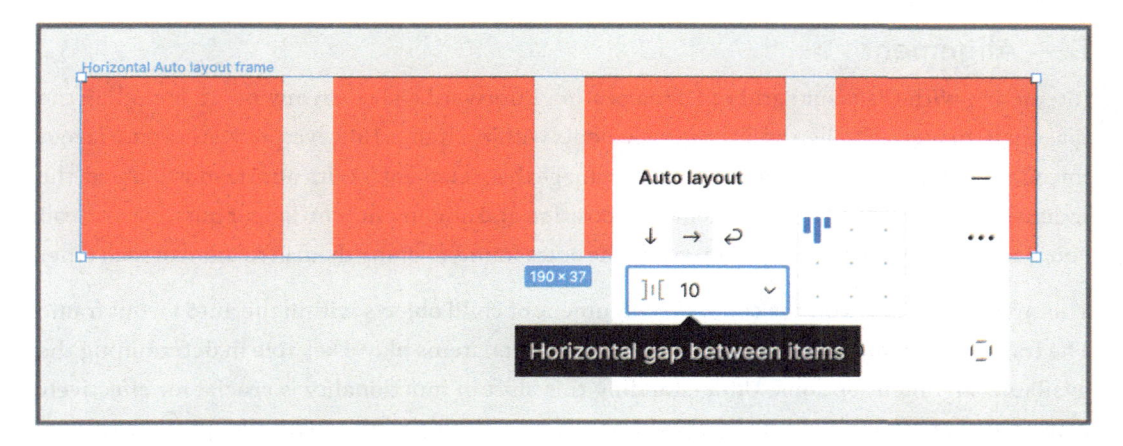

Figure 6.3 – The Horizontal gap between items option

C – Padding

Padding is a common design concept, often familiar to those with some design experience. In Figma, when you adjust the padding parameter, it applies horizontal or vertical spacing inside the borders of a frame. This internal spacing affects how elements within the frame, such as text or images, are positioned relative to the frame's edges. If you're new to this concept, think of padding as the inner spacing before the stroke of the frame. This is distinct from a margin, which is the outer spacing after the stroke. The following figure will help illustrate the subtle yet important difference between padding (inner spacing) and margins (outer spacing), enhancing your understanding of how each affects the layout and appearance of your designs:

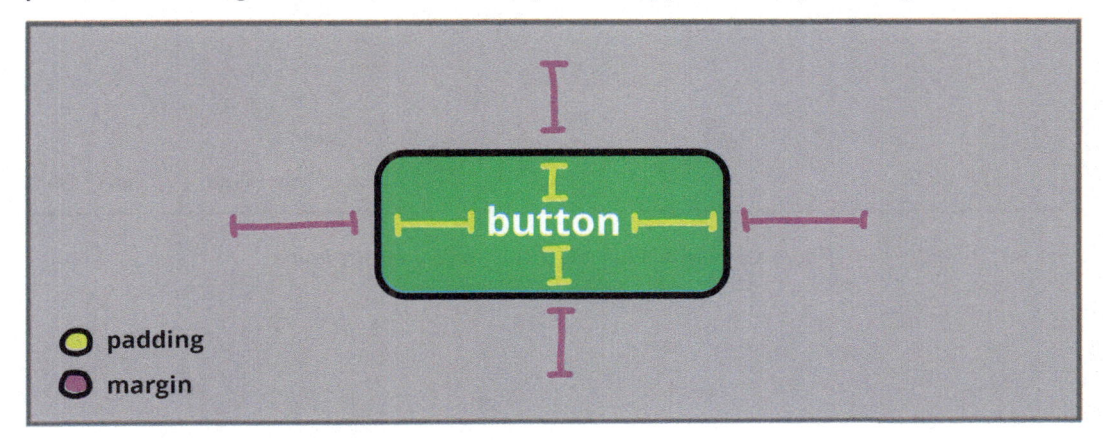

Figure 6.4 – Padding and margin differences

D – Alignment

Interacting with the visual grid in Figma is straightforward – click on any point, including the diagonals, to precisely align and arrange elements within a frame. However, activating auto layout introduces a significant change in how you manage these elements. With auto layout enabled, the independent adjustment of each element's position and alignment is no longer possible. Instead, you manage the elements as a group within the outer frame, aligning them in relation to each other.

This approach focuses on the collective alignment of child objects within the auto layout frame. The frame's direction and the spacing or gaps between items play a key role in determining the available alignment options. Understanding this shift in functionality is crucial for effectively using auto layout. For a visual demonstration of how this impacts your design process, refer to the illustrative figure below:

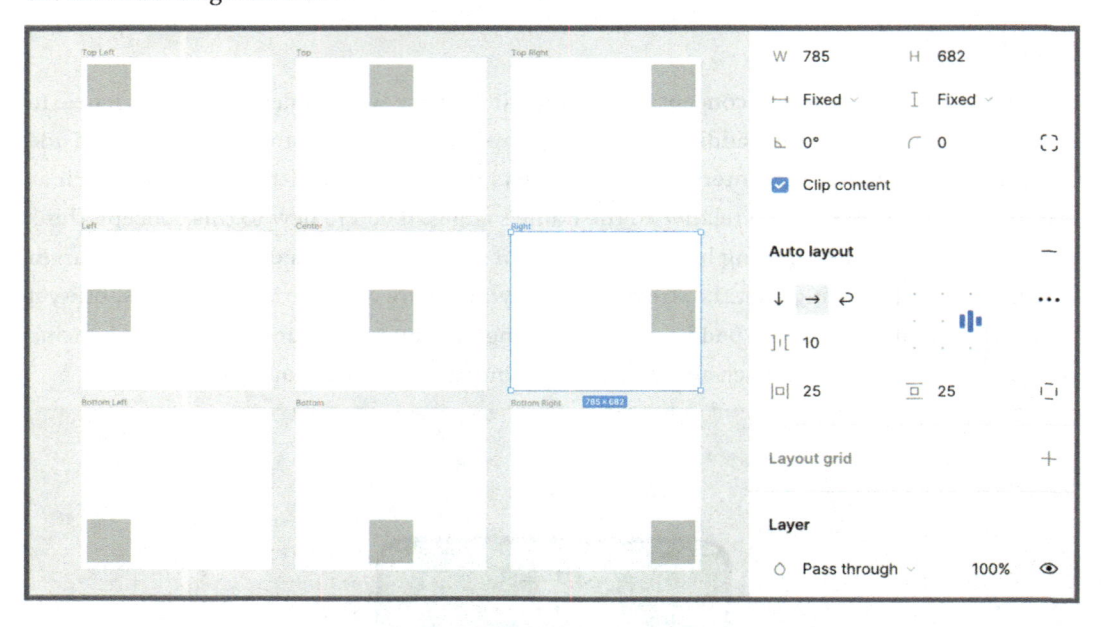

Figure 6.5 – The different alignments on a fixed-size frame

Chapter 6　　147

In a frame containing multiple elements, they naturally cluster and move together. However, this behavior can be adjusted by selecting the **Gap between elements** (*B*) option, or setting it to **Auto**. Enabling **Auto** ensures that all the elements within the frame are automatically and evenly spaced to fit within your frame. For a convenient shortcut, you can achieve this by double-clicking on the alignment box.

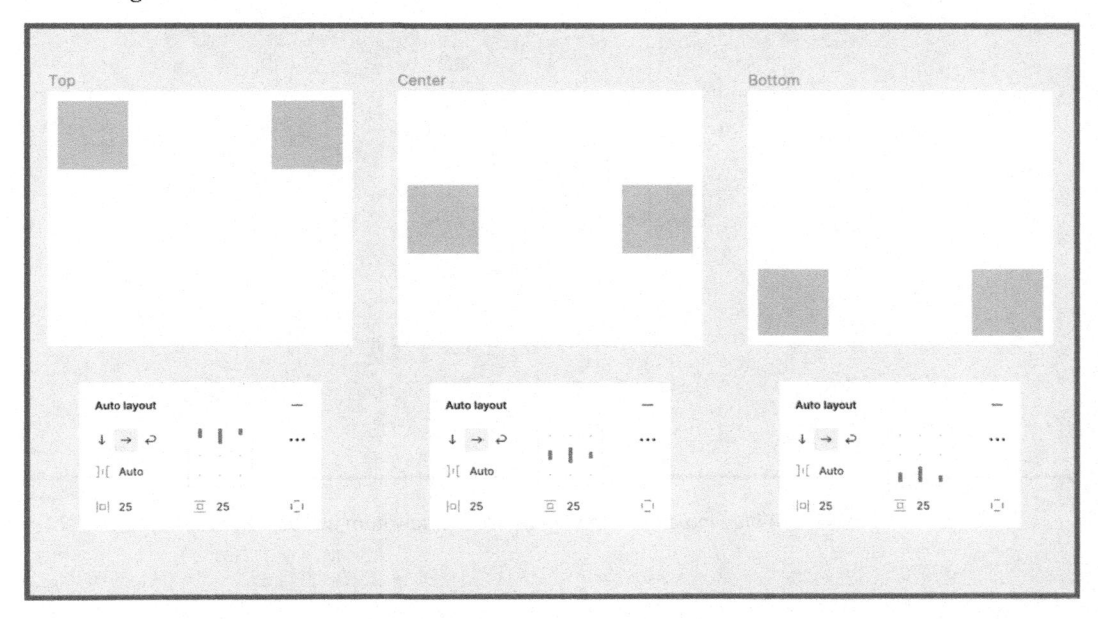

Figure 6.6 – Horizontal gap between properties

The options also differ depending on the direction of the auto layout. Also, note that distribution and alignment have a visible effect on the frame only if it is not adapted to the elements it contains and is larger. You may be confused at this point, but you will learn more about these cases in the *Resizing and constraints* section.

Adding, removing, and rearranging elements

Once auto layout is applied to a frame, you can no longer freely position the inner elements, as they will all follow the set auto layout rules. On the other hand, from this point on, the frame becomes more flexible and stable, which allows you to quickly create complex but very accurate layouts, so you can be sure that everything is consistent with the logic.

If, at any point, you need to add a new element to the horizontal or vertical stack, all you have to do is simply drag that element into the auto layout frame. What's more, you can choose exactly where to insert the new element.

As you drag your element and move it over the existing ones, a blue indicator appears to help you place the object where you want it to be:

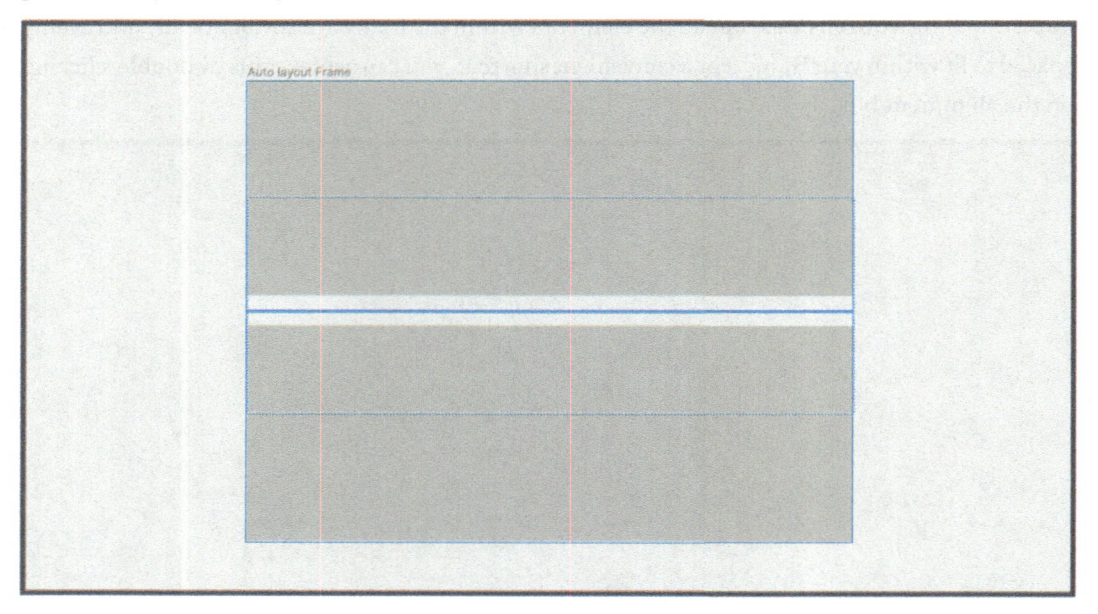

Figure 6.7 – A blue indicator showing where the new item will be added

> **Note:**
> You can also duplicate any element in the auto layout frame by selecting it and pressing *Command + D* (macOS) or *Ctrl + D* (Windows). The new element will be placed right next to the original one.

Deleting elements is also very easy. Just select one and press *Backspace* on your keyboard. If you just want to remove it from the current frame without deleting it, you can simply drag it out of the container. Your stack will change accordingly.

It's just as easy to reorder elements in an auto layout frame. For example, to swap the positions of the second and third elements of the stack, simply drag the second element onto the third. You can also do this by selecting the element and using the *Arrow* keys on your keyboard.

Chapter 6

Without auto layout, moving elements and keeping the correct gap between them would be much more time-consuming and risky.

Nesting auto layout

Nesting, a key design concept used in Figma and other design tools, involves placing elements or groups of elements inside one another, creating a layered structure. This approach is akin to stacking boxes, where each box can contain other, smaller items. When you apply this principle to Figma's auto layout frames, it allows for the creation of intricate and well-organized designs. By nesting an auto layout frame within another, you can build complex layouts with multiple layers of structure.

Take a classic card layout as an example: it might be vertically composed of an image, text, and two buttons. In this layout, the outer card is the primary frame, arranged vertically, and within it, the two buttons are grouped together in a secondary, horizontally oriented auto layout frame. This nested structure demonstrates how efficiently different design elements can be organized within a single cohesive unit.

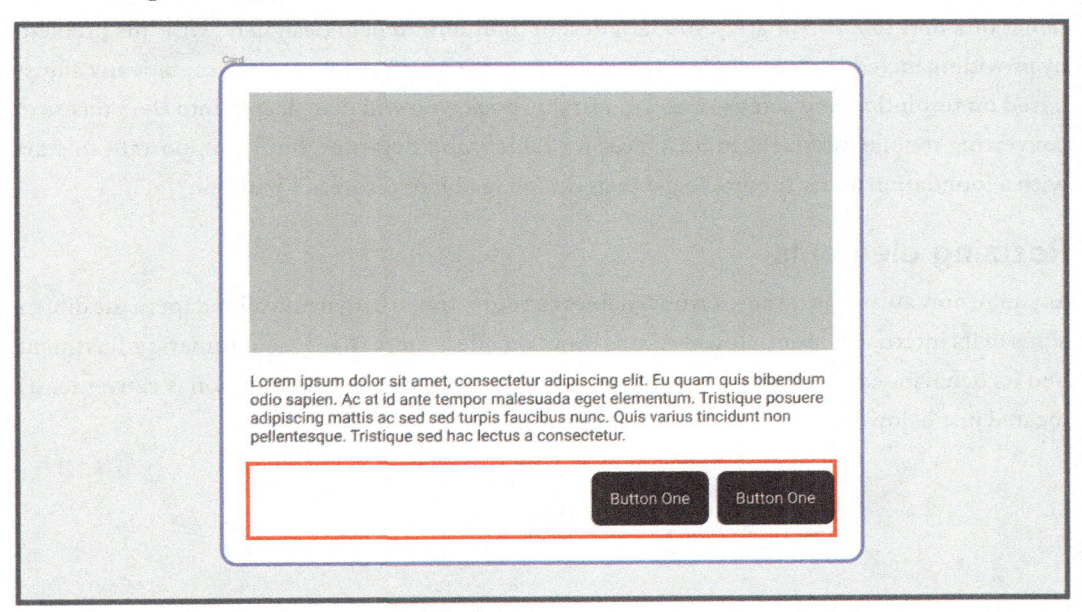

Figure 6.8 – A vertical auto layout frame containing a horizontal one

This way of designing makes it easy to change the layout at any time and really makes Figma a high-end design tool.

Using and mastering auto layout is certainly not an easy task for both beginners and more experienced designers who are used to other tools without this feature. The more you use it, the more you'll understand how this tool can make your workflow easy and enjoyable. Later in this chapter, you will practice more with auto layout, and your understanding of this function will become much clearer for you. But first, you need to explore other important features directly related to auto layout, namely, resizing and constraints.

Resizing and constraints

Responsive design is essential in a world where screen resolutions and device orientations vary widely. Imagine a simpler scenario with only one screen resolution; designing for it would be straightforward, without the need for additional features. However, in the real digital world, things are different, and you should consider all resolutions, if possible, as well as the cases of switching from portrait to landscape mode with devices, or even from a mobile phone to a tablet or a desktop. Fortunately, modern design tools aim to help designers with this problem by providing incredible features for creating responsive interfaces that can automatically adjust based on resolution and screen size. Later in this book, you will dive deeper into the process of converting mobile interfaces to interfaces for tablets and desktops, but it's important to start with a foundation and structure to get your design ready for future adaptation.

Resizing elements

As you're now aware, using auto layout enables the outer frame to dynamically adapt to the dimensions of its internal content. However, this function offers more than just automatic adjustment, and its behavior can be further customized in the **Resizing** section. This option is conveniently located just below the width and height values:

Chapter 6　　151

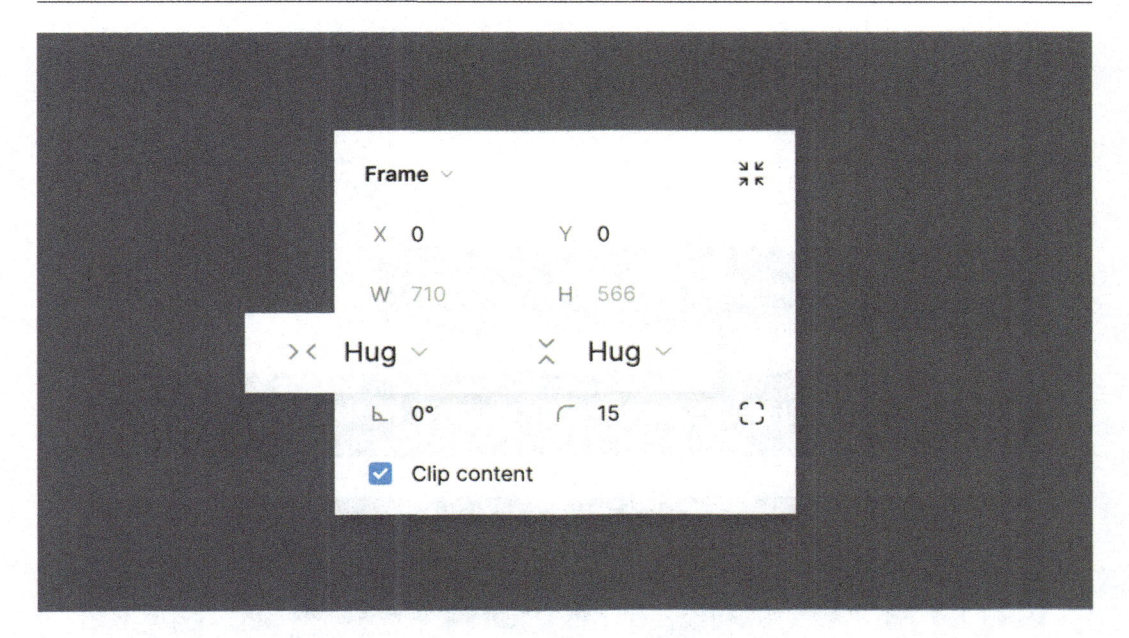

Figure 6.9 – The Resizing options

By default, you have the **Hug** contents option, which results in the outer frame dynamically adjusting its size based on its content. This feature grants you the flexibility to specify distinct behaviors for the width and height of the chosen frame. For instance, you can set it to hug contents in width while maintaining a fixed height in pixels.

> **Note:**
>
> In an auto layout frame, padding is integral to nested elements, ensuring consistent spacing as the frame resizes. This inclusion of padding in size calculations maintains visual balance and coherence, regardless of content changes.

Setting the **Hug** contents parameter for your frame means that its width and height will be automatically determined by the content inside it. But if you manually (or visually) change the width or height of this frame in your workspace, the properties will change to the **Fixed width** or **Fixed height** value, respectively.

This may seem confusing to you at this point, and you might be wondering when you need to use a fixed-size auto layout instead of **Hug** contents, so let's take a look at a few examples in the following figure to get a better understanding of this:

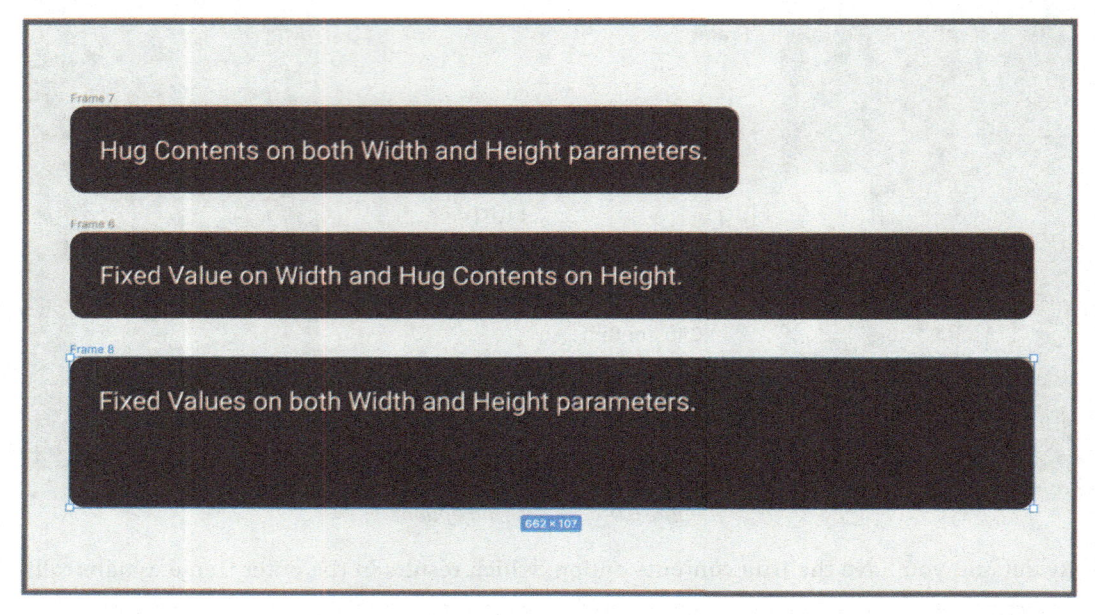

Figure 6.10 – Hug contents and fixed sizes

Resizing in Figma offers a valuable third option beyond fixed width and variable height, or vice versa. This option is the **Fill container** property, which can be applied to the inner elements of a frame. It enables nested elements to stretch and adapt to fit the width and/or height of the parent frame. This flexibility is particularly useful for responsive design. To illustrate this, the following example compares how this option functions with the hug contents one in both the horizontal and vertical directions:

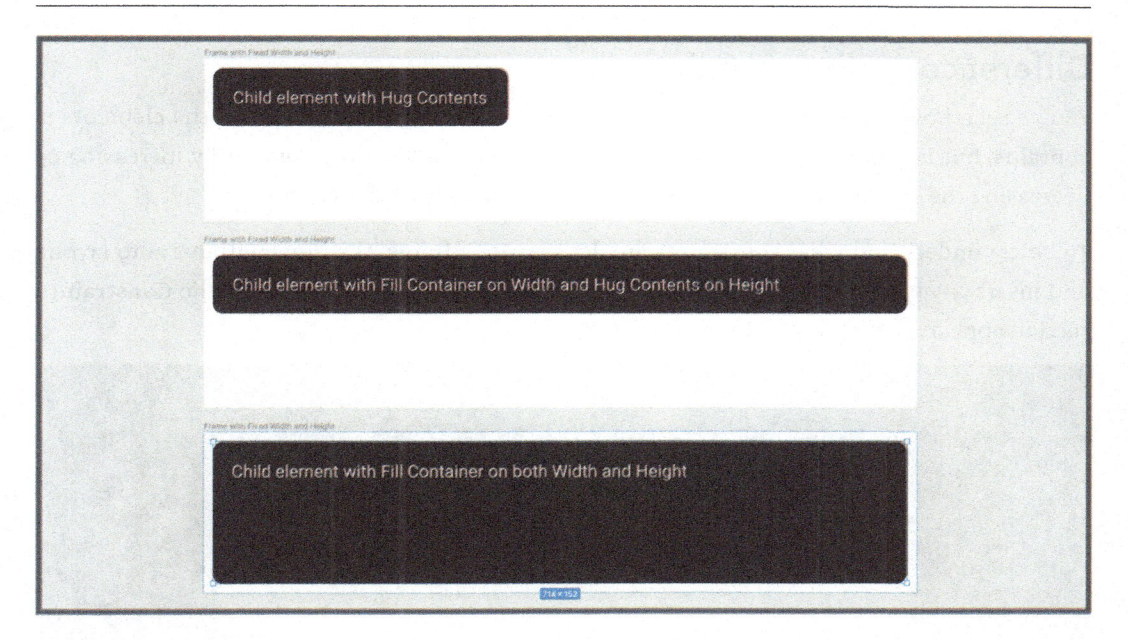

Figure 6.11 – A Fill container example

Among the many Figma features you've seen so far, auto layout is the most complex one, and there is only one way to fully master it – a lot of practice. It will be even more effective if you can combine what you have already learned to find out how different tools can work together and impact one another. For example, try nesting multiple auto layout frames and applying a specific behavior to each one, or set different **Resizing** properties for the elements in the group – one can be flexible in size and the other fixed. Remember that experimenting with the tools is extremely important because it is the only way to get the most out of them.

Differences with constraints

You've seen how auto layout allows you to change the outer frame based on the elements it contains, but is there a reverse way? Is it possible to resize the inner content by increasing or decreasing the size of the outer frame? The answer is yes, with **Constraints**.

To better understand what constraints are, let's create a frame, this time without auto layout, and insert any type of element inside it. After you select the inserted element, the **Constraints** section appears in the right sidebar:

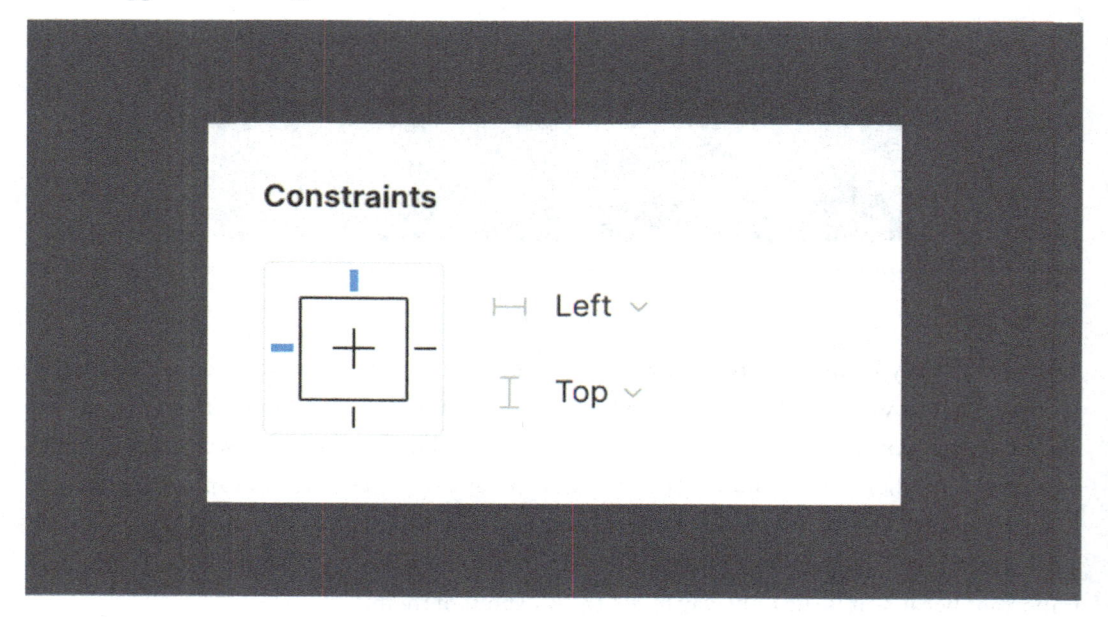

Figure 6.12 – The Constraints section

When using a constraint, you are essentially locking the inner object at a specific position. This means that when the outer frame is resized, the element inside will keep its position.

Chapter 6

In the following figure, you can see a visual representation:

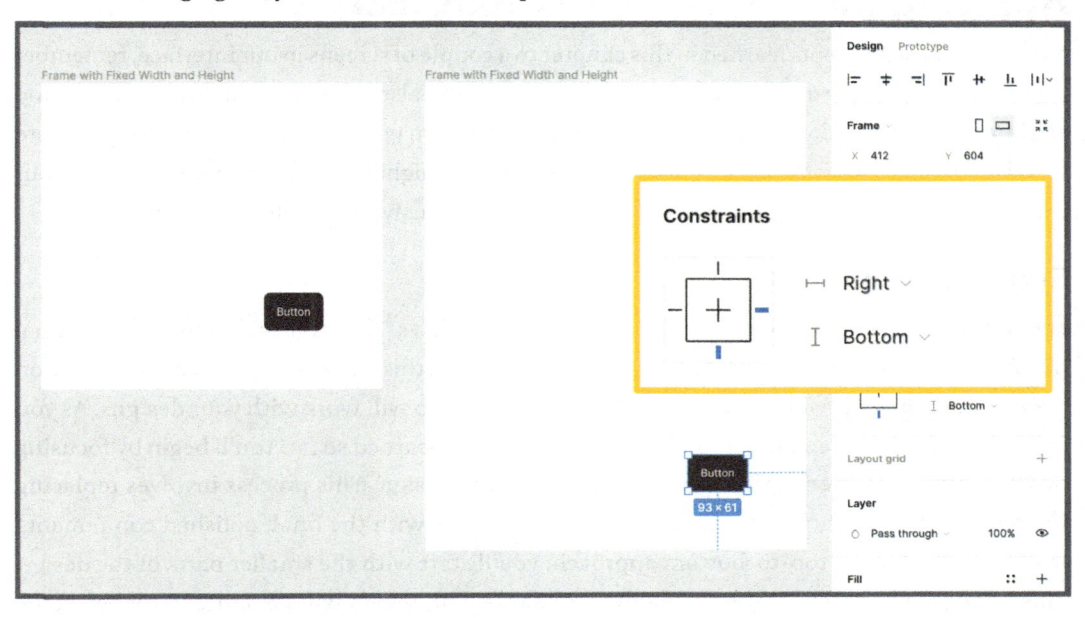

Figure 6.13 – Resizing a frame with right and bottom constraints

This way, you can choose whether to block the element vertically or horizontally, on one side only, or in the center. If you deactivate all the constraints instead (by left-clicking the active constraints while pressing *Shift*), the behavior will be changed to **Scale**, which means that the inner element will be scaled in the same way as the outer frame.

Now we know enough about auto layout, resizing, and constraints to get started on the interface of our application and structure the elements in the best possible way. You'll do this in the next section, but you will also have the opportunity to practice these features more in *Chapter 8, User Interface Design on Tablet, Desktop, and the Web*.

Applying auto layout to our interface

As you apply the concepts learned in this chapter to a couple of screens in our interface, remember that step-by-step instructions are not just for following but also for understanding and analyzing the impact of each action. This part of the chapter focuses on working with the **Hi-Fi** page, where you'll learn the best practices for auto layout. Let's dive straight into applying auto layout to your interface, enhancing your practical skills in creating responsive and well-structured designs.

Shaping a button

For now, your **Hi-Fi** page contains only four wireframed views. This page will showcase the actual polished layouts that will be handed off for development. In this phase, precision and organization are key, both for your workflow and for the developers who will work with your designs. As you embark on this task, remember to apply all that you have learned so far. You'll begin by focusing on the simplest elements, then gradually build up the design. This process involves replacing the temporary, placeholder elements in your wireframes with the final, polished components. Instead of the typical top-to-bottom approach, you'll start with the smaller parts of the design. This strategy allows for creating a highly modular layout, which will be particularly beneficial when you start using the components discussed in the next chapter.

Let's start with the **Login** page first and create a **Login** button. To do this, follow these simple steps:

1. Make sure you are on the **Hi-Fi** file page. Since you are going to fill the frame with new elements and want to keep a visual reference of them, select all the elements of the **Login** frame and move them aside to the left:

Chapter 6   157

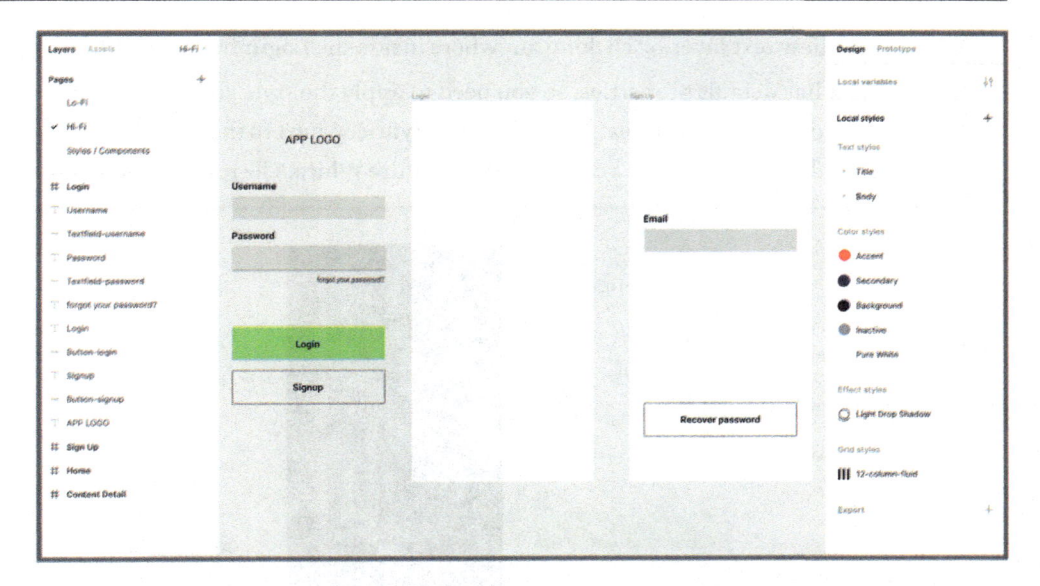

Figure 6.14 – Preparing a blank frame on the Hi-Fi page

> **Note:**
> We'll hide layout grids for better readability. However, in a real work environment, it's a good practice to always keep them active in your layouts, especially in the initial stages when you have to be very accurate. You can quickly turn on/off grids from time to time to see your progress better by using the shortcut *Shift + G*.

2. Select the **Login** frame and apply your first color style to it. To do that, go to the **Fill** section, click the **Style** icon, and select the previously created **Background color** option. Remember that you can quickly check the color names by hovering over them in the panel for a few seconds. You can also change the view mode by clicking the **Show as list** icon next to the **Color Styles** dialog header so that the color appears in the list along with their names.

3. Create a new text layer by clicking anywhere inside the **Login** frame and enter Login.
4. This text has default properties, so you need to apply the style you created earlier for the text. To do this, select this text layer, click the **Style** icon next to the **Text** section, and select **Title/Medium**. Then, apply a color style to it of **Pure White**. The result should look like this:

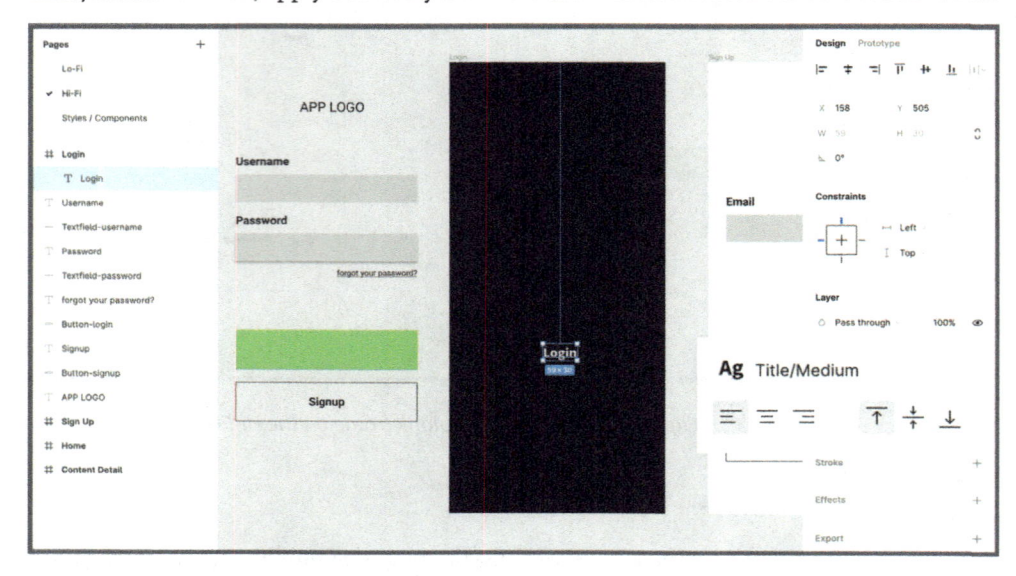

Figure 6.15 – A text layer placed on the Login page

It's time to create a real button. While you might initially consider drawing a rectangle underneath the text, just like we did in the wireframe, there's a more efficient and straightforward approach, as explained in the following steps:

1. Right-click the text layer and choose **Frame selection** to quickly wrap the text in a new frame. Rename this frame layer Button / Primary / Default (you will learn more about this naming convention in the next chapter):

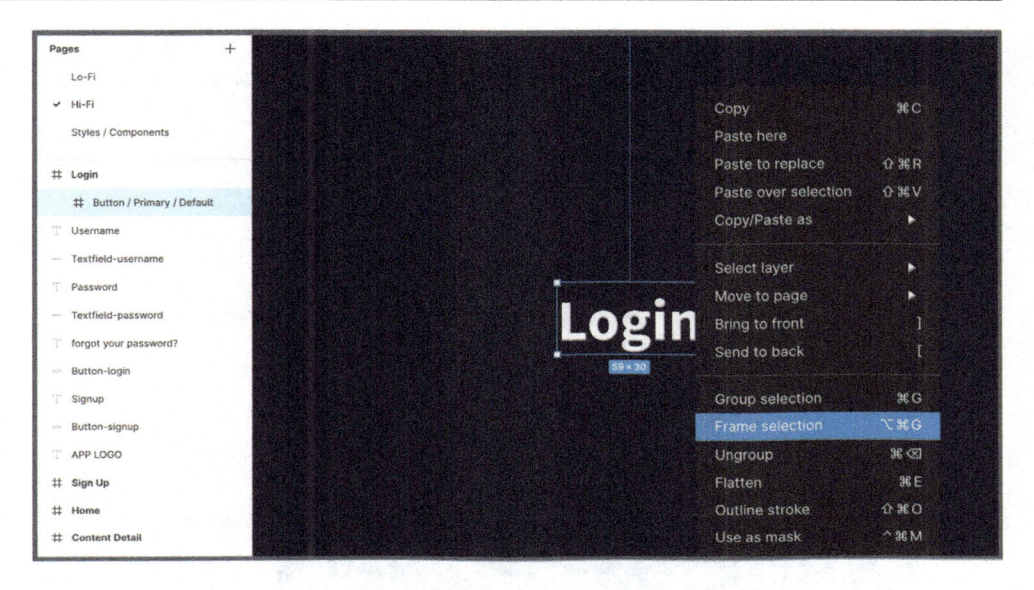

Figure 6.16 – Framing a selection

2. Select this new button frame and add the auto layout to it by clicking the + button next to the auto layout section heading. Then, add some padding so that the text stays exactly in the middle of the frame. To do this, click the **Padding** values and enter 16 both horizontally and vertically (remember that we are working with a grid in multiples of 8).

Lastly, click on the **Alignment grid** and set it to **Center**.

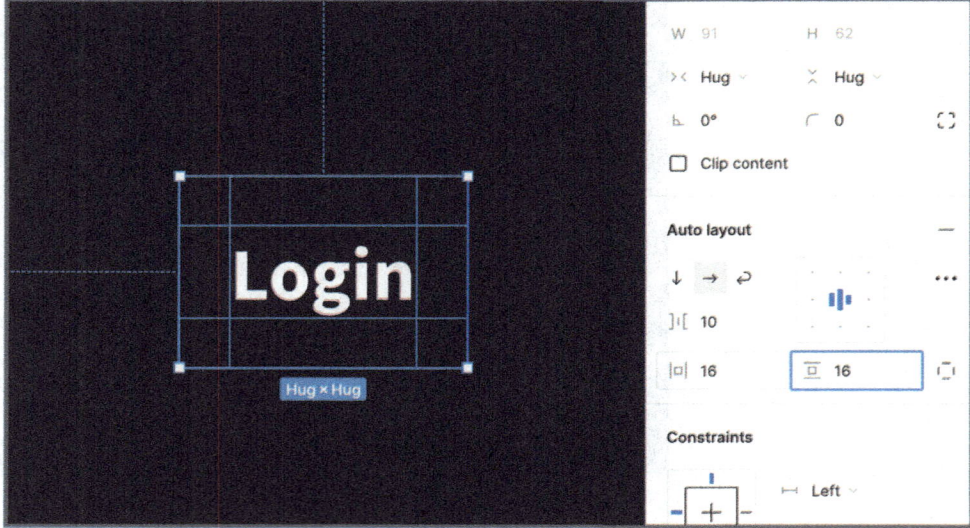

Figure 6.17 – Adding an auto layout to the text layer

3. Now, apply a **Fill** style to the button to make it visible. Since this will be the primary user action in this view, let's use an **Accent** color.

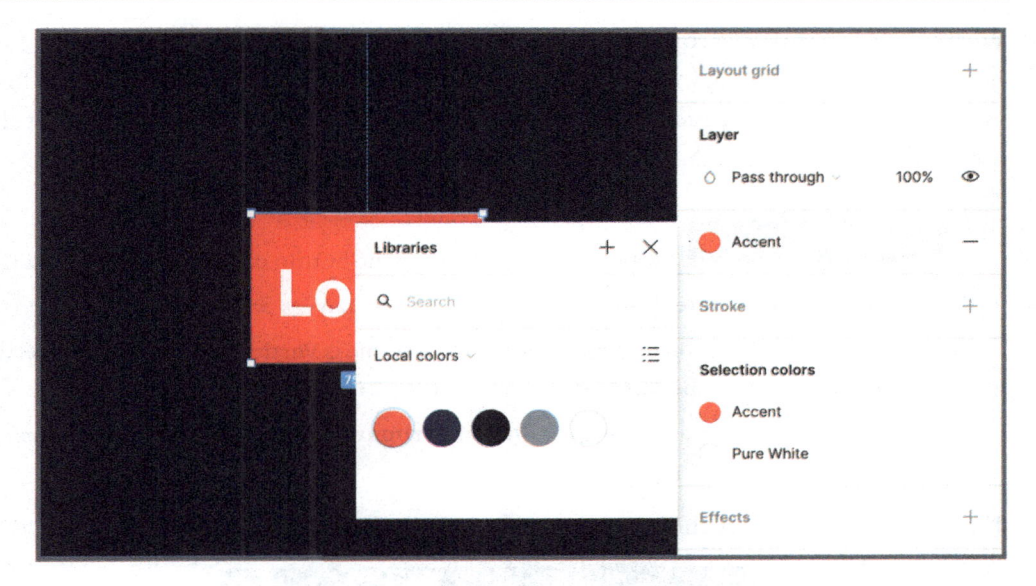

Figure 6.18 – Applying a previously created color style

Note:

There's a quicker method for crafting your button too! Simply select the text and hit *Shift + A*, and voilà! A new auto layout frame will instantly envelop it. By default, it will also feature `10 px` padding all around. This handy trick is especially useful for speeding up your workflow, and it'll become a common trick in your design arsenal.

What you have been doing so far has not been difficult, has it? And with time and practice, it will become even easier for you! You now have the perfect **Login** button, so let's go a little further and work on a secondary action button, which is **Sign Up**. This time, you won't just repeat all the previous steps to create it; there is another quick and easy way:

1. Select the **Login** button frame you just created.
2. Press *Shift + A* on your keyboard to quickly wrap the button in another auto layout frame.
3. Rename this new outer frame Button Group in the **Layers** panel.
4. Make sure the direction in the new auto layout frame is **Vertical** and set the **Gap between items** value within the **Auto layout** properties to **16**.
5. Now comes the fun part. Select the **Button / Primary / Default** layer and press *Command + D* (macOS) or *Ctrl + D* (Win).

The result should look like this:

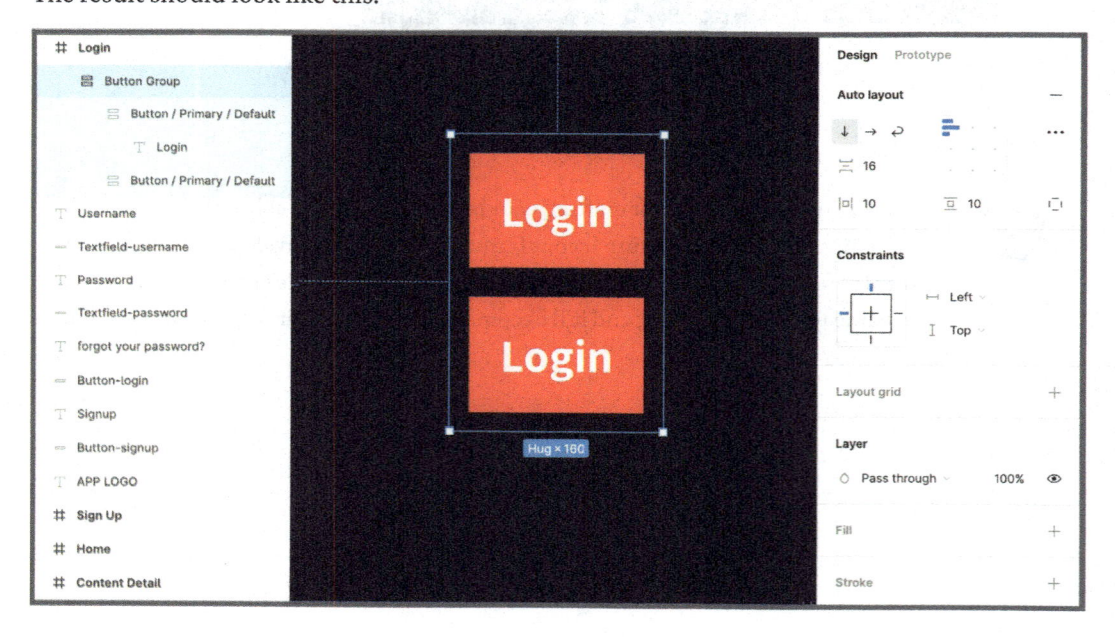

Figure 6.19 – Duplicating an element with auto layout

As you can see, auto layout helps you get the job done quickly with minimal effort! There are just a few more steps left to do before the button is finally ready:

1. Select the bottom button and rename it Button / Secondary / Default in the **Layers** panel.

2. Now, change the text in the new button – by double-clicking it – to Sign Up. Note how the wrapper frame automatically adapts based on what you type. This happens because of the default **Hug contents** option, and it is the real magic of auto layout.
3. With the **Sign Up** button selected, open the list of the color styles in the **Fill** section. Since this is a secondary action, choose the **Secondary** color style:

Figure 6.20 – The Sign Up button styled as a secondary button

Looks good enough already, doesn't it? You will take a few additional steps to make your layout even better:

1. Increase the size of the **Button Group** layer so that it is the same width as your outer frame:

Figure 6.21 – Resizing Button Group to fill the parent frame

2. You may notice that your design doesn't fit the layout grid. Let's solve this problem by changing the general padding of **Button Group** to **16 px**.

3. Now, click on the **Alignment** box and set the alignment to **Center**. This way, the buttons are perfectly aligned to the center of the view:

Figure 6.22 – Aligning elements to the center

4. Select both **Button / Primary / Default** and **Button / Secondary / Default** and change their horizontal resizing options to **Fill container**. You should get this:

Figure 6.23 – Applying Fill container to our child elements

Great! The buttons look much better now! With the functions we have tried out so far, we have created a piece of the interface with the ultimate precision in a short time. Moreover, what you have just created is a real modular block of elements, in which you can add, delete, and invert objects at any time without worrying about losing the gap, alignment, and size.

However, you have not yet practiced constraints. To understand the best use case for them, first, select a **Login** screen frame and try to manually enlarge it in width. Here's what you will see:

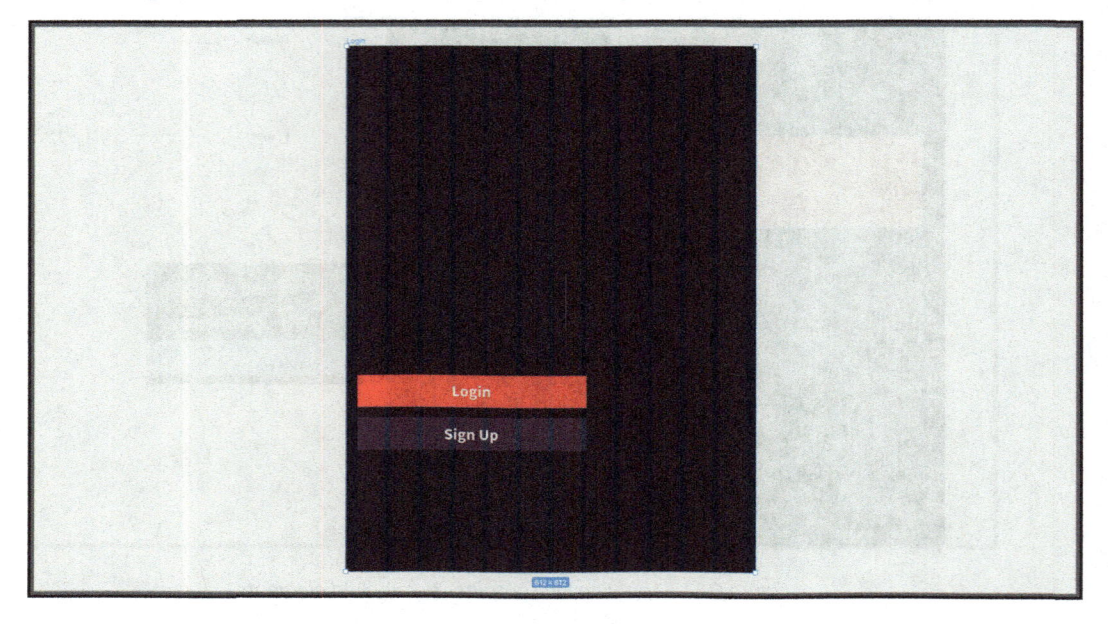

Figure 6.24 – Resizing the outer frame to reveal unexpected behavior

This is not what you expected, or at least not exactly what you want your layouts to be. This is about responsive design, and as mentioned earlier, you will explore this topic in more detail later in the book. Anyway, to fix the problem at this point, we can use the **constraints** feature:

1. Select the **Button Group** frame.
2. In the **Constraints** section on the right sidebar, change the horizontal behavior from **Left** to **Left and right**. Basically, this is how you tell Figma to anchor the elements on both sides and scale them proportionally. The result should now be more solid:

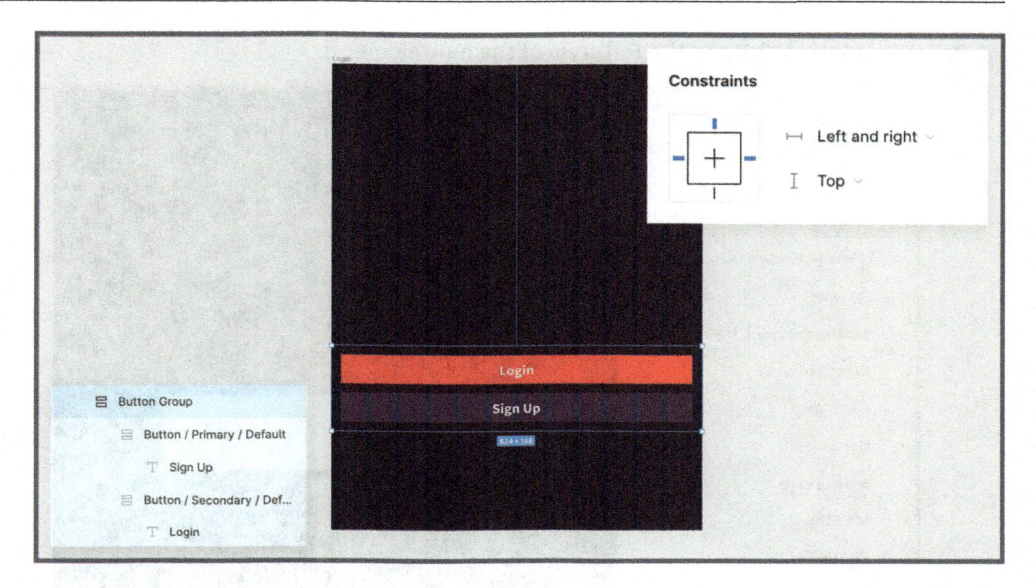

Figure 6.25 – A proper resizing

Now your design not only scales proportionally horizontally and looks nicer but also fits perfectly into the basic layout grid structure you created earlier. Be aware that you still don't need to resize your frame's width – we'll do that in a later chapter – so before proceeding to the next section, bring back the previous **375 px** width to your **Login** frame.

Completing the view

The first view of our application is starting to take on a finished look, and we're now going to replace the lo-fi text fields and labels with the elements of the actual design. The next steps will not be very difficult for you as they are more or less similar. So, let's move on to the final part of working on the interface of the first screen:

1. Create a new **Rectangle** shape vertically in the center of the interface. Make sure its height is **50 px** (the width value is not important for now). Rename this layer `Text Field`.

2. Apply **Pure White** as the **Fill** style of the new element:

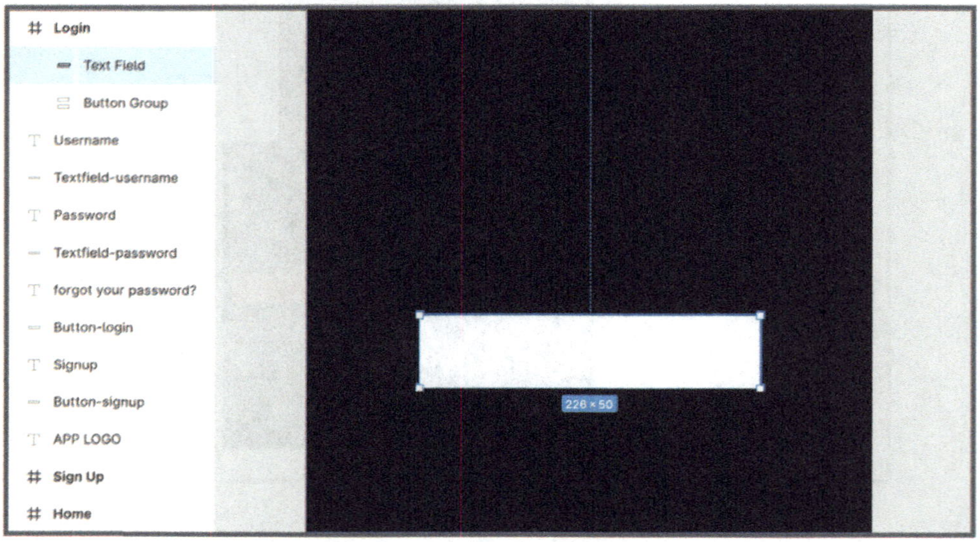

Figure 6.26 – Creating a text field

3. Create a new **Text** layer just above the text field and enter Username. Apply a **Pure White** color and a **Title/Medium** text style to it.

4. Select both the text label and the text field, and then add an auto layout to this selection by clicking the + icon next to the **Auto layout** label on the right sidebar; or, more simply, use the *Shift + A* keyboard shortcut.

5. As a result, you should have a new frame containing both elements, which should be left-aligned by default. Rename this new frame Form Element.

6. Set **Gap between items** with the corresponding auto layout property to **8**:

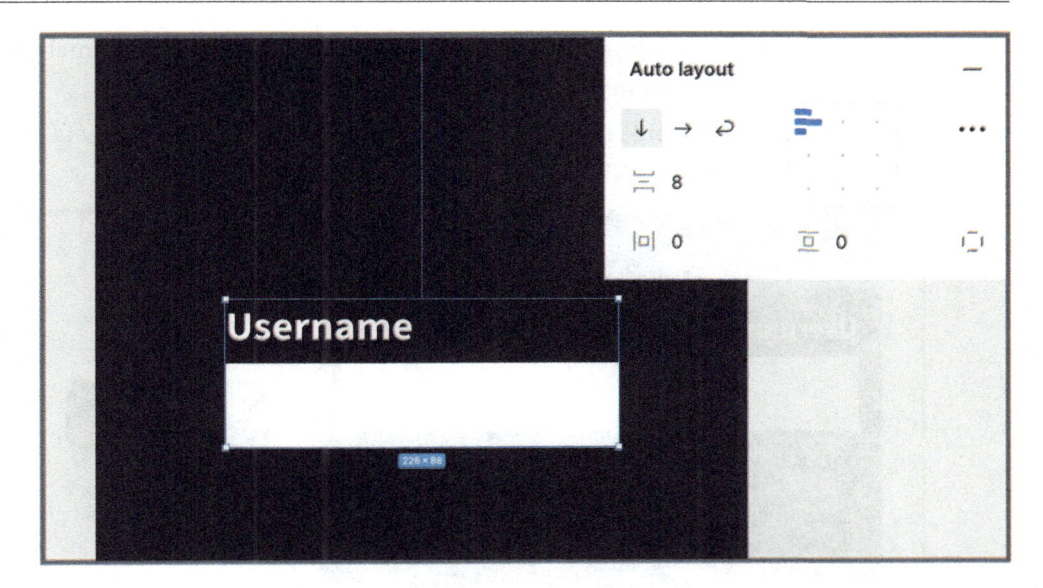

Figure 6.27 – Adding a text label

7. Now, wrap the **Form Element** layer in another auto layout frame. This will again create a new frame around the selection, and you will soon see why this is relevant.

8. Rename this new frame Form (since this will be our parent form container) and change its global padding to **16** to fit your layout grid:

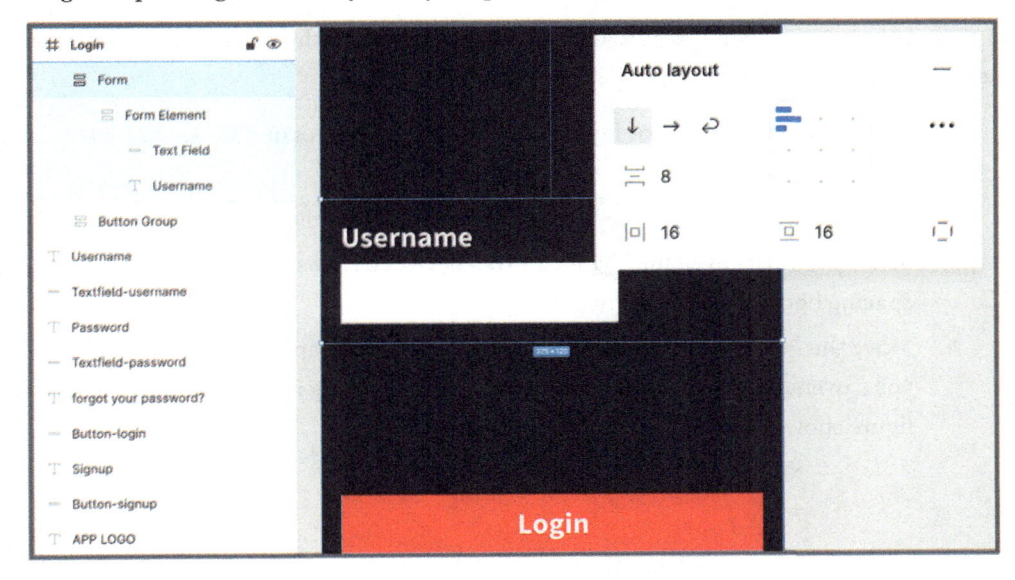

Figure 6.28 – Structuring our form element

9. Select the **Form Element** layer, set its width to **375 px**, and change its horizontal resizing property to **Fill container** instead of **Hug contents**.
10. Now, select the **Text Field** layer and change its horizontal resizing property to **Fill container** instead of **Fixed width**:

Figure 6.29 – Applying Fill container to the child elements

The first of your text fields is ready, and now it's time to create the second. Since you've used auto layout correctly, the following step will be incredibly simple:

1. Select the **Form Element** layer and duplicate it by pressing *Command + D* (macOS) or *Ctrl + D* (Windows).
2. Double-click the **Username** label in the lower field and replace it with Password.
3. Select the **Form** layer and change its **Gap between items** property to **32** to add the proper spacing between all the form fields.
4. Move the **Form** layer up a bit so that it does not overlap with **Button Group**. To do this, you can change the **Y** value on the right sidebar, setting it to about **180 px**. The following figure shows the end result of these operations:

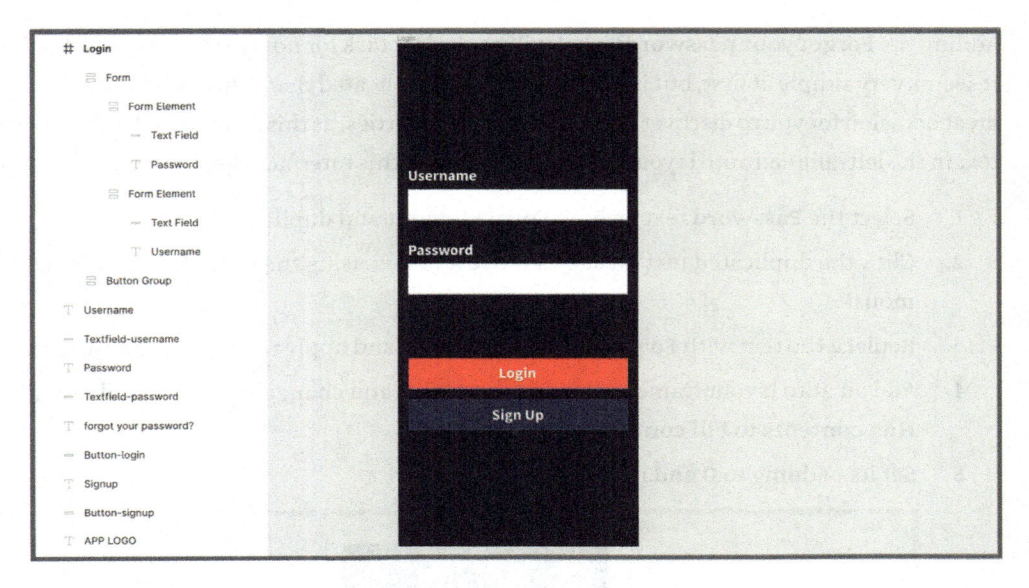

Figure 6.30 – The resulting Login view

> **Note:**
>
> You can quickly adjust input field values using the scrubbing feature over properties like position, dimension, rotation, or any other numerical field. This is done by clicking and dragging your mouse over a field holding the *Option* (macOS) or *Alt* (Windows) key. Don't forget to add the **Left** and **Right** constraint to the **Form** layer so that it will quickly adapt to any resizing of the outer frame.

So, how easy was that? Of course, this is not the limit of all the capabilities of Figma, but you can already see how advanced features can speed up your design process. Using auto layout is, of course, optional but still highly recommended, as the result will be easily editable and scalable. It is also handy for code because all the auto layout frames in your files will automatically be converted into flexbox items for web development.

Adding the **Forgot your password?** label will be the last task for now to complete the **Login** page. It seems very simple at first, but it's actually more complicated than you expect. Anyway, this is a great occasion for you to discover new auto layout properties, as this element will be right-aligned text in the left-aligned auto layout container. To create this interface element, follow these steps:

1. Select the **Password** text layer in **Form Element** and duplicate it.
2. Click the duplicated text layer and move it below using the *Down* key, or drag with your mouse.
3. Replace the text with `Forgot your password?` and apply the **Body/Light** text style to it.
4. Add an auto layout frame to this new text layer and change the horizontal resizing from **Hug contents** to **Fill container**.
5. Set its padding to **0** and its alignment to **Right**:

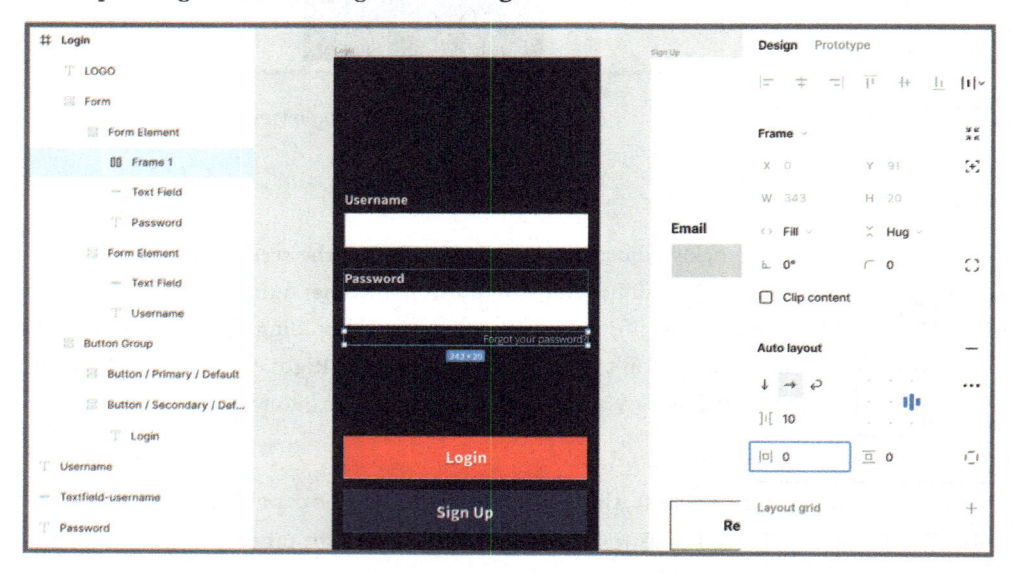

Figure 6.31 – Adding a nested auto layout frame

Nesting auto layout frames may seem tricky at first, but it can help you create complex interfaces in a very short time with exceptional precision.

The view is almost done, and all you need to do now is just polish it up a bit to achieve a more convincing visual result. So, what can you do to accomplish this? Well, it might be a good idea to add a logo at the top of the page and tweak the vertical gap of the elements. Also, if the text labels seem too large, you can create a new text style on the **Styles + Components** page, just as you did in the previous chapter. For example, you can go with **20px** and **Bold**, saving it as a new text style named **Body/Bold Label**.

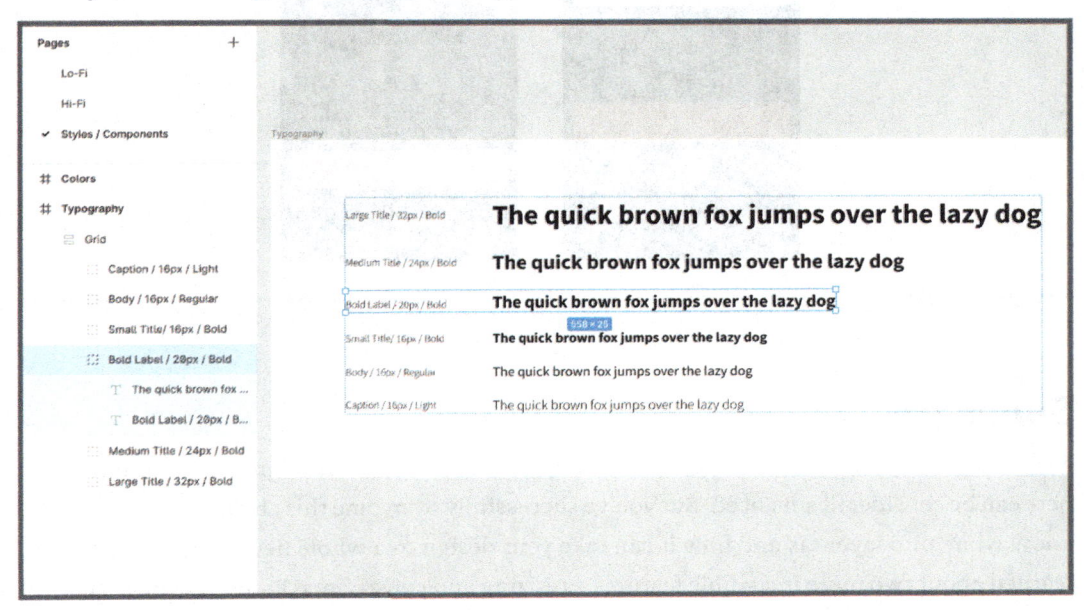

Figure 6.32 – Inserting a new text style

Feel free to experiment with your first interface to practice your skills better. Before moving on to the next chapter, try converting the **Sign Up** page from lo-fi to hi-fi, which shouldn't be much different from what you just achieved.

Your final result should be something like this:

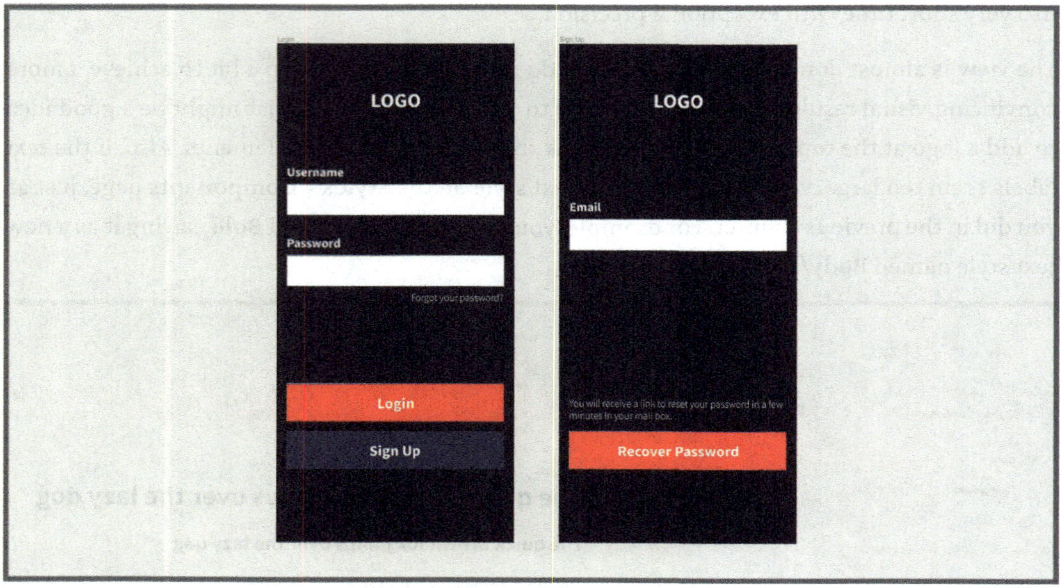

Figure 6.33 – The Login and Sign Up views

Summary

As stated earlier, the topic of this chapter was quite complex, and the Figma features presented here can be considered advanced. But you've successfully overcome this challenge, and now you know what auto layout is and how it can take your design to a whole new level. You have also learned about two more incredible features – resizing and constraints. Proper use of all three of these makes any layout flexible, responsive, and highly structured. And that's exactly what you did in the hands-on part of this chapter, by creating two views for our application – great job!

Obviously, all the other views will also be created using auto layout, so you will practice this function many more times throughout the book to discover even more incredible design options. The learning process will become even more effective if you experiment from time to time with different automatic layout properties and elements in drafts.

So, using auto layout, resizing, and constraints in your design makes it a lot easier and faster to create an interface. But what if there was another feature that could further improve our workflow? There is – Components (which has already been mentioned several times in this book)! Soon, this feature will no longer be a mystery to you, as you will learn all about it in the next chapter!

Learn more on Discord

To join the Discord community for this book – where you can share feedback, ask questions to the author, and learn about new releases – follow the QR code below:

`https://packt.link/figma`

7
Building Components and Variants in a Collaborative Workspace

You are now right in the middle of your Figma journey, where you are facing the most difficult but exciting challenges. You've already used advanced features such as styles and auto layout, and even successfully applied them to your project's design. Remember that mastering Figma, as with any other design tool, means not only knowing its functions but also having a deep understanding of the purpose of its use. So, it's better to think first, analyze the created wireframe, and then move on to building the interface elements.

In this chapter, we'll discover components – a fairly common feature for modern design tools, but Figma has put in a lot of effort to deliver them elegantly and smartly. Components are great, but when combined with the other features you've learned about, they make it possible to create something extremely powerful. From now on, you will be practicing a lot, and you will create components in the best possible way by using auto layout and styles together! Plus, you'll learn about the collaboration, sharing, and auto-save features in Figma. Get ready – this chapter is as interesting as it is intense!

In this chapter, we are going to cover the following main topics:

- Creating and organizing components
- Extending components with variants
- Multiplayer mode, libraries, and version control

Creating and organizing components

Your journey started with basic shapes and tools and then moved on to more advanced features, such as **layout grids**, **styles**, and **auto layout**, that you need to know about, as they all make your design much better. At the same level, there are **components**, which are quite a common feature for design tools (the name of this function can differ – for example, in Sketch, it's called **Symbols**), as it is truly indispensable.

In this first section of this chapter, components in Figma will no longer be a mystery to you and you will learn mostly by using them directly in your project! So, open up Figma, and let's get started!

What are components?

Components in Figma are powerful tools that allow you to reuse design elements across your project efficiently. They are essentially individual elements – ranging from a simple button to a complex layout block – that you can replicate and manage consistently throughout your designs. Unlike styles, which apply uniform property rules (like colors, text styles, and effects) to elements, components encompass the objects themselves. This means that when you create a component, you can transform any design element into a reusable unit that retains its properties and structure wherever you use it.

To convert an element into a component, select it and use the *Command + Option + K* (macOS) or *Ctrl + Alt + K* (Windows) shortcut, or click on the **Create component** icon in the top bar, as shown below:

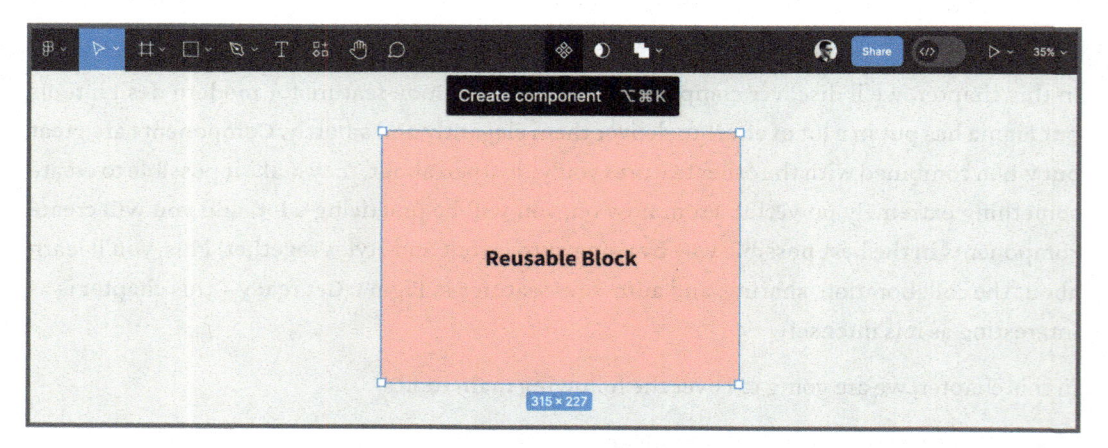

Figure 7.1 – Creating a component

Chapter 7   179

Once you do this, your element becomes what is called the main component – the source of truth, or the foundational element, from which all its instances will derive their properties and updates. The main component can be identified by the **Component** icon (the four-sided, diamond-shaped icon) that appears next to the object name, both on the canvas and in the **Layers** panel. Moreover, if you switch from **Layers** to **Assets** in the left-hand side panel, you will see the component that you just created in the library:

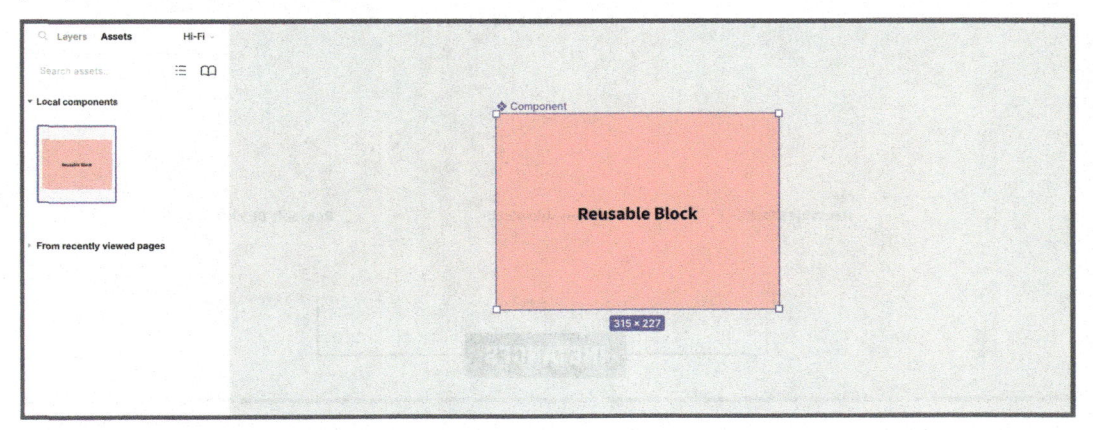

Figure 7.2 – The Assets panel

Note:
Unlike Sketch, Figma doesn't automatically move a component to a separate dedicated page but instead leaves it where it was created, and from now on, it's up to you to decide where it should be stored.

You can reuse your component as many times as you like by dragging and dropping it from the library into your workspace. All the elements created in this way will be instances of the component and will automatically inherit any properties and styles of the main component.

180   Building Components and Variants in a Collaborative Workspace

The following figure shows an example of a main component and its three instances:

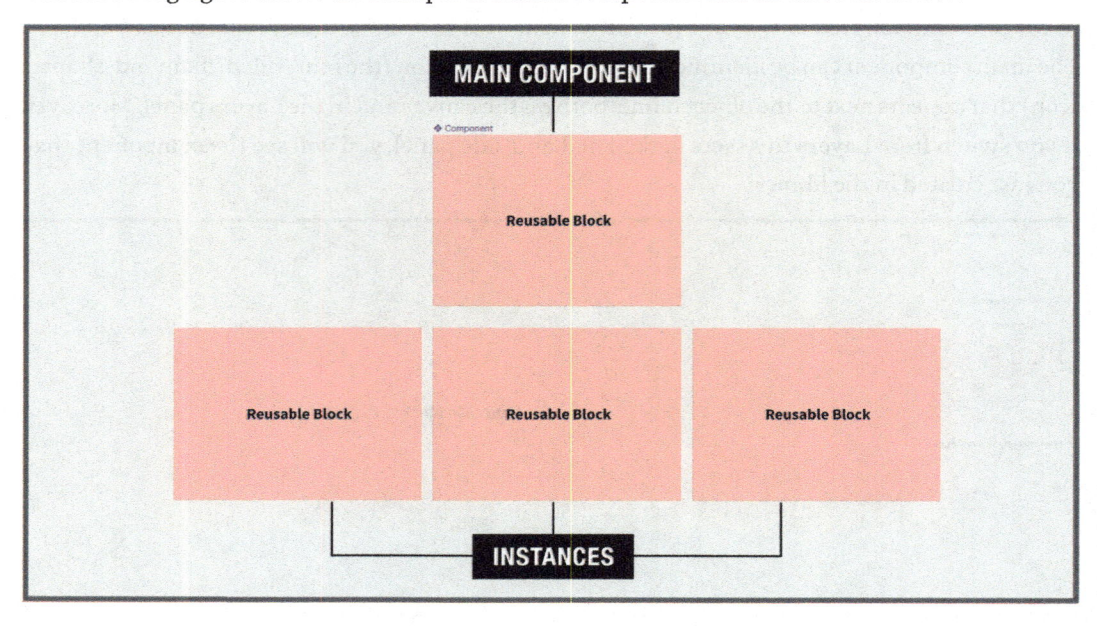

Figure 7.3 – The main component and its instances

So, what's the big difference between a main component and instances? It's very simple. A component acts as a parent for all the instances created from it. Thus, if you change something in a main component, these changes will be applied in the same way to all its instances. In the following figure, the color of the main component has been changed, so all instances have inherited this property automatically:

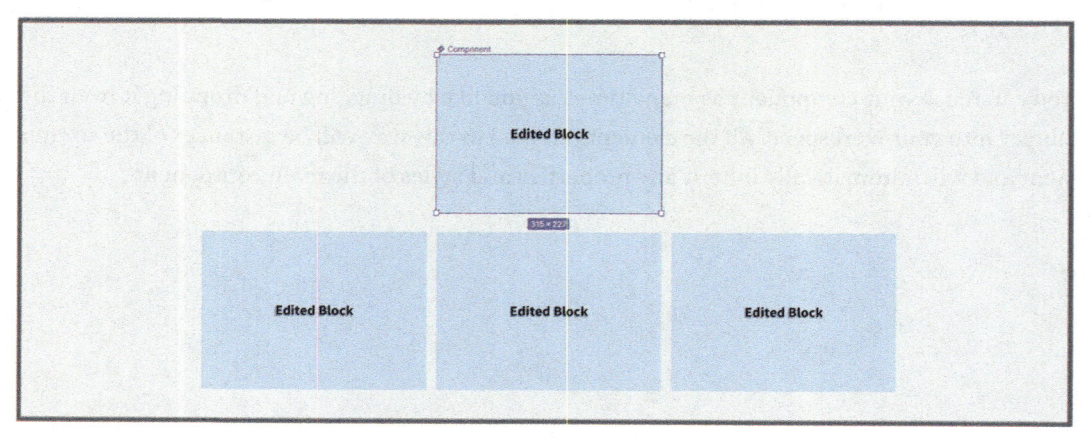

Figure 7.4 – Editing the main component

Chapter 7 181

As you can see in this example, all objects are now blue. However, if you do the opposite and change any property of an individual instance, those changes will be applied exclusively to that instance, without affecting the others and the main component itself:

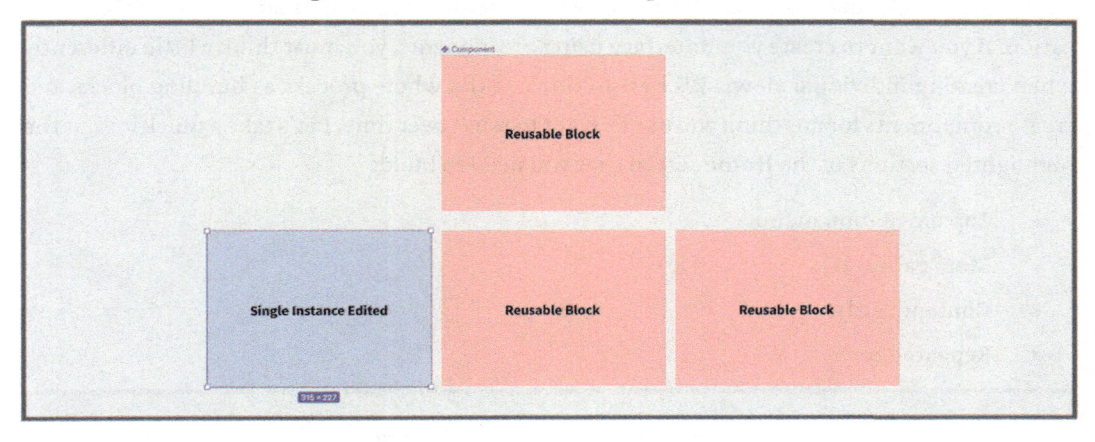

Figure 7.5 – Editing a single instance

And this is precisely the great potential and flexibility of components, which have the ability to change each instance of an element. Note that after you override an instance property, that specific property will no longer be modified through the main component. For example, if you change a color, the color property will no longer change based on the parent, but all other properties will still be controlled by the main component.

> **Note:**
> You can create multiple components at the same time; just select all the items you want to convert to components and select the **Create multiple components** option after clicking the dropdown near the **Create component** icon in the top bar.

Now that you know the basics of components and instances and how they relate to each other, it's time to try it all out and see how you can optimize and improve your workflow using this powerful feature!

Building a view using components

This part of the chapter will be all about practice; you will learn how to use components while working on the **Home** screen **Hi-Fi** layout – the main interface of your streaming service application. If you want to create your interface using components, you must think a little differently when creating individual views. It's best to think of the whole process as building blocks and create components for anything you might want to reuse over time. Let's take a quick look at the highlighted sections of the **Home** screen that you need to build:

- Top navigation menu
- Main carousel
- Content cards
- Repeated rows

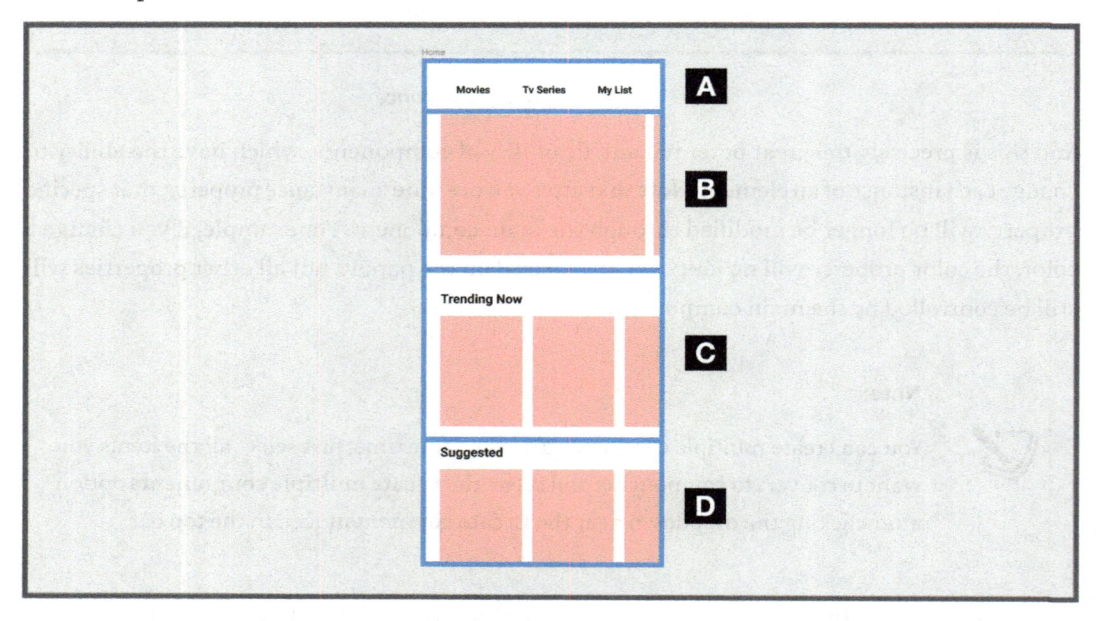

Figure 7.6 – Our Home view structure

Chapter 7

Before you start, it is very important to thoughtfully consider the best approach to optimize your work. Carefully plan the creation of elements, styles, and components. Taking time to thoroughly analyze and strategize at this stage will prevent the need for future revisions and ensure a more efficient design process.

The initial step in working with the **Home** view is to clear all existing elements. You have two options: either delete everything and refer back to the **Lo-Fi** page as needed, or duplicate the view for a constant visual reference. To duplicate, drag the view while pressing *Option* (macOS) or *Alt* (Windows). Once you've prepared your workspace, you can proceed with the following steps:

1. Select the outer frame of the **Home** view and enable **Auto layout** (by pressing *Shift + A*). Make sure it has a vertical direction.
2. From the **Color Styles** library, set the frame **Fill** color to **Background**.
3. In the **Padding** options, set the horizontal values to **16** and the vertical values to **0** to align with your layout grid.
4. Change the **Resizing** option from **Hug contents** to **Fixed width** and **Fixed height**. This ensures that the frame size never changes and represents the screen of a real device:

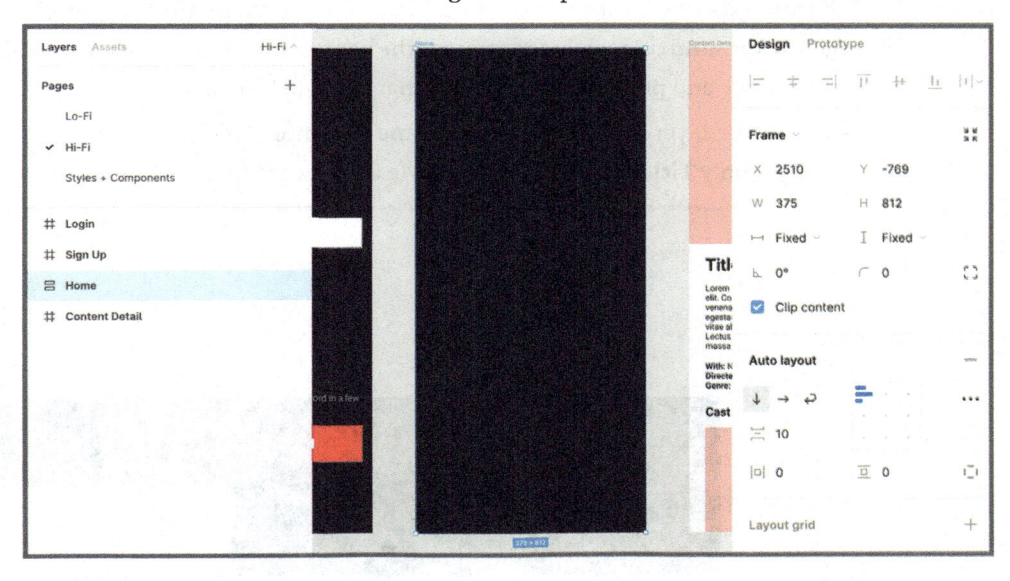

Figure 7.7 – Setting up the parent frame

> **Note:**
> You can also duplicate any element in the auto layout frame by selecting it and pressing *Command + D* (macOS) or *Ctrl + D* (Windows). The new element will be placed right next to its original one.

Great! Now that the parent frame is ready to go, you are ready to create the first section!

A – top navigation menu

When creating your interface, simply pasting text and applying styles might seem straightforward, but it's important to plan for dynamic elements and their interactions. For instance, in a navigation bar, one tab might be active while others are not. To efficiently manage these variations, using components is key. Let's proceed with implementing our first one:

1. Go to the **Styles + Components** page. There, create a new frame to house all the components for your navigation elements. Name this frame `Navigation`.
2. Since the interface of your app is mostly dark in color, you can set the **Navigation** frame's fill to the **Background** color style to represent the background of the views. This will make it easier to create and preview the elements that you will be using.
3. Create a new text layer in the **Navigation** frame and enter `Item` (this will be your placeholder text). Apply **Title/Small** as the text style and **Pure White** as the fill style:

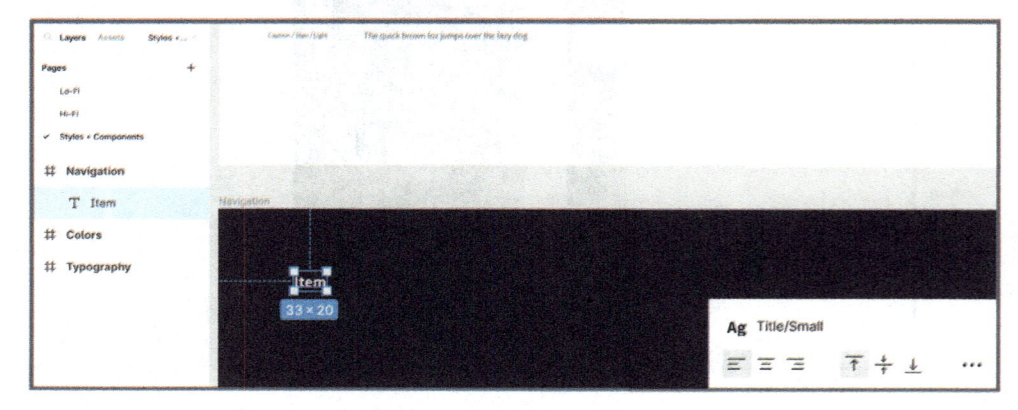

Figure 7.8 – Creating your first menu item

Chapter 7   185

4. Wrap this text layer in an **Auto layout** frame using the *Shift + A* keyboard shortcut. Set its horizontal and vertical **Padding** values to **16** and rename it `Menu Item`. The padding is critical here as it will also be the interactive element area.

5. Now, select **Menu Item** and click the **Create component** icon in the top bar, or use the *Command + Option + K* (macO)/*Ctrl + Alt + K* (Windows) keyboard shortcut.

Great! Your first component is done, and you can check it yourself by going to the **Assets** tab, or by using the **Resources** tool:

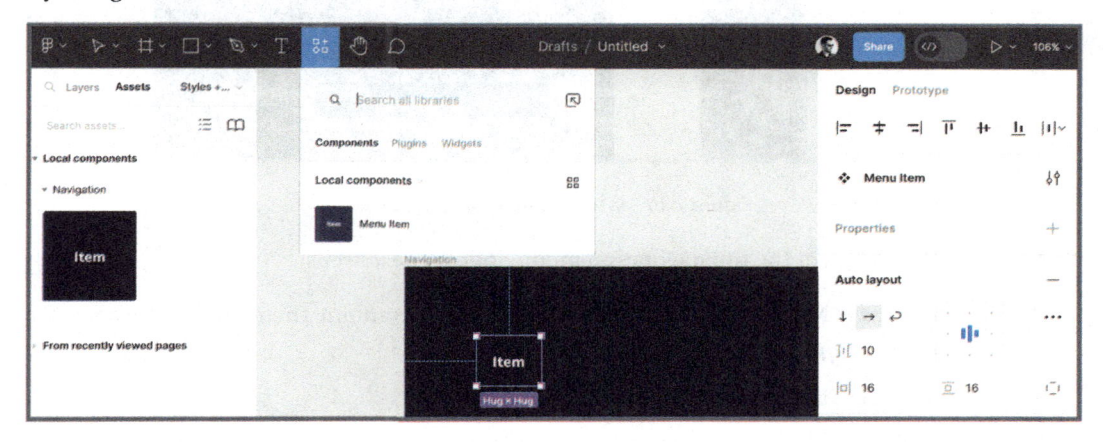

Figure 7.9 – Your menu item component

Now it's time to try this component in an interface. Go back to the **Hi-Fi** page, and then simply drag your menu item from the **Assets** panel three times into the **Home** page frame. You can also drag it just once and then duplicate it the way you learned, and the result will be exactly the same.

> **Note:**
> An easier way to access your **Components** library is with the *Shift + I* keyboard shortcut. This will immediately open up the **Resources** tool, a drawer containing all of your components, so you can quickly add them to the canvas.

At this point, your **Home** page should look like the following figure:

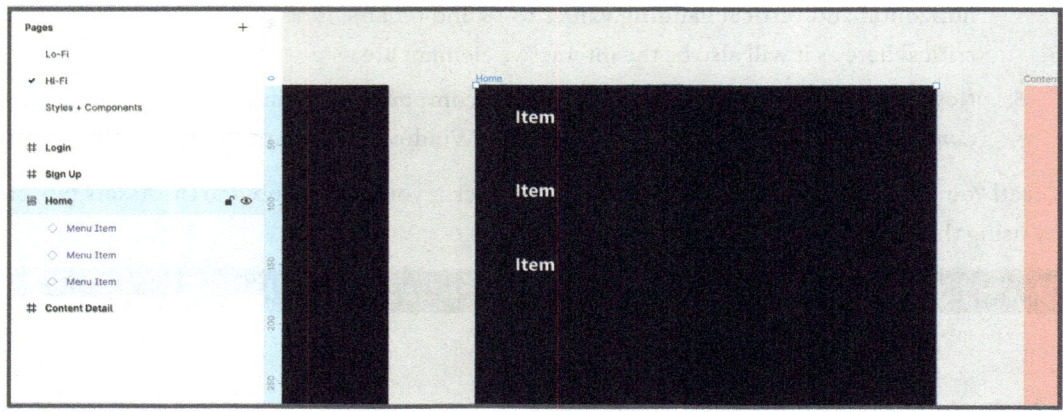

Figure 7.10 – Inserting multiple instances

To complete the design of the top navigation menu, follow these steps:

1. Select all three **Menu Item** layers you just added and combine them into an **Auto layout** frame with *Shift + A*. Rename it `Top Navigation`.

2. Set the frame direction to horizontal.

3. Set the **Top** padding to **32**, the **Bottom** padding to **0**, and **Horizontal** to **0**, and then set **Gap between items** to **8** and **Alignment** to **Center** by clicking on it in the visual grid.

4. Set the **Resizing** horizontal option to **Fill container**.

5. Finally, change the text in the text layers of each component instance to `Movies`, `TV Series`, and `My List` in order from left to right:

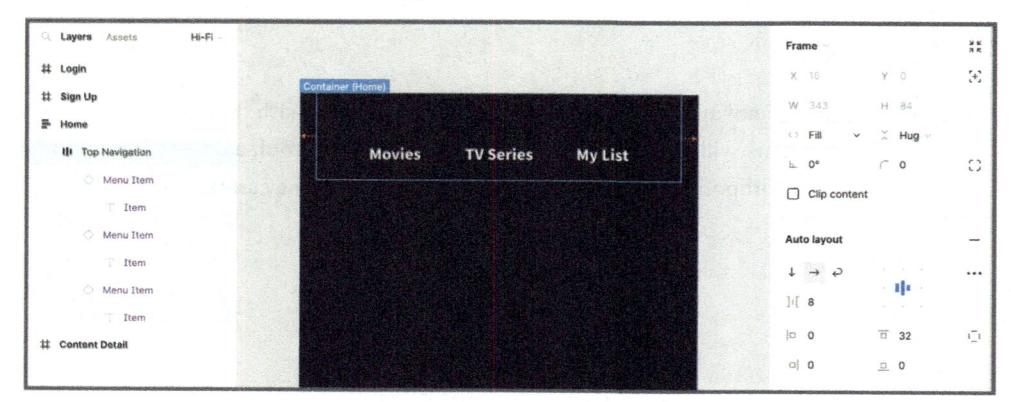

Figure 7.11 – The top navigation menu

Chapter 7

The top navigation menu is complete and looks great. Take a moment to think about what you have just achieved. Look at how clean, editable, and scalable your complex layer is thanks to the combination of components and auto layout. Without these tools and features, you would have spent a lot more time and effort to achieve the same result.

B – main carousel

The second block will be the main content carousel that shows featured shows in your application. Go back to the **Styles + Components** page and create a new frame; this time, rename it **Cards** and fill it with the **Background** color style as you did earlier. This frame will store all of the card elements of your layout. When you're done, follow these steps:

1. In the newly created **Cards** frame, insert another frame (*F* key) with a size of **300 px** (width) x **200 px** (height).
2. Enable **Auto layout** and change its **Padding** (both horizontal and vertical) values to **16**.
3. Enable **Fill** and change the type from **Solid** to **Image**:

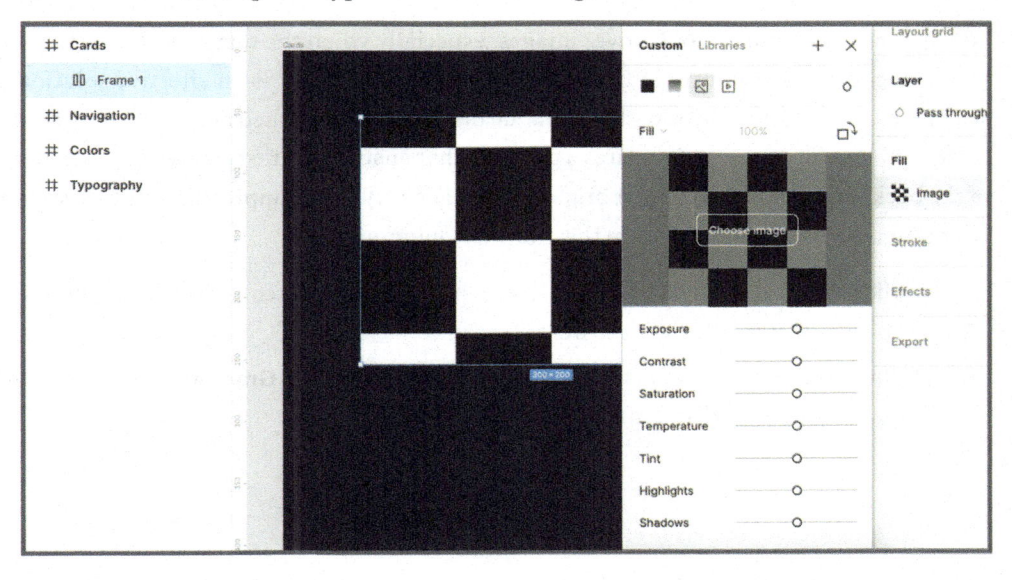

Figure 7.12 – Inserting an image for a card element

4. Drag and drop an image into the preview area in the **Image** panel. You can choose any image that resembles a movie poster. You can easily find something like this on the `unsplash.com` website, which has many free images for both personal and commercial use.
5. Make sure you give the newly created frame a clear name, such as `Carousel item`.

6. Set the **Corner radius** value of your carousel item to **8**. The frame should now look like the following figure:

Figure 7.13 – Adding the corner radius to the element

(photo by Michael Oeser on Unsplash)

To enhance the visibility of text over images, especially when the text is at the bottom and the image backgrounds can vary in brightness, using a "text scrim" is an effective solution. A text scrim is essentially a fill layer with an opaque black gradient applied at the bottom of the image. By setting this fill correctly, it creates a contrast that ensures the text remains visible, regardless of the background image's color or brightness. In Figma, you can apply multiple fills, strokes, and effects to the same layer to achieve this. Here's a quick guide:

1. Click on the + icon next to the **Fill** label. This will create a second **Fill** overlay, with a default opacity of **20%**. Change it to **60%**.
2. Click on the fill you've just added and change the type to **Gradient**. Then, edit the linear gradient points, as shown in the following figure:

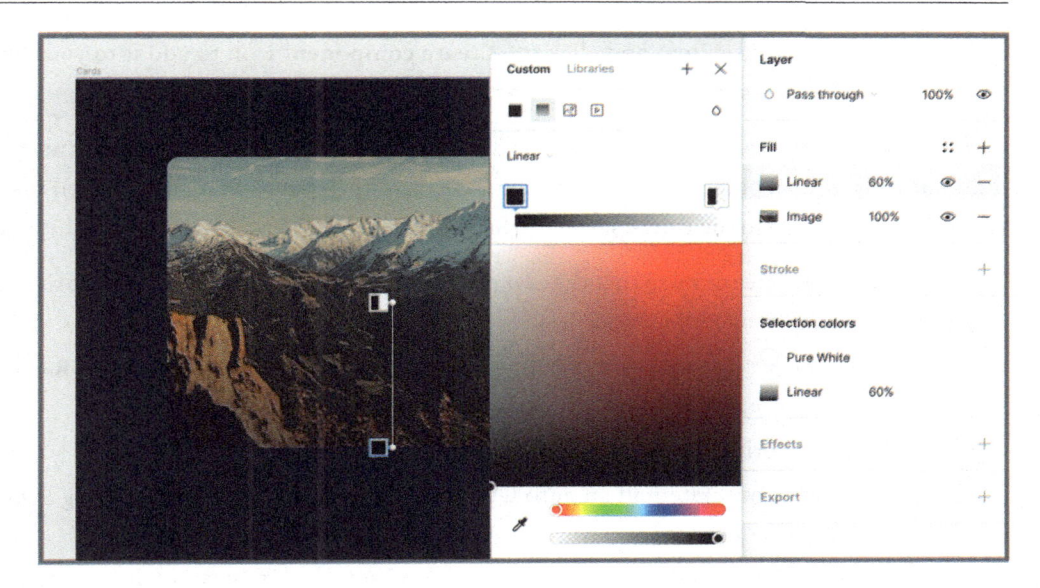

Figure 7.14 – Adding a Linear gradient for text readability

This way, the bottom half of any image will be slightly darker. Let's add a title to the card and see how it looks on your image:

1. Change the carousel item **Resizing** option to **Fixed** both vertically and horizontally. This will ensure that its size is not automatically adapted to the text you are about to add.
2. Add a **Text** layer in the carousel item frame, enter `Movie Title` as a placeholder, and then apply a **Title/Small** text style and **Pure White** as a fill to it.
3. Set the **Alignment** of the **Carousel Item** to bottom left, as shown in the following figure:

Figure 7.15 – Alignment and Padding options

4. Select the carousel item and click the **Create component** icon to add it to your library and make it reusable.

Just like earlier, your component now appears in **Assets** (note that it takes the layer name and automatically adds a parent folder with the name from the canvas that contains it). It's now ready to be inserted into the **Home** screen, so head back to the **Hi-Fi** page and follow these steps:

1. Select the **Home** frame so that the component will be already inserted into the right spot, as the lower item of the stack.
2. Through the **Assets** tab, drag the carousel item into the stack, or add it from the **Resources** menu using the *Shift + I* keyboard shortcut.
3. Change the horizontal **Resizing** option to **Fill container**.
4. Wrap your carousel item in an auto layout frame by selecting it and pressing *Shift + A*; then rename it Carousel.
5. Change the **Carousel** direction to horizontal and set the **Gap between items** value to **16** and **Padding** to **0** at the top, left, and bottom, and to **16** on the right. This way, your stack will have some distance from the edge of the screen, which will remain even when scrolling.
6. Select the inner carousel item and duplicate it twice with the *Command + D* (macOS) or *Ctrl + D* (Windows) keyboard shortcut:

Figure 7.16 – Inserting multiple carousel item instances

7. Fill them with different images and set each title accordingly.

The duplicate elements in your carousel are now out of view, but don't worry – it is absolutely normal. These cards will only be visible to you in prototyping mode when you simulate a real horizontal scrolling carousel.

Chapter 7   191

If you are having trouble editing these hidden elements, simply select the appropriate one in the **Layers** panel and change the images and text directly from there. Later in the chapter, you will learn about the **Clip content** function, which makes it easier to edit elements that are placed outside of their parent frames.

C – content cards

Structuring your content cards is a straightforward process, similar to what you've already experienced. For our wireframe, the top stack is reserved for featured videos, which means these card previews should be larger. Now, we'll shift our focus to designing a smaller type of card. This new card will house elements arranged differently, requiring the creation of a new component. Despite being a distinct component, it will still fit within your existing card's frame. Let's return to the **Styles + Components** page and proceed with the following steps:

1. Create a **120 px** (width) x **140 px** (height) rectangle and rename the layer Poster Image. This time, we're not using a frame because we don't need any text laying on top of it.

2. Set the **Fill** type to **Image**. You can leave the default black and white checkerboard background for it, since you will customize it in each component instance individually.

3. Use the *Shift + A* keyboard shortcut to wrap the shape in an **Auto layout** frame and change the **Padding** values to **0**. Name it Content Card by pressing *Cmd + R* (macOS) or *Ctrl + R* (Windows):

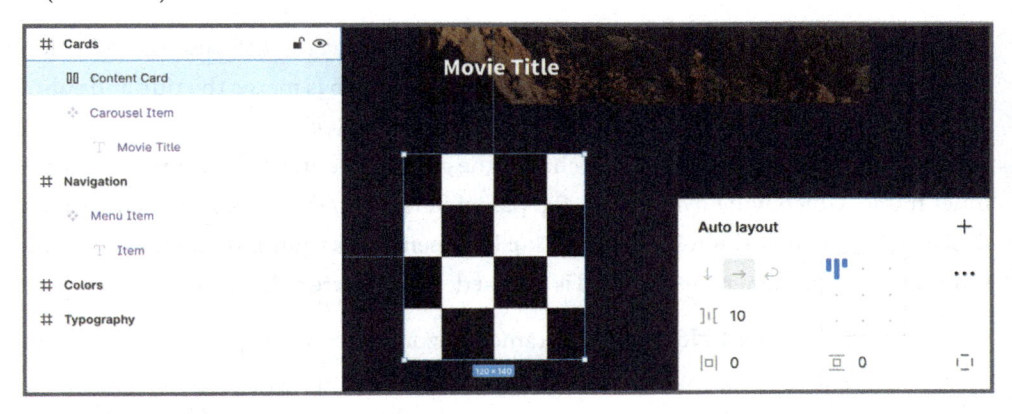

Figure 7.17 – The Content Card element

4. Change the **Auto layout** direction to vertical, since the title and subtitle will be placed below the image.

5. Add a first **Text** layer in the **Content Card** frame below the image and enter **Content Title**. Apply **Title/Small** as a text style and **Pure White** as a fill style.

6. In the **Content Card** frame, add a second **Text** layer below the content title and enter **Content Subtitle**. Apply **Body/Regular** as a text style and an **Inactive** color as a fill style.

At this point, it would be great to use the auto layout **Gap between items** option to set the appropriate hierarchical spacing between your elements. But this option will simply allow you to set the gap between every item, and this is not the best option when you want to visually group some elements and separate them from the others. In the following figure, you can see how the card will look if you use the **Gap between items** option for the entire auto layout frame:

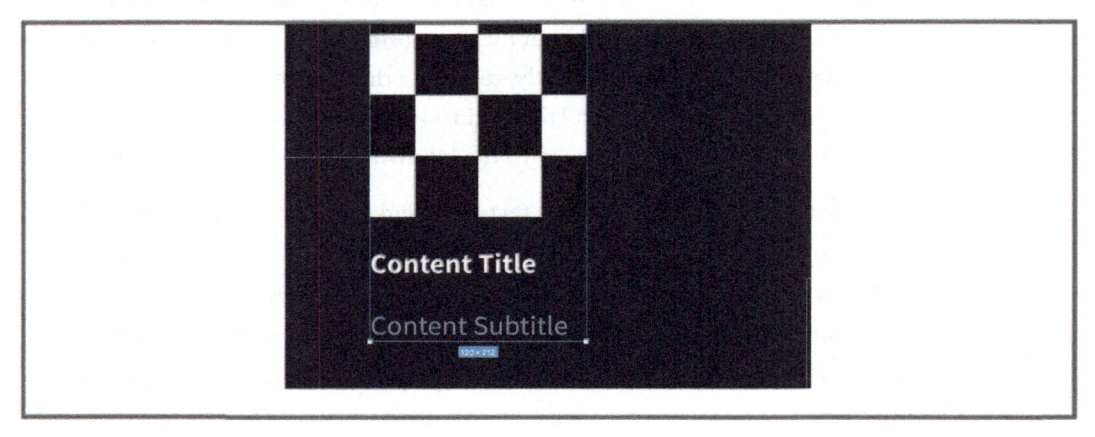

Figure 7.18 – Gap between items

The space between the image and the title looks good, but the title and the subtitle are now placed too far from each other. To fix this, all you have to do is merge the title and subtitle in an auto layout frame by selecting both of them and pressing *Shift + A*, and then rename it `Title + Subtitle`. From now on, you can still change the gap in the outer frame, but it will not affect the inner frame, which will have its own gap parameters. With the right alignment, it looks better, doesn't it? To achieve this result, set the **Gap between items** value to **16** for the outer auto layout frame and **8** for the inner one. The card is almost done; there are only a few steps left to complete it:

1. Set the internal **Title + Subtitle** frame horizontal **Resizing** option to **Fill container**.
2. Select all the inner elements of the card – the image, the title, and the subtitle – and then set the horizontal **Resizing** option to **Fill container**.

Setting the **Fill container** option ensures that the card will still look nice when resized. What's more, if the actual title and subtitle text are longer than the placeholder, the card layout won't fall apart, as you can see in the following figure:

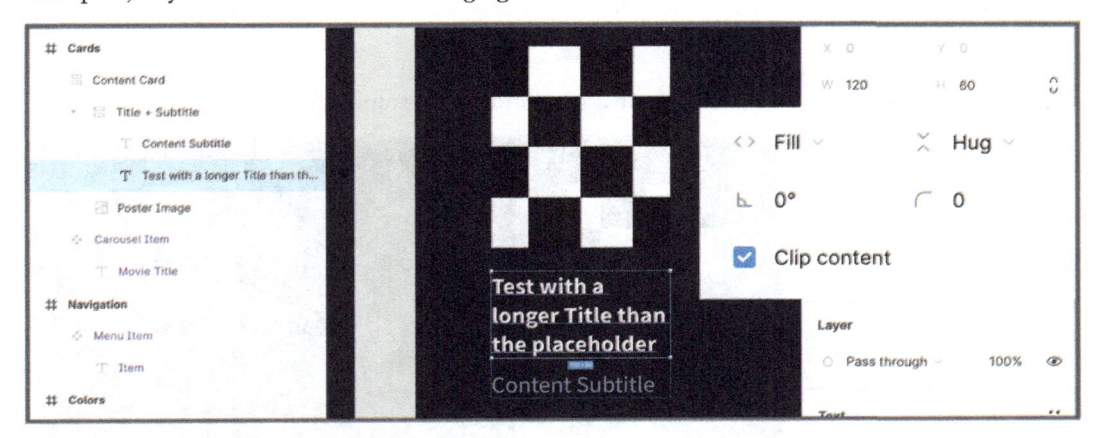

Figure 7.19 – Testing out the structure with a longer placeholder text

Great! Now that your **Card** layer is ready, transform it into a component by selecting it and clicking the **Create component** icon at the top center. Upon doing this correctly, all layers inside will turn purple, indicating they're part of the component. A **Component** icon will also appear next to the **Content Card** frame on the canvas and in the **Layers** panel. This new component will be accessible in the **Cards** folder of our **Assets** library.

For the content cards designed to appear as a sliding row, simply dragging multiple instances into a frame and arranging them horizontally in the **Home** view might seem straightforward. However, this method can be inefficient, especially when you need to replicate or modify the entire carousel for different media sections. The solution lies in creating a nested component. This involves designing a master carousel component that contains individual card components. This way, any changes made to a single card or the master carousel will automatically reflect in all instances where it is used, streamlining the process and ensuring design consistency across various sections.

D – repeated rows

Let's take a look at how you can optimize your work even better by taking full advantage of the component's capabilities. For now, stay in the **Cards** frame on the **Styles + Components** page and do the following:

1. Drag a **Content Card** instance from **Assets** and drop it somewhere inside the **Cards** frame:

Figure 7.20 – Duplicating our component to create an instance

Note that the main components and their instances have different icons next to the layer names in the **Layers** panel. You are now going to work only on the instances without touching the main **Content Card** component.

2. Select an instance and wrap it in an auto layout frame using the *Shift + A* keyboard shortcut.
3. Rename this new frame **Cards Row**, and set **Padding** for all sides to **0** and **Gap between items** to **16**. Make sure that the auto layout frame direction is horizontal.
4. Select the **Content Card** instance within the frame again and duplicate it by pressing *Command + D* (macOS) or *Ctrl + D* (Windows). Repeat this action three times. You should now have the same result as shown in the following figure:

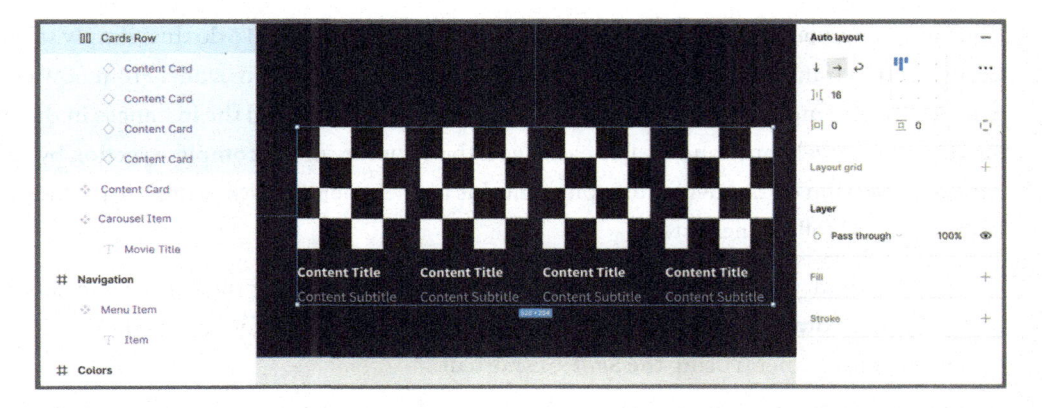

Figure 7.21 – Cards Row

5. Select **Cards Row** and press *Shift + A* again to place it in the auto layout frame. Rename this new outer frame `Cards Section`.
6. Set its **Padding to all sides** value to **0**, direction to vertical, and **Gap between items** to **32**.
7. Add a **Text** layer on top of **Cards Section** and enter `Section Title`. Apply medium **Title/Bold** properties as the text style and **Pure White** as the fill style:

Figure 7.22 – Structuring the section

Great job! Now, you are going to create your first nested component. To do this, simply select the **Cards Section** frame and click on the **Create Component** icon button. Done! From now on, you can modify the single **Content Card** component, which will affect all the instances in the **Cards Section** row as well, but you can also easily edit the structure of the complete section by editing the **Cards Section** component. To implement this new element into your design, go back to the **Hi-Fi** page and follow these steps:

1. Place your **Cards Section** component instance right below the carousel in the **Home** view by dragging and dropping it from **Assets**. Alternatively, you can quickly access the **Resources** menu using the *Shift + I* shortcut.

2. Repeat the first step (or just duplicate the first element) to create a second row of cards under the first one.

3. Select the outer **Home** screen frame and change **Gap between items** to **32** to evenly space each element in your view.

4. Customize each title, subtitle, and image. We can follow the example in the following figure:

Figure 7.23 – Our finished Home view

(photos by Kristaps Ungurs, Zachary Delorenzo, Perry Kibler, Daniel J. Schwarz, Tasos Mansour, and Daniel Sessler on Unsplash)

Chapter 7

The **Home** view now looks complete. Moreover, this view is modular and flexible, so if you need to change something on this screen, it will be very easy to do so through the main components, even if they are crucial changes. Also, if you select any component's instance in the frame, you will discover many new features, as you can see in the following figure:

Figure 7.24 – The component's options

Let's take a closer look at the actions in the right panel that you can now do with any instance in your design:

- First, if you click on the instance name in the properties panel, a dropdown will appear with all the components in your library, allowing you to swap that selected instance with any other component.
- To the right of the instance name, you can see the **Component** icon, and after clicking on it, you will be taken directly to the page where the main component is located (for example, our **Styles + Components** page).
- The three-dot (**...**) **More** icon contains all the other manipulations you can do with your instances. **Detach instance** is a destructive action that disconnects the selected instance from the main component, and from then on, this instance becomes a regular frame. The **Push changes to main component** action allows you to quickly update the main component with the changes made to the selected instance. The last option, **Reset all overrides**, returns the instance to its original state, resembling its main component source. This function can be useful if, for example, your instance behaves in an odd or undesirable way after editing and you cannot determine the exact reason.

Note that if you change the width and/or height of any instance, a new option will appear, **Reset size**, which allows you to reset the size of the instance as its source of truth but not any other edit you may have done. As you experiment more with components, you'll discover many other properties that can be reset, expanding your understanding and control over component behavior.

This section of the chapter was your first and most important step in mastering components. You learned what components are, why and when to use them, and how the main component and its instances affect each other. You have created several components for the **Top Navigation**, **Main Carousel**, **Content Cards**, and **Repeated Rows** blocks of the application's **Home** view. Finally, you've explored the additional functionalities that Figma allows you to apply to instances. This is a big step! And of course, it's completely okay if you're feeling overwhelmed by all this new information, so don't rush to the next section – try playing a little bit more with the components in your drafts. You can create some of them from scratch, from simple to nested ones, and then experiment with their instances as you want.

In the next section, you will learn even more about components and, of course, immediately try out this feature to improve your design.

Extending components with variants

As you've seen, components are incredibly powerful, especially when they are nested or combined with other features such as styles. However, they can do even more to improve your design and make your workflow more efficient. At this point, you have created a few components, and they were quite easy to implement in your layouts. But when you are working on a more complex project or creating an entire design system, the number of components immediately begins to grow very fast. This means that your **Assets** library will be full of similar components, and it will be very difficult for you to navigate them. To solve this problem, Figma has another great feature called **Variants**. In this section, you will learn everything about this amazing feature by implementing it in our app design!

Why use variants?

Variants in Figma allow you to group similar components that serve the same function but have slight differences, such as color variations or text changes. This grouping creates a cohesive set, simplifying your Assets library by reducing clutter and enhancing navigation. Each variant within the set is distinct but shares core properties with others in the group. However, it's important to use variants judiciously. Not every component needs variants, especially if the differences between them are substantial. Overusing variants for components that don't logically fit together can lead to confusion and reduce the efficiency of your design process.

To better understand the concept of variants, let's look at a case when it is appropriate to use them. A common practice for using variants is a button component, as it is a design element that has many types and states, all of which need to be presented in your design. So, since this is such a convenient case, you will learn about variants by creating them for the button component, but first, you need to build a **Content Detail** page, using a few new tricks.

Setting up our Content Detail view

Before getting to know variants, let's set up a new view to take advantage of our new feature. As with all the other views you have built on your Hi-Fi page, the first thing you need to do is empty the **Content Detail** frame by moving all the wireframe elements to the side or deleting them. Next, you are going to customize the view by following these steps:

1. Select the **Content Detail** frame and enable **Auto layout**.
2. Set **Direction** to vertical.
3. Set **Gap between items** to **0**.
4. Set **Padding** to all sides to **0**.
5. Set the horizontal and vertical **Resizing** options to **Fixed width** and **Fixed height** respectively.

Great! Now the parent frame is ready to position the inner elements in a better and more flexible way. Make sure your settings match those shown in the following figure:

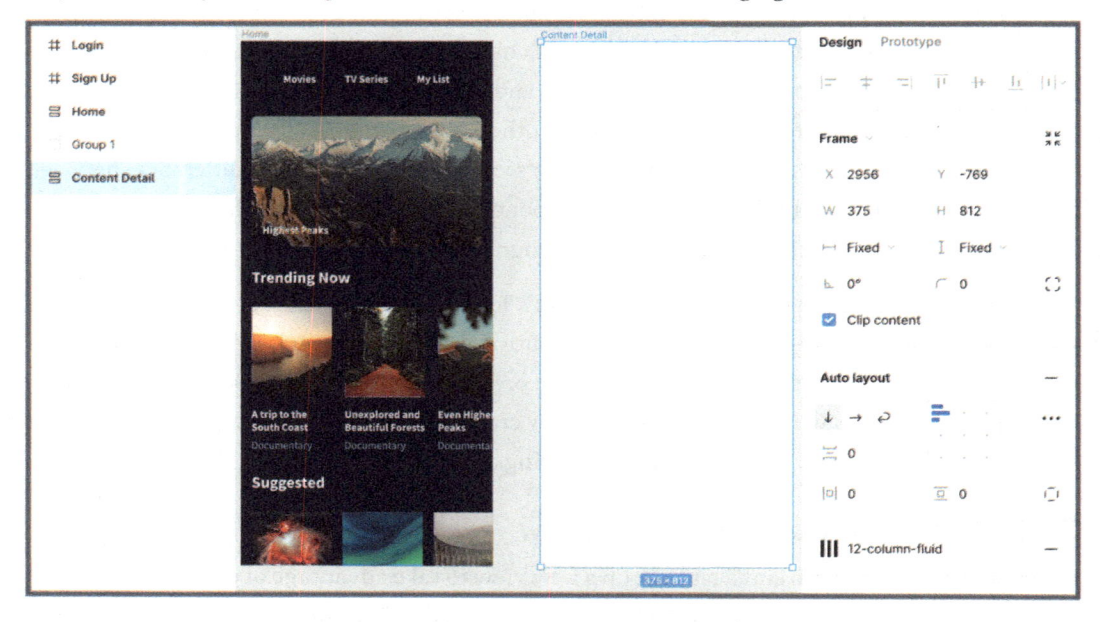

Figure 7.25 – Preparing our Content Detail parent frame

> **Note:**
> If you want to set aside wireframe elements in Figma while keeping your **Layers** panel organized, consider creating a **Wireframes** group or even a section. This can be done by clicking **Section** in the toolbar or using *Shift + S*, then positioning it on the canvas. It's a neat way to group and manage these elements separately from the rest of your design components.

The top elements of the **Content Detail** view are very similar in design to what you have done for the **Home** view, so this stage should be pretty clear to you. However, the points that differ will be explained in detail. Now, let's get the job done by following these steps:

1. Select the **Content Detail** frame and set its fill style to **Background**.
2. Create a **Rectangle** shape of **375 px** (width) x **360 px** (height) and rename it **Poster Image**. Set its horizontal **Resizing** property to **Fill container**.

Chapter 7

3. Change the **Poster Image Fill** type to **Image**. You can choose any image you like, but since there will be detailed information about one of the videos from the **Home** page, picking the same image that you previously used for the **Home** view will be more consistent. Your frame should now look something like the one shown in the following figure:

Figure 7.26 – Poster Image

You may have noticed that, in this particular case, you did not set the padding from the right and left edges of the parent frame, unlike what you did earlier for your layout grid. This is because the **Poster Image** element does not have side spacing but will fill the screen from edge to edge.

4. Now, let's create a new container for the elements that should fit the layout grid. Add a frame of any size right below the **Poster Image** element. Rename this layer **Container**.

5. Enable **Auto layout** on the **Container** frame. Set **Direction** to vertical, **Gap between items** to **16**, **Padding** to **16** (vertica) and 0 (horizontal), and the horizontal **Resizing** property to **Fill container**, as shown in the following figure:

Figure 7.27 – Preparing a container

At this point, you are going to try to complete the view in the same way as when working on the **Home** screen. Take this opportunity to practice what you have already learned, and if you have any difficulties, refer to *Chapter 6, Creating a Responsive Mobile Interface Using Auto Layout*, where you can find out everything about the auto layout feature. I understand that this task may seem complex, but it presents an opportunity for you to ensure that you are truly learning and not just mechanically following step-by-step instructions. Consider the structure carefully; you can even sketch it on paper to visualize all the containers properly. The final **Content Detail** view should look like the following figure:

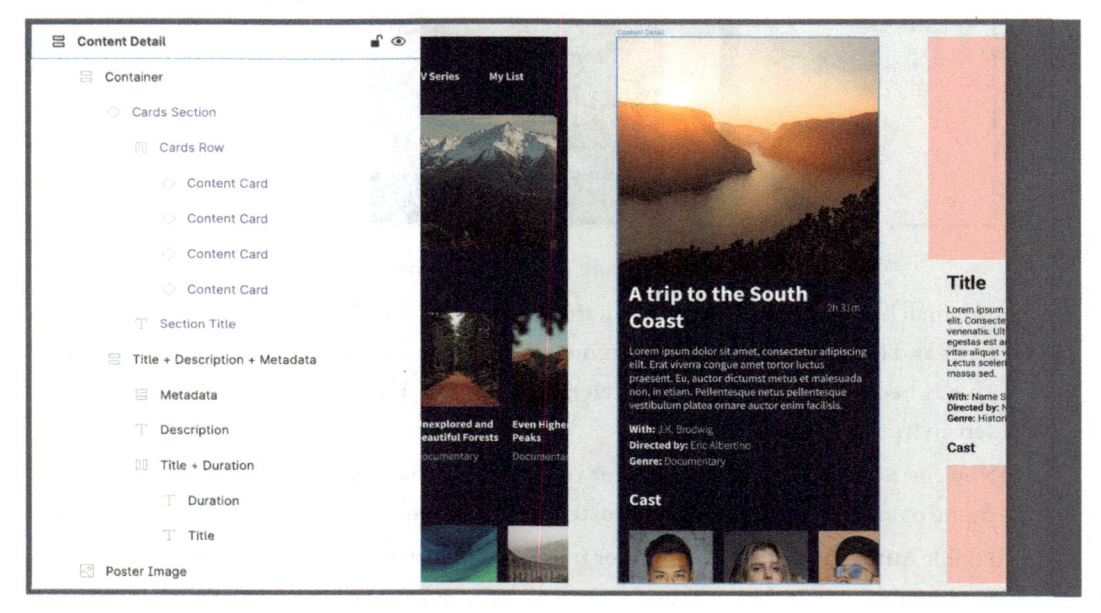

Figure 7.28 – An overview of the final Content Detail results

While comparing your result with *Figure 7.28*, take a look at the layer structure to make sure you did everything right. Note that **Cards Section** was used as the basis for the **Cast** section. It is possible that getting the right result will be a challenging task, but with a lot of practice, attempts, and even mistakes, you will definitely succeed! In any case, you can always make your own small design changes or simplify the whole structure if you run into problems.

The content in your interface grows noticeably, and you will reach a point where the vertical space of the frame is almost filled, making it extremely difficult to add new elements to the view.

Chapter 7

It happens because the canvas automatically masks anything outside the parent frame, which is great for prototyping, but while you're working on a design, you might find it very convenient to see elements outside of the vertical scroll. Don't worry – you can fix this problem simply by selecting the **Content Detail** frame and unchecking the **Clip content** option on the right sidebar, as shown in the following figure:

Figure 7.29 – The Clip content option

(photos by Joseph Gonzales, Raffaella Mendes Diniz, and Ivana Cajina on Unsplash)

When the basic interface of our application is complete, you are ready to create and implement variants in the most useful way by adding key actions to your layout.

Implementing variants

In the **Content Detail** view, according to the wireframe, there are two action buttons located at the bottom of the screen. The primary button is designed for the main action, which is to access and view multimedia content. The secondary button, in contrast, is meant for a less prominent action, providing the option to download the video for offline viewing. Remember that you already created a button when working on the **Login** and **Sign Up** views, but you weren't using components at the time, and so now is a good time to fix that.

As stated earlier, button elements required in any interface design need to have different styles, types, and states, and this is a typical case when it makes sense to use variants. To better understand the importance of this feature, let's think about the buttons in our app.

You know that you need to create at least two buttons, primary and secondary, but each can have a set of different features– for example, with or without an icon – which doubles the number of components. Also, each button certainly has different states that you need to show when prototyping, such as **Hover** (when the mouse pointer hovers over an element), **Focus** (when an element is selected), and **Disabled/Inactive** (when an element is disabled and not clickable). Each of these states must also be explicitly applied to each style and size of your buttons. Now, you may have lost the number of components for a button element that you need to create, and this is where variants come into play to help you organize and set all the components that have similar characteristics.

To start creating your variants, let's move to the **Styles + Components** page and follow these steps:

1. Create a new frame that will contain all the button components and rename it Buttons. Set the fill style to **Background**.
2. On the **Hi-Fi** page, copy the **Login** and **Sign-Up** buttons from the **Login** frame and paste them directly into the new **Buttons** frame.
3. Change their text labels to something less specific like Button, as shown in the following figure:

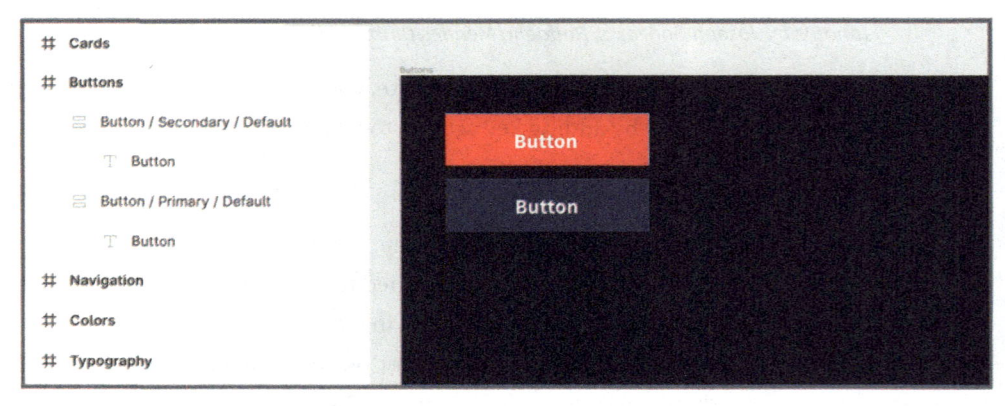

Figure 7.30 – Preparing buttons

The layer names that were previously assigned to your buttons are very important because they tell Figma that these elements are part of the same button class, allowing us to create a set in just seconds. Basically, from now on, you can structure your button element with two different styles but in the same state, which is **Default**. Instead of creating components from each of the buttons individually, select both, and now a new **Create component set** option will magically appear on the top panel, as shown in the following figure:

Chapter 7 205

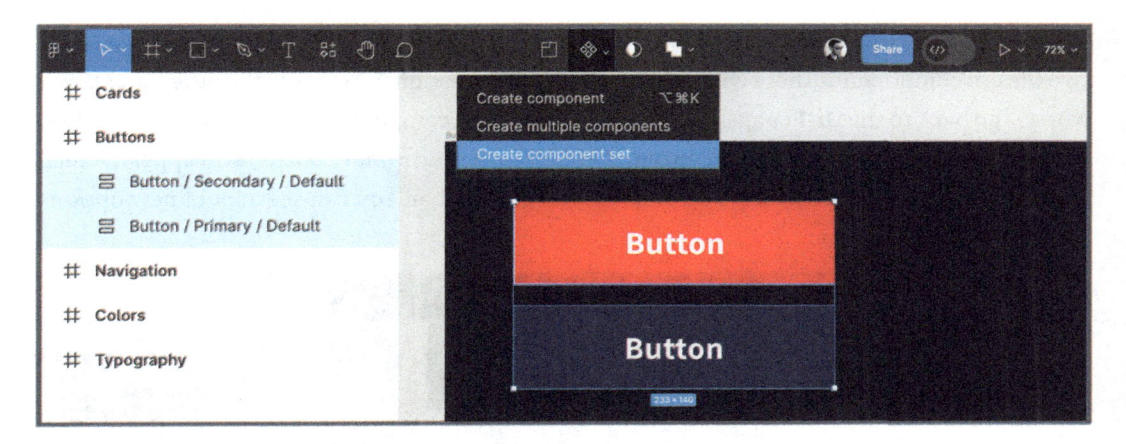

Figure 7.31 – Creating a component set

After this action, a lot happened in the **Buttons** frame that you had not seen before. The elements are now combined with a dashed stroke, and if you look at the layers, you will notice that they have been grouped together. In addition, when this area is selected, the right sidebar now shows many new options, as you can see here:

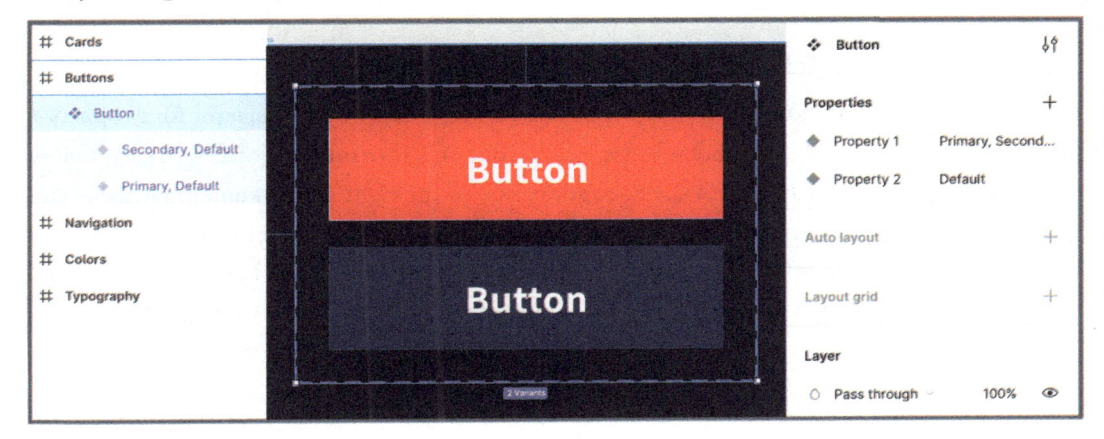

Figure 7.32 – An overview of the component set

> **Note:**
> No need to worry if you've already created individual button components. You can easily consolidate them into variants to achieve the same outcome. Simply select multiple components, and in the right sidebar, click the **Combine as variants** option.

Now, if you open your **Assets** library, you will again find an unusual situation there – instead of two button components, there will only be one. So the question is, where is the other one? Don't worry – go back to the **Hi-Fi** page and just drag the button component from the library and drop it right below the **Cast** area in the **Content Detail** frame. The primary button will appear, which is quite predictable, but select it and look at the right sidebar. You can see a lot of new options, as in the following figure:

Figure 7.33 – Switching between two buttons' properties

As you can see, you can now easily swap your button in the drop-down selector for **Property 1**. Let's see how this works! Drag another instance of your new **Button** component, place it below the **Primary** one, and swap it with the **Secondary** one in the right panel. Remember to set the horizontal **Resizing** property to **Fill container** for each button. It's also better to wrap the two buttons in an **Auto layout** frame and set their gap to **16**. Change the button labels to **Watch Now** and **Download**, and you're done with the **Content Detail** view! The final result should look like the following figure:

Chapter 7

Figure 7.34 – Details of the final results

When you're done, select the main **Content Detail** frame and re-enable the **Clip content** option to temporarily mask all the elements outside of the view.

Variants are incredible, and you can already easily implement them into your designs, but there is still more you can do to further organize them. Go back to the **Styles + Components** page and select your **Button** set. In the right-side panel, change the names of **Property 1** to **Style** and **Property 2** to **State**. This will make your button component even more accessible and easier to understand its properties. The renaming result is shown in the following figure:

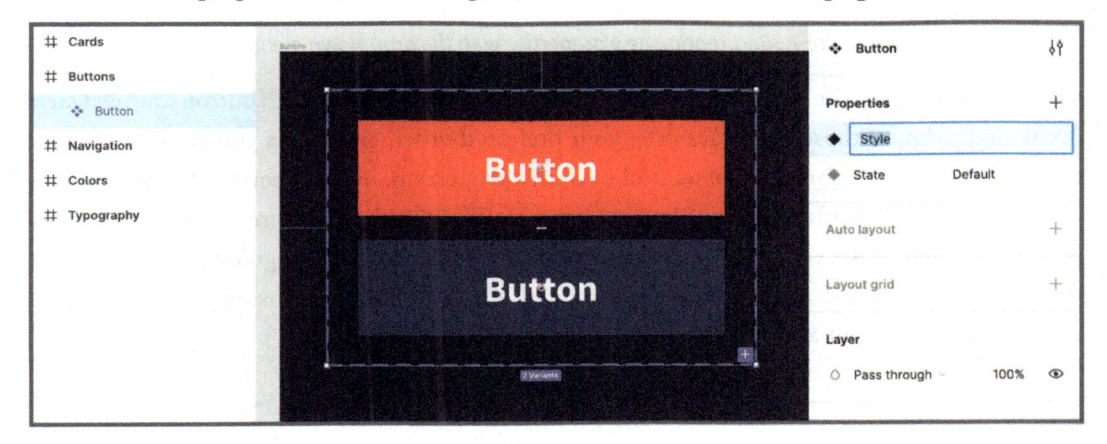

Figure 7.35 – Renaming our variants

Let's go back to the button components and think about states. Besides **Default**, you need to create the **Hover** (which will only be available on the web/desktop, since touchscreens have no cursor), **Focus**, and **Disabled** states. The easiest way is to manually expand the width of the set's external dashed stroke and duplicate both buttons as many times as needed for all states (or alternatively you can also use auto layout to better manage the set structure). Figma will warn you that some conflicts are occurring, which is perfectly normal, since you have elements with the same property names at the moment. Select each button individually, and in the **State** drop-down list, create a new value for each state. You can achieve that by simply entering the name of each new state, as in the following figure:

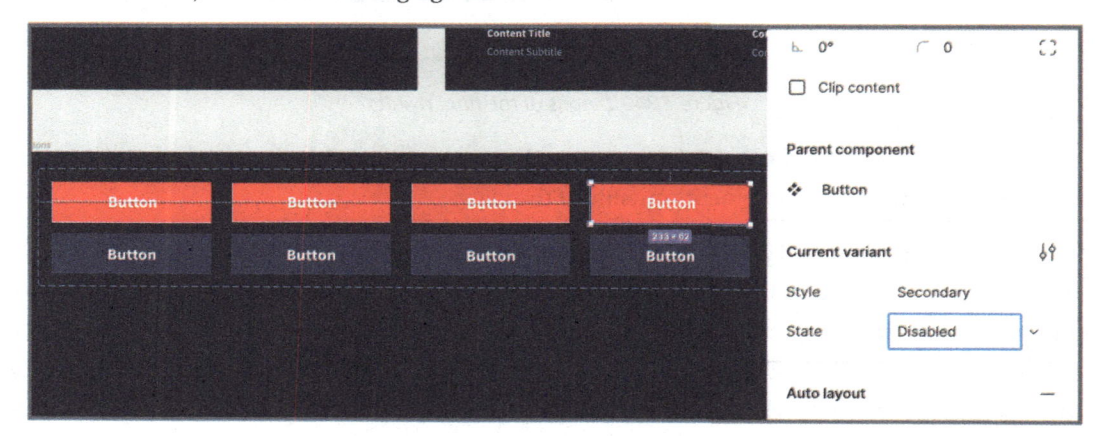

Figure 7.36 – Creating new properties with the drop-down menu

After you've assigned the **Default, Hover, Focus**, and **Disabled** states to each button, the next step is customization. If these states aren't in your preferred order, Figma lets you easily rearrange them. Just select the component set and drag the property names to reorder. For styling the buttons, the existing colors in your library may not suffice. You'll need to create new color styles, particularly lighter **Accent** and **Secondary** colors for the **Hover** state. To guide you, refer to the **Color Styles** example shown in the figure provided. This approach will ensure your buttons are not only functional but also visually appealing.

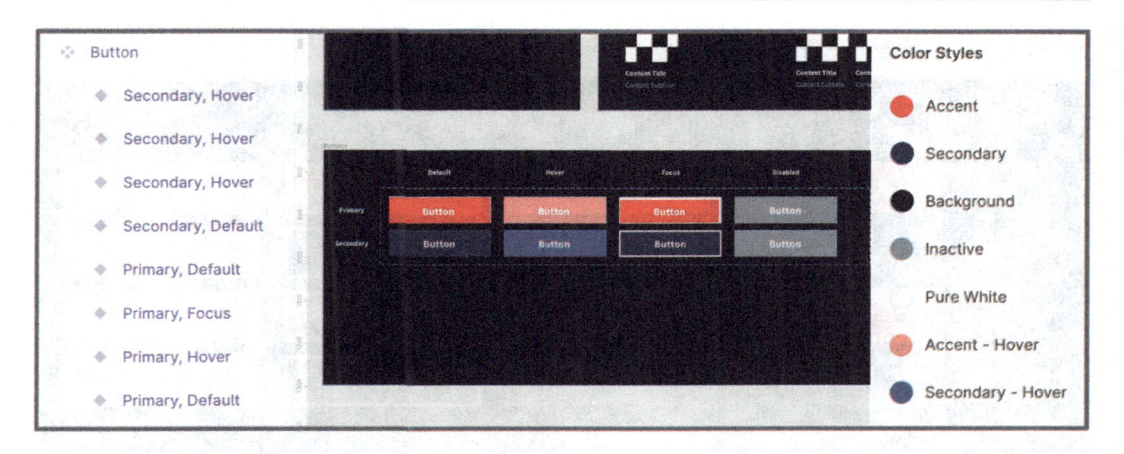

Figure 7.37 – An overview of the results with new color styles

No matter how many button component variants you add, the **Assets** panel will still show only one element. However, once added to the canvas, you'll not only have the choice to select a style but also the ability to access a state that may not be immediately useful but will certainly be essential during the prototyping phase. If you're looking to expand your design options, you can create a new unique button type, such as one with an icon positioned beside the label. This can be especially valuable in specific design scenarios. To do this, duplicate the two rows of buttons that you already have, and upgrade those new rows by adding a fun star (using the **Star** tool) in the button's frames. Then, click the + icon next to **Variants**, and then select **Add new property**. You can name this new variant property **Icon**, which should just have two options – **True** to show the icon on the button, or **False** to hide it. Finally, it's time to set everything properly by turning on the **Icon** property where needed. Before trying it yourself, make sure that you have enough knowledge and practice of using variants.

Take your time to exercise and replicate what you see in the following figure:

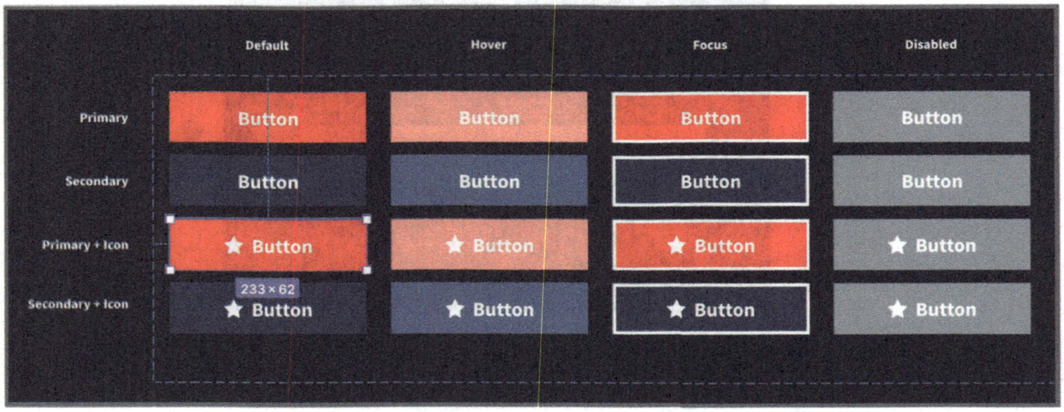

Figure 7.38 – Pushing variants and properties even further

> **Note**
> Once you set **True** and **False** as values, this property will appear as a cool toggle button in the right sidebar, not a dropdown. You can literally turn the **Icon** element on and off with the button!

What you now have in the **Buttons** frame can be created simply by using **Components**, but the end result in this case will be a library filled with tons of different button components to accomplish every single combination of properties. The benefits of variants will become more apparent to you as you advance to complex interfaces or, more significantly, design systems.

Well, now you have covered everything you need to know to start using components efficiently by implementing variants to your design. For sure, using these functions requires a lot of practice, but eventually, you will find your own system to decide what elements need to be converted into components, which of them can have variants, and how to organize everything in a library.

In the next section, you will learn about some other amazing features that Figma has, namely collaboration, sharing, and version history. This way, you'll take a little break from our project and explore new Figma functionalities.

Multiplayer mode, libraries, and version control

It was a lot to manage, wasn't it? And yet this project is a simple one. It is likely that your future projects will be more complex, and you will not be working on them alone. Collaborating with other people is always a fun but challenging process, and it's also an important part of your design journey. In this section, you will discover what solutions Figma offers for effective teamwork and real-time collaboration.

Working with multiplayer features

From the very beginning, Figma tried to outperform other tools by building its entire software architecture on modern web technologies. This, on the one hand, turned into significant limitations, such as the need for a constant internet connection, a condition that no other design tool requires. But, on the other hand, it presented an incredible number of advantages, such as the immediate synchronization of files and projects, the ability to work directly from the browser without downloading anything, and above all, multiplayer features.

In Figma, as well as in FigJam, you can invite up to 500 collaborators in one file, which is too much to handle for other design tools.

You can see other editors or viewers working in the same file as you, by seeing their avatars appearing in the top bar, as well as their cursors moving in real time on the canvas.

Figure 7.39 – Multiplayer mode and active editors/viewers

Looks cool, doesn't it? So, in this section, you will learn how to share a file with friends and colleagues, as well as what other collaboration opportunities Figma can offer you. It's easy to invite someone to a file; all you have to do is click the **Share** button in the upper-right corner.

Then, a pop-up window similar to the one you see in the following figure will appear:

Figure 7.40 – Adding new editors/viewers to the file

There are two ways to invite people to your file through this dialog:

- You can do this by typing in your teammates' emails, specifying their roles in the drop-down menu right in the textbox (editor or viewer), and clicking **Send invite**.
- Alternatively, we can choose the **Copy link** option and then send direct links to the people you want to share the file with. Do not forget to specify the role before copying the link in the drop-down list on the right side of the window, as shown in the following figure:

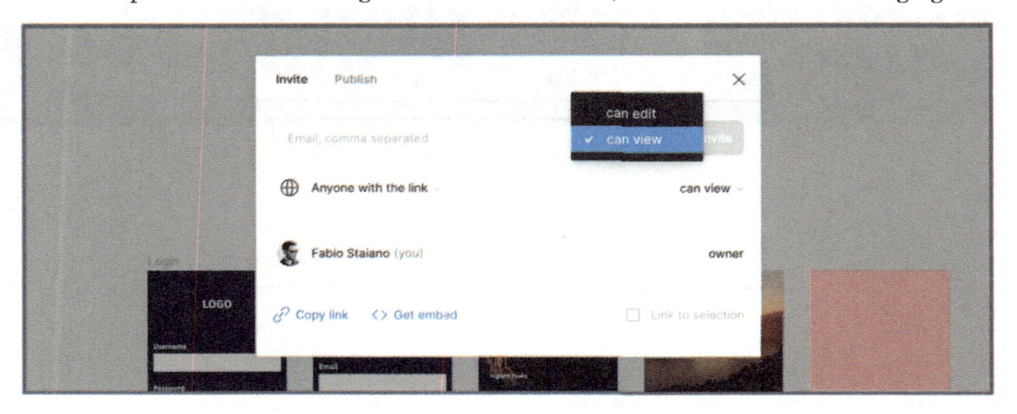

Figure 7.41 – Choosing a default rule for people joining via a link

Sending the same link to others is undoubtedly a quick and easy way but also very risky, as you may end up unwittingly giving unwanted people access to your file.

Also, at any time, you can change the roles for each individual participant in the file, from editor to viewer or vice versa, close access, or even transfer ownership of our file to third parties, simply by selecting the option you need from the corresponding drop-down list.

What has been said so far in this section relates to your individual personal files, but sharing and collaboration are even easier when you're working in a team! In fact, if you create a new team in the Figma welcome screen (refer to *Chapter 1, Exploring Figma and Transitioning from Other Tools*, to brush up on this), you can add your colleagues directly to the team, after which they will have access to every project and file that already exists and is added afterward. The team owner can always manage team members and all permissions, plus create private/invite-only projects if needed. You can see an example of a team management page in the following figure:

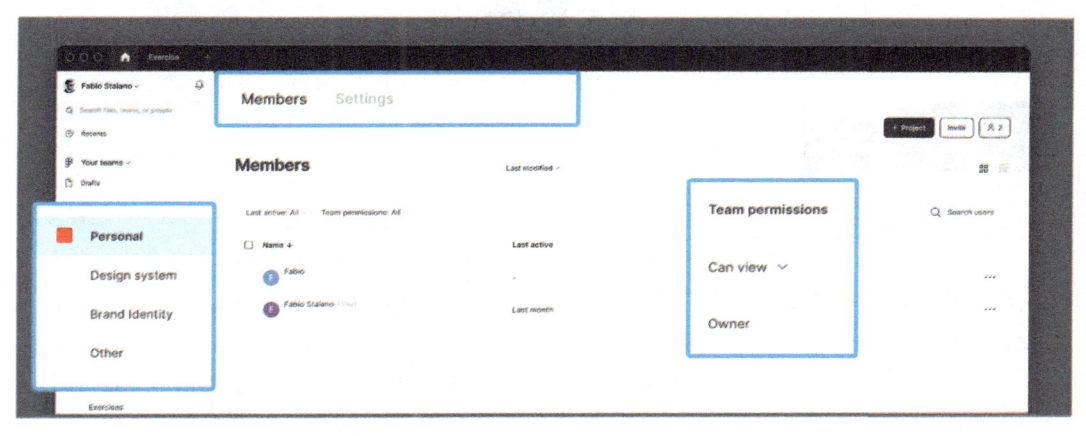

Figure 7.42 – Team members and permissions

That's pretty much everything you need to know about multiplayer mode at the moment, since Figma has everything very clearly organized in its interface. However, sharing in Figma is a big topic, and it doesn't end there, so the next thing you need to learn is how to publish and manage libraries.

Managing libraries

Through practice, you have seen that components as a function have limitless potential – they behave like building blocks, allowing you to create reusable elements. Styles are also a very powerful feature, although they are nothing more than a set of properties that can be applied to elements. After creating your components and styles, you can easily use them in the file in which they were placed. But what if you could go beyond and extend this behavior by sharing them across other files and projects? All this is possible thanks to libraries in Figma!

Let's see how this works in action. On the **Styles + Components** page, you have saved all your components and styles, and those are always accessible locally in this specific file. Now, you will create a library that will contain all of those elements. First, open the **Assets** panel, and then click the **Team Library** icon (the book-shaped one). You should see a popup, as shown in the following figure:

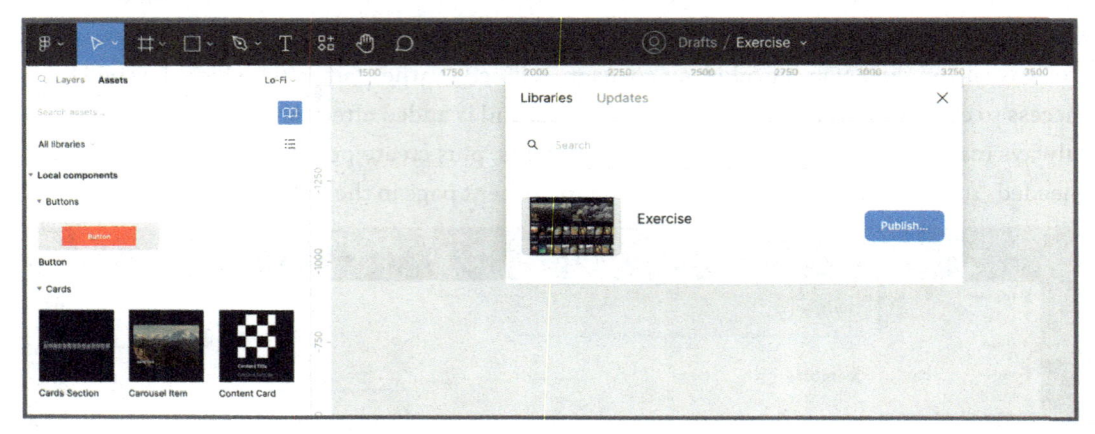

Figure 7.43 – A team library

In this dialog box, you will see the name of your file with a **Publish...** button next to it. Publishing the entire library is only possible if your file is in a team and not in **Drafts** (in this case, you will be asked to move your file to a team). If you don't want to move it from **Drafts**, you will be prompted to choose to publish styles only, which is always possible. To check out all the features of the library, move your file to any team.

Okay, great, you're ready to go! So, the next thing you will find is a long list of all your previously created styles and components that you are about to publish to this new library. There is a helpful description textbox at the top of the dialog, which should always be used for a quick comment on what you intend to publish or update in the library. As you can see, the entire list is presented as checkboxes, so in the end, you can even select the ones that you really want to publish.

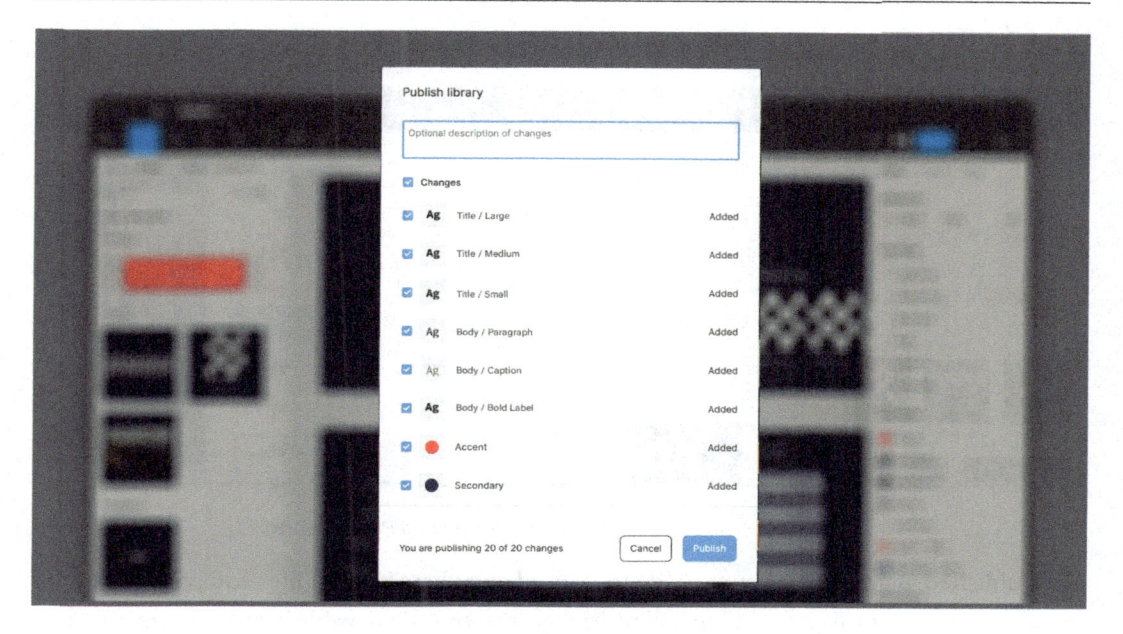

Figure 7.44 – Publishing a library

Note:

Any errors, particularly those involving the incorrect creation of variants or properties, can result in conflicts when attempting to publish. You'll receive a notification next to the problematic element, prompting you to address the issues before proceeding. Alternatively, everything except the flagged items will be published.

If you make any changes to any component or style after the library is published, you will see a notification on the **Team Library** icon. By clicking on it, you can easily submit all your updates – and describe them in the text field – to the shared library.

You can try it yourself or refer to the following figure:

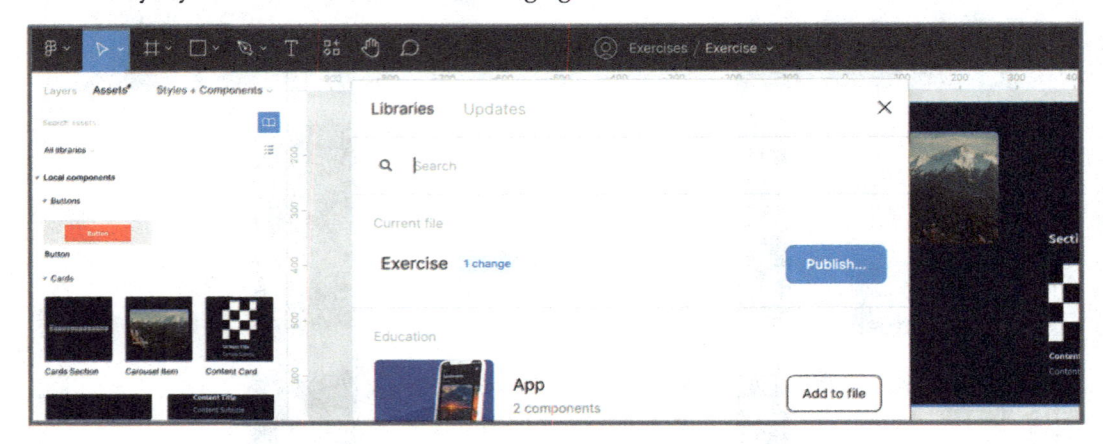

Figure 7.45 – The team library's notification and Publish button

The published team library is now ready to be used anywhere in team files and projects in your Figma. You can test this by opening – or ultimately creating – a new file in the same team. Then, go to **Assets** and click on the **Team Library** icon. In the popup that appears after that, you will see the name of your library and the toggle button next to it, so once you enable it, you and your team members can instantly use all the styles and components that you previously created in the new file. In the following figure, you can see an example of this popup:

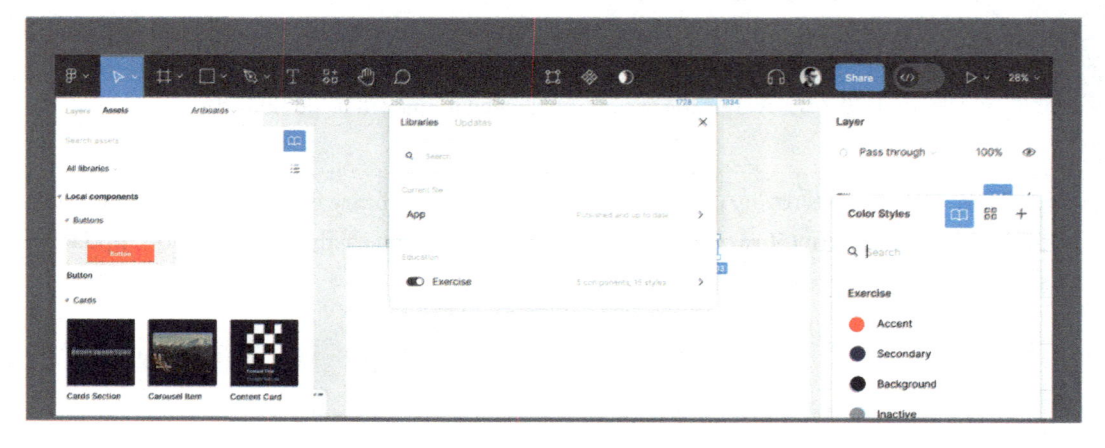

Figure 7.46 – Components and styles activated in a new file

Note:

You can edit main components and styles only in the source files in which they were originally created, except when they're moved or detached.

Now you finally know the full potential of styles and components and how to create shared libraries. This last feature helps a lot when working on, for example, different projects for the same client. Therefore, you can create a base of styles and components only once and then reuse it over time. If, one day, a client decides to change something, such as the main brand color, all you have to do is change its style in the source file and publish the update to the team library. This way, you can be sure that the color will change in every project in which it is used.

You will discover even more about libraries in *Chapter 12, Discovering Resources, Plugins, and Widgets in the Figma Community*, which is dedicated to the Figma community!

Preserving your work with version history

When you worked on the project in your file, you may have noticed that you never had to save your work in progress. This is one of the incredible benefits of a web tool that removes once and for all the worry of saving, and you don't lose your last changes. But Figma doesn't only do that; it also keeps your **version history** as well. To see it, open the drop-down menu next to the filename in the top bar and click **Show version history**.

Figure 7.47 – The Show version history option

Once clicked, the version history will be shown as a new right panel, where you can see and navigate past versions of your file. You can see an example of this panel in the following figure:

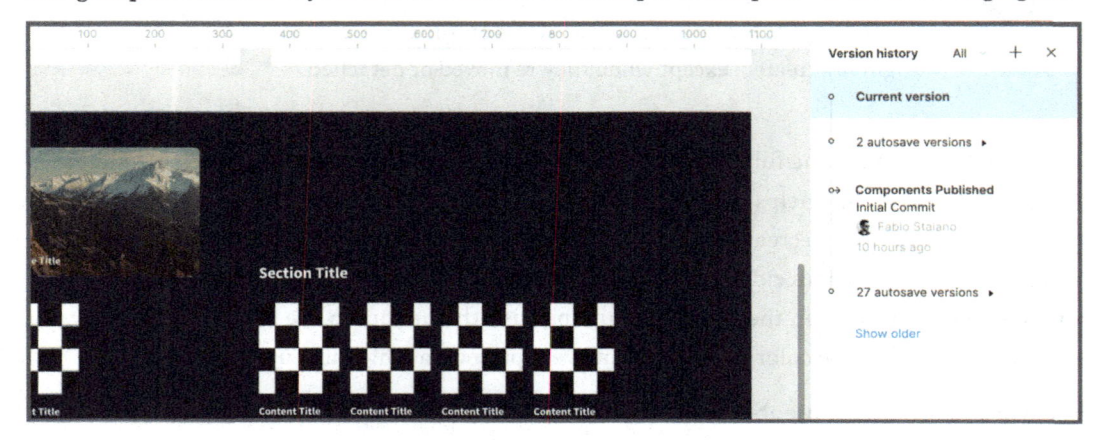

Figure 7.48 – The Version history panel

As you can see, **Current version** is now selected, which means that you are using the most recent version of the file. Also, you can see the save point that Figma created automatically when you published the library (every time you publish an update, the new version will be added to the history with your descriptions from the update notes). Finally, below that is an expandable list that contains all the autosaves that Figma has done from time to time.

Version history allows you to go back in time with just one click, and you can see everything you've ever previously done in your file. You can now even copy/paste elements from the past, without having to completely restore a previous version. In addition, from here, you can access many new options by clicking the **...** icon next to the current save point, as shown in the following figure:

Chapter 7   219

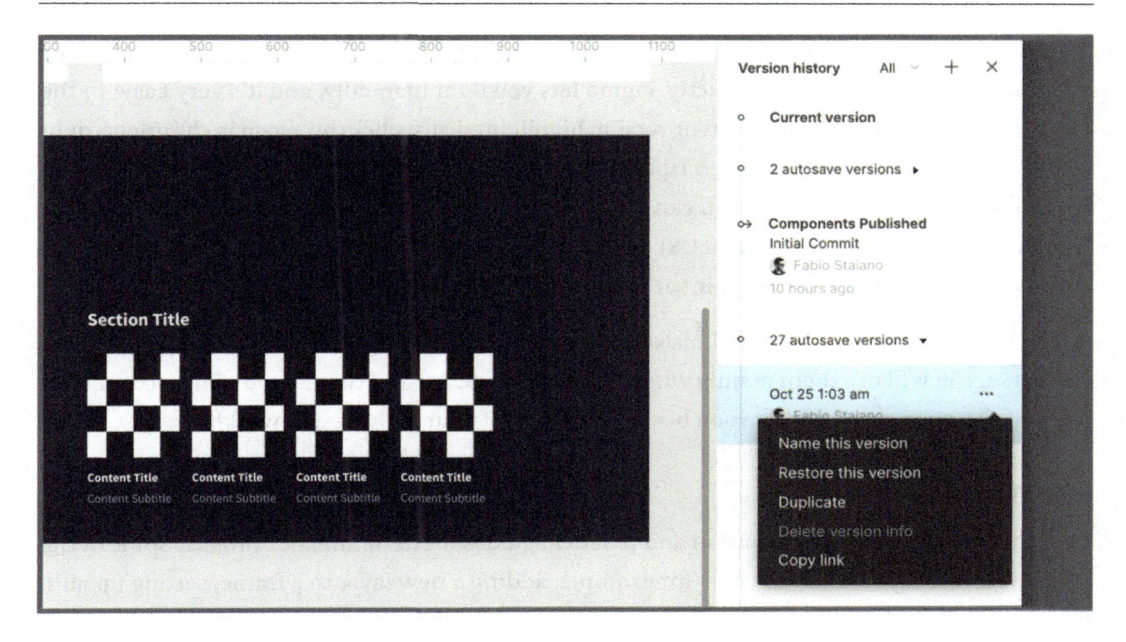

Figure 7.49 – The history version options

From this menu, you can give a name to a specific save point (to make it more recognizable), or you can click **Restore this version** to bring the selected version back to life. If you're not working on the file alone, you'll see not only your personal editorial history but everyone else's (you can change this to show only your history by clicking the **All** drop-down menu at the top of the sidebar and choosing **Only yours** instead).

> **Note:**
> It is important to know that for **Drafts** and free team plans, the version history will be limited to 30 days. Upgrading to the paid plan gives you unlimited access to version history.

The autosave function is great and prevents you from losing anything, but if you want to be doubly sure that everything is saved correctly, Figma lets you do it manually, and it's very easy! In the **Version history** panel with the current version highlighted, just click the + icon in the upper-right corner, then give it a name and description, and that's it! From now on, you can return to that specific save point at any time. You can also access it, bypassing the **Version Control** panel, by using the *Command + Ctrl + S* (macOS) or *Ctrl + Alt + S* (Windows) keyboard shortcut. I would suggest creating a manual save point at each milestone of a project.

All the collaboration, sharing, and history features in Figma are great and very easy to operate. Of course, you will use them mainly when working in a team, and that is, you will discover even more of their potential, with it soon becoming a part of your daily design workflow.

Summary

This chapter was full of information and practical guides for designing our project. Some of the steps were already familiar to you – for example, adding a new layer to a frame, setting up auto layout, and changing properties of elements according to styles. But at the same time, there has been a lot of new information to take in about possibly the most difficult subject on your journey. As always, don't worry if you feel overwhelmed – components and variants are huge, very complex topics, and no one really masters them right away!

It was a rich chapter, and you not only learned about components and variants but also greatly advanced our project by building the **Home** and **Content Detail** views – the most important screens of the application – using all the advanced features that you learned about in the previous chapters and this one. Also, now you know how to work with the library and even how to publish it for use in other team files. Plus, you explored multiplayer mode. Finally, you discovered version history and saw how you can restore and save your work at any stage of your design.

In the next chapter, you will learn how to design for different platforms so that our application can be opened on large screens without falling apart.

Learn more on Discord

To join the Discord community for this book – where you can share feedback, ask questions to the author, and learn about new releases – follow the QR code below:

`https://packt.link/figma`

8
User Interface Design on Tablet, Desktop, and the Web

In the previous chapter, we made significant progress in designing layouts for our mobile app by completing two more views, and we also created some important reusable components that are now easily accessible from your library. According to the brief that was defined in *Chapter 2, Structuring Moodboards, Personas, and User Flows within FigJam*, our application should run not only on smartphones but also on tablets and desktops, so in this chapter, you will learn what you need to do to make your design responsive and how to make it look good on large screens. You are already familiar with functions like constraints and resizing, which prevent your interface from breaking when adjusted for different dimensions. Correctly applying these functions can help you avoid numerous issues when scaling your layouts across various platforms. However, this is not enough to make your design fully responsive, especially if you are creating a product for different platforms, as in our case.

In this chapter, you will discover many important tricks on how to optimally scale an application to larger devices without risking and impacting the functionality behind the design elements and/ or interrupting the UX. You will start by testing your mobile interface on different smartphone models, and then move on to customizing it for tablets and the web while making improvements to your design. As usual, you'll be guided by "how-tos," but this time, you'll have more room to work on your own using provided illustrated examples and tips. So, open up Figma and get ready for a new challenge!

In this chapter, we are going to cover the following topics:

- Discovering responsive design
- Adjusting the interface for tablets
- Adjusting the interface for web and desktop

Discovering responsive design

In this section of the chapter, you will be introduced to the concept of **responsive design**, which is essential for ensuring that digital products function effectively across various devices. This understanding is key when designing adaptable and user-friendly interfaces. You'll learn the fundamental techniques for making your interface design as flexible and responsive as possible. Although this is a broad topic to tackle, you will start with simple tasks, such as adding missing elements and ensuring your app looks good on various screen resolutions on your mobile device.

As you recall, on the **Hi-Fi** page, you designed your application for streaming video within a specific screen size, that of the iPhone 13 Mini. However, as mentioned earlier, it's crucial to ensure that your product appears well on all major device resolutions it may be used on. You don't need to create new views from scratch for this; instead, you'll focus on optimizing the existing ones so that they work seamlessly on any screen size.

Even when a design is done neatly and accurately, there may be some minor aspects that might seem insignificant but turn out to be important in the later stages of the work. From time to time, for example, you will work with constraints and then resize frames to see if everything looks good, but while concentrating on other features, that aspect inevitably fades into the background. Don't worry, this is absolutely normal when you are learning and it is not easy to take things into account at the beginning, but with experience, it will become smooth and natural to anticipate what needs to be implemented in your design. For now, let's just take a step back to fix the missing points.

In the following sections, you will learn how to quickly check whether constraints and everything else in your layouts are set correctly, by scaling the frames to a size similar to other smartphone devices.

Design to code with fluid layouts

You should never forget that your design will eventually be implemented in code, so it makes sense that design and development should relate to each other. Developers, like designers, look for ways to create scalable interfaces that easily adapt to multiple screens and resolutions without too much trouble.

Chapter 8

It is for these purposes that new programming languages such as **React**, **SwiftUI**, and **Flutter** were developed, and designers more or less follow the same path, creating responsive interfaces with fluid layouts and breakpoints.

To better understand these new concepts, you will start with the current **Hi-Fi** interface. If you copy the **Login** frame, make several – temporary – copies, and then use the frame presets, you can easily test the same view on many other similar smartphones:

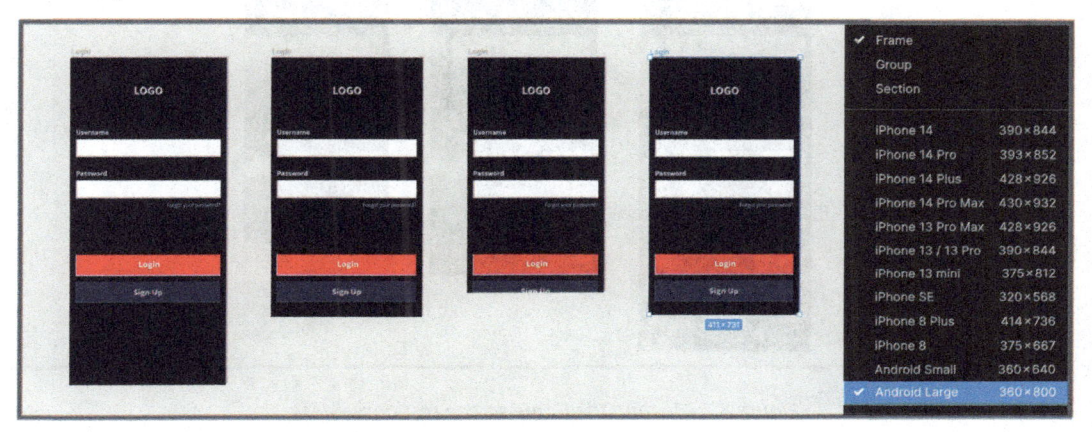

Figure 8.1 – Testing on similar devices

As you can see, on the larger iPhone, as well as on the smaller one, and even on Android devices, this interface does not break but adapts to these screen sizes. This is due to a combination of resizing rules and constraints that you applied to your interface in *Chapter 6, Creating a Responsive Mobile Interface Using Auto Layout*, so all the elements resize their width according to the selected device. With this kind of testing, you can easily check if there are any issues that need to be fixed for resizing and/or constraints. What's more, it's a nice way to see how your layout changes across different devices.

Now you know how to quickly and easily check if your layout looks good on different mobile devices. Keep in mind that Figma has many popular presets for this, and that's usually enough, but if you need to test for a specific screen resolution that isn't listed, you can always manually enter its width and height in the appropriate fields. In addition, the **Login** view is pretty simple, in which the elements are simply resized to fit the parent frame. But this does not mean that other views and the elements within them act in the same way. Let's go ahead and see how to test more complex views.

If you are happy with how your **Login** view looks in different presets, you can remove all the test screens and repeat the same process with other views. Even for complex views, such as the **Home** one, created with **Auto layout,** switching to a preset frame from the list now ensures smooth adaptation to various sizes. The following screenshot demonstrates how the **Home** screen adapts to different sizes, showcasing the seamless functionality of auto layout:

Figure 8.2 – Testing the Home screen responsiveness

If done correctly, you should see a result similar to the one shown in the preceding screenshot. Also, you won't see as much re-adaptation here as you would in the **Login** view, since the **Home** page is composed of scrollable rows that stay the same across all smartphone frames.

This is how a fluid layout works. After you finish quick resizing and testing, clean up your workspace (or restore a previously created save point in **Version history**). Now, let's get down to creating a few elements to complete the design of our mobile interface. Immediately after that, you will discover breakpoints in the tablet section.

Mobile first

Now let's go back for a moment to the reason why we started our project with a mobile design. Since, nowadays, more and more development frameworks are created primarily for mobile devices, the first design version of our application was mobile. Plus, it's much easier to create a small interface first and then scale it up, rather than struggling to shrink things down when you start with a large design.

Chapter 8 227

Before you start making your application fully responsive, there is still something missing in the mobile interface, so now you are going to polish and complete the **Home** and **Content Detail** views by adding navigation elements, allowing the user to easily move from page to page at will. For our application, you will create the typical bottom tab bar that you can find in most mobile applications. Apart from the **Login** and **Sign Up** views, all other screens in our application will have a tab bar. This time, you don't have many views in your file, but it is still better to create components for the navigation elements, as this is what you will be doing in your future, more complex projects. So, now, go to the **Styles + Components** page and follow these steps:

1. In the **Navigation** frame, create a new **Text** layer and type Home. Apply the **Title/Small** text and **Pure White** color styles to it.

2. Using the **Ellipse** tool, draw a 38 px X 38 px circle directly above the text, remove the **Fill**, and apply a 3 px Pure White stroke. This will be your icon's placeholder. As a result, you should end up with something similar to the following screenshot:

Figure 8.3 – Structuring an icon's placeholder

3. With the **Ellipse** layer selected, press *Shift + A* to wrap it in an **Auto layout** frame. The frame is necessary because the icons you will choose could have different sizes or ratios, so it is better to wrap them in a container.

Rename this frame to `Icon`, set **Alignment** to **Center**, and, most importantly, set **Horizontal** and **Vertical Resizing** to **Fixed** to lock its width and height:

Figure 8.4 – Creating an Icon wrapper

4. Now select both the **Icon** frame and the **Home** text layer, and apply **Auto layout** to it with the *Shift + A* keyboard shortcut. Rename this frame to `Tab Item` and change **Alignment** to **Center**:

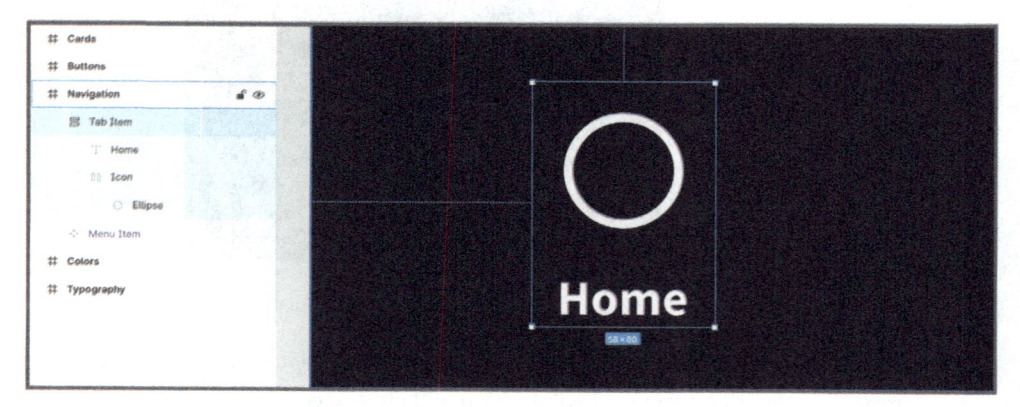

Figure 8.5 – Preparing Tab Item

5. Select **Tab Item** and, once again, press *Shift + A* to wrap it in another **Auto layout** frame. Rename it to `Tab Bar`. Make sure **Direction** is set to **Horizontal** and change its **Fill** style to **Secondary**.

6. Using the *Command + D* (macOS) or *Ctrl + D* (Windows) shortcut, duplicate **Tab Item** three times and change each label, as in the following screenshot:

Figure 8.6 – Creating Tab Bar

7. Customize each icon as you wish by replacing each ellipse with the actual icon and setting **Horizontal** and **Vertical Resizing** to **Fill container**. You can draw icons with the **Pen** tool or use the `.svg/.png` icons you may already have (you can use a free set of icons from *Google Material Icons* at `fonts.google.com/icons`). Later, in *Chapter 12, Discovering Resources, Plugins, and Widgets in the Figma Community*, you'll discover a plugin that makes finding icons incredibly easy right in Figma.

The tab bar seems to be done, doesn't it? But don't forget that it has to adapt to different screen resolutions. So, let's try manually resizing it to make sure everything is fine. Once you stretch it, you get something like this:

Figure 8.7 – Testing the tab bar resizing

This is not what you want your tab bar to look like in a real interface. Don't worry – you can fix it in a few clicks.

8. First, select the **Tab Bar** frame and set the **Gap between** value to **Auto**, as shown in the following screenshot:

Figure 8.8 – Alignment and padding on the tab bar

9. Great, now you can finally move on. Select the tab bar and convert it to a component so it can be easily reused in any view you need.

For this exercise flow, you are only designing the main views that relate to the **Home** page, so you can simply change the **Fill** color style of both the **Home** text label and its **Icon** color to **Accent** to make it clear which tab item is selected. If you want to push yourself even further, you can follow a best practice by creating variants of this component so that you have an **Active** state for each of the tab items, as in the following example:

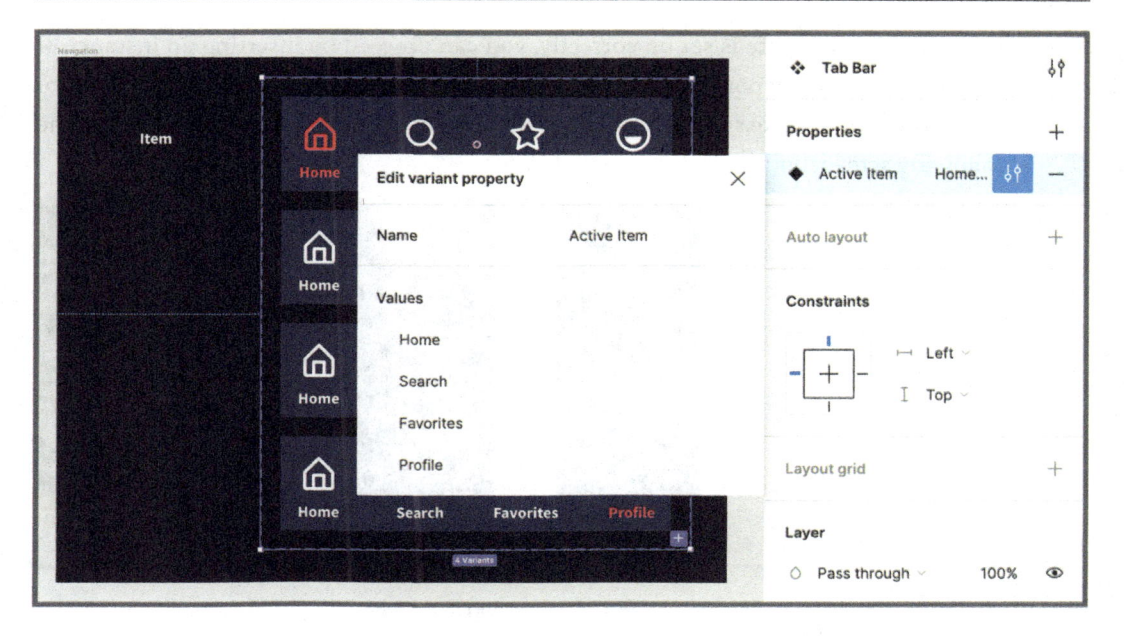

Figure 8.9 – Tab Bar variants

Your new component is now included in your assets and ready to be added to the **Home** screen on the **Hi-Fi** page. But before proceeding with that, you need to make a small adjustment. Since the tab bar is a static element and does not scroll with the rest of the page content, the current **Auto layout** structure of the **Home** frame is not appropriate for it. Follow these steps to fix its **Auto layout** settings and properly add **Tab Bar** elements to the view:

1. Select the **Home** frame and disable **Auto layout**.
2. In order not to lose all the advantages of **Auto layout**, select all the inner layers of the **Home** frame and press *Shift + A* to wrap everything in a new auto layout frame, which you will rename to `Container`. This way, no customized auto layout settings will be lost.
3. Manually resize the container to fit the screen width (375 px), add **16 px** padding to **Left** and **Right**, and finally, set the **Left and right** constraint so it scales correctly later.

4. Now that the structure is set up correctly, you can proceed by inserting an instance of the new **Tab Bar** component by dragging it from the **Assets** panel and dropping it into the **Home** frame. Make sure the **Tab Bar** is placed outside the container, as shown in the following screenshot:

Figure 8.10 – Inserting the tab bar

5. Change the width of the tab bar to fit the frame. Change its **Horizontal** padding to **16**. Then set its constraints to **Left and right** horizontally and to **Bottom** vertically. This will ensure that when your screen resizes, the tab bar will not change its size accordingly and stick to the bottom of the screen:

Figure 8.11 – Fixing the tab bar

That's all. Now the tab bar has to be added to the **Content Detail** page. You can do this by simply copying the element from the **Home** view and pasting it in the **Content Detail** screen, but remember to disable **Auto layout** for the parent frame first.

Moreover, to make the interface consistent across all views, the **Content Detail** screen will need a top navigation bar since this is an internal page, and the user must somehow return to the previous screen. The final result should look something like this:

Figure 8.12 – Overview of the result

It is also better to create a component for the top bar as it could be used for every child view of the application. In addition, you can place the **Add to Favorites** button in the upper-right corner, as you can see in *Figure 8.12*.

It's really important to use the right tools to make your design work well on different screen sizes for mobile devices. When you set up a flexible layout at the beginning, it will handle most of the adjustments for you. You might still need to make a few small changes, but your mobile design will be pretty much done. Any fine-tuning can happen later when you work on the interactive prototype, where you'll decide exactly how the tab bar should behave.

Well, you already know what a responsive interface is and why it is so important to make sure that all your layouts follow this principle. You have tested your views on various mobile presets, and you have also created and added a new scalable **Tab Bar** component to your library. Now that you've started diving into the topic, let's move on to a bigger task and scale your app interface to fit a tablet!

Adjusting the interface for tablets

In this section, you will take a step further and learn how to design your tablet app using ready-made Hi-Fi mock-ups for your mobile app. You'll discover optimal methods to adapt your design to much higher resolutions, ensuring it looks exceptional in all views, from the simplest to the most complex. This might sometimes involve reinventing the layout for better suitability.

In the previous section of the chapter, you saw how a fluid layout adapts to different mobile resolutions, so it was pretty easy to properly configure our interface for each smartphone model in the presets. But just because our interface can scale automatically doesn't mean it will look good on larger devices, such as an iPad, without additional adjustments. Want to see a practical example?

The following screenshot shows the **Login** screen of the app immediately after switching to the **iPad** preset, without additional changes to the originally existing interface design:

Figure 8.13 – Testing the Login view on an iPad

This is not what you want the user to see on the iPad, is it? Would you use an app that looks like this? Always ask yourself this question to deeply understand whether something is wrong with your design. Don't worry, in this section, you will learn about another concept of responsive design – namely, **breakpoints** – that can help you solve this problem.

Introducing breakpoints

As you already know, a fluid layout is great when working with similar devices that are only slightly different from each other. But when you decide to move to other platforms instead, you need to stop and think about how to optimize everything in a special way. A breakpoint is the width of the screen at which a crucial and explicit design change occurs, a real leap between different UI views.

So, to ensure that your design is perfect for every device and every platform, you'll create your first breakpoint, which is a parallel, yet separate, user interface specifically designed for tablet layouts. Obviously, unlike a fluid layout, a breakpoint actually doubles the layouts that need to be managed; therefore, it's important to set additional breakpoints only when needed. To decide how many breakpoints you need to have, refer to your UX research results, which should include the types of devices and platforms your product will run on.

It's time to scale our interface and make it as enjoyable for a tablet as it is for smartphone screens. The first thing to do is to duplicate all views. The best way to organize parallel flows is to create separate pages for each platform so you can name them appropriately. But now you may be using the free plan and, at the moment, you may have reached a maximum of three pages per file; therefore, this time, you can store everything on one **Hi-Fi** page. So, let's select and duplicate all four of our views. With multiple selections active, you can then click and drag the handles between frames and position them farther apart to make room for much wider interfaces, as shown in the following screenshot:

Figure 8.14 – Spacing the views

When you're done, select all of the screens and switch to a new frame preset by clicking **iPad Pro 11"** in the list of presets:

Figure 8.15 – Testing all the views on an iPad

If each element has the correct constraints and resizing rules, the preceding image (*Figure 8.15*) should represent the result you get. If an issue occurs, remain calm and identify the container frame that is misconfigured. Pay attention to the **Content Detail** view, which you almost completed independently as a learning exercise. Don't worry if this view is not the same as in the image; it will take much more time to remember the important steps regarding resizing and constraints aspects. The good news is that you can always fix it in a few clicks without breaking your work. Right now, you will understand how important it is to work with fluid layouts. If, for example, your **Content Detail** view has **Fixed** width settings and no constraints, it would look like the example on the right compared to the correct one on the left in the following screenshot:

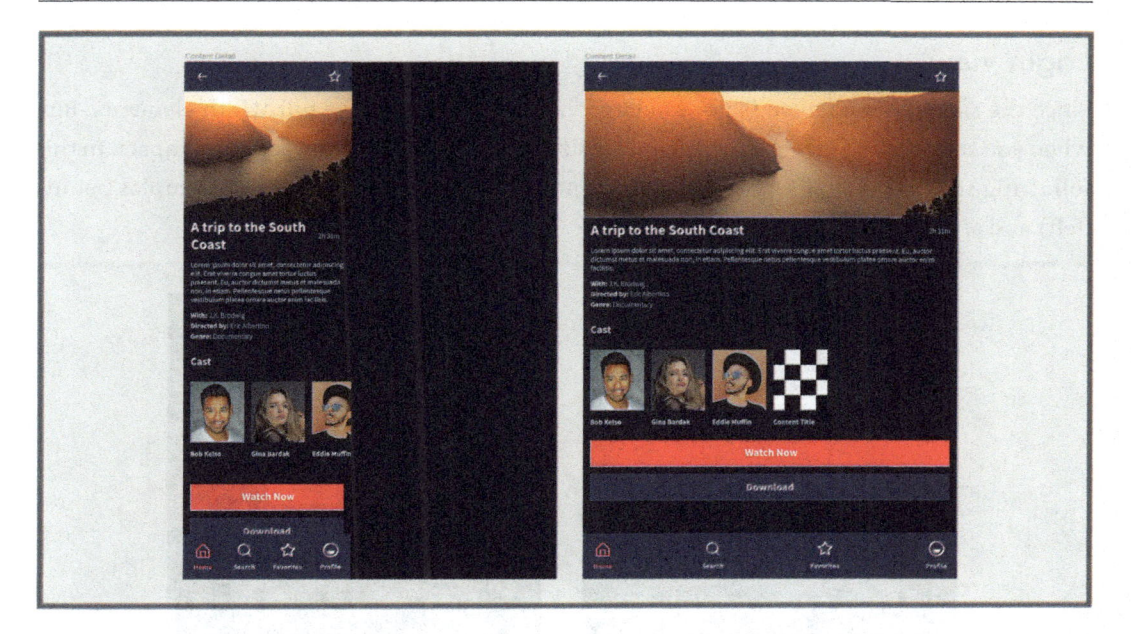

Figure 8.16 – Content Detail page without (left) and with (right) constraints

Take your time and make sure everything looks right. Keep calm if something doesn't work out at first. Check and fix all your **Auto layout** settings in the smartphone interface, and then duplicate and rescale the correct one to avoid any problems in the future.

When the base is ready, the next step is to decide what needs to be changed to improve the tablet layout. We'll examine, analyze, and address each screen separately.

Login view

Since the smartphone screen is not too large, it is convenient to use full-width elements. But when you start scaling this interface to tablet size, the elements should be more compact. In the following screenshot, you can see one of the possible redesign options with examples before (left) and after (right):

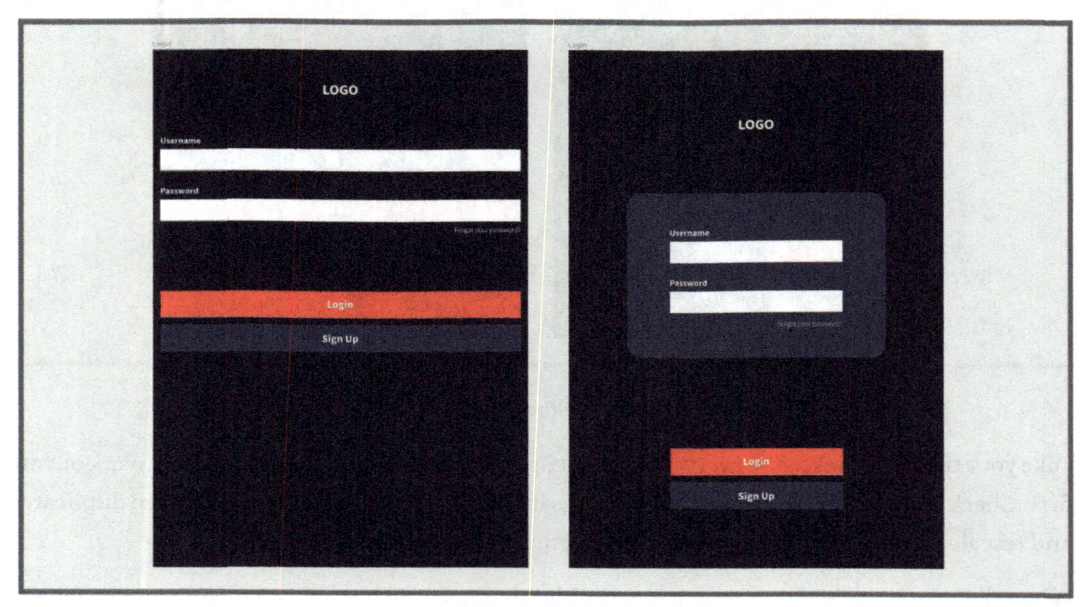

Figure 8.17 – Login view : fluid layout (left), redesign (right)

In the redesigned example, horizontal padding of **224 px** has been added to both text fields and buttons, so each element is better distributed over a larger space. In addition, a card has been added to make the form section even more compact and pleasant to the user.

Try to recreate the example breakpoint yourself. You don't have to go into the details; use the image as a guide and pay more attention to the **Auto layout**, **Constraints**, and **Resizing** settings.

> **Note:**
>
> When you're done, don't forget to test your interface by temporarily resizing it to make sure **Resizing** and **Constraints** are set correctly. For example, in this way, you may notice that **Button Group's Constraints** need to be changed to **Bottom**.

Chapter 8

Great, you've just created a breakpoint view for tablets! Now you know why this is needed when scaling up for a larger screen and what it might look like in reality. Let's move on to the **Sign Up** view.

Sign Up view

The **Sign Up** view has elements very similar to the **Login** frame, so the adjustments will be more or less the same. Here's a screenshot comparing the design before and after:

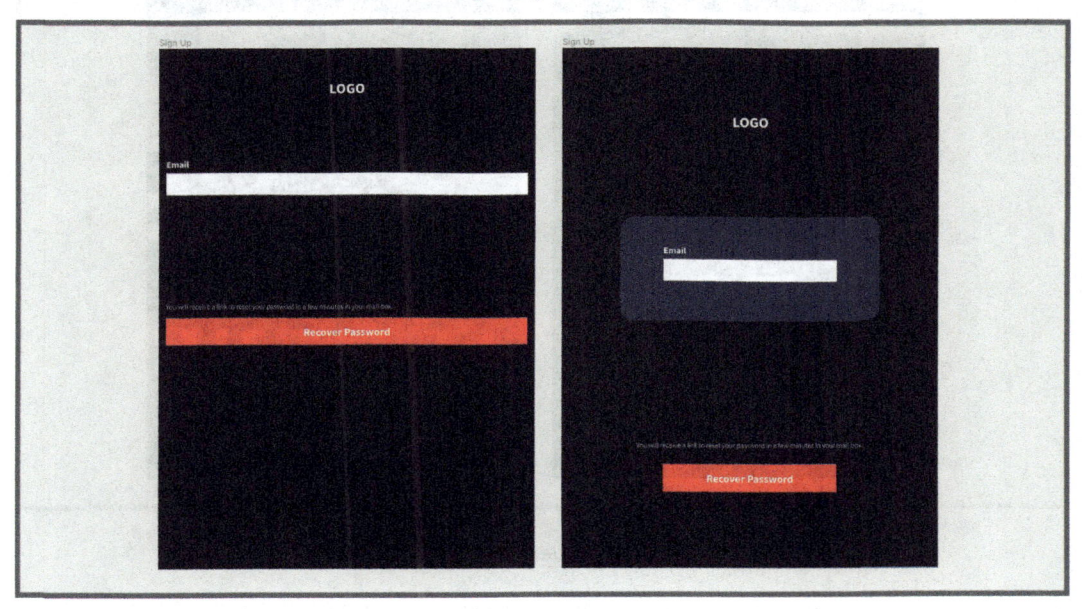

Figure 8.18 – Sign Up view | fluid layout (left), redesign (right)

Nothing fancy, but still way better than the unedited fluid version.

Again, follow this example to design the breakpoint view yourself. To be consistent, stick to the same values for padding, text field, and button width that you applied for the **Login** screen.

Home view

Unlike the two previous pages, the **Home** view requires more work as it has more complex elements, so you need to make the following changes:

- Change each carousel item's size to **700 px** (width) x **320 px** (height).

- Add more elements to the **Cards Row** component (on the **Styles + Components** page) to simulate the scrolling behavior.
- Add **horizontal** padding of **164 px** to the **Tab Bar** element.

Here is a comparison of the default scaling interface (left) and the configured one (right):

Figure 8.19 – Home view | fluid layout (left), redesign (right)

As you can see in the example on the right, the carousel is more impactful, there are enough items in the cards row to simulate scrolling, and the tab bar is more compact and accessible.

Before moving forward, there is an additional improvement you can make in your design. Now that you know how to simplify the process by creating complex nested components, it would be great and really helpful for what's coming next – to convert the top navigation to a component.

Chapter 8 241

To do this in the best way, follow these steps:

1. Go to the **Home** frame (smartphone) and select the **Top Navigation** frame:

Figure 8.20 – Selecting the Top Navigation layer

2. Copy the layer with *Command + C* (macOS) or *Ctrl + C* (Windows) and paste it with *Command + V* (macOS) or *Ctrl + V* (Windows) in the **Navigation** collection on the **Styles + Components** page.

3. Convert it to a component by clicking **Create component** or use the shortcut *Option + Cmd + K* (macOS) or *Ctrl + Alt + K* (Windows):

Figure 8.21 – Creating a Top Navigation component

4. Copy your new component.

5. Go back to the **Home** view (smartphone), select the **Top Navigation** layer, then right-click and choose **Paste to replace**:

Figure 8.22 – Paste to replace function

6. Repeat the last paste action on the top navigation bar in the tablet **Home** frame.

Great, you just created a more flexible view, and now, having **Top Navigation** as a component makes it easier and faster to make more complex changes.

Content Detail view

Now that you know the tricks and have practiced scaling up, you can also experiment with the **Content Detail** view, which is not too difficult to adjust correctly. For example, you can dedicate more space to the main poster image. Since the buttons are too wide as well, you can change the **Button Container** auto layout **Direction** to **Horizontal** so that both buttons are on the same row, as shown in the following screenshot:

Figure 8.23 – Content Detail view with fluid layout (left) and with a breakpoint redesign (right)

Note that in the preceding example, the positions of the **Download** and **Watch Now** buttons have been reversed because, in the case of multiple actions on the same line, users tend to consider the action on the right more as the main action leading to the next step. For most users, this direction of movement is natural, and the same concept applies to horizontal scrolling, where left leads backward and right leads forward.

Well, the adaptation of our interface for tablets is complete. As you may have noticed, only one specific iPad model was used for this, but since each layout is still fluid, the design will automatically adapt to all devices with similar screen sizes.

Also, only portrait mode was taken into account (that is, when you hold a tablet vertically), but it is also possible to customize the app for landscape mode if needed.

To summarize, you now have two parallel flows in your file: one for mobile and the other (which is a breakpoint) for tablets. There is one more set of layouts left to add, which targets browsers and the desktop. Since computers are fundamentally different devices than portable smartphones and tablets, this will be very different from what you have done so far. But since you already know the basics of responsive design, it shouldn't be too hard for you to complete this task, so let's get on with it!

Adjusting the interface for the web and desktop

In the previous section of the chapter, you crafted the tablet app interface, aiming for seamless integration with the mobile ecosystem. Now, it's time to take a stride toward larger screens, the desktop environment, and the vast world of web browsers. While web and desktop applications are distinct entities, the lines between them have blurred significantly in recent years. The evolution of scalable frameworks and programming languages has made it increasingly challenging to draw a definitive distinction between the two. So far, you have worked on the interface as if it were an application, but the application itself can be easily rendered in a browser and turned into a web application, with most of the functionality still present. Practical examples of this include platforms like YouTube, Facebook, and Twitter/X, which can be accessed from a smartphone, either through a browser or as their own standalone applications. These platforms are regularly used by many and demonstrate how an application's design can fluidly transition between web and mobile environments.

It is always efficient to work in a hybrid way since the final product will be scalable and available for any platform. Plus, modern browsers have evolved significantly and are capable of supporting even the most complex content. Think about Figma itself, available both on browsers and as a standalone app. Still, it's important to know that browsers are limited in some of the more integrated device features, such as personalized notifications or, trivially, the ability to use them offline, which is critical in some cases. Thus, from a design point of view, it is always important to remember that technologies must be selected initially and based on users' needs and product requirements.

So, for the current project, let's define that you need to deliver a native app design with a consistent web experience accessible directly from the browser – from desktop to mobile.

Scaling up to the web and desktop

Regardless of whether your application is launched on a large screen – in a web browser or in a standalone application – in both cases, the user experience will be very different from what you have seen so far. First, while on a computer, users typically exhibit a heightened level of concentration compared to their interactions with mobile devices. Moreover, it's essential to remember that most desktop and laptop computers do not have touchscreens, with touch-enabled systems being the exception rather than the rule. In these cases, users rely on the accuracy provided by a mouse or trackpad for their interactions. Also, the cursor can move through objects without any actual click/action, and that adds an extra state to the UI elements. This and more should be considered when setting up a design for desktop. But don't worry, this section will walk you through the process step by step with hands-on exercises and detailed explanations of each adjustment solution.

Before you start working on scaling, there are a few other things to consider. Until now, you have strictly respected your layout grid as there was not much horizontal space – especially on smartphones – and you needed to use it as efficiently as possible. On huge screens with large aspect ratios, this problem no longer occurs. Instead, you may even have the opposite problem – you have to distribute a small amount of content in a wide space at the risk of creating an unpleasant look. So, depending on the amount of content, you can use two different types of basic containers: fluid or fixed-width layout. You can see the grid difference between the two in the following screenshot:

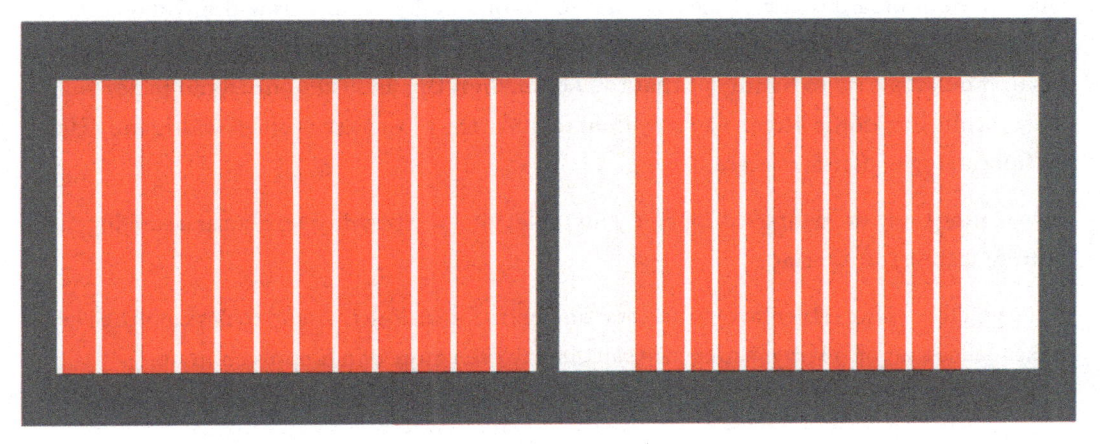

Figure 8.24 – Fluid (left) and fixed width (right) layout

You already know what **fluid** is, as you've followed this method so far by creating containers that scale content based on the size of the parent frame. The boxed type, very common on desktop websites, makes everything more compact so that the elements are not too far apart. Imagine browsing the website on a 65-inch TV. It would be an incredibly large interface. Here's what happens to our app's **Login** page if you enlarge it to a similar resolution with a fluid layout:

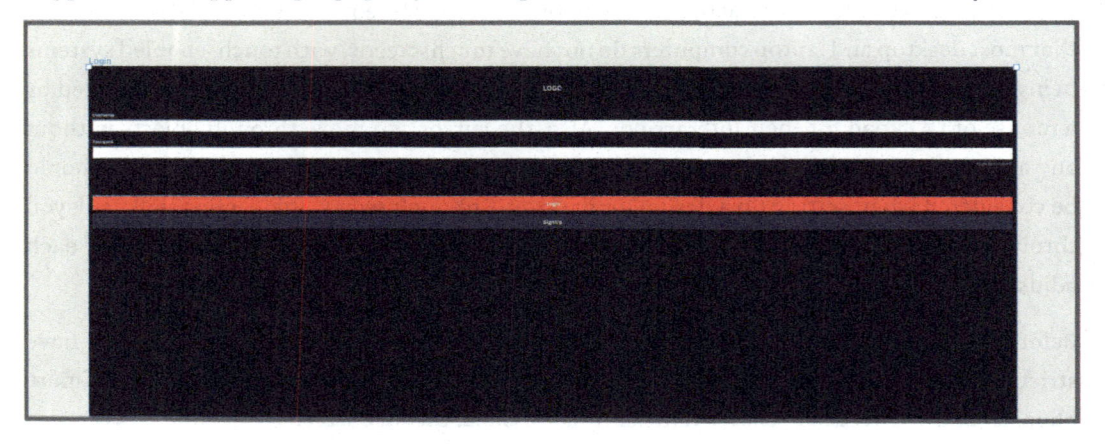

Figure 8.25 – Scaling our Login view on a TV

It is impossible to imagine a worse interface for this page, right? But you can fix this by setting a fixed-size container inside the frame. For example, you can set up an inner container of 960 px, which is the standard width of the base size for a computer screen. This width will remain the same regardless of the monitor size, and the content will always be compact and centered. With this in mind, it's easy to figure out that the **Login**, **Sign Up**, and **Content Detail** pages will be boxed, while our **Home** screen can stay fluid to make the most of the screen width and display the full catalog of digital content.

Once scaling types are defined, duplicate your tablet views – you will use them as a starting point for fully scaling the interface.

While you'll be using tablet layouts as a starting point for scaling them up to desktop/the web, it makes sense that on a larger screen, we can display even more of our app's content.

Follow these steps to find out how best to do this:

1. Select the **Login** frame and, in the **Frame** presets list, this time, you can select **Desktop (1440 X 1024 pixels)**.

To work better with boxed layouts, you can also create a new layout grid style by setting **Type** to **Center** and doing some math to get a 996-pixel grid. You will learn about some helpful resources that can help you to make the process easier in *Chapter 12, Discovering Resources, Plugins, and Widgets in the Figma Community*.

> **Note:**
>
> Every value field in Figma supports math operations. This is incredibly handy because you can, for example, calculate the width in the layout grid properties by entering `996/12 - (gutter value)`.

By now, you should know how to properly configure the elements in the interface, so use this section as an additional exercise on scaling. On the desktop/web interface, you have a lot more room to use, so you can certainly add more elements to the composition to make it look less empty and visually better. Just remember not to radically change the entire structure as it is necessary to keep things reusable. For reference, you can use the following screenshot where an additional side image was added on the **Login** page:

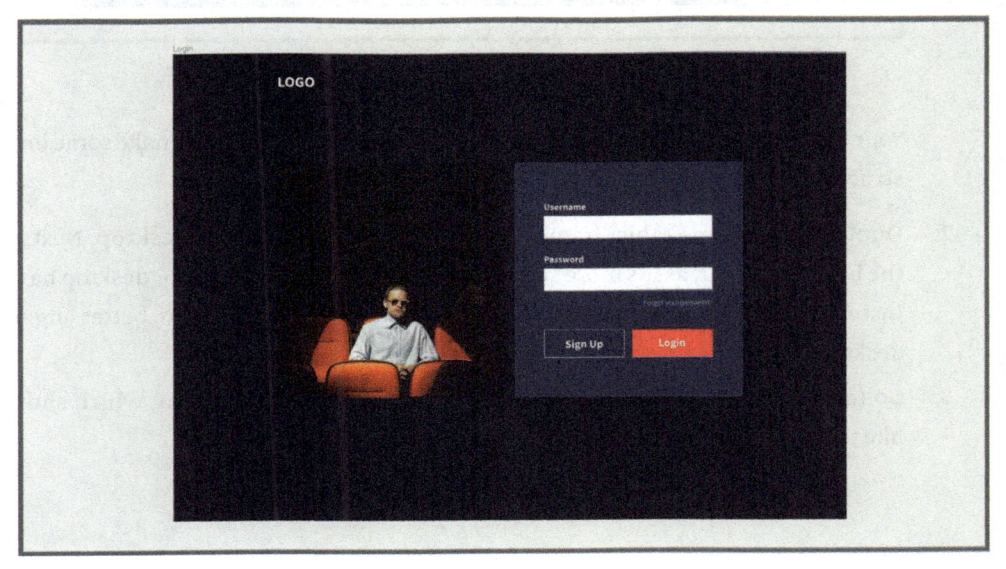

Figure 8.26 – Redesigned Login view for desktop (photo by Gabriele Stravinskaite on Unsplash)

Of course, this is just one of the many possible design options for this page. So, feel free to play with this view as much as you like and customize it your way. Just keep in mind that all of your pages must be consistent and have the same styling, so here is what the **Sign Up** page might look like if it had a structure like the **Login** view example:

Figure 8.27 – Redesigned Sign Up view for desktop

Your next task is to work on the **Home** view, where you will need to make some important structural changes.

2. Duplicate the **Home** tablet frame and swap the **Frame** preset to **Desktop**. Next, remove the bottom tab bar, as it's more suited for mobile and not relevant for desktop navigation. Instead, we'll shift our focus to crafting a redesigned top navigation, better aligned with desktop usability.

3. Go to the **Styles + Components** page and create a new component, which should look like the following screenshot:

Figure 8.28 – Creating a desktop Top Navigation component

If you have any difficulties creating a new **Top Navigation** component, here are some tips:

- You can start by duplicating the mobile **Top Navigation** component and building a new one from it. This ensures that any possible future changes you may make to the mobile navigation will automatically be applied to this new element as well.
- The red circle you see in the preceding screenshot represents a placeholder for the current user profile picture.
- The main frame's **Gap between items** must be set to **Auto** so that when you scale, each element will have its own position. In addition, the **Search** and **Profile** icons must be on the same side, next to each other, so they need to be framed together.

1. When you are satisfied with the result, select the element, rename it to `Top Navigation - Desktop` to distinguish it from mobile, and click on **Create component**.
2. Now, on the **Hi-Fi** page, go back to the desktop **Home** view and select the current **Top Navigation** layer.

3. With the selection active, click the component name in the right panel. This action will open the **Swap component** dialog box, and from there, simply select **Top Navigation - Desktop** to instantly replace it:

Figure 8.29 – Swapping components

Done! As a result, you should have a nice **Home** screen desktop version of our interface, as in the following screenshot:

Figure 8.30 – Redesigned Home view for desktop

Chapter 8 251

> **Note:**
> To swiftly add images to all your interface cards, just press *Command + Shift + K* (macOS) or *Ctrl + Shift + K* (Windows) to open the dialog. Select your images, click **Open**, and then easily insert them into each field by clicking.

Let's move on to the last view, the **Content Detail** page. Since it contains less information, a fluid layout might not be as effective. However, consistently alternating between fluid and fixed layouts between the **Home** screen and **Content Detail** view can be impractical. The optimal approach here is to create a hybrid page. This involves encasing **Content Detail** in a type of invisible card, providing a seamless transition in layout design. The appearance of this hybrid layout is demonstrated in the following screenshot:

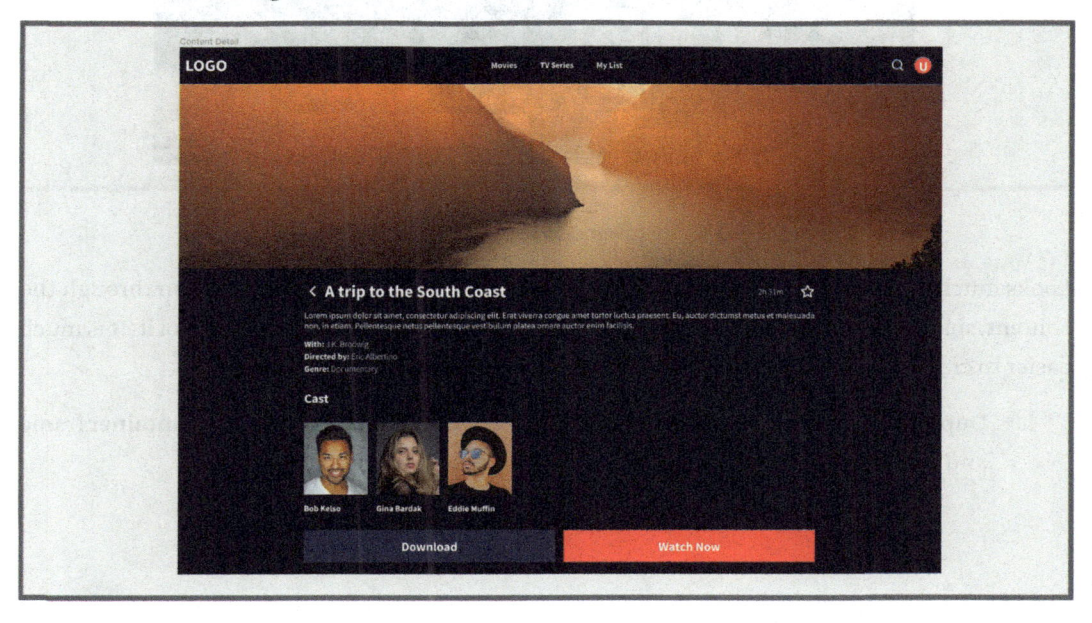

Figure 8.31 – Redesigned Content Detail view for desktop

It makes sense (remember to insert navigation back and the ability to add content to favorites in this view), but it could still be improved.

For example, you can present **Content Detail** as a modal dialog that opens directly on top of the **Home** view, blurring the content behind it:

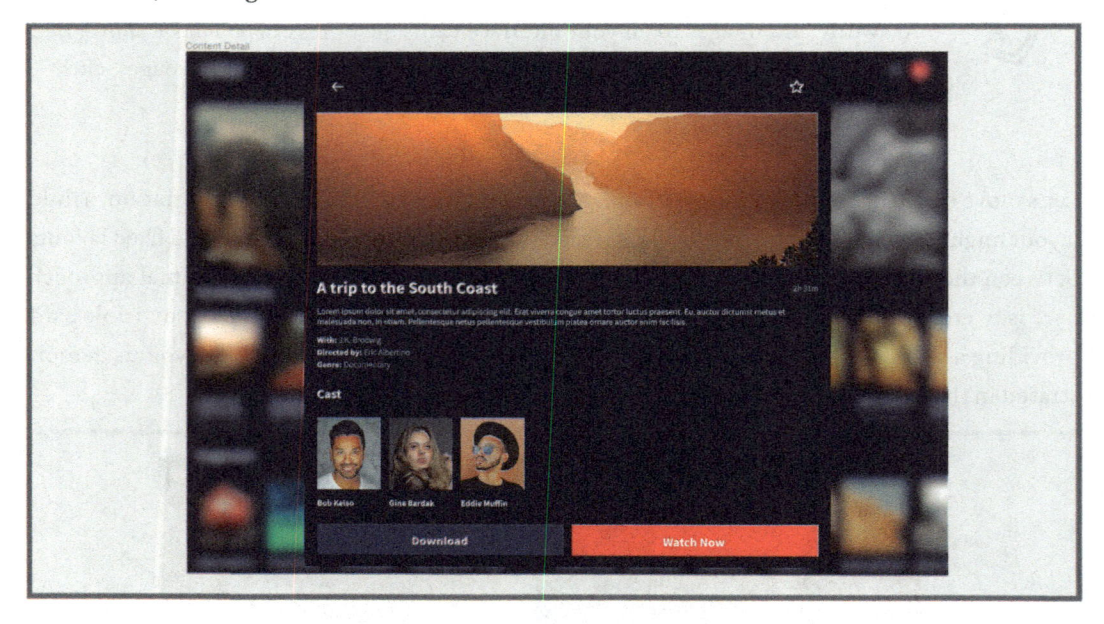

Figure 8.32 – Improved Content Detail view for desktop

Looks much more interesting, doesn't it? Moreover, it greatly speeds up navigation through the content, since the user always stays in the **Home** view and opens the dialog on top of it. It is much easier to create such a structure than you might imagine. Follow these steps:

1. Duplicate your **Home** view, rename it to Content Detail, then select the **Container** frame and add a **Layer blur** effect to it, changing its value to **22**:

Chapter 8

Figure 8.33 – Adding Layer blur to the inner container

2. Select the **Container** frame in the tablet **Content Detail** view and copy and paste it into the newly created **Content Detail** desktop frame.
3. Add a **Secondary** style as a background color to it, bring the **Image Poster** here as well, and add a **Top Bar** for the **Back** and **Add to Favorites** elements. Remember to set both **Constraints** to **Center** so that when you scale the interface, the popup stays exactly in the center of the page.

It's completely up to you whether you stick with the simpler, hybrid-styled **Content Detail** page or try something more advanced. Feel free to experiment and you may eventually come up with your own solution.

Polishing details

In this chapter, you've added numerous new views, and they're all sharing the same page, potentially causing clutter in your workspace. This might be problematic if you haven't had the chance to organize and group these frames. If you're using one of Figma's paid plans, you can consider placing the high-fidelity frames for each platform on separate pages. However, regardless of your plan, a fantastic method to maintain clarity is to assign appropriate names to each frame.

Let's start with your smartphone mock-ups. Go to these frames and rename them by adding `Mobile` to the name, for example, `Login - Mobile`, `Sign Up - Mobile`, and so on. You can do this faster by selecting All Frames and using the keyboard shortcut *Command + R* (macOS) or *Ctrl + R* (Windows), which will launch the **Rename Layers Modal** window, allowing you to rename multiple layers at once. There are many options for renaming layers, but for this specific purpose, you need to first click the **Current name** button and then type `- Mobile`. In the same way, you can add `Tablet` to the tablet frames and `Desktop` to the desktop frames. Try to keep them visually separate in your working area, and stick to the correct order of the views, as shown in the following screenshot:

Figure 8.34 – Overview of the workspace

Note:

To keep your file neat on a single page, consider using sections. Group your mobile, tablet, and desktop frames in separate sections and use distinct colors for clear differentiation.

Chapter 8   255

So, the base of the application interface for the different platforms is finally complete. As you can imagine, if you are going to design and structure a complete application with every required page, the flow can instantly become much larger and more complex, so organizing it, renaming each layer, and keeping your workspace clean are very important.

For even smarter organization, you can make each file more recognizable at a glance among all your files in the Figma welcome screen. To do this, you can set a thumbnail using any frame in the file or by creating a new one for this purpose. Let's set up a thumbnail for our file. To do this, you can right-click the **Home - Desktop** frame and select **Set as thumbnail**:

Figure 8.35 – Setting a file thumbnail

Now, open Figma's **Home**, and you should see the frame image you just selected to preview the file:

Figure 8.36 – Thumbnail result

If you wish, you can create a new frame with a design for a suitable cover image to make it even nicer and more recognizable. Remember to set the frame's dimensions to 1600 x 960 pixels for optimal display. It might happen that the installed thumbnail doesn't show up immediately. In that case, simply close and reopen your current file to clear the cache and update the thumbnail view.

Well, adjusting the interface for desktop and the web was pretty tricky, wasn't it? And now you can understand why it is set aside from applications for mobile devices and tablets, which means that it requires a more thorough analysis. As you can see, you even had to rethink the anatomy of one of the pages and make it a hybrid or even a dialog. In addition, you always need to redesign the navigation for the web due to the different ways of interacting with the computer. Again, it's okay if you made some mistakes or didn't fully understand something; you always have the opportunity to come back to the difficult points and try again. Plus, the more you get into design, the more you pay attention to details while using your smartphone, laptop, or any other device. So, give yourself time, and those tasks that seemed difficult to you will not be so after a while!

Summary

Responsive design is one of the principles that a designer must always stick to when working on any interface. An app or website you create might have a great user experience and a stunning user interface, but if it's not properly adapted for all the resolutions and devices it needs to run on, your good work will be diminished all at once. In this chapter, you have done everything to prevent this from happening with your application. You have completed your mobile app interface by creating additional reusable components and making sure all layouts are fluid by testing the views in different smartphone presets. Also, you have adjusted the design of your app for tablets by redesigning a couple of views specifically for this platform (that is, creating a breakpoint), so now you know when and why it is worth doing it. Finally, you've learned how to scale the interface correctly for desktop and the web while maintaining the harmonious and consistent look of your designs across all platforms. It was a lot of work, but you successfully completed all the tasks!

So now that you have a static user interface for multiple platforms, you might be wondering what comes next. You can be sure that the next stage of the design will be just as fun and interesting because you are going to make everything dynamic! If you're thinking about prototyping, the functionality that Figma has turned into pure magic, well done! You will soon learn how to make your components interactive and also bring all your views to life, by creating a dynamic flow with smooth transitions between screens and cool animations of some elements in your layouts. You will explore this, and much more, in the next chapter, after which you may even feel like a wizard!

Learn more on Discord

To join the Discord community for this book – where you can share feedback, ask questions to the author, and learn about new releases – follow the QR code below:

`https://packt.link/figma`

Part 3
Prototyping and Sharing

In this final part, you will make your prototype live and interactive by using triggers, transitions, and interactive components. You will also learn how to test, publish, view, and export your project. You will also get an opportunity to go advanced with Variables and Conditional Prototyping.

This part comprises the following chapters:

- *Chapter 9, Prototyping with Transitions, Smart Animate, and Interactive Components*
- *Chapter 10, Testing and Sharing Your Prototype in Browsers and Real Devices*
- *Chapter 11, Exporting Assets and Managing the Handover Process*
- *Chapter 12, Discovering Resources, Plugins, and Widgets in the Figma Community*
- *Chapter 13, Going Advanced with Variables and Conditional Prototyping*

9

Prototyping with Transitions, Smart Animate, and Interactive Components

In the previous chapter, you adapted the design of your app for tablets and desktops, making it responsive, which was a big step forward. Now, on your **Hi-Fi** page, you have not one but three beautiful flows, and you may be wondering what comes next. This is the ideal moment to dive into prototyping, a significant and engaging phase in a designer's workflow. Think of this as you needing to package what you just created in order to present it in the most impressive way possible. However, you should also keep in mind that prototyping can be very helpful not only for others but also for you. It often happens that while building an interactive flow or seeing it in action, you realize that you need to fix something. Don't worry if this ever happens; this is completely normal, as designing is not a linear process.

In this chapter, you'll explore the essential prototyping features available in Figma and learn how to apply them to your interface. While Figma offers a wide range of prototyping tools, we'll begin with the basics and gradually progress to the more advanced features. You will find that creating a dynamic flow with impressive animations and cool tricks behind the scenes is a very exciting journey, and the results can be amazing! As before, in this chapter, you will find guides on how to best implement some of the techniques in your interface, as well as suggestions and ideas for self-practice. It might sound challenging but with everything you've learned about Figma, it will be as fun as it is useful for you!

In this chapter, we are going to cover the following main topics:

- Mastering transitions and triggers
- Animating with smart animate
- Structuring interactive components
- Creating interactive overflows and overlays

Mastering transitions and triggers

We have reached the point where we can say that the main interface design of our product is complete, and even from the static layouts, it is very clear what our application is about. However, the design is not complete yet, as there is still some work to be done. In this section of the chapter, you will take the first step into a new stage of your workflow. Before we dive into this new topic, let's summarize what you should have in your design file so far.

First things first, you should have a flow for a mobile app that contains four views – **Login**, **Sign Up**, **Home**, and **Content Detail** – plus two more parallel flows for tablet and desktop, the interface you have created by redesigning and scaling your screens for smartphones. Of course, we didn't create all the views that such applications might actually contain, as some of the design steps would take longer to be fully ready for development, but it was a great start that allowed you to learn about and practice basic and advanced Figma tools and features.

When you work on real projects, you will have to devote much more time to the UX phase and, possibly, come back to it more than once in order to dive deeper into analysis and research, especially if the product is more complex. Therefore, the whole process of designing a real application may not be as smooth and purely phased as the current one, and it will take a lot more effort to get to the prototyping stage. However, suppose the static design you have now is approved, and we can go further and make the interface come alive with **transitions** and **triggers** for a start. You are already quite familiar with the functionality of the **Design** tab in the right sidebar, which allows you to edit the visual part of the interface. In this chapter, you will discover the **Prototype** tab, which is also in the right sidebar, as shown in the following screenshot:

Figure 9.1 – The Prototype tab

If you open the **Prototype** tab without selecting any items on the canvas, you will see general prototyping settings for the current file. In this section, we'll start with the basic prototyping functions, namely transitions, which allow you to switch from one frame to another, making the navigation more life-like.

Moving between frames with transitions

Our interface views for different platforms are currently standalone, lacking any connections or interactive elements. In *Chapter 2, Structuring Moodboards, Personas, and User Flows within FigJam*, you built the user flow in FigJam and stuck strictly to it until now, but the app layouts themselves are static, therefore, they do not successfully simulate a flow of a real application.

What you need to do now to get one step closer to an interactive prototype is to connect views to show Figma which paths users can follow and how they should actually proceed. This is what you will use transitions for.

Let's begin by selecting the **Login - Mobile** view – obviously, this will be your starting point and the very first user step when the application is launched for the very first time.

Then, switch the tab from **Design** to **Prototype** in the right sidebar.

Figure 9.2 – Prototype options for the selected frame

You will see that with an active selection, the context in the **Prototype** tab has now changed. You can no longer find editable properties of forms and texts like in the **Design** tab, but a number of settings dealing with flows and user interactions. What's more, you may have noticed that there are some changes to your canvas now – a new indicator, a small round marker that appears in the middle of your chosen frame, to the right of it. It's called a **hotspot**, and it's thanks to this handle that you can implement your first frame-to-frame transitions in a few clicks.

Click and hold the hotspot, then drag it into the **Sign Up - Mobile** view to draw a connector that links the two views, from the source where the hotspot is located to the destination:

Figure 9.3 – Creating a connector

This way, you can be sure that after performing an action in the **Login** view, the user can navigate to the **Sign Up** view, which sounds logical. But don't you think that there is still something wrong with that? In fact, you don't want the entire **Login** view to generate the transmitting action, but only a part of it, or rather a specific element, which is the button. So, if instead of clicking on the entire **Login - Mobile** view, you only select the **Sign Up** button, you will see that it now has a hotspot as long as the **Prototype** tab is open. Each element (as long as it is inside a frame) has a hotspot, no matter whether it is nested or external.

Since the **Sign Up** button will take the user to the appropriate view, you can remove your previously made connector by clicking it and simply pressing the *Backspace* or *Delete* key. Then, set the right transition by selecting the **Sign Up** button in **Prototype** mode and creating a connector to the **Sign Up - Mobile** view, as shown in the following screenshot:

Figure 9.4 – Connecting the Sign Up button

Great, you've just made the **Sign Up** button element interactive by linking it to another view! Immediately after this action, near the right sidebar, a dialog window will automatically open, which displays the default configurations for the newly created connection, as you see in the preceding screenshot.

Right now, you have an interaction that is triggered **On click/On tap**, which means that you will need to click or touch an item, and this allows you to navigate to the destination page – in this case, the **Sign Up - Mobile** one. That's enough to get the flow working, and you'll see exactly what it looks like when you play the prototype by clicking the **Play** button in the top bar (in the next chapter, you will learn more about this function).

Another important option that you can see in the same dialog is **Animation**. By default, it is set to **Instant**, which means that after you click the button, you will immediately switch to the **Sign Up - Mobile** view without any transitions or animations. In many applications, this is actually the default behavior for navigating between views, but in certain cases, such as when using the native iOS development framework, you may want to move between views with right-to-left or left-to-right navigation, depending on the direction of flow.

Let's try to change the **Animation** parameter. Whenever you switch to **Prototype** mode by selecting the corresponding tab, you will see all the connectors on the canvas that you previously configured for your elements.

Chapter 9

This means that you can access the interaction parameters of any element by simply selecting any connector that you might want to edit. So, now select the one you created, and all the options will immediately be visible again. Click the **Animation** drop-down list:

Figure 9.5 – The Animation drop-down list

Aside from **Instant**, there is a huge list of different **Animation** options available: **Dissolve** is a subtle and smooth transition where elements gradually fade into each other, creating a seamless shift between views; **Smart animate**, on the other hand, is something more complex but powerful, and you will explore it in detail later in this chapter. Next, you can see the **Move**, **Push**, and **Slide** animations block. To better understand each of them, here's an illustrative example:

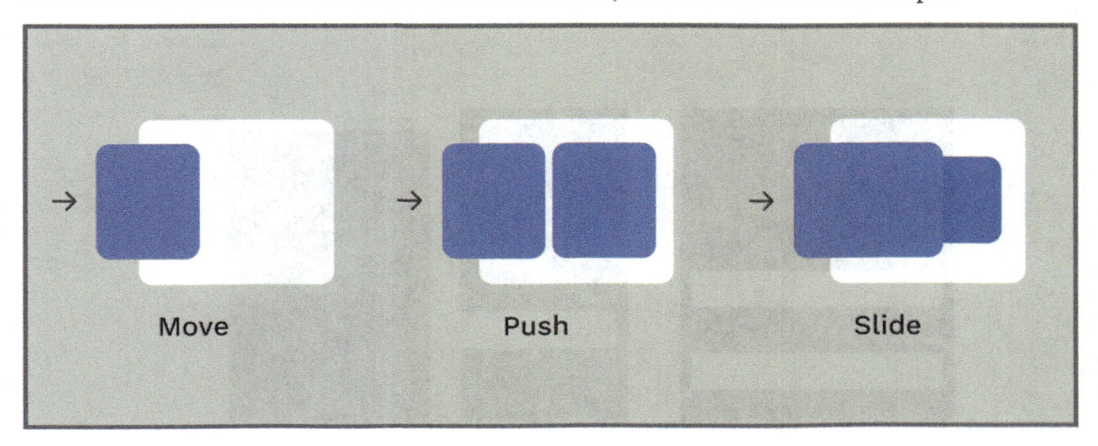

Figure 9.6 – Move, Push, and Slide animations

Using these different transition types allows you to give the user a better idea of how the flow is occurring, or to simulate some specific behavior such as dialogs or activity views. Now select your connector and try changing **Animation** from **Instant** to **Move in**, and once you do, many new additional settings will appear, as shown below:

Figure 9.7 – Animating the Sign Up transition

As you can see, here, you can adjust the **Direction** and **Timing** parameters for **Animation**. To add more depth, the **Ease** options allow you to refine transitions by controlling their acceleration, much like the changing speed of a thrown ball due to gravity and air resistance. These settings apply physics principles to make animations feel more natural and engaging:

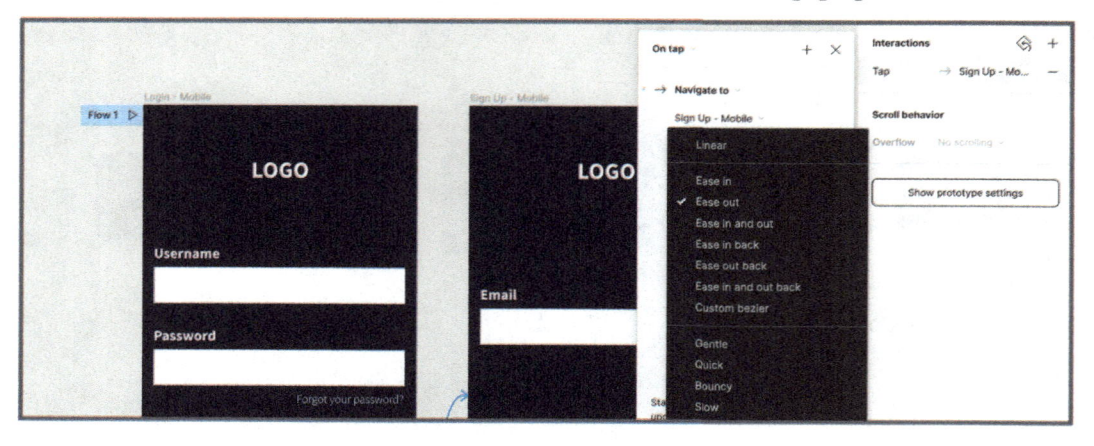

Figure 9.8 – Animation's Ease options

If you want to go even further, instead of **Ease** parameters, you can create an animation in **Custom Spring** mode, which gives you many additional options for manually creating your own easing curves by setting the **Time** and **Speed** values:

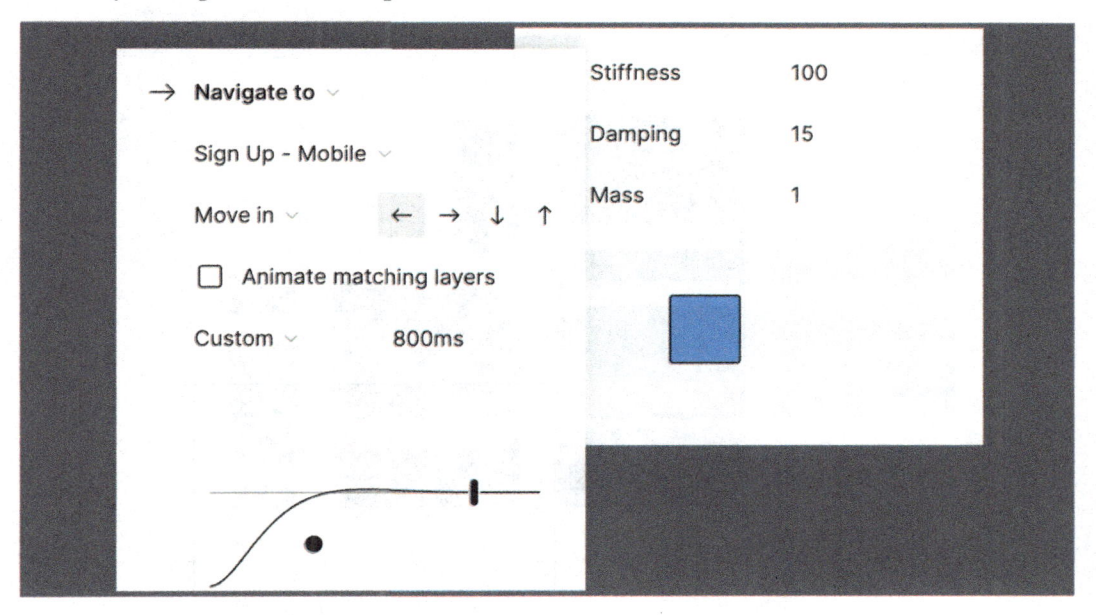

Figure 9.9 – Custom easing

> **Note:**
> The small preview window right below the graph editor is a cool and quick way to check what your animation looks like without even launching your prototype. You just need to hover over it to see it live.

We'll keep it simple for our app and use mostly **Instant** transitions, but if you want to test out all the different ways to animate your frames, feel free to do so.

Let's connect all the views together by following these steps:

1. Make the transition from the **Login** button to the **Home** view as shown in the following screenshot:

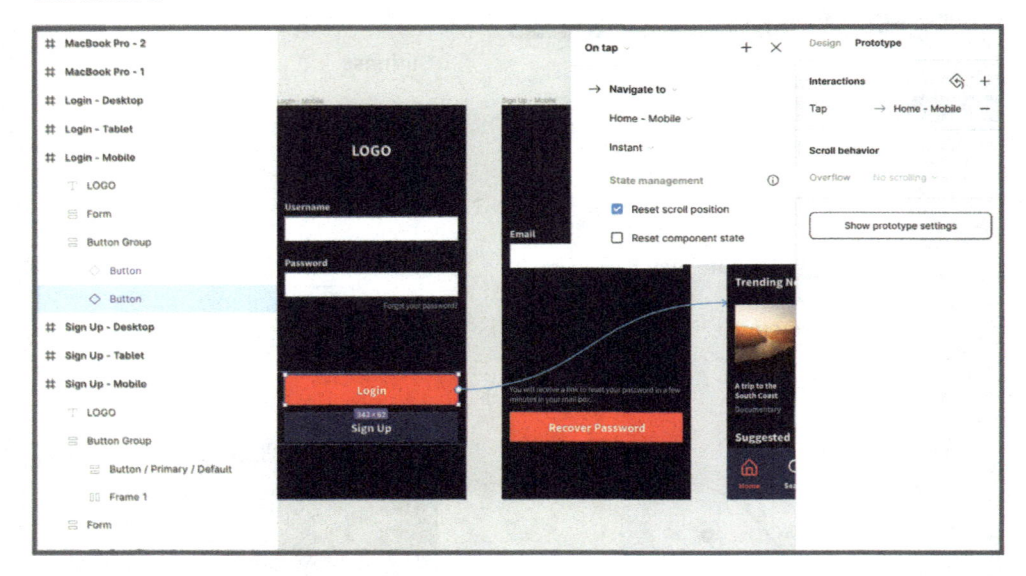

Figure 9.10 – Connecting the Login button to the Home view

2. Connect the **Recover Password** button in the **Sign Up** view to the **Login** view, then change **Animation** to **Move out** and **Direction** to **Down**. Thus, you simulate confirmation of the end of the password recovery process, after which the current view is discarded, returning the user to the **Login - Mobile** page:

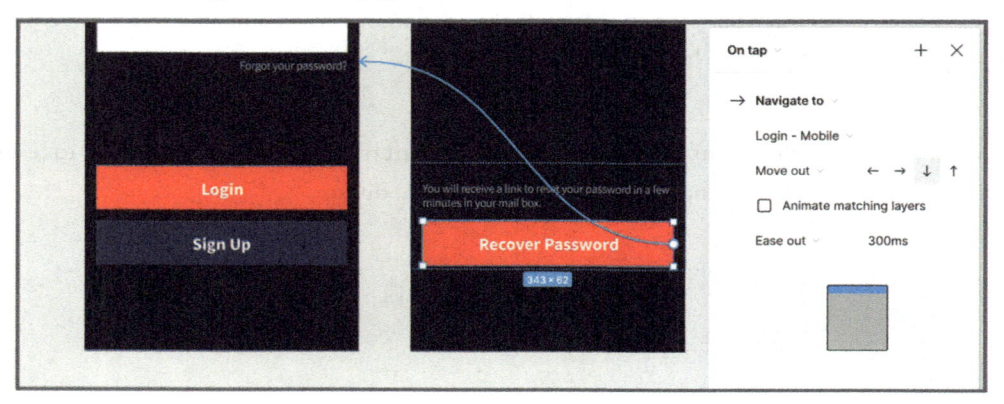

Figure 9.11 – Connecting the Recover Password button

3. Finally, in the **Home - Mobile** view, choose one of the individual content cards, rather than selecting the entire frame. Next, link this selected content cards to the **Content Detail - Mobile** page.

> **Note:**
>
> To select an inner element more efficiently, hold down the *Cmd* key (on macOS) or the *Ctrl* key (on Windows) and click the element. This method bypasses the need for multiple double-clicks, streamlining your selection process.

Figure 9.12 – Connecting a single Content Card to the Content Detail view

Great! Now all your views are connected, and you have your first flow, so you have already completed the first iteration of the interactive and usable prototype that you will very soon see in action. It was quite fast and easy, right? Later, in the *Structuring interactive components* section of this chapter, you will continue to work on this with a few more details, but before moving on, repeat the same steps for the tablet and desktop interfaces, creating similar flows.

Exploring triggers

Having mastered frame transitions, this section introduces you to triggers in Figma. While you're familiar with the basic **On click/On tap** trigger, there's a wealth of other interactive possibilities to explore.

You will get many completely different results using triggers, but first, let's get to know all of the ones available in Figma and how you can activate actions/animations on elements. So, click on the **Login** button connector and then open the drop-down list of available triggers by selecting the current option, namely **On click/On tap**:

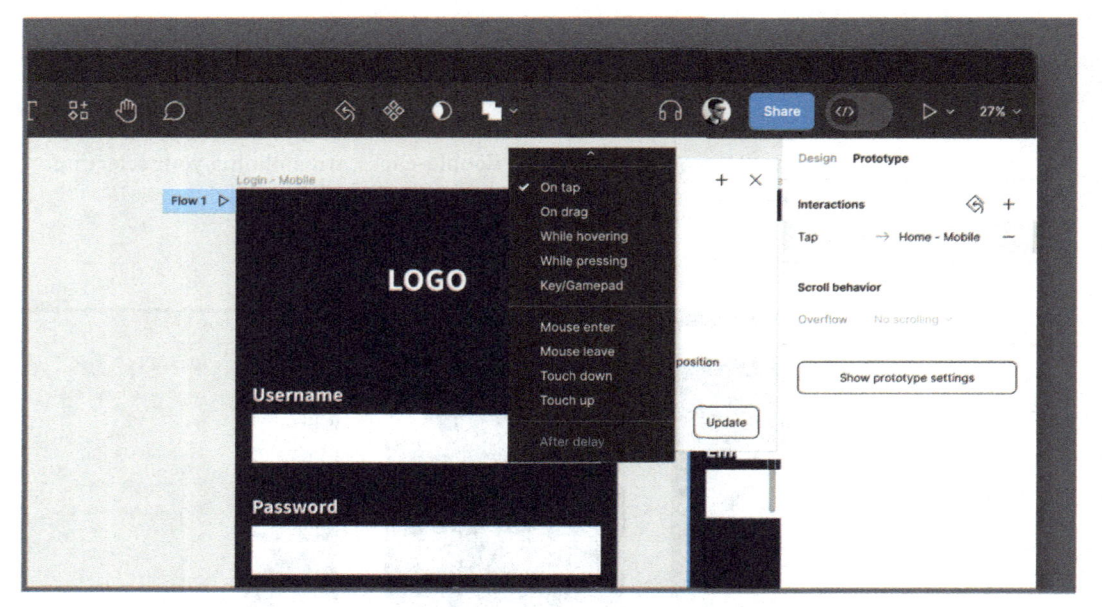

Figure 9.13 – List of available triggers

In this drop-down list, you can see a whole new set of ways in which your elements can interact. Let's take a closer look at each of the triggers to better understand the difference between them in the following sections:

On click/On tap

The default action, triggered by either a click or a tap, launches a response upon interacting with an element. This action covers both mouse cursor and touch input, with the specific input method displayed depending on the device chosen in the overall prototype options.

On drag

Once this trigger is set, the interaction begins when the user clicks and drags the selected item. This is the right trigger to use if you need to simulate behavior such as sliders, drawers, or any slide gesture. It works best in combination with the smart animate features, which you'll learn about in the next section of this chapter.

While hovering

This option triggers an action while the user's mouse hovers over a hotspot, so as soon as the cursor leaves it, the user will return to the previous state. You could see this interaction in tooltips, image previews, and more, but remember that like any hover action, it is not supported on touchscreens.

While pressing

In this case, the user initiates the interaction by clicking (with the mouse) and holding, or by touching and holding on a touchscreen device. This option is useful for simulating reactions like those in social media apps, or accessing specific settings/menus. Similar to the **While hovering** trigger, this one returns you to the previous state once you release the mouse click or lift your finger from the screen.

Key/Gamepad

This trigger is very special and powerful, although an underrated one. In fact, it allows you to associate an action with a specific key on your keyboard or with a key combination (for example, Press *A* to continue). Moreover, it is possible to use gamepads (Xbox One, PS4, and Nintendo Switch Pro controllers are officially supported, but other generic pads may work fine as well) and associate actions with their keys. With this feature, you can prototype not only applications designed for consoles (see, for example, streaming services also available on PlayStation and Xbox) but even games!

Mouse enter/Mouse leave

These actions are used for interactions triggered by the mouse cursor moving into or out of a specific area. **Mouse enter** activates when the cursor enters a targeted area, while **Mouse leave** is triggered as the cursor exits. They are separate triggers and, unlike **While hovering** and **While pressing**, they do not automatically return the interface to its previous state after the interaction.

Mouse down/Mouse up

These triggers are associated with the start and end of a mouse click or screen touch. **Mouse down** is activated at the beginning of the click or touch, and **Mouse up** is triggered when the click is released or the touch ends. This enables distinct interactions at the start and end of a user's click or touch action.

After delay

This trigger functions like a timer, initiating an interaction once a set delay period ends. It's a tool to be used judiciously; excessive use can cause your prototype to auto-play, which may not always be desired. Typically applied to top-level frames, it's great for simulating situations like an app's splash screen. An interesting use of the **After delay** trigger is in simulating animation frames using the same object with **Smart Animate**, such as creating the effect of a spinning progress indicator. This adds a dynamic, animated aspect to your prototype, showcasing potential motion and interactivity.

These are triggers that you can use to make your design not only dynamic but also simulate maximum interaction with a real product. It is very important to remember all possible user actions with your design elements and reflect them in the interactive prototype. Now that you know what transitions and triggers are in Figma, it shouldn't be difficult for you to quickly build an interactive flow and make it pretty convincing with just these functions. But still, there is one more thing that can make your prototypes even more outstanding, and this is such a huge and interesting topic: smart animate. Let's dive into this!

Animating with smart animate

In this section, you'll dive into **smart animate**, a feature that's initially easy to use but requires practice to fully harness. Its versatility and the range of creative possibilities demand a nuanced understanding of animation concepts like timing, sequence, and layer dynamics. A well-organized workspace with correctly named layers is vital. Initially, you'll test **smart animate** on separate frames to avoid issues. Beyond the exercises in this section, personal experimentation is key, as it is a vast topic. With enough practice, you'll uncover new ways to use this powerful feature. Once confident, you can then integrate **Smart Animate** interactions into your current project as appropriate.

What is smart animate?

All of the animations and transitions you've seen so far are excellent and effective prototyping tools of all kinds. However, in some cases, it may happen that you have to simulate the more complex behavior of your elements, which is not like anything that is present in Figma presets. This is where smart animate comes in.

With smart animate, you can easily create your own animations by specifying starting and ending points, and Figma takes care of the rest. What smart animate does behind the scenes is keep track of the layer names and hierarchy of elements that need to be animated and, if there is a match between the start frame and end frame, it will handle the transition between them as best as possible.

Let's take a look at a practical example to better understand how this works. In our current interface, in the **Home - Mobile** view, we have a tab bar and top navigation that can guide the user to other views. In those target views, the tab bar and top navigation will still keep the same position. If you set the **Move in** transition from the **Home** view to the **Search** view, and then take a hypothetical snapshot in the middle of that transition, you get the following:

Figure 9.14 – Overlapping two views

The target screen will overlap the entire **Home** view, whether it contains the same elements or not, which would be bad practice, not at all like a real application. You can fix this very simply by leaving the **Move in** effect but enabling **Animate matching layers**.

It is a minor version of smart animate that can be embedded directly in all other animation methods, as shown in the following screenshot:

Figure 9.15 – Using smart animate with a Move in animation

With **Animate matching layers** enabled, the animation will run as normal, except that each matching layer in two views, such as the tab bar and top navigation, will stay in place without switching between views. In other words, Figma recognizes the matching layers within two views, then determines what has changed and applies the appropriate animation between the frames.

Smart animate can be applied both to entire elements and components and individual layers inside a component or group. Of course, the full functionality of smart animate doesn't end there. There are many other aspects that it can dynamically change, such as **Position**, **Scale**, **Opacity**, **Fill**, and **Rotation**, and this will be the next thing for you to learn about with a few visual examples.

Getting advanced with smart animate

Imagine creating complex animations in your interactive prototype for elements like sliders, swipeable cards, and interactive graphics. This may sound challenging, but smart animate greatly simplifies it. Consider animating a toggle known to have **OFF** and **ON** states. Begin by crafting a frame with a styled toggle element, such as a circle and a rounded rectangle, as shown in the example below. Next, duplicate this frame, ensuring the inner layers have the same names for animation coherence. The parent frame's name can vary. Finally, adjust the duplicate to depict the **ON** state by repositioning the circle and changing its color, following the screenshot example if needed:

Chapter 9

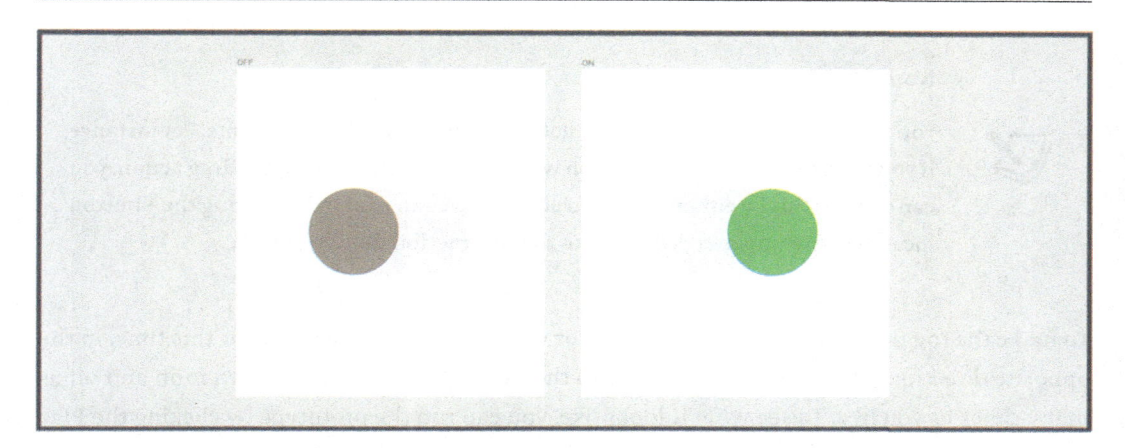

Figure 9.16 – Drawing two toggle states

To link these two toggle elements, you need to switch to **Prototype** mode and then create a connector from the first toggle element to the **ON** frame. The right trigger for this case would be **On drag** and in the **Animation** section, **Smart animate** must be selected, as shown below:

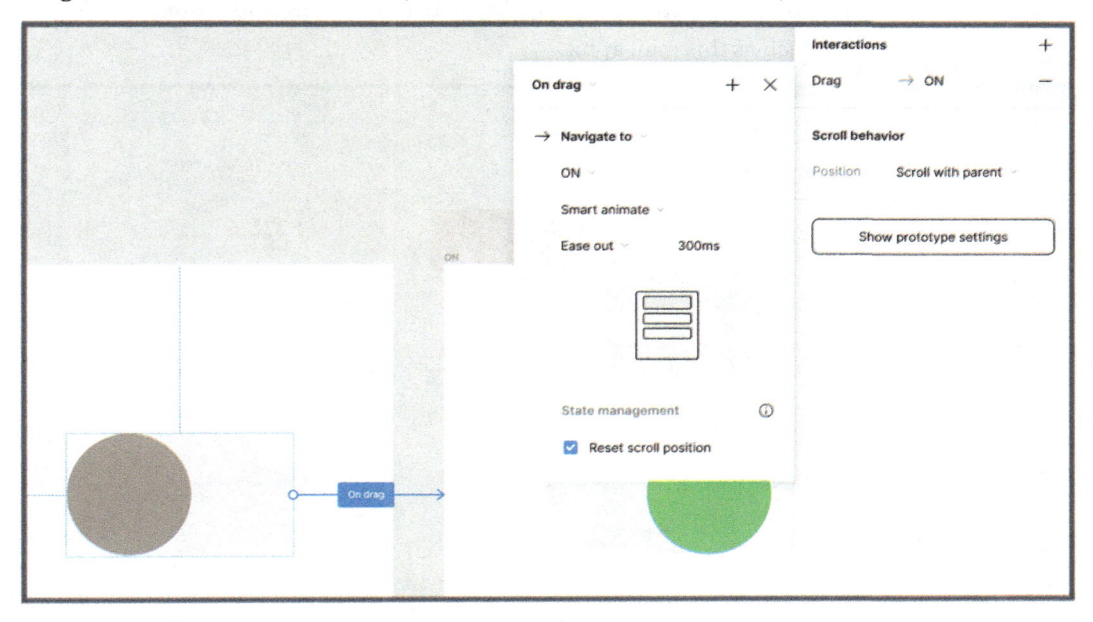

Figure 9.17 – Animating the toggles with smart animate

> **Note:**
>
> You can also establish multiple connectors between the same elements. For instance, if you wish to initiate the animation with both an **On tap** and an **On drag** action, you can achieve this by either adding an additional connector or by clicking the + button located in the upper-right corner of the **Interaction details** section.

To make the toggle complete, create a connector with the same properties, but this time, in the opposite direction – from the second frame to the first. This way, you can turn it on and off as many times as you like. To see what it looks like, you can run the prototype by clicking the **Play** button in the top bar and try switching it on and off. The result is incredible: even if the two states are actually different frames, the animation makes them act as if they were the same element, and your **Toggle** gradually changes its color and the position of the element's slider, like magic.

Everything you just learned is just the tip of the iceberg. The possibilities of smart animate are endless with all the supported properties. You could even combine more animations in a flow to achieve greater results, such as this mail app:

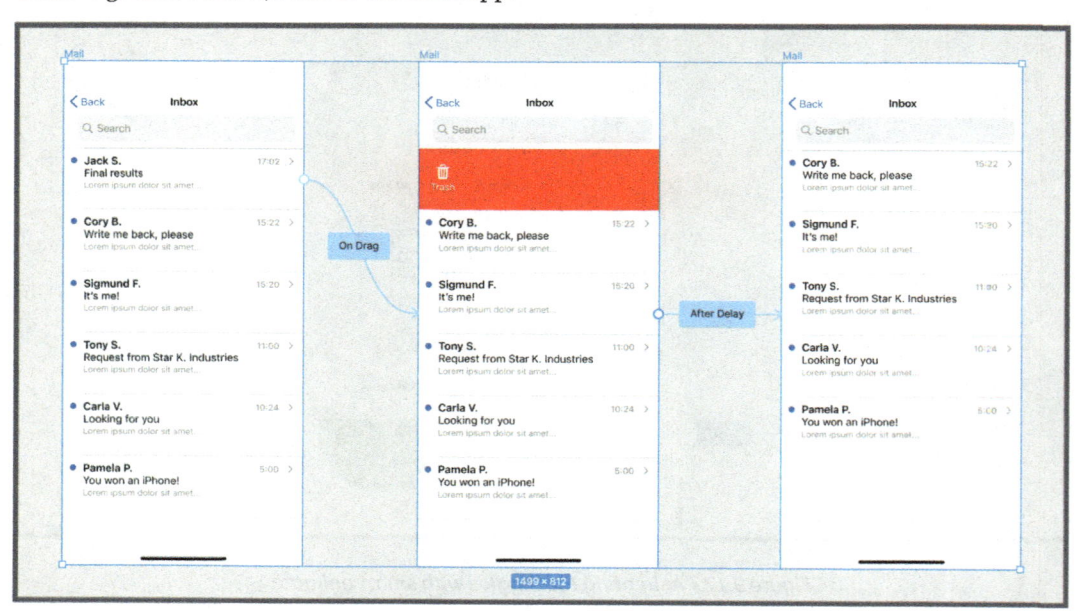

Figure 9.18 – A more complex smart animate and triggers example

Here's what happens in this prototype scenario: when you drag the first email, a trash can row appears indicating that that email has been removed, and immediately after that, with an **After delay** transition, the list automatically scrolls up. Note that if you are in **Prototype** mode, when you hover over an object, Figma will highlight identical elements in other frames, so you already know how smart animate will affect your interface:

Figure 9.19 – Highlighting one element and its duplicates

These were just quick examples of what you can do with smart animate. You can of course go further by using and adding more complex elements, or even combining them all with components, variants, and so on. The only limitation of smart animate is your experience with it!

Now that you know how to use the features Figma offers you to create a dynamic flow with smooth transitions, unique triggers, and impressive animations, it's time to learn how to prepare your layouts for prototyping, manage them in a clean and efficient way, and optimize your workflow process. There is one feature that can help you with all of this, and that is interactive components, which you are about to learn about!

Structuring interactive components

In this section, you will be introduced to Figma's most powerful feature: interactive components. This breakthrough has revolutionized the way designers work, streamlining project workflows to an astonishing degree. How exactly did it achieve this? Let's delve deeper into this topic to discover the details.

What are interactive components?

As you've seen, making a prototype interactive and navigable in Figma isn't all that difficult, but if you want to create a flow with complex, detailed animations, you have to duplicate many frames, sometimes repeating entire views over and over again. For example, imagine you need to create and then show in your prototype hover states for all buttons present in our streaming app interface. Sounds intimidating, doesn't it? And it still wouldn't be the worst thing you can imagine since our application is not that complicated!

Let's see how it would look if we wanted to display a hover state for one button:

Figure 9.20 – Duplicating views to animate button states

Wait, there are secondary buttons with hover states too! Adding another flow might seem excessive, leading designers to focus on prototyping just the essential parts, a choice that previously caused issues like limited user testing and ambiguities for developers. However, with Figma's introduction of interactive components, these challenges are alleviated. Now, you can apply interaction rules directly to the main components. This means all instances inherit not only the component's properties but also its animations and triggers. Let's dive into a practical example to understand this feature better.

Creating interactive components

Beginning with the basics, we'll transform your existing buttons into interactive components. This involves integrating animation directly into the main components, utilizing the structured variants you've already set up. Go to the **Styles + Components** page and follow these steps:

1. Select the **Primary Default** button and – while in **Prototype** mode – draw a connector that has the **Primary Hover** button as its destination. Set the trigger to **While hovering** and make sure that **Smart animate** is selected. The settings in your dialog should match the following:

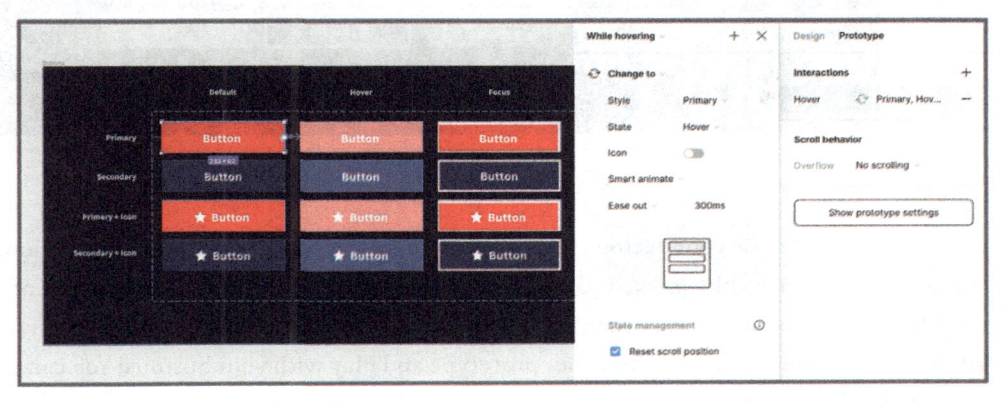

Figure 9.21 – Connecting the Default button with the Hover button

2. Select the **Primary Default** button again and create another connector, but this time, with the **Primary Focus** button as the destination. Set **While pressing** as the trigger:

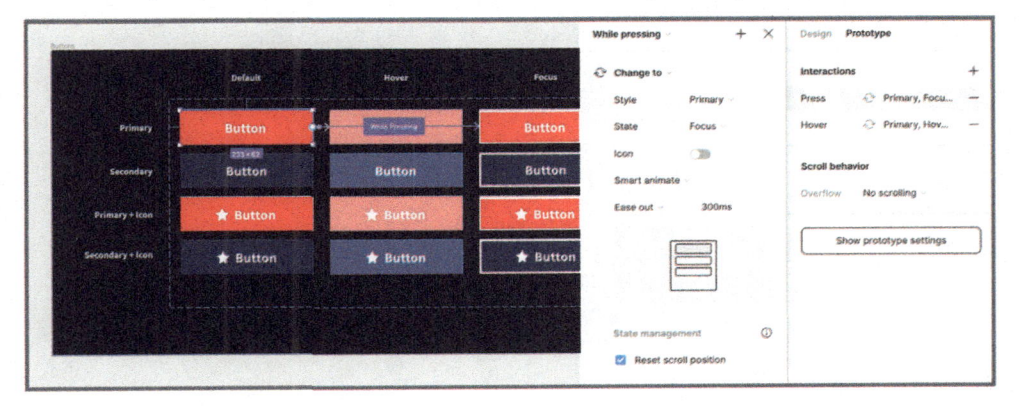

Figure 9.22 – Connecting the Default button with the Focus button

3. Repeat the same process for the **Secondary** button (and, if you created variants for buttons with icons, also for them), connecting the **Default** state with **Hover** and **Focus** and setting the right triggers:

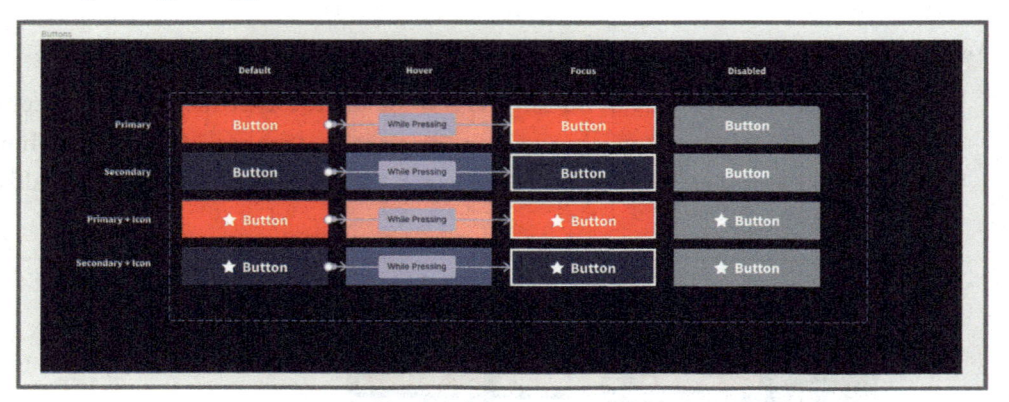

Figure 9.23 – The final outcome

Done, you've just made your buttons interactive! You have just set all the basic interactions right inside the component blueprint, and now, wherever you use that particular component, it will have **Hover** and **Focus** states in each of its instances, so you don't have to duplicate any of your views. Want to see it in action? Run your prototype and play with your buttons! You can see that each button in the interface now has interaction states, and it works for both desktops, which require **Hover**, and mobiles and tablets, which require **Focus** states:

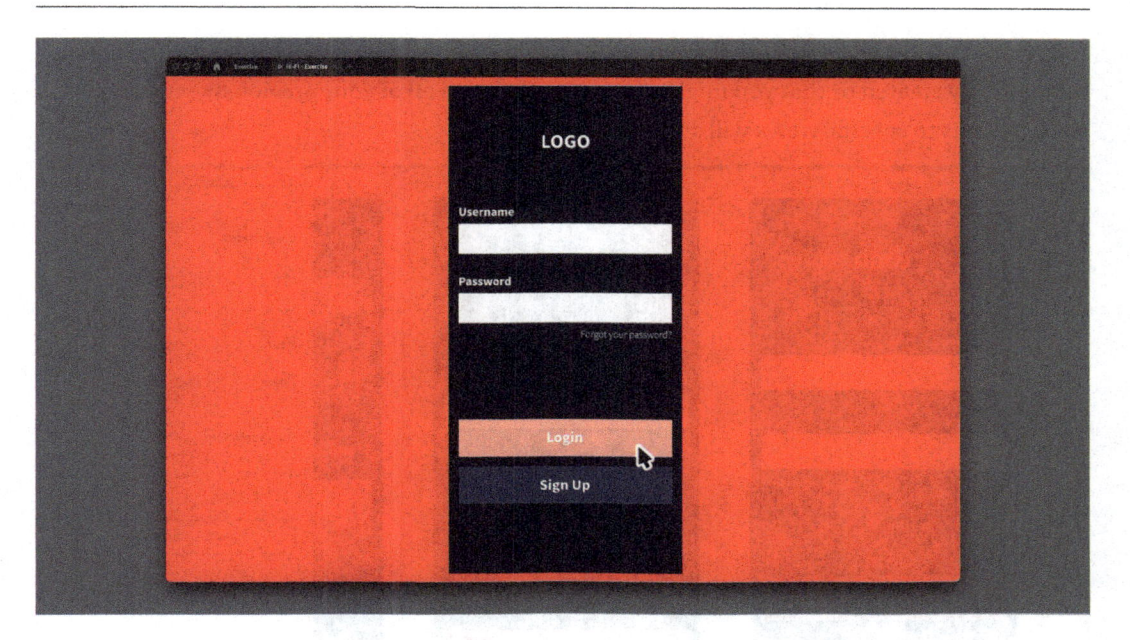

Figure 9.24 – Previewing the Hover state on a button

Interactive components are an incredibly powerful feature that takes prototyping to a whole new level and allows you to avoid huge increases in views in your flows. However, not all interactions need to be set right inside the component. For example, the **Login** button, while having states like any other button, still needs to be pressed to bring the user to the **Home** view. This is what makes this particular button different from others in your interface because, obviously, each of them has its own destination views.

Don't worry, because interactive components do not interrupt flow interactions that you might have already created or that you might want to create. And all of your previously set transitions from buttons to specific views will still work correctly:

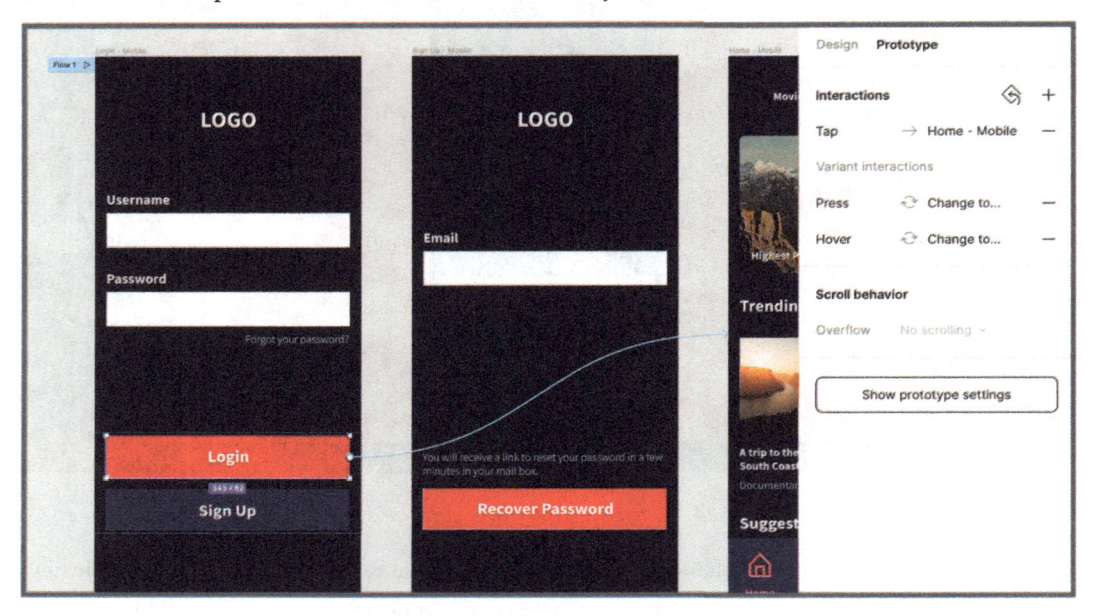

Figure 9.25 – Individual and variant interactions

When you include interactive components in your prototype, the **Prototype** sidebar will show your flow interactions as well as variant interactions. By combining these two, you can reach a completely new level of your workflow optimization since it will become much easier to manage, plus you can make it as close as possible to the real product that will be released.

Just like you created interactive components for your buttons, you can do the same with any other element that you previously converted into a component. For example, if you want to make the tab bar interactive, instead of changing its states in each separate view, you can add triggers for it right in the variants, as follows:

1. Select each **Tab Item** individually and create a connector to the corresponding active state variant (that is, the **Search** tab should be linked to the variant with an active **Search** icon, and so on). Set **On click/On tap** as a trigger and **Smart animate** must be selected:

Chapter 9

Figure 9.26 – Making the tab bar interactive

2. Proceed to the next variant, and then to the rest in sequence, connecting each **Tab Item** (except the active ones) with the corresponding **Tab Bar** variant. The final result should look like this:

Figure 9.27 – The outcome of our tab bar prototyping

It might look pretty messy, but all the connectors remain in the component set and don't appear in the UI flow itself, so in the end, it won't be that annoying.

Well, now you know about the concept of interactive components, but there is a way to optimize your prototyping even more. In the previous section, you built the main flow by adding transitions. This flow follows one direction, not letting the user return from the **Content Detail** to the **Home** view, for example. This is not how our app is going to work and there is actually a back arrow for this action, but for now, this is just a design element, not an interactive one. Of course, you can easily fix this by simply adding a connector back to the **Home** view and that will work too. But in fact, **Top Bar** is used in many other views, and you would have to connect each of its instances over and over again. What if you could simplify it by setting this interaction to the main component, which will return the user to the previous view, whatever it is?

To do this, go to the **Top Bar** component on the **Styles + Components** page and follow these simple steps:

1. In **Prototype** mode, select **Tab Item** inside the **Top Bar** component, as shown in the following screenshot:

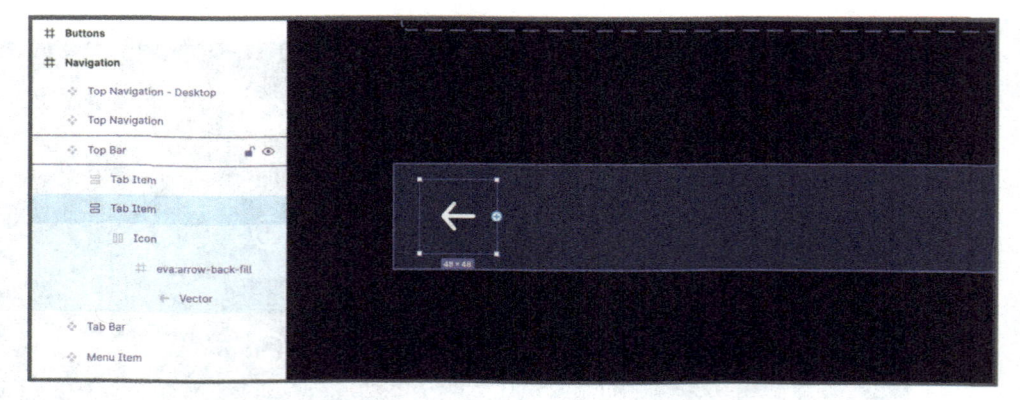

Figure 9.28 – Selecting the back Tab Item element

2. Add an interaction by clicking the + button on the right sidebar.
3. Set the trigger to **On click/On tap** and the action to **Back:**

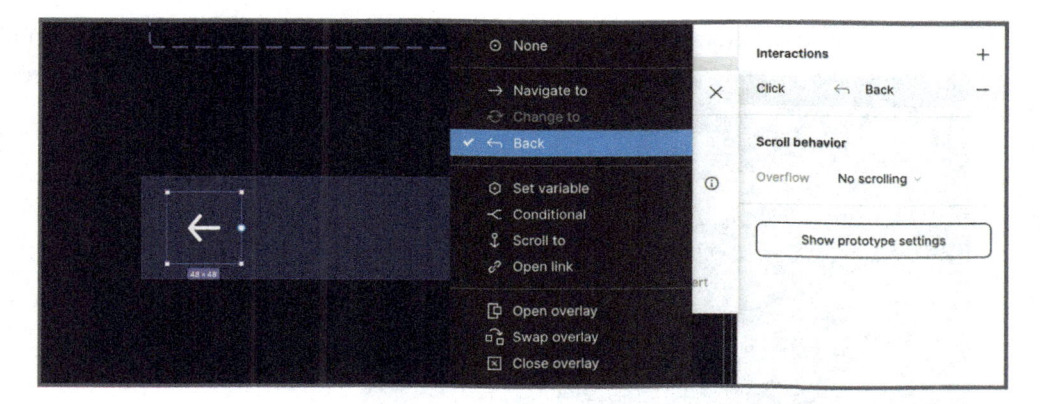

Figure 9.29 – Setting the Back action

And that's all! In just a few clicks, you have assigned a *go-back* command to all instances of the component. If you look at your interface right now, you will find that the **Back** action is automatically applied to **Mobile**, **Tablet**, and **Desktop** frames too:

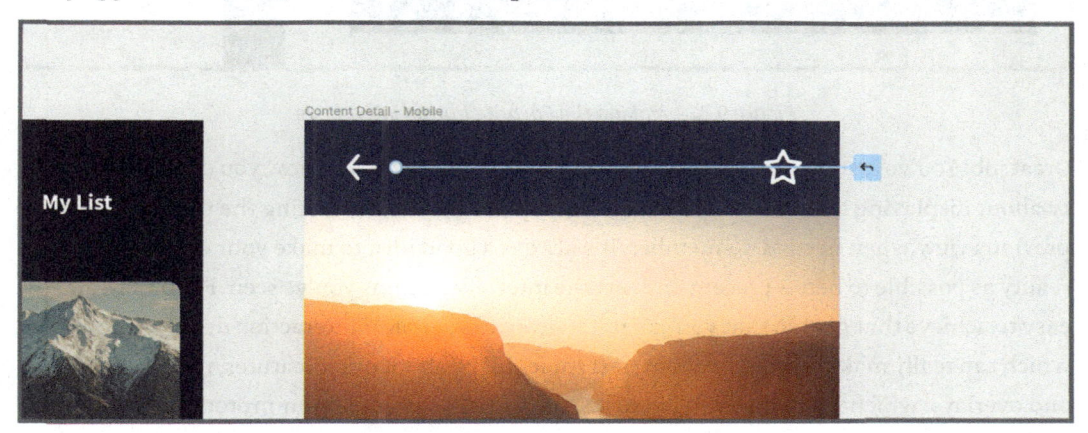

Figure 9.30 – The outcome on our frames

To make the **Content Detail** view even better, it would be a good idea to add interaction to the **Add to Favorites** icon as well. You can start converting the star icon to a component, after duplicating it from the **Top Bar** component, and then create a **Filled** variant of it. Replace the star icon in the top bar with the component you just created. Then you just need to add the **On click/On tap** interactions in the newly created variant to switch from **Default** to **Filled** and back.

In the following screenshot, you can get a more specific overview of what you need to achieve:

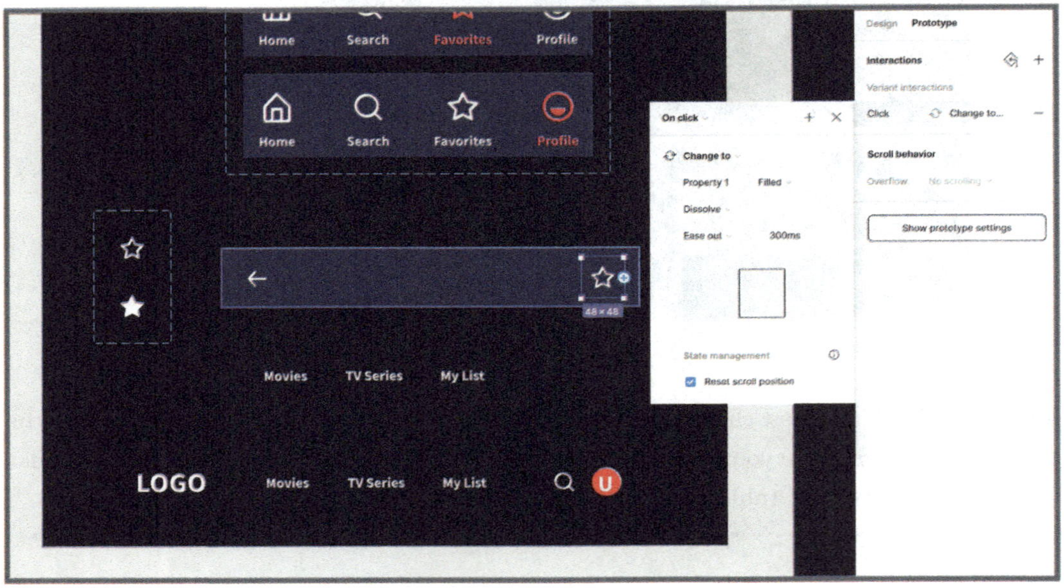

Figure 9.31 – Making the Favorite button interactive

Great job! You've just taken your prototype to a whole new level, and now you don't have to worry about displaying the states of your buttons in your layouts and letting the user return to the previous view when needed. Remember, it's always a good idea to make your design as close to reality as possible to better present and test the interface. And, as you've seen, Figma can make it easy to achieve that goal so that you can reflect even the smallest interaction details in your flow, which can really make a difference. Our next topic will be about other features, namely overflows and overlays, which you will also need to add, and it will complete your prototyping work.

Creating interactive overflows and overlays

You have now reached the point where your application interface is almost finished and most of the prototyping is done. However, there are a few more important details that you need to add. In this section, you are going to do that by creating scrollable views and setting interactive overlays on top of all other elements.

Making our view scrollable with overflows

As you're aware, some of our views contain extensive content that exceeds the initial vertical space, concealing elements outside the initial device viewport. Previously, to access and manage these elements, you had to disable the **Clip content** function. However, when playing your prototype, this isn't an option because the interface must faithfully represent the actual device resolution.

To address this, we need to introduce scrolling functionality to navigate through views that extend beyond the screen. Currently, scrolling hasn't been implemented in your views, but we'll now solve this. As a starting point, you are going to apply scrolling on mobile, and then you just need to do the same for tablet and desktop. Since our **Login - Mobile** and **Sign Up - Mobile** views do not contain long content, they do not require scrolling. However, you should keep in mind that some views might perfectly fit smartphones with bigger screen resolutions, with everything inside, but they would not necessarily be displayed the same way on much smaller screens, such as older iPhone models. So, in this case, scrolling might still be needed. Therefore, it is extremely important to test your interface on different devices, as you did in *Chapter 8, User Interface Design on Tablet, Desktop, and the Web*.

You will now start with the **Home - Mobile** view, which certainly requires the user to scroll down to see all of the content. So, open the file and do the following:

1. Select the **Container** layer and manually change its height to the top of the tab bar. It is important that the content exceeds the **Container** limits, otherwise, the view will not scroll:

Figure 9.32 – Selecting and resizing the Container element

2. Switch to the **Prototype** mode and – with **Container** selected – change the **Overflow** setting to **Vertical**, as shown in the following screenshot:

Figure 9.33 – Changing the Container behavior to Vertical scrolling

By setting this option, you simply told Figma that your interactive prototype can be scrolled vertically. Moreover, since **Container** does not include the tab bar, this element will automatically remain at the bottom of the frame when scrolling through the content of the view itself. Alternatively, you could apply scrolling behavior for the entire **Home** frame, but then you must set the tab bar's **Position** to the **Fixed (stay in place)** option. This option is actually very good in many situations, allowing you to lock an element at its current position even when the whole view is scrolling:

Figure 9.34 – The Fixed position when scrolling option

The next view that needs scrolling is our **Content Detail - Mobile**. Repeat the steps for this screen and make sure everything except the tab bar is in the **Container** layer (if you don't have one, you can always select the needed elements and frame the selection to create a new container), and then change its **Overflow** option to **Vertical**. To ensure that the scrolling behavior will work fine across the entire screen, even if the parent frame is resized, set the **Container** vertical constraints to **Top and bottom**.

The scrolling work is not completely finished yet, as there is still something to do. Both the **Home - Mobile** and **Content Detail - Mobile** views also have a set of sliders and rows that require horizontal scrolling. The procedure for working on this is almost the same as the one you have already done:

1. Select a row you want to make scrollable.
2. Resize its width to match the outer frame width.
3. Switch to the **Prototype** mode and, this time, set **Overflow** to **Horizontal**:

Figure 9.35 – Changing the Carousel behavior to Horizontal scrolling

Note:

Since your **Cards Section** is a nested component, you cannot manually resize and change its behavior in layouts. To make it scrollable, go to the **Main Component** on the **Styles + Components** page and apply the changes. Alternatively – but it's almost never suggested – you can detach its instances to get a simple frame with a row of **Content Cards** inside, and then resize it directly on the canvas.

Great, you're done for the mobile views, and now they are scrollable! As you've seen, doing that in Figma is very fast and easy, so you can easily add scrolling behavior to tablet and desktop screens wherever it's needed.

Creating interface overlays

Prototyping in Figma offers many ways to make your interface come alive and covers most of the possible user interactions in apps, websites, and even games. All of the prototyping features you've used so far are essential to professional dynamic flow building. But there is another simple, but no less interesting, addition that needs to be implemented in our prototype – namely, **overlays**. Just like interactive components, overlays are very useful when you want to keep your flows clean and have a limited number of frames in your work area. Overlays are great when you want to add additional elements to your prototypes, such as popups or tooltips, without duplicating additional views for this purpose. Let's jump right into practice to better understand this new concept.

Go to the **Styles + Components** page, create a new frame, and rename it to Overlays. Here, create a simple **Dropdown Menu** like the example shown in the following screenshot, and then make it a component:

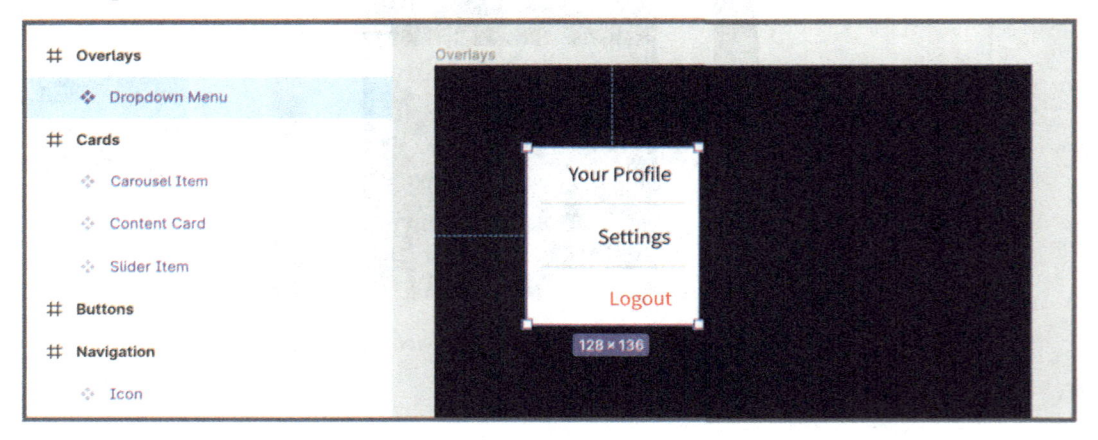

Figure 9.36 – Creating a Dropdown Menu component

Now go back to the **Hi-Fi** page and drag an instance of the component you just created from the assets. Place it directly above the **Home - Desktop** frame, but this time, not inside it, as shown here:

Figure 9.37 – Placing an instance of Dropdown Menu on the Hi-Fi page

Why does it make sense to put it there? The fact is that it must exist as a separate frame, which, after you set the appropriate parameters, Figma will use as an overlay element to open it on top of all the items to which it will be attached. In our case, it should appear when clicking on the **Profile** icon. So, select the icon, switch to **Prototype**, and create a connector from it to the **Dropdown Menu**. Set the trigger to **On click/On tap** and choose **Open overlay** as the action. This allows users to easily dismiss the overlay by enabling the **Close when clicking outside** option. Optionally, the **Add background** checkbox is available to introduce a transparent color behind the overlay, enhancing its readability.

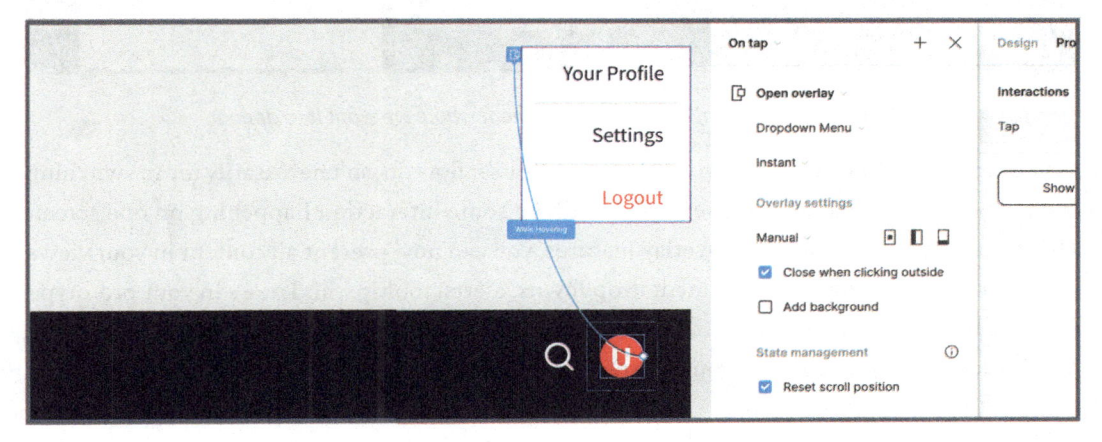

Figure 9.38 – Connecting the Profile icon to the Dropdown Menu instance

Okay, now there are a bunch of new options to manage the overlay. Here, you can make it appear exactly in the center of the screen (for example, for modals, popups, and alerts), on the left border (for example, boxes and menus), or even at the bottom (for example, smartphone keyboards). But in our case, it should have a very specific position, so click the **Overlay** position drop-down list and select **Manual**. A transparent clone of the **Dropdown Menu** element will appear in the **Home - Desktop** frame, which you can drag across the screen to drop in the exact location where you want it to be displayed. Place it just below the **Profile** icon, as in the following screenshot:

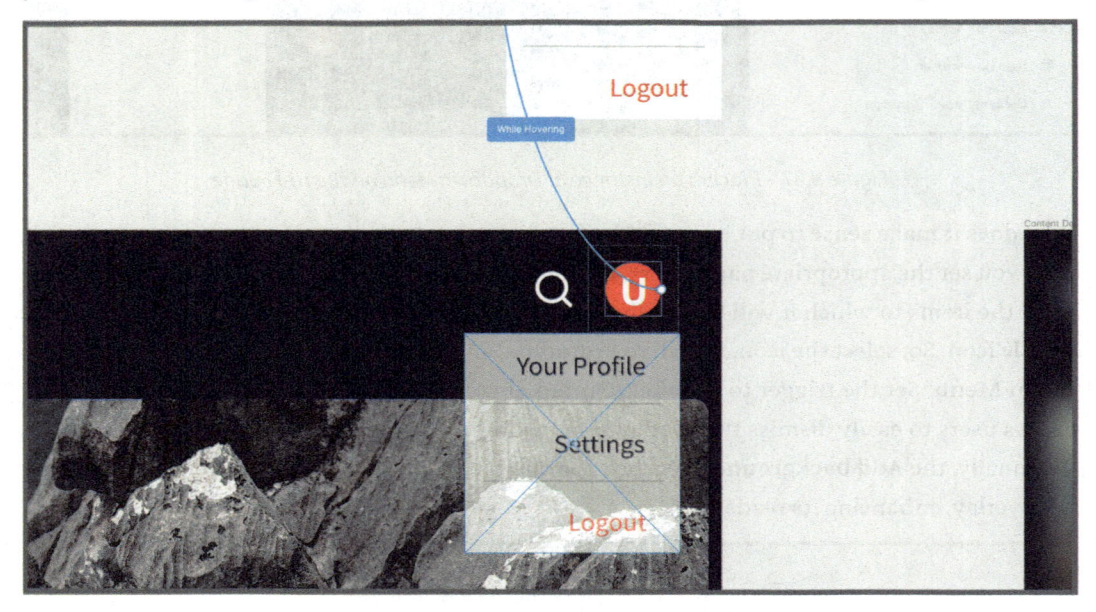

Figure 9.39 – Manually moving the element where we want it to appear

As you work on any prototype, keep in mind that the user flow doesn't necessarily mean switching from one screen to another, as there might still be some interaction happening on one screen. Thanks to Figma's overflow and overlay features, you can now present all content in your views with working scrolling and implement dropdowns, alerts, tooltips, and more in your prototype without having to create additional views to do so. Finally, we can say that the design of our application has come to life, as you will see for yourself in the next chapter!

Summary

This chapter was your first step into the world of prototyping in Figma, which is just as important a design phase as UX research and UI creation. You have learned how to connect views to each other to build dynamic flows using transitions and triggers, and when combined with smart animate, this can give outstanding results. You have also learned how to create interactive components that significantly simplify your workflow, making interactions within frames so much better. In addition, you have discovered that each view, depending on its intended use and the content inside, can be prototyped differently, since the user can stay on the same screen longer, scrolling the content or performing additional interactions with some interactive elements. Figma brilliantly takes this aspect into account, offering you overflows and overlays, which you have also successfully implemented in your interface.

Having explored the foundational and intermediate prototyping techniques in Figma, you're now prepared to delve deeper. In the next chapter, we'll focus on preparing your three key flows – for mobile, tablet, and desktop – and making them ready for sharing and testing on various devices. This step is crucial for ensuring a seamless user experience across all platforms.

Learn more on Discord

To join the Discord community for this book – where you can share feedback, ask questions to the author, and learn about new releases – follow the QR code below:

```
https://packt.link/figma
```

10
Testing and Sharing Your Prototype in Browsers and Real Devices

In the previous chapter, you learned how to prototype your interfaces in Figma using interactions, transitions between views, and animations. You also converted static layouts into live flows for the interfaces of all three devices, which was a pretty challenging but interesting task, and you learned a lot along the way. As a result, you not only linked all screens together but also made some components interactive, as well as adding missing elements to the application. At some points during this practice, you ran the prototype to make sure everything was set up correctly – this is absolutely the right strategy, since constant monitoring of the prototype is necessary to prevent errors.

While we briefly touched on prototyping earlier, we didn't delve deeply into launching a prototype, a topic deserving its own detailed exploration. This chapter is dedicated to just that. You'll not only learn how to run a prototype but also discover new Figma features for sharing your work, gathering feedback, and preparing your interface for testing. Additionally, you'll be guided on how to execute the prototype on a real device and enhance its effectiveness by strategically structuring the flows within your file.

In this chapter, we are going to cover the following main topics:

- Viewing your interactive prototype
- Sharing your prototype with others
- Working with feedback and reviews

By the end of this chapter, you will be able to view and test the interactive interface you created in Figma directly on small devices such as tablets and smartphones, as well as provide access to your prototype in a variety of other ways.

Viewing your interactive prototype

Now that your app's design and prototyping are complete, it's time to see the results come to life. This section guides you on configuring prototype parameters in Figma for a dynamic interface preview. You'll explore using Figma's device presets for a realistic experience and the Figma mobile app for testing on smartphones or tablets. Let's start by focusing on the **Prototype** tab and understanding how to effectively run your prototype

Running prototypes on desktop/web

Although in the previous chapter you created a whole flow connecting views to each other and using interactions and **transitions**, so far, you have only seen the static version of the application design (with a few minor exceptions). Now, it's time to view the dynamic version of the prototype. But first, let's see what settings are available for it. With no layers selected on the canvas, switch to the **Prototype** tab to see the general prototyping options:

Figure 10.1 – General prototype options

You should already be quite familiar with this tab, but let's take a look at it once again and see what else you can manage with these parameters. The first section you will see is the **Device** selector, where you can choose from a list of device presets for how the prototype will be framed.

Figure 10.2 – Device selector

It is important to understand that choosing one of these real device mock-ups will not affect the actual resolution of the interface you are about to run. To better understand this aspect, select **iPad Pro 11"** from the list and launch your prototype for mobile devices, and this is what you will see:

Figure 10.3 – Selecting the wrong device for the current resolution

In the preceding figure, you can see that the view does not match the preset, and whenever you have something like this (they do not fill all the space, as in the preceding example, or on the contrary, they are cropped and you do not see all the content), you can fix it right in the **Device** selector by switching to the right device.

In this case, since you worked with the **iPhone 13 mini** preset frames from the beginning, to see the interface at its best, you should also select the same from the **Prototype** list. After choosing the preset, a **Model** selector will appear just below, in which – if available – you can even change the color of the device. Once you've got everything set up, you can finally run your prototype. To do this, you should select the initial mobile frame (**Login - Mobile** view) and click on the **Present** button – the one with a **Play** icon on the right side of the top bar. As a result, you will get a fully functional prototype:

Figure 10.4 – Playing a prototype

As you will have noticed, the prototype opens in a separate new Figma tab (or browser tab if you're using the web app). This dedicated space is called **Presentation view**.

> **Note:**
> In the general **Prototype** settings, you can also customize the Background Color of the **Presentation view**, which is the surface on which the device is displayed. In addition, you can change the **Orientation** of the device to be able to show the prototype in both **Portrait** and **Landscape** modes.

It's amazing how impressively realistic your interface looks when framed in a device mock-up, so it's a great way to present it to your customers or stakeholders. However, when you are still in the internal testing stages, using a specific preset can be limiting and inconvenient. For example, if you want to quickly switch between interfaces with completely different resolutions to test versions for mobile devices, tablets, and desktops in real time, you need to go back to the settings each time and manually select the most appropriate preset.

To avoid this problem, you can use the last two options from the device list: **Custom size** and **Presentation**. The first one, **Custom size**, lets you define specific width and height values for each prototype run. The second, **Presentation**, is more straightforward and often more useful. It displays the entire prototype at its actual size, ensuring no part of the design is cropped or scaled. With **Presentation**, you won't get layout mock-ups, but you'll always see the full, true-to-size screen of your prototype. For now, let's switch to **Presentation** mode as it is most suitable for our current testing phase.

Now that your **Presentation** view is set up and ready to use, we can finally try our mobile prototype interactively. In the **Presentation view** tab, you can easily share your prototype and leave comments. You will learn more about this in the section ahead, *Sharing your prototype with others*, dedicated to this topic. But for now, let's focus on the view settings.

In the top-right panel, click **Options** and a dropdown will appear with a whole bunch of new options, as shown in the following screenshot:

Figure 10.5 – Prototype view settings

From this menu, you can choose to display the interface of the desired zoom while maintaining the original interface proportions or filling the entire screen as much as possible. If you want a much cleaner, non-distracting way of presenting, you can disable the **Show Figma UI** option, and the entire Figma interface will be hidden. Make sure the **Show hotspot hints on click** option is enabled, as we'll use and talk about those soon in this section. You may also notice that some of the options are grayed out, but don't worry; once you start working with **flows** and **comments**, all of these options will be enabled.

Now, let's try to navigate the frames to see whether everything that we have done in the prototype works in the expected way. You can use the *Left* and *Right* arrow keys on your keyboard to move through all the frames in the file, but this will be similar to viewing a slideshow presentation. What if, instead, we want to actually test all the interactions that we implemented earlier? This is very easy to do. You just have to click where the **hotspots** were set in our design. Remember the elements you linked using **connectors**? They are now clickable!

In our design, you can test the interaction right on the very first screen. Just try hovering over the **Login** button and it will immediately change its state to **Hover** as this is the interactive component you created earlier! If everything is right, the **Sign Up** button should act the same way:

Figure 10.6 – Testing the hover state

Continuing with your testing, let's now click on the **Login** button, after which you will be taken directly to the **Home - Mobile** page, as this is the exact scenario set up during the prototyping phase. Now that you are on the **Home** page, you can see it live with all of its scroll behaviors, both horizontal and vertical. It works great, as if you had it on a real device. Here, however, you might get a bit confused about continuing the flow, since you haven't made every card clickable, and therefore it becomes problematic to determine which one to click on. Don't worry; in that case, there are **hotspot hints** to help you see all the interactive areas.

To see them, you just have to click anywhere on the screen (even outside the interface's frame) and Figma will highlight all the **hotspots** on the current page in blue for a second, as shown in the following screenshot:

Figure 10.7 – Blinking blue hotspots

Hotspot hints are certainly very useful for the prototype creator, but they also make it incredibly easy for any external viewers to follow the flow.

> **Note**
> You can quickly restart your prototype from the beginning at any time by pressing *R* on your keyboard.

With these simple navigation techniques, you can now easily view your entire interactive prototype on mobile, tablet, and desktop pages. Take a moment to quickly test all the views to see if everything is working well. If necessary, fix any small bugs you might encounter. Common issues could include misaligned elements, incorrect transitions or animations, or broken links between frames. For example, remember to test opening the dropdown menu you created for **Home - Desktop**, the one that appears after clicking the **Profile** icon, and see if it works and opens in the right place. When working on real projects, it is best to test interactions as you work on them by keeping the **Presentation view** open next to your design file tab. This way, you can directly check if the transition from page to page is done correctly and the animation of the elements performs the way you want. You can always change something for the better in your prototype if you feel like it is necessary.

Now that you know how to launch and navigate your prototype in **Presentation view**, let's see how to do the same thing, but without even leaving our main workspace!

Using the inline preview

In our journey through Figma's prototyping capabilities, one essential tool at your disposal is the **inline preview**. This feature empowers you to witness your interactive prototypes in action and offers real-time insights that can significantly enhance your design workflow. You've painstakingly crafted your prototypes, incorporating interactions, transitions, and dynamic elements. Now, it's time to see the results come to life in an even easier way than before. The inline preview serves as your window into this dynamic world, allowing you to experience your design directly within the Figma canvas.

One of the key advantages of the inline preview is its seamless integration with your design process. As you make changes or refinements to your prototype, the inline preview keeps pace, providing an immediate, real-time reflection of these adjustments. This dynamic connection ensures that you can fine-tune interactions and animations with precision and ease.

Accessing the **inline preview** is straightforward. While working on your design, simply click the dropdown arrow near the **Play** button, then click on **Preview**, and your prototype springs to life within the canvas.

> **Note:**
>
> A quick press of *Shift + Space* summons the inline preview of the currently selected frame or component's instance, making it incredibly accessible and efficient for all designers. However, be mindful that the inline preview might not always be as reliable as the Presentation view, especially for intricate designs or complex interactions. Still, using a desktop preview for a smartphone or tablet app has its limitations. Let's find out how to make testing more realistic by running your prototype on your actual mobile devices. This way, you can assess how your design performs in its intended context and gain valuable insights.

Running the prototype on a smartphone/tablet

Viewing prototypes in Figma is convenient and efficient, but it doesn't always capture the real-world user experience. This is particularly noticeable when testing mobile interfaces on a computer. For example, hover states on buttons, designed in Figma, don't apply to actual mobile devices where interactions are touch-based.

To bridge this gap, Figma offers a solution: the Figma mobile app. Available on both **iOS** and **Android**, this app allows you to test your designs on smartphones and tablets, providing a more realistic user interaction experience. Here's a glimpse of what the Figma mobile app looks like on a device:

Figure 10.8 – Figma mobile app

So, what can this app actually give you? In fact, it is a standalone portable viewer for your projects that allows you to access all designs directly from your portable device. Of course, this app cannot replace the Figma desktop or web app, as it only allows you to view, not edit, your files. But its main advantage is that you can run an interactive prototype right in the app, so your mobile interfaces will look and feel as real as possible in the Figma mobile app, and your tablet views in the tablet app version accordingly.

> **Note:**
>
> The Figma app requires you to be signed in with the same credentials you use with your Figma desktop/web app in order to access all of your files and connect to the **Presentation view** in real time.

Chapter 10

If your smartphone or tablet is running an iOS or Android operating system, find and download the Figma app from the store, and then log in with your account. The first thing you will see is a list of your recent files. If you find and enter our project, it will look like this:

Figure 10.9 – Viewing a file on the mobile app

On this file page, you can see the tab bar with only a few tabs. On the first, you can freely move, pan, and scale the layouts, and on the second, you can run the prototype directly from your device. The third and fourth are related to comments and sharing options.

> **Note:**
> If you want to restart the prototype or exit this mode, tap and hold anywhere on the device screen to bring up the quick actions menu.

This app has another incredibly useful feature, namely **Mirror**. There used to be an app of the same name, also from Figma, the only purpose of which was to reflect the frames that you select in Figma on the screen of your smartphone. Now, this feature is built into the Figma app itself, and from here, you can constantly view your frames and interactions between views directly on your device in real time.

To try this, head back to the main app's page and go to the **Mirror** tab. In the following screenshot, you can see its initial state:

Figure 10.10 – The Mirror tab

Now you can simply open any file on your desktop or web Figma and select the frame you want to view. The app will automatically recognize your choice and update the prototype on your device in just a few seconds. With this fairly simple yet powerful tool, it becomes incredibly easy to design interfaces while constantly monitoring how they appear on the actual target device. This way, you can always check the actual sizes of the elements, transitions between the pages, interactions, and the states of each element. However, don't expect a hassle-free experience, since some interactions may work differently from the desktop counterpart.

The Figma application lets you view and test all your frames regardless of their size, since they will always adapt to the width of your device screen. Of course, if you test on a real device that you are prototyping for, it will be a better and more natural experience.

As you can see, Figma makes it as efficient as possible to test your prototypes by inviting you to not only view your product in Figma with all those fluid interactions and cool animations but literally test it with your fingers in the Figma app!

Take some time to explore this app, playing around with the Mirror feature. Once you're ready to move on, you'll learn how to share your prototype in the next section.

Sharing your prototype with others

Now you know how to view and test your prototype in Figma, with **Presentation view** and **the inline preview**, right on your device. During testing, you might come across issues or improvements in your design or screen transitions that you'd like to address. This is normal, since prototyping should primarily be useful for you, in order to identify and correct inaccuracies or change something. If everything is in order and you are happy with your work, it is time to move on to the next step, which is to show your prototype to other people. This could be colleagues, friends, clients, or stakeholders. So, in this section, you will learn about the best practices on how to share your prototype with others in Figma.

Linking the prototype and managing permissions

In *Chapter 7, Building Components and Variants in a Collaborative Workspace*, you learned how to share your design files by sending email invitations and giving others either full collaborator rights (with an editor role) or limited access to third parties (with the role of a viewer, without the possibility of editing). Thus, it makes sense that everyone you invite will have access to the prototype as well, since access to the project automatically provides the ability to play and view your prototypes.

However, there are times when you only want to share an interactive prototype without showing your design files, even in read-only mode. This feature is also provided in Figma. To do this, while in the **Presentation view**, you should click on the **Share prototype** button in the upper-right corner:

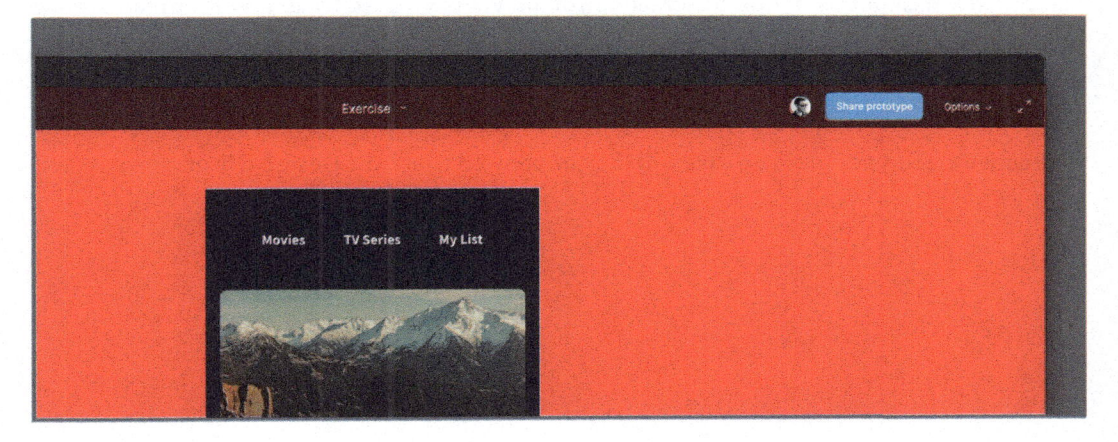

Figure 10.11 – Share prototype button

This will open the sharing options dialog box, which you have already seen in the previous chapters. If you already have co-editors and/or viewers listed, they can view and try the prototype, but at the same time, see (or even edit) the original file. To give someone access only to the prototype, you should paste their email address and click on the **can view** dropdown menu item. You will see that you now have an additional completely new option, namely, **can view prototypes**:

Figure 10.12 – Viewing permissions

Note:

The **can view prototypes** option is only available for Professional teams and organizations.

You can also assign this option to someone you previously added as an editor or reader, thus changing their permissions. By setting the **Anyone with the link** rule to **can view prototypes**, you can then click on **Copy link** in the lower-right corner and send the generated link directly, which you now have copied to your computer's clipboard. Whoever gets it can only access the interactive prototype, but in no case will they be allowed to see the **Design editor** view.

Chapter 10

Embedding the prototype

In **Presentation view**, just like in the design file, you will also find the option to create embedded code. But what does this incorporation consist of? How is this different from what we can do with the file itself? And how can this be useful? Now, you will receive answers to all these questions, point by point. Go ahead and click on the **Get embed code** option at the bottom of the same sharing dialog in **Presentation view** and you will see something like this:

Figure 10.13 – Embed code

This is HTML code that you can just **Copy** in a block, and once you do it, you can paste it into any website or application that supports HTML blocks. For example, you can use it on your personal website to create an interactive portfolio of products, or in any documentation tool to display interactive examples. What you do is entirely up to you.

> **Note:**
> An embedded prototype can be public and accessible to anyone who sees the page or application that includes it, or private, and this will require the user to be signed in and have access permissions.

If you're looking to embed your prototype in FigJam, you have a convenient option. Although you can copy and paste the HTML embed code, it's not necessary. FigJam simplifies the process for you. Just copy the share link of your Figma prototype and paste it directly into a FigJam board.

FigJam automatically converts this link into an embedded, interactive prototype, streamlining your workflow:

Figure 10.14 – Using an embed prototype on FigJam

Note that embedding a prototype (using the **Share prototype** button in the **Presentation view** tab) and embedding the entire file (using the **Share** button in the main design workspace) will give you different results. In the second case, once your code is embedded and pasted anywhere, you can only view and navigate but not edit anything:

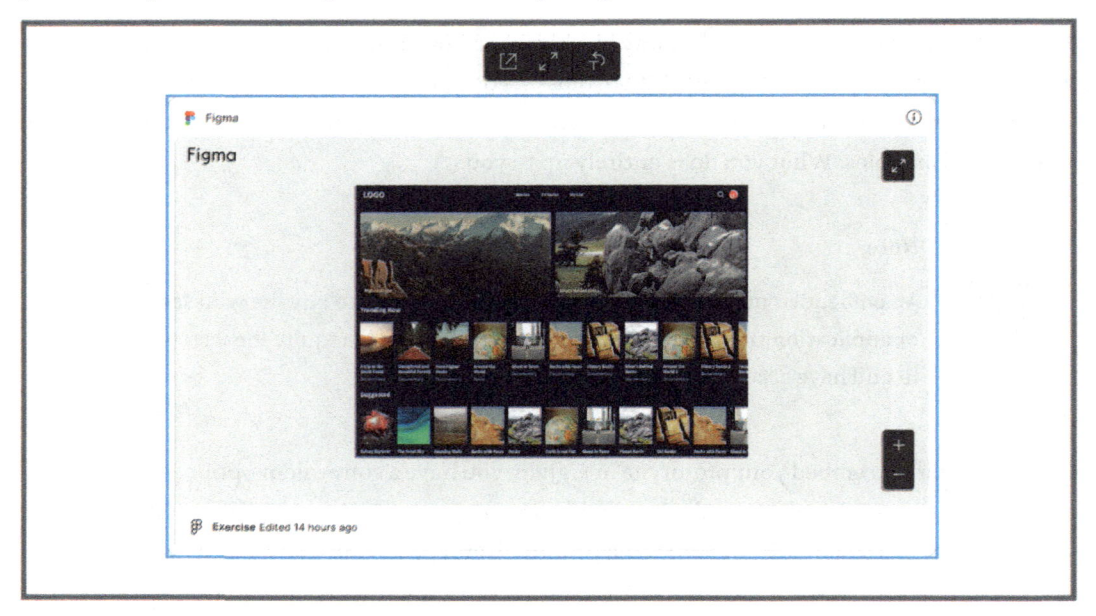

Figure 10.15 – Embedding a Figma file in FigJam

When considering these two functions – embedding the design view and the prototype link – it's crucial to understand their distinct differences. Each serves a unique purpose: one for detailed design insights and the other for interactive experience, ensuring you can tailor the presentation of your work in FigJam according to specific needs and contexts. Plus, it's a good way to let anyone who's not familiar with Figma see your work, and it doesn't even require account creation (as long as you give access to your embeddings with public permissions).

> **Note:**
>
> In Figma and FigJam, you can add password protection to files for secure sharing. Set the access to **Anyone with the link and password**, then either create your own password or use one generated by Figma. This feature ensures only intended recipients can view your shared designs, prototypes, or boards.

That's all you need to know in order to share your work the way you like, setting whatever access rules you need for any occasion possible. Sharing in Figma is a generous feature that goes beyond the app itself and makes it easy to implement, show, and present your designs and prototypes to anyone. But in most cases, you will be sharing your work to get feedback and reactions from customers, target users, or stakeholders. Once again, Figma has made it easy to collect feedback and collaborate with others in an easy and fun way. In the next section, you'll learn how to do this and about all the tools and tricks.

Working with feedback and reviews

At this point, you have gone through the main stages of the design workflow. Our interface is designed, interactive, shareable, and completely ready for the stage of user testing, review, and comparison. However, collecting feedback is a very important part of a designer's job, and you should take it seriously. Other people may see and appreciate your design in a different way, often unexpectedly, so it can be challenging at times. It is also very important to know how to analyze comments and see what is behind them – such as a simple note about the style or a whole UX case. So, don't be afraid to ask the right questions, respond, empathize with user needs, and try to take criticism as an opportunity to look at your work from a different perspective and possibly make it better. It can be overwhelming at first but don't worry, it all comes with experience. Plus, Figma can help you make collaboration and communication with others a greatly organized and fun process. You will learn all about these techniques in this section.

Viewers and comments

When working in a team, or when your file is shared with other collaborators, each of you can use the appropriate **Add comment** function to add notes and feedback anywhere in the workspace. In the following screenshot, you can see what an example comment might look like:

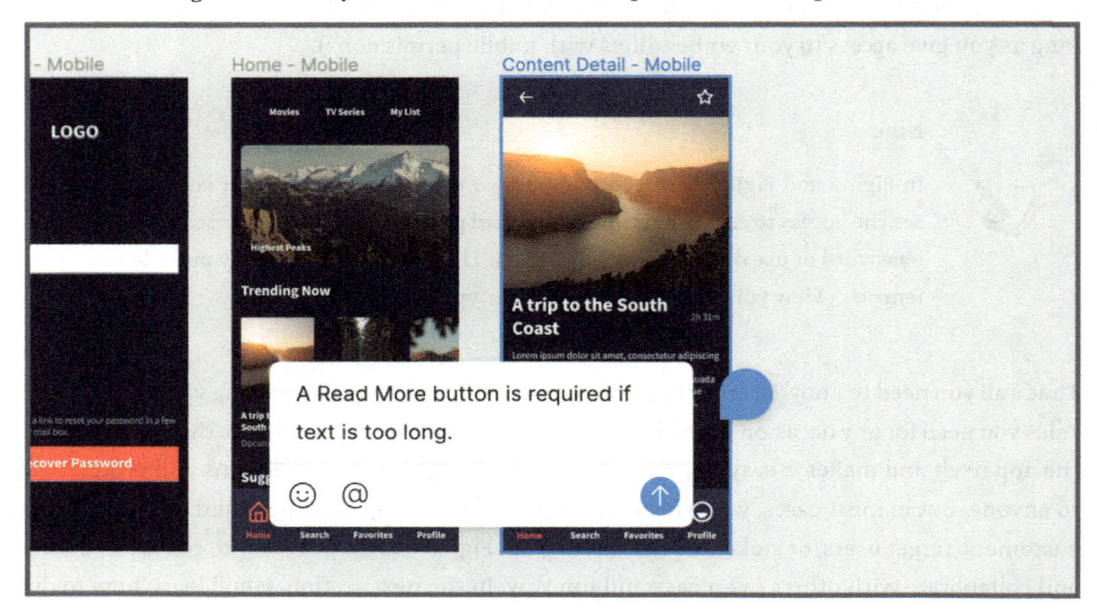

Figure 10.16 – Inserting a comment

When you activate the **Add comment** mode, the right sidebar will allow you to view, scroll, respond to, and resolve (if the requested change has been made) all comments from all contributors on the current page:

Figure 10.17 – Comments panel

Figma has enhanced its comments feature, significantly improving readability. Now, it includes the ability to use reactions and directly tag team members for targeted feedback. And, notably, they've introduced formatting options. These options include bullet and numbered lists, text styling with bold, italic, and underline, and the ability to add hyperlinks to selected text. Feel free to explore every feature!

During the phase of collecting feedback, it often happens that for some reason you do not want to provide access to the source of the file, but still want someone to be able to view the design interface, share their opinion, and leave feedback.

This can be a common case where customers or stakeholders need to see the product and leave feedback or suggest corrections that need to be made. In this situation, you can simply provide a link to the prototype only (keep in mind that the prototype always starts with the view that you see in front of you when you create a shared link), and from the **Presentation view**, even those who do not have access to the original file will be able to insert comments using the appropriate tool on the top bar:

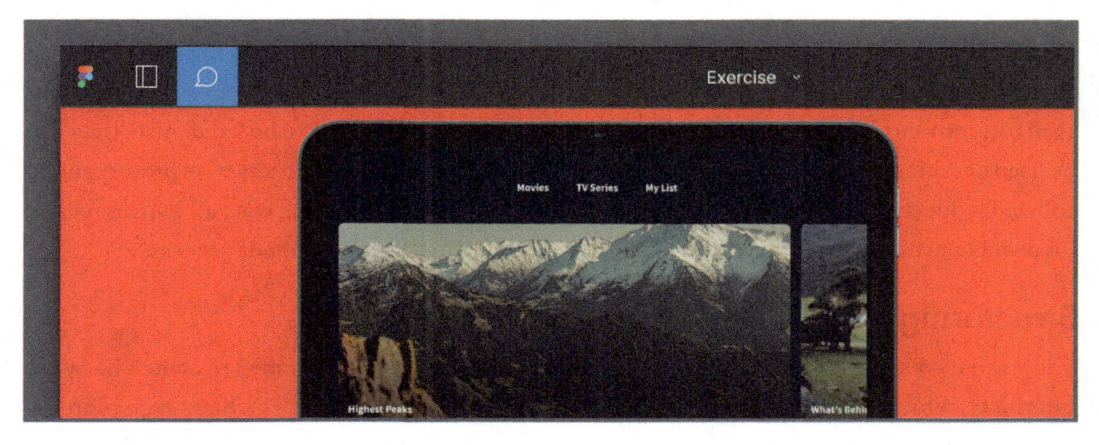

Figure 10.18 – Add comment function for viewers

Remember that even if someone only intends to leave comments in your file or prototype, and nothing more, a Figma account – any, even a Starter one – is required. Thus, there will be no unpleasant surprises such as anonymous and unwanted comments.

All reviews collected in this way will be automatically added to the list, which is available from the design file, and whoever has edit rights will see a badge on the icon, indicating the presence of new comments:

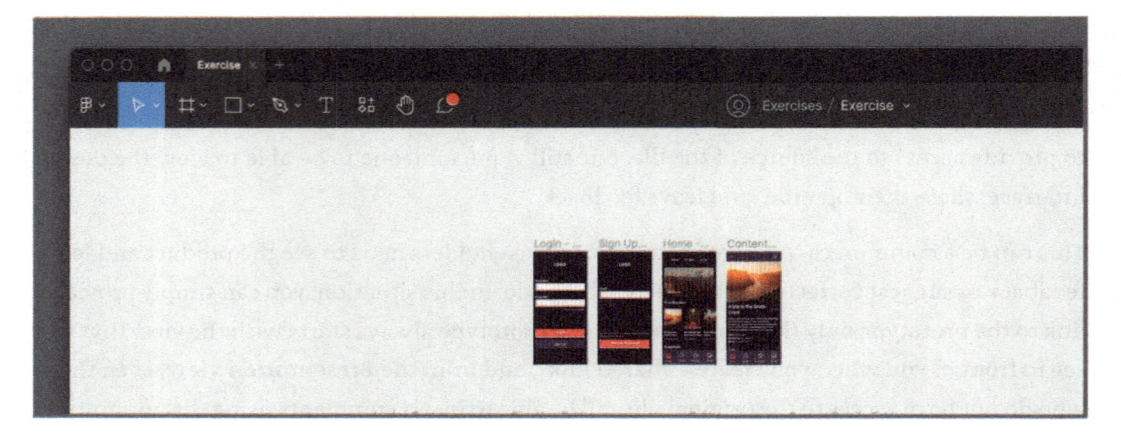

Figure 10.19 – New comments alert badge

In summary, comments can be used in two different and equally useful ways. First of all, they can be for internal use, for collaboration between everyone who works on the interface design so that they can communicate, suggest, review, and keep track of what needs to be fixed. Also, they can be used at critical stages (such as completing a wireframe, interface, or interactive prototype), to collect feedback and reactions from customers and stakeholders. In this way, all parties will be involved to avoid any problems and misunderstandings in the development process.

Structuring flows

Since you have three different flows (mobile, tablet, and desktop), you need to switch between interfaces, which may not be so easy and fast. In complex projects, you can have even more dynamic flows, and often, at first glance, they can look almost the same. In such cases, it is quite easy to send the wrong link by mistake, and as a result, the recipient will see the wrong prototype. How can you avoid this confusion?

To solve this problem, Figma has created **flows**, a function with which you can label, structure, and manipulate your flows in a file. To see exactly how this works, let's implement flows for our prototypes. To do this, follow these steps:

1. Temporarily exit the **Presentation view** and return to the **Hi-Fi** page. From here, switch to the **Prototype** tab and select the first view of the mobile flow, that is, **Login - Mobile**.

Chapter 10

2. In the upper part of the panel, you will find the **Flow starting point** option. Click the **+** button and the first flow will be added:

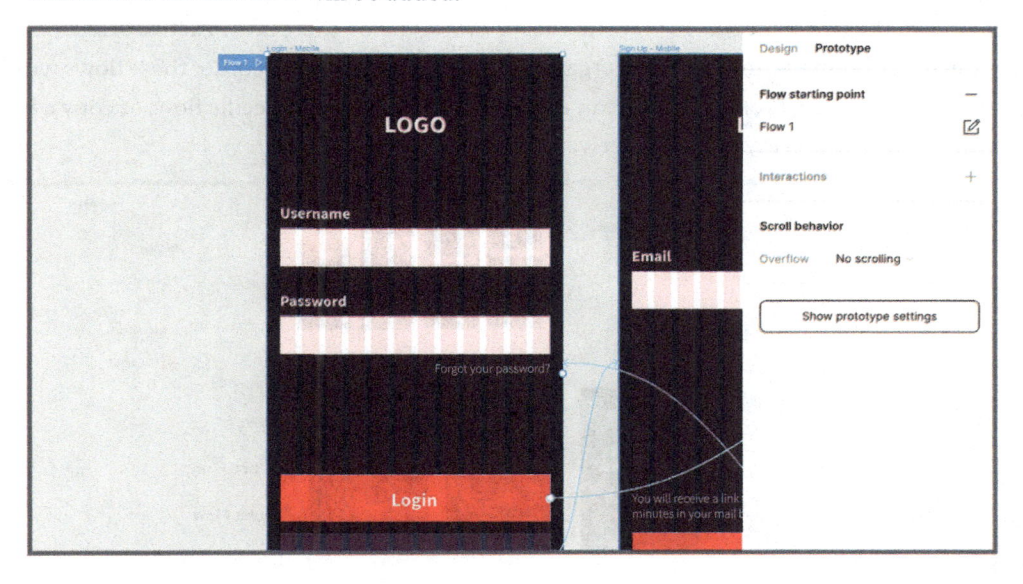

Figure 10.20 – Adding a flow

3. From now on, Figma will know that the **Login - Mobile** view is the starting point for one of our user flows. By default, this flow was named **Flow 1**, but to make it more specific, you can rename it to `Mobile Flow` simply by clicking on the name and entering a new one.

4. Then click the **Edit** button and add a description. This way, you will make everything clear even to those who are not involved in the project, but they will only see the finished prototype, so that they can quickly get the idea:

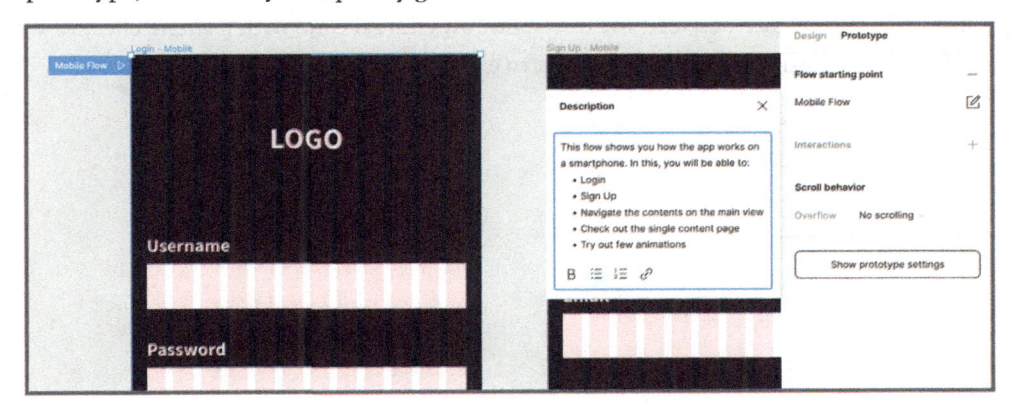

Figure 10.21 – Setting a description for a flow

Repeat the same operation for the tablet and desktop flows, giving them the appropriate names and descriptions. After completing your work, all the flows you've created in the project will be visible in the right sidebar. To view this list of flows, ensure there are no active selections on the canvas. Additionally, for enhanced organization, you can drag and reorder these flows within the sidebar as needed. From here, you can even run a prototype of a specific flow, or copy a link to it, which will direct everyone who receives it exclusively to this flow:

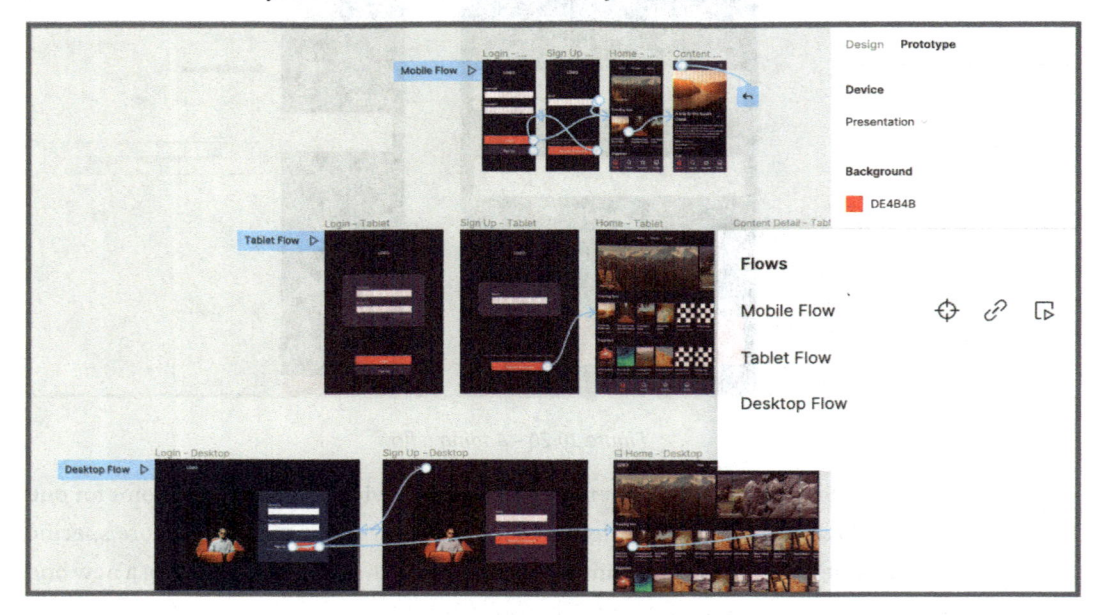

Figure 10.22 – Flows overview

In addition, from now on, a new left sidebar will be available in the **Presentation view**, which allows you to navigate between the different flows in real time with a single click, as well as to read their descriptions so you know what to expect:

Figure 10.23 – Presentation view with flows

Flows are a great addition to the prototype feature that makes your interactive interfaces more organized and easier to manage. As long as you use appropriate names and clear descriptions, even in a file with multiple flows, it will be easy for you and your teammates to navigate.

Advanced user testing

User testing of a product – and at different stages of design – by those who represent the target audience is an important step for every project, as well as an excellent opportunity to detect critical issues and problems long before the product is released. **Flows** in Figma are also an undoubtedly useful function for this case, as you can offer a user two or more flows to perform the same operation within your application or website. By doing this kind of comparative analysis, you can investigate user behavior more deeply, as well as identifying bugs and problems.

In fact, when prototyping very large and complex applications, it is impossible and not very efficient to provide users with the entire prototype, consisting of a huge number of possible paths, and tell them to try it. So, it is best to structure real tasks, that is, a list of goals that the user must complete in the application. Only after defining all of them can you then create specific prototypes for these purposes and provide the user with this set of flows from various parts of the application. For example, the first flow might be to register a new user and log in to the application, the second to select and view streaming content, and so on. In this way, the flow description can be strategically used as a numerical step-by-step list that the users must be able to follow on their own.

However, there may be circumstances when **flows** in Figma aren't enough, for example, when there is no way to closely observe the testing phase or to interview each individual user to determine their satisfaction with the user experience. In this case, there are some very interesting alternative tools that you can use alongside Figma for creating user tests and carrying out user research. The most famous is definitely **Maze** (`maze.co`):

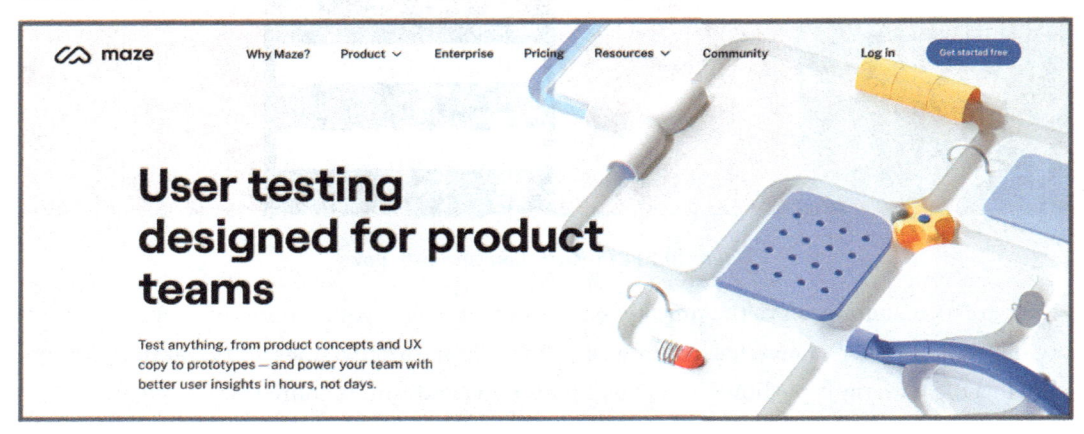

Figure 10.24 – The Maze tool

Maze is an extremely interesting tool with a free plan that allows you to send real structured tests to a significant number of people. It allows you to try out different flows of your prototype by asking the users to complete the assigned tasks, and finally, have them fill out short surveys that you can prepare in advance, so you can gather ideas and opinions and analyze the general level of satisfaction. Obviously, the prototypes you'll be using in Maze can be created in Figma, and in fact, it will be enough to use the link to the Figma prototype when requested by Maze.

As you know, one of Figma's greatest strengths is its powerful collaboration features, and perhaps this section has made you even more convinced of this by seeing how easy it is to leave and manage comments. You will use comments a lot when working in a team, and as you've seen, Figma is still developing them to make them even better. You also learned about another easy-to-use but very useful feature, namely, **flows**, and even implemented them in your prototype, so now everything is better structured and understandable. And if you ever need or want to go further with user testing, you can always refer to external tools such as **Maze**, which, in collaboration with Figma, can give you better user testing results!

Summary

Perhaps this chapter was special for you because here, you finally saw the live result of your work. There will surely have been a lot of pleasant surprises – you had already implemented amazing prototyping techniques before this, but it can still be impressive to see how it all works in practice. Even if you found something that didn't work as planned, don't worry; you now have enough experience to correctly identify the source of the problem and fix it quickly. In the future, you will find such errors earlier, because now you know how to monitor and test a prototype in real time, both in the **Presentation view** and in the Figma application.

Apart from that, you also learned how to share your prototype, embed it to give easier access to it, and let others comment and share their opinions right in Figma. You also learned how to structure your prototype better using flows. Now your prototype is even better prepared for user testing.

In the next chapter, you will be exploring Dev Mode, and you will learn how to export assets and prepare your design files for further development.

Learn more on Discord

To join the Discord community for this book – where you can share feedback, ask questions to the author, and learn about new releases – follow the QR code below:

https://packt.link/figma

11
Exporting Assets and Managing the Handover Process

So far, you've successfully completed the prototype for your interface, configuring and testing it, possibly within the Figma mobile application as well. Your journey has been significant, marked by extensive learning of Figma and a comprehensive understanding of design principles and workflows. Therefore, we can safely say that your future projects will be easier in terms of working with Figma, since you can now not only use all the necessary functions of this design tool but also the more complicated ones, as real projects require much more detailed work at each stage of product design.

While working on complex products, the team's composition and communication are as crucial as design skills. A team of professionals, including key player designers, must collaborate effectively to realize a project's full potential. Excellent layouts and user experiences can fall short if not properly developed or communicated, rendering the design effort futile. To address such challenges, Figma offers functions to efficiently export and prepare assets, facilitating a smoother handover to developers, and minimizing misunderstandings within a team. This is what this chapter will focus on, and beyond that, you will also learn how to make your design files easily accessible and understandable to both you and others.

In this chapter, we are going to cover the following main topics:

- Exporting from Figma
- Exploring Dev Mode
- Handing over the project for development

By the end of the chapter, you will have learned how to distinguish Figma's save and export formats, export assets and code snippets, and apply best practices for smooth handover to the development team.

Exporting from Figma

At this point, you have a pretty clear overview of the exact work behind the analysis, design, interactive prototyping, and product testing. Now, you will focus on the very last stage – working on the handover of all resources and assets, which happens after you have made sure that your design is absolutely ready for it. The first thing that you need to know about is the Figma tools: these allow you to prepare and export a file and individual elements to everyone, who will then work on the actual development of the application or website. There are several ways to do this, as well as several formats that Figma offers for it. This and more will be presented to you in this section of the chapter.

What formats are supported?

First, we need to define an important difference between saving and exporting in Figma, as well as other design tools. By clicking on **File** in the menu bar (desktop version only) or on the **Figma** logo in the upper-left corner and then **File**, you can save a local version of a project:

Figure 11.1 – Save As .fig… and Save local copy…

When you opt for saving, you're essentially creating a local version of your project, downloading a backup of its source. This backup can be stored locally or potentially shared with third parties, transferring the file's ownership on a permanent basis. In essence, saving means working with source files, granting you the ability to open and edit your Figma creations.

It's important to note, however, that saved files won't encompass comments, rules/permissions, or version history – these are excluded from the saved .fig (Figma file extension) files. The export option is available from the same **File** menu, just below the save options. The first function, **Export…**, allows you to specify your choice, and you will explore it in more detail later in this chapter. Another option, **Export frames to PDF**, exports a single PDF file containing all the frames of the current page, even if they are of different sizes. **PDF (Portable Document Format)**, as you probably already know, is an extremely versatile format type, but above all, it is absolutely compatible with any system, old or new. This format is very convenient, as it can collect text, fonts, vectors, and images.

In addition to PDF, Figma allows you to export some of the most common formats, such as these:

- **.PNG** – a lossless raster format that keeps any eventual layer transparency.
- **.JPG** – a compressed raster format that gives a smaller file size but may reduce image quality and flatten transparencies.
- **.SVG** – a vector format that can be scaled without loss of quality, since it is based on numeric values and coordinates. It is not pixel-based and does not work with bitmaps.

Now, after this brief overview of the formats available in Figma, let's move from theory to practice and learn how to export single and multiple assets.

Single- and multiple-asset export

In addition to the capability to export an entire document or entire pages of a file, you can also selectively export specific components of a design and gather the assets used within a composition. This can be valuable when collaborating with a development team or for various other purposes. You have the flexibility to carry out this operation by either selecting items individually or in bulk, depending on your specific requirements. Let's begin by exploring the process of exporting a single element.

It happens quite often that you need to provide the development team with a set of icons used in your design, so now, you will try to simulate this action with a single asset. To do this, go to your **Hi-Fi** page and follow these steps:

- Open your layouts and select any icon, such as the star, provided in our **Content Detail** view. Keep an eye on the right-hand panel, where you'll notice the **Export** section, which is presently inactive. To activate this feature, simply click the + symbol next to it.

- Now, Figma will show you some of the options available to export this single asset. Given that this icon is in vector format, you have the choice to select the **SVG** format to maintain its editability. Alternatively, you can opt to save it as a bitmap while retaining transparency by selecting the **PNG** format.

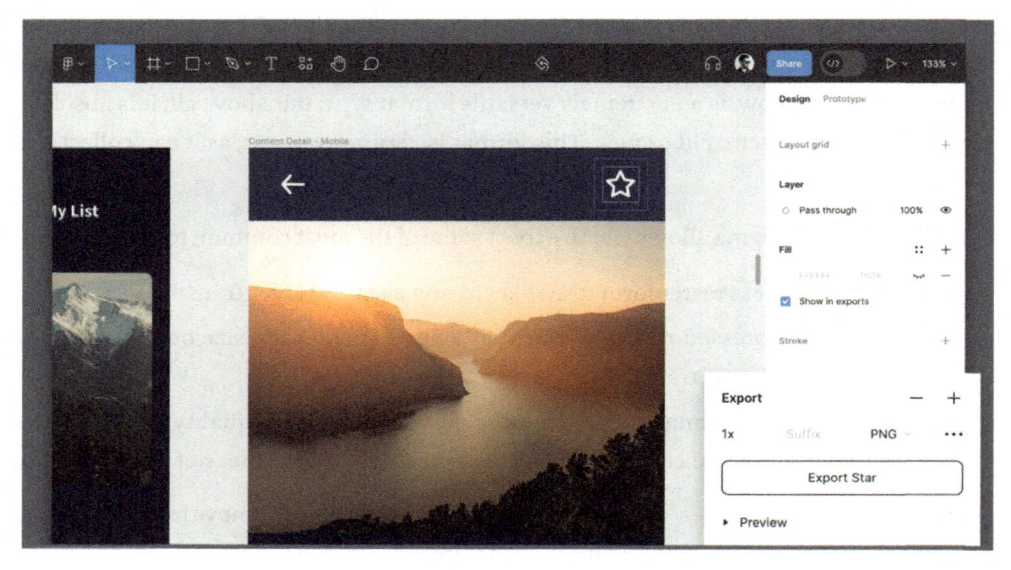

Figure 11.2 – The Export section

- Next to the format selector, you can see the scale setting. Click **1x** to open a list with some asset scaling presets.

   In this list, you'll notice several choices, each with different letters at the end of the value. Here's what they mean:

    - Values with an **X** at the end, such as **2x**, act as multipliers. Choosing one of these options will proportionally increase or decrease the size of the icon. For instance, if you select **2x**, the icon will become twice its current size, which may result in a larger file size. This scaling can be useful to ensure that the icon looks crisp and clear on devices with higher pixel densities.
    - Values with **W** and **H** indicate a fixed width and height, respectively. If you choose one of these options, the object will be set to a specific width or height, maintaining its aspect ratio while adjusting the other dimension accordingly.

If none of the preset options suit your needs, you also have the flexibility to enter your custom scale value in this field. This allows you to fine-tune the size of your asset based on your specific design requirements. For now, just go on with the default **1x** option.

- When you're done, just click the **Export** (+ *Layer Name*) button, choose where to save this individual asset, and confirm, and your file will appear right there in just a few seconds.

> **Note:**
>
> You can add more than one **Export** option to each item by simply clicking the + button in the appropriate section on the right sidebar. This allows you to easily export the asset in different formats with one click, or export in the same format but at different scales, such as **1x** and **2x**.

After exporting an icon or any element in Figma, the export settings persist, keeping all the details you filled in. This feature is particularly useful for future exports of the same element, eliminating the need to re-enter settings. However, what's even more useful is the ability to customize the export options directly during the design process, ensuring that all the elements will be immediately ready for the export phase. Thus, you can preconfigure the export parameters for you and anyone else who would like to export assets from the file, even with view-only permissions:

Figure 11.3 – Export section for users with view-only permissions

One of the main benefits of this feature is that developers can remain autonomous in exporting assets directly from Figma. And this is not the only advantage of this feature.

If you set the correct export options for each asset (for example, **PNG** on **1x** – for each icon, for all card images, and maybe some full parent frames in PDF to have a quick preview of the interface), each element will be ready to be extrapolated from Figma, and you can even do it with one click. Exactly for this purpose, there is the previously mentioned **Export...** function, which you can find by clicking the Figma icon menu at the top left and choosing **File**. To access it faster, you can – with no active selections - press *Shift* + *Command* + *E* (macOS) or *Shift* + *Ctrl* + *E* (Win), and a bulk export window will appear. This dialog collects all the assets on the current page, with relative settings set for each, and performs a bulk export:

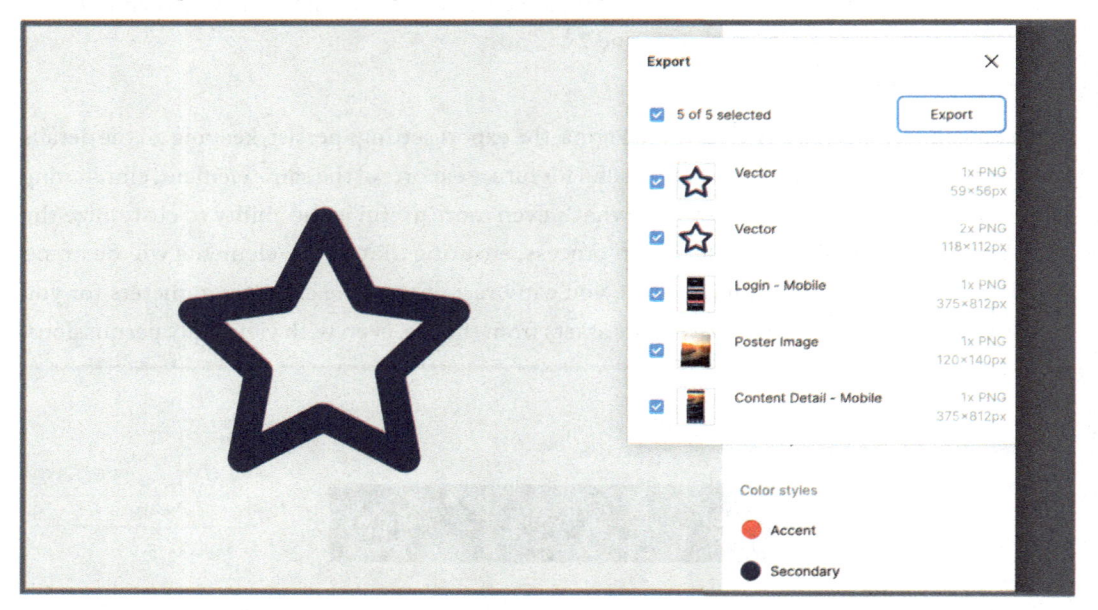

Figure 11.4 – Bulk-exporting assets

The list of assets is presented with checkboxes, allowing you the flexibility to selectively export the assets you need. You can also, if necessary, uncheck items that you don't wish to export at the moment.

Alternatively, you have the option to select one or more items directly on your canvas and then initiate the **Export...** function. In this case, the export window will only display the selected items, making it a convenient way to export specific elements.

This functionality extends to selecting a single layer that may contain multiple assets within it. For instance, if you choose the **Content Detail** frame and then open the **Export** dialog box, it will exclusively show the exportable assets contained within that particular view, streamlining the export process for your chosen elements.

Let's recap all the possibilities Figma offers you for your assets and files. So far, there are five formats – **FIG, PDF, PNG, JPG**, and **SVG** – to save or export the elements you want. The first one is for downloading a local copy of your file, and its further use can be exclusively in Figma. Other formats are easy to open outside of Figma and are completely independent after export, so you can share them without any special restrictions. Each format has both advantages and limitations, and your choice depends on your needs and the goals of that export. Also, you can export items individually or in large quantities, as well as export the same item in several formats and scales with one click, if you have configured everything correctly beforehand. Finally, you have learned how to make it easier to work with elements that you might need to share by setting all the **Export** options for them at the interface design stage. Moreover, this way, you open up the ability to others to freely save these elements in Figma, even users.

Take some time to delve further into the export functions as needed. Once you feel comfortable with these options, you can proceed to explore the **Properties** panel and way more features for the final project phases.

Exploring Dev Mode

As you've likely noticed, the right panel is a treasure trove of functions, settings, and tools, carefully designed to enhance your design workflow. It encompasses everything, from crafting aesthetically pleasing and functional interfaces to efficiently organizing your files for seamless collaboration with your team, and simplifying the handover process to developers. Your journey so far has been a voyage through multiple chapters and extensive practice, uncovering a multitude of tips and hidden gems to elevate your proficiency with layers, styles, components, and more.

Now, all that hard-earned knowledge is about to become even more valuable as it translates into actionable insights for the next phase. Let's start by exploring what happens when you share your file with external viewers with no editing permissions.

This unveils a range of features neatly organized in a tab called **Properties**.

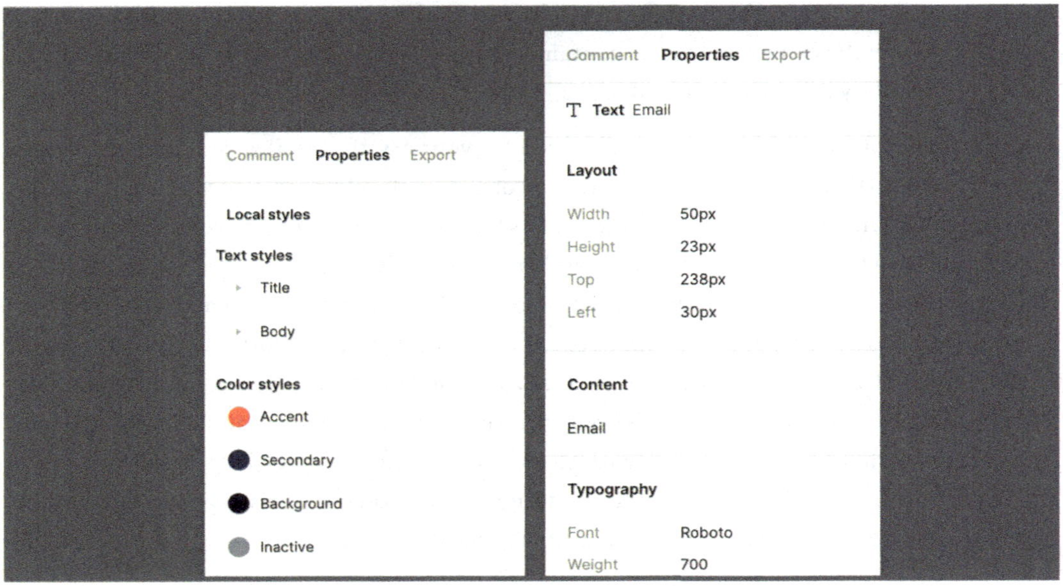

Figure 11.5 – The Properties tab

Essentially, it offers a straightforward and swift way to access the style library. By selecting specific elements, you can delve into the nitty-gritty of their layout rules. While this summary might be useful for collaborators seeking a more in-depth design understanding, it may not hold as much appeal for developers aiming to supercharge their workflow. To significantly enhance the handover process between teams, it's advantageous to transition to **Dev Mode**. This dedicated workspace is equipped with numerous features designed to streamline collaboration.

Switching to Dev Mode

Dev Mode stands as an evolved platform designed for the seasoned developer. It's a sophisticated yet intuitive environment, now fully integrated into Figma's suite of tools. This feature-rich space is tailored to enhance the developer's workflow, and it's accessible through Pro and higher-tier subscriptions or available as an individual offering for developers.

Making the switch to this mode is as simple as a single click. Just glide your cursor to the top bar of your Figma interface, and there, on the right, awaits the **Dev Mode** toggle (or press *Shift + D*), as you see below:

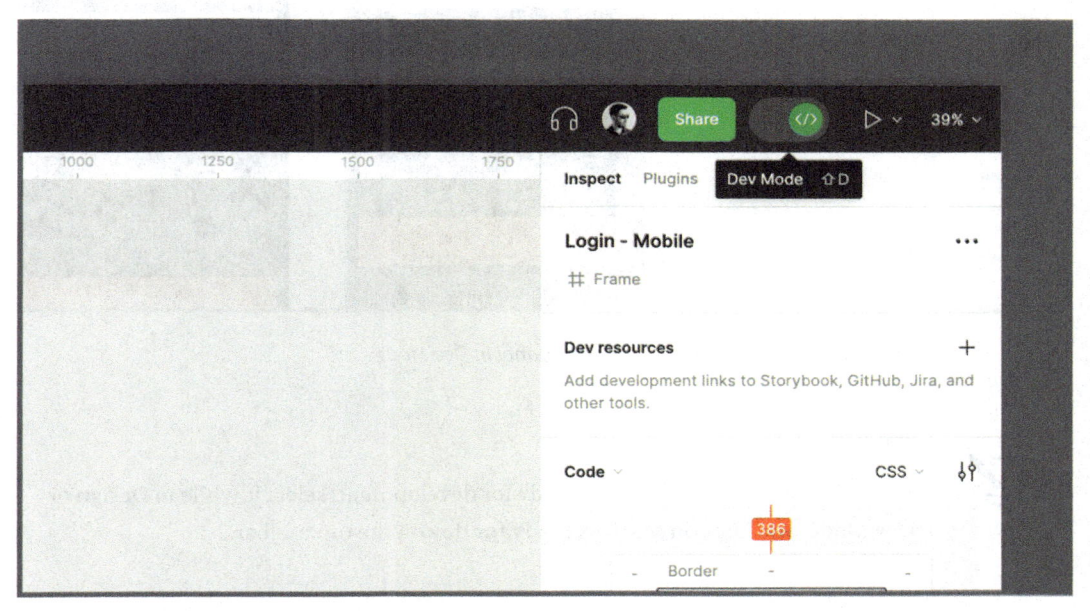

Figure 11.6 – Switching to Dev Mode

Starting now, your interface will look a bit different, all with the benefit of making handover easier. Your toolbar has been simplified, keeping only the most important tools for selection and comments. The left panel has been divided vertically, displaying all the frames and sections marked as **Ready for development** on the top. This makes it easier for designers to communicate which views are completed and which are still in progress.

The layers section has also been modified, now showing only the layers of the currently selected frame and its contents, streamlining your workflow.

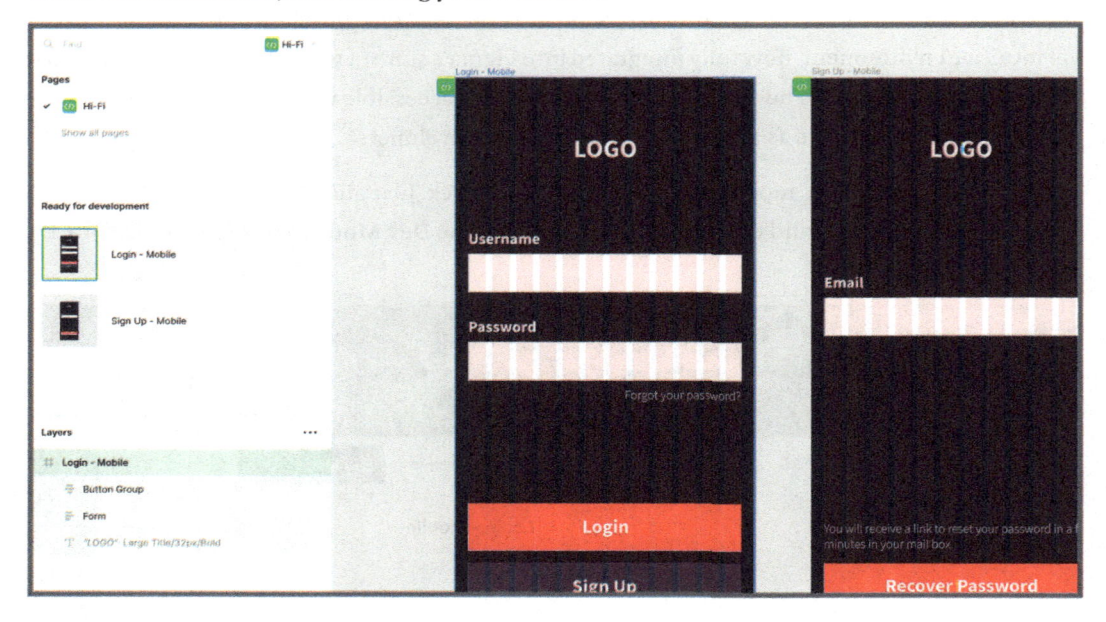

Figure 11.7 - Left panel in Dev Mode

> **Note:**
> To mark any frame or section as ready for development, select it while in Design or Dev Mode, and click on **Mark as ready for dev** on the top toolbar.

On the other side, in the right panel, you will not find Design and Prototype anymore but, instead, **Inspect** and **Plugins**. Here is where all the main stuff happens, allowing you to dive deeper into layouts, styles, and elements and access a wealth of valuable design insights and code snippets. Let's start by delving into the design aspects first.

Overviewing the file

Without any active selection, the right panel in **Dev Mode** may not appear particularly exciting, primarily displaying the flows of the current page and some code options we'll delve into later. However, once you select a frame or inner element, a set of new information related to your current selection comes to life. For instance, if you choose a complex component like our button element, complete with variants, you'll gain access to a comprehensive overview of everything associated with it. This includes all the properties, any linked descriptions or documentation, and even a playground for live-testing the component itself.

Figure 11.8 - Inspecting a button component

At the bottom of the panel, you can check out colors and assets and adjust export settings. Plus, while inspecting your canvas in real time, you'll easily see guides, padding, margins, and spacing details, just like you would do with any browser's live inspector.

Figure 11.9 - Design-related info

As the name suggests, **Dev Mode** is tailored for developers, and where it truly shines is in handling various aspects related to code. This is the precise direction we're heading next – delving into the rich array of code-related features and functionalities it offers.

Design to code

As a designer, you will most likely rarely use the Dev Mode's **Inspect** panel, as it is primarily intended for developers. Of course, the property summary can be useful, but its main purpose is to provide the development team with all the values they might need to write the actual code. At the beginning of your journey, it was mentioned that Figma may seem limited in comparison to, for example, Adobe Illustrator, but the truth is that these products are slightly different and complementary. In Figma, the limitations are dictated by a specific need, namely the ability to easily convert everything we design into code. All elements you create in Figma are almost automatically converted to the best(mostly web-based)rules using the latest **HTML5** and **CSS3** standards. So, if, for example, you can't find a specific filter or effect in a code snippet, it might not be possible to reproduce it in HTML and CSS, and Figma won't support that.

Chapter 11

Does this mean that what designers create in Figma is already automatically turned into a complete and functional product? No. For these purposes, there are, for example, plugins that export entire frames in HTML/CSS, React, and other programming languages, but this way is still recommended exclusively for really basic products such as quick landing pages or simple testing prototypes. In this context, automatic systems never guarantee high quality compared to what we can achieve with targeted development.

However, what is really useful in the **Inspect** tab is the ability – while in **Dev Mode** - to select specific items and inspect, copy, and use the same properties for different purposes. For example, after clicking on any **Button** element, the following will be displayed immediately below the component's summary in the right panel:

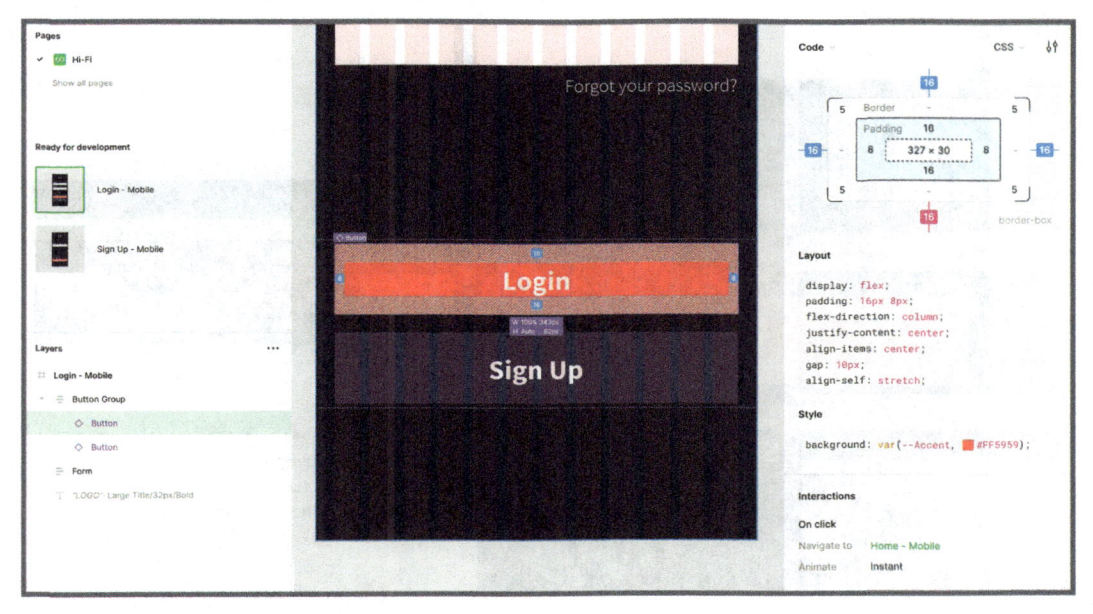

Figure 11.10 – Code snippets for the Button element

In the **Code** section, **CSS** rules are set by default, as this is the most useful and commonly used option. **CSS** stands for **Cascading Style Sheet** and is a style rule sheet that combines the structure created in HTML (which serves to create the "skeleton," the foundation of your layout) to structure and style a website or web application. What is especially remarkable about it is that the highest-quality code is achieved here when using **Auto layout** at the design stage. In fact, **Auto layout** corresponds to a 1:1 **Flexbox** web system and, therefore, allows you to already have at your disposal all the rules you need to create the prototyped layout.

If you didn't use **Auto layout**, values would be suggested with absolute value coordinates in **Frames**, which should be avoided where possible, as this results in unresponsive interfaces or harder work at a later stage. The **CSS** rules that we have access to range from color rules (even converting color styles to CSS variables) to text, effects, sizing, and positioning. Each property and function presented in the **Design** tab is equivalent to a rule that you will find here later.

As you can see, the **Code** section can make web development a bit easier. But what if instead of a website, we need to develop mobile applications? It is also possible to get the code for these purposes; just click on the **CSS** option and a dropdown will appear, where you will find both the **iOS** and **Android** options and, thus, can access small snippets – based on the selected layer – of the code in Swift/SwiftUI and Compose/XML, respectively:

Figure 11.11 – Switching to iOS/Android code snippets

Dev Mode is indeed tailored for developers, offering a dedicated environment for coding within Figma. However, its benefits extend to the entire team. A comprehensive understanding of **Dev Mode**'s tools and functionalities can significantly enhance communication with developers. Familiarizing yourself with its features, especially the **Inspect** panel, is a valuable practice not just for developers but for designers too. By doing so, you'll gain a deeper insight into the development process, which can lead to more efficient collaboration and potentially spark new ideas to streamline your team's workflow.

Extending Dev Mode

However, we're not finished yet! We've already discovered lots of cool features that make it easier for designers and developers to work together. And now, we can take it even further by using **Plugins** in **Dev Mode**. These Plugins help developers get all the info they need in one place to bring a design to life. They're like handy tools that can take inspecting and generating code to the next level, making these tasks even easier.

We'll delve into Figma's Plugins in the next chapter, but here, we're talking about special plugins created or adjusted specifically for developers. You can access these in the right panel by switching from the **Inspect** to the **Plugins** tab.

Figure 11.12 - Plugins tab

If you're a designer, these plugins won't impact your workspace or interfere with your design-oriented plugins. However, some of these plugins are available for both design and development. In the development section, they are customized to automatically gather data from the design side and present it in a format that's easy for developers to work with, without requiring any additional input from you.

I won't make specific plugin recommendations because it primarily caters to developers, and the choice really depends on their specific needs.

For instance, your development team might need plugins to convert components to React, integrate with Jira for project management, or connect Figma with GitHub. The possibilities are virtually limitless, and it all depends on what works best for your team's workflow and requirements.

Furthermore, if your development team is looking to push the boundaries, they can explore **Figma for VS Code**, which is available as a Visual Studio Code plugin. This integration takes the connection between design and code to a whole new level.

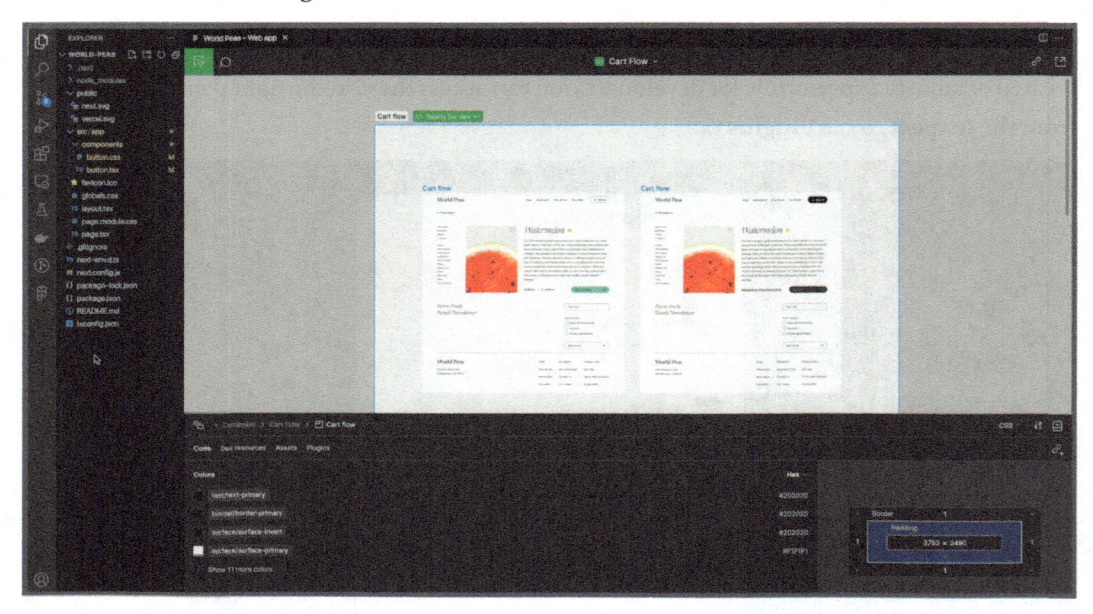

Figure 11.13 - Figma for VS Code

In the next section, you'll learn how to make your design project in Figma even more development-friendly, and you'll find out why it's important to keep it that way even if the product is already on the market.

Handing over the project for development

Your journey was as exciting and interesting as it was intense, wasn't it? You have gone through the important steps in designing a generic product. Of course, all phases have been minimized to keep the overview for you as complete as possible. Nevertheless, we can say that, at the moment, you have keys with which you can approach any other projects on your future path, which will be devoted to the creation of real products, and therefore, the designs will be much more detailed and elaborate.

In addition, it is likely that you will be a part of a whole team working on a complex digital product, and it will also be a very interesting journey in which you will combine tools that you already know with the discovery of new, more advanced features.

So does our work really end here? Can we really consider the project closed? Of course, even after testing a product, getting approval, and providing developers with the necessary resources, there are still very few cases where a designer actually "stops" working on something that has been created. So what will happen next?

There are no universal answers to this question, and it all depends on the type of job and whether you are a freelancer or an in-house designer. However, while there can be many scenarios, we can give you a general overview of how things usually work if a designer is part of a team that manages an entire product or a part of it, as seen in the next section.

What's next?

In the early days of digital technology, professionals were only hired to design a product, and once it was developed, it was no longer necessary to maintain a working relationship. Often, designers did not even provide the source files of a project; instead, they only sent representative images of how the product should ultimately look. Year after year, the value of digital products increased, and companies began to invest more and more in them, and with that, the approach to design and development completely changed.

A digital product today represents a full-fledged ecosystem. Research and analysis are its foundation, and the design and prototyping phases are constant aspects that make it come alive, as the product will always be updated and improved. This is what defines a successful product – one that is built based on flexibility, modularity, and continuity in its development.

For this reason, more and more companies and agencies are no longer starting with the product itself but with a **design system**, or rather, a system of building blocks that helps create one or more products with scalability in mind. We have also built the foundation for a modest design system, chapter by chapter, by structuring typography, colors, grids, and components. The design system grows with the product; it is constantly expanding and evolving through the creation of new blocks and may even contain more abstract aspects of it. In addition, the design system can be used to create a range of products that fit together to provide more than one service, without making the user feel pushed into an unfamiliar environment.

Speaking of design systems, we must differentiate them from **UI kits**. While a comprehensive comparison would warrant its own book, I'll give you a basic idea of their main principles. A UI kit is essentially a collection of design elements like components and styles. At first glance, you might think this sounds quite similar to a design system. However, there's a fundamental difference you should be aware of as a designer.

As mentioned earlier, a design system evolves alongside the product and encompasses both standard and custom elements specifically created for it. It can even extend to include guidelines for other aspects like user communication, tone of voice, inclusivity, design patterns, design tokens, and much more. What's noteworthy is that a variety of professionals beyond the design team, such as copywriters, psychologists, marketers, and others, can contribute to a design system's development.

On the other hand, UI kits are usually less tied to a specific product. They may offer a set of text styles, colors, grids, and components that can be easily reused across various apps or websites, perhaps with some style customization or minor adjustments, like a development framework. UI kits are often employed as a rapid solution for creating generic digital products or as a starting point for crafting and adapting your unique design system.

Thus, a UI kit can speed up the initial process, but as your product gets more complex, you run into tough constraints, so it is often worth investing in the creation of a design system.

Documenting, reiterating, and improving

It is normal that while a project grows, improves, and develops, the composition of the team that works on it may change, and the number of professionals can also increase. When this happens, project files and resources are frequently and repeatedly passed from hand to hand among other designers and developers. You should never underestimate this aspect and always take it into account in your future work process. What you can do is organize your projects, files, and folders, always clear them of useless items, and rename layers, styles, and components in the best way. However, this is not always enough. Especially when you are working on a product that has a design system based on styles, components, and variants, it is very important that they are all clear, transparent, and documented.

But what exactly does this mean? Well, you can make it easy for anyone new to a project by specifying when to use each library item specifically. Thus, if you go to the **Styles + Components** page and select any element – for example, **Carousel Item** – you can add a code snippet for it, or perhaps indicate the use case in a few words or sentences for this component:

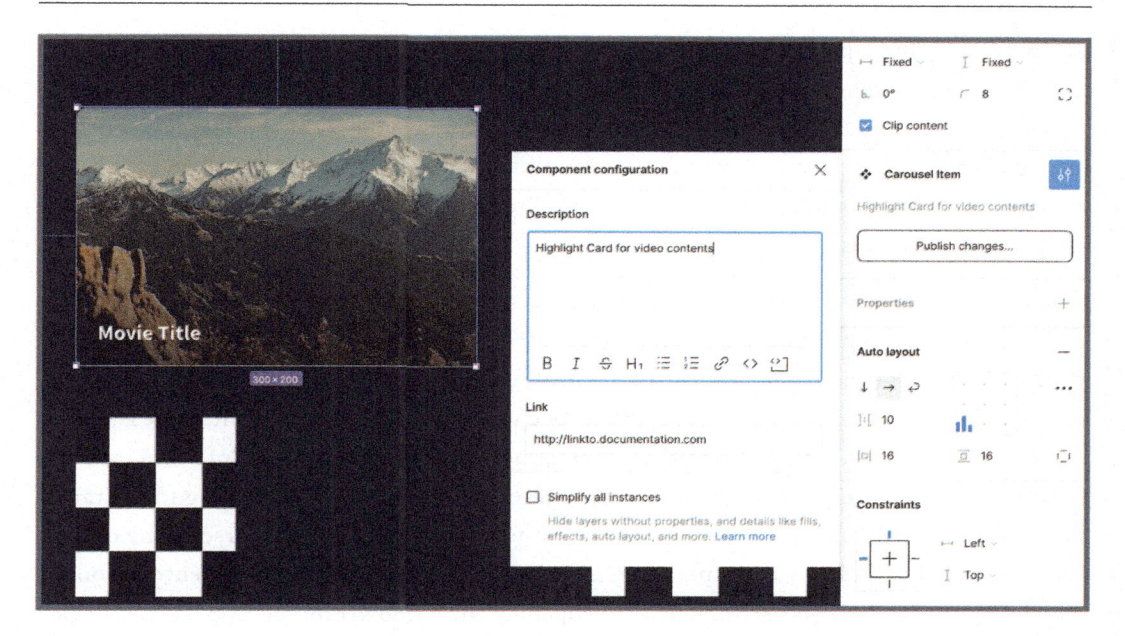

Figure 11.14 – Adding documentation to a component

For more complex cases, you can add a direct link – and this will appear directly in Dev Mode - to any more extensive documentation that can be created in an external platform, such as **Notion**, **Zeroheight**, or in a separate Figma file, depending on the needs of the project.

In addition to components, it is best to apply accompanying information to styles as well, where you can describe the purpose of a specific typography or color. In larger projects, even text styles, colors, and spacing are converted into so-called **design tokens**. In fact, thanks to design tokens, Figma styles can be converted to code in real time, and in the case of some changes, they are automatically replaced in all instances of them in the actual source of the application. This is a very advanced concept, but it's worth exploring with the developers on your team, and we'll have a deeper look at this in *Chapter 13, Going Advanced with Variables and Conditional Prototyping*.

As you can imagine, there is always room for improvement in any product, which is great because you, as a designer, can strengthen your skills, acquire new ones, and grow professionally. And even when you've created a mature product with an incredible design system (which itself takes years of work), there will always be something to change, develop, and improve. This is due to the fact that user needs are constantly changing, technology develops at a tremendous speed, and standards are often revised. Therefore, it is useless to try to create the perfect product right away, as you risk never going into the release phase.

When you feel that a product is well designed, it's important to launch it to market, study user reactions, conduct market research with your target audience after launch, and see if everything works as expected. Your preliminary analysis may seem perfect in theory even after a few tests, but in practice, it may fail due to unforeseen events or miscalculated variables. However, you should always use this as an opportunity to take advantage of the new data that the market provides to solve critical problems.

That way, even when a product does well in the market, the designer's job is never over, and you will continually repeat the design process and try to improve what you already have. There will always be many questions and problems to be solved. Is there any way to improve the conversion rate? Can it be influenced if you move a button or change its color? At this point, there is a great way to get useful data – an **A/B test**, that is, creating another version of the interface that will be compared with the current one and presented to a group of people belonging to the target audience, enabling you to understand whether it will perform better or worse in the market. Large companies conduct such experiences expensively, releasing slightly different versions of the same product. You can see for yourself by opening the Facebook mobile app on your device and a friend's one: do you have the same interface, the same icons, the same arrangement of the elements on the tab bar? Probably not. As you can see, the designer always has something to do, and design in general has a huge impact on the life of the product and its users.

As you can see, being a designer means always being ready to take on challenges, knowing that there is always a way to improve the user experience and meet the users' needs on a deeper level. It's also important to empathize not only with your audience but also with your teammates, by giving them your files in an organized and understandable way. Thus, it will be much easier for you as well as other designers to navigate through documented and descriptive resources, rather than through something messy, especially if you need to create a design system, which is almost inevitable and indeed necessary if your product constantly evolves.

Summary

In this chapter, you discovered that Figma can not only be an efficient and fast design tool but also go beyond that, considering the needs of other team members who might work in collaboration with designers. Thus, you learned how to export a whole file or its individual elements from Figma in several possible formats, as well as how to set up elements for subsequent export while still at the active design stage. Also, you finally explored the functionality of **Dev Mode**. In addition, you learned about what a design system is and how to document and assign descriptions for styles and components in your projects, ensuring that everything is well organized and easy to use.

In the next, you'll see how to extend Figma by discovering the amazing Figma Community, where you can explore hundreds of cool UI kits, templates, widgets, and plugins from creators around the world. Using Figma Community resources, you can not only speed up and optimize your workflow but also find inspiration to create something amazing yourself!

Learn more on Discord

To join the Discord community for this book – where you can share feedback, ask questions to the author, and learn about new releases – follow the QR code below:

https://packt.link/figma

12

Discovering Resources, Plugins, and Widgets in the Figma Community

In the previous chapter, you completed the interface design of our video streaming application by learning about exporting assets and preparing files for further development work. Of course, in real life, your design routine will be full of other aspects that this book cannot cover, but now, you clearly understand how product design begins, what stages it consists of, and when we may (or may not) call it completed. You should understand, however, that in reality, things can be different. Thus, in some cases, you could work in a team of designers who are engaged in only a single feature of a huge digital product, or you could get a job in a company that has already launched projects, and you will need to work on improving them from the design side. Yes, you will have many challenges along the way, but as you gradually overcome them, you will open up tremendous opportunities to learn something new, and you will grow professionally and personally.

Another reason why you shouldn't worry too much and take more risks is that, now, designers prefer to be open, share experiences with each other, and support and guide beginners. This happens in a variety of ways – meetups, conferences, open talks, mentoring, and more. Figma goes the extra mile in bringing designers from all corners of the world together. It provides an entire platform to share resources, and that's what we'll dive into in this chapter. What makes this chapter unique is that we won't focus on the application's interface this time. Instead, we'll embark on an exciting journey into the captivating realm of the Figma Community.

Therefore, for the activities offered in the chapter, you only need your drafts, so open up Figma and get ready to dive in!

In this chapter, we are going to cover the following topics:

- Exploring the Figma Community
- Finding useful resources
- Extending Figma/FigJam with widgets and plugins
- Speeding up your flow with AI

By the end of this chapter, you will be able to freely navigate the Figma Community, find and duplicate helpful files for personal use, and select and run widgets and plugins for your needs that can help you improve your workflow.

Exploring the Figma Community

As you know, Figma was created from the very beginning as a collaboration tool. It was revolutionary not only in terms of the concept of the design tool itself, but also in encouraging designers to share and communicate with each other. The fact is that, in the beginning, unlike developers, designers remained reserved and rarely opened their resources for public use. However, today, we can finally say that designers are developing a strong sense of community, just like developers, so their mindset is changing, and they are increasingly sharing their knowledge.

And it is for this reason that the Figma Community was created, a special public space within Figma itself that contributes significantly to the interchange between designers around the world. The Figma Community allows you to make your creations available to others in a very simple way, possibly inspiring someone to do something of their own in a similar way. Isn't that amazing?

So, in this section, you will explore the Figma Community and learn how to search and duplicate resources from it for personal use in Figma and FigJam, as well as how to publish your files.

Accessing and publishing to the Figma Community

It's incredibly easy to explore the Figma Community space. Just go to your Figma main tab – where **Teams**, **Files**, and **Projects** are located – and click on **Explore Community** in the left sidebar. This is what you will see immediately after:

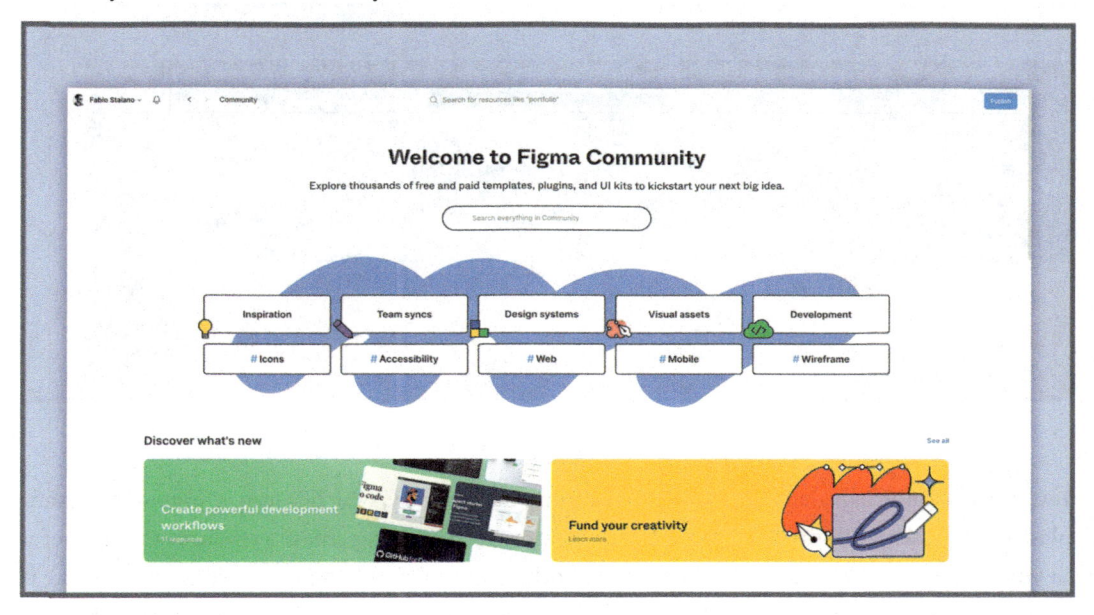

Figure 12.1 – Figma Community (in dark mode)

This is your starting point in finding a wide variety of resources (most of which are free, but there are some that are view-only available and have to be paid for to be used) that other designers, like you, publish to a wider audience. You can freely explore the different categories available here or use the search bar at the top to look for something specific, such as files, plugins, widgets, or creators.

Let's start by talking about files, which are basically designs created in Figma. Search for anything you might need, look at the read-only preview on its details page, and when you're done, just look at the top right for the **Open in Figma** button, as shown in the image below, which allows you to duplicate this resource in your drafts to use and modify however you want:

Figure 12.2 – Duplicating a resource file

You, as a designer, can also contribute to the Figma Community, which is now a hugely important platform that depends on the efforts of each creator. So, if you ever create a resource that is useful to you, it is very likely that it will be useful to others as well, and you might consider making it available publicly to the Figma Community. This is easily achievable with the **Sharing** feature in Figma from any open file you want to publish. After clicking the **Share** button – if you want to invite contributors to the file – in the tab at the top, switch to **Publish to the Figma Community**:

Figure 12.3 – Publishing a file to the Figma Community

From here, all you have to do is select the appropriate thumbnail, add the name and relevant details such as the description, tags, and co-creators, and validate the publishing. Right after that, your file will be available to everyone in the Figma Community.

> Note
>
> By default, every file published in the Figma Community will be licensed under a *Creative Commons Attribution 4.0 International License*, which means anyone can use, edit, and republish your file as they wish, simply by indicating the authorship. Be careful not to publish files that you have created under a contract with any client or company.

The Figma Community is an amazing place, and you will soon discover many valuable resources you can find for any purpose. At first, you may feel lost in all this diversity, which is growing more and more every day. Don't worry: later in this chapter, you will learn more about the different types of resources so that you can easily navigate this space.

Starting off with FigJam and templates

So, now you know how easily you can duplicate Figma Community resources to your Figma, but in fact, this space is not limited here, and it offers us many useful resources for FigJam as well, including extremely interesting templates that you can use in the very early stages of a project. By heading into the dedicated FigJam section of the Figma Community, you can find tons of starter whiteboards to kick off everything we did in *Chapter 2, Structuring Moodboards, Personas, and User Flows within FigJam*, in even less time. For example, you may want to build a user persona, and you just have to search for that. Here's a great example of such a foundation:

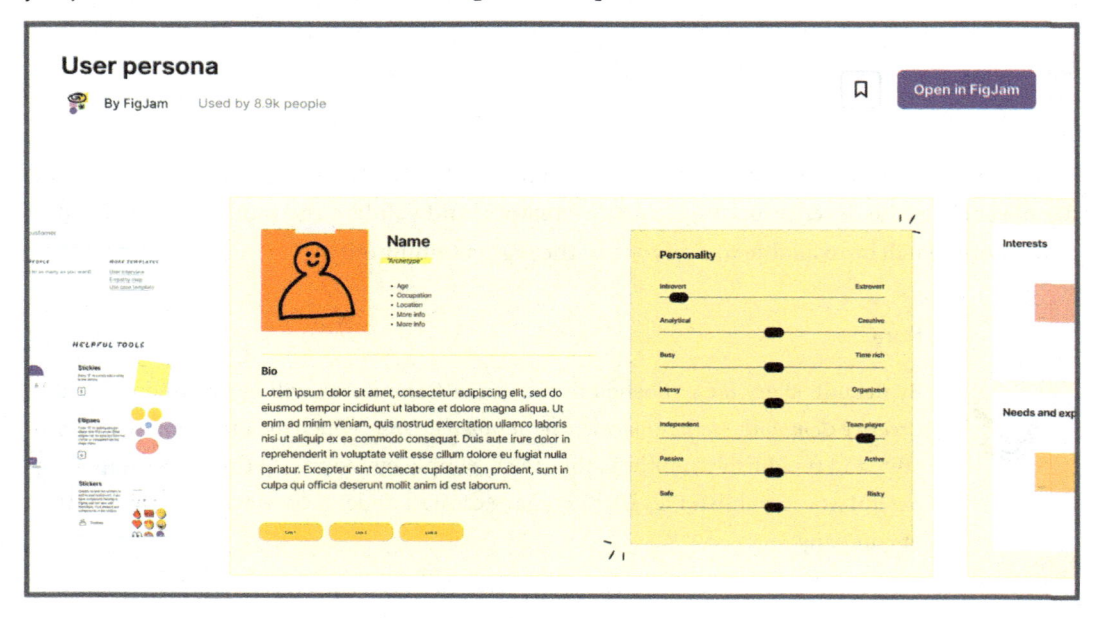

Figure 12.4 – User persona by FigJam

The amount of such amazing resources is endless, and you can get flowcharts, team agendas, empathy maps, or even ice-breaking activities and other cool templates to improve teamwork, or just let everyone take a fun break for a few minutes. Those kick-off resources are even available right inside your FigJam board itself, under the **Templates** icon. Take some time to explore these presets, paying attention to how they were created, and you will surely learn a lot from it. When you feel more confident in the Figma Community space, move on to the next section for some great examples of quality resources.

Finding useful resources

Now that you know how to find and copy files from the Figma Community for personal use, let's take a look at exactly which resources you might be interested in most. Since you've seen how easy it is to share in the Figma Community, you'll find a wealth of resources available. However, it can be tricky to distinguish the good from the not-so-good. In this section, we'll explore some helpful resources to guide you through this valuable but potentially confusing landscape.

UI kits and design systems

Speaking of the most useful resources to be found in the Figma Community, the first we should mention is the numerous **UI kits** and **design systems** created by professionals, large companies, or well-known brands. Using these files, you can start designing a new project but not from scratch, speeding up and simplifying the initial process. This can be done in two ways. First, you can find those files that are real starter kits, consisting of basic elements and styles. This way, you will have a starting point for the subsequent creation of a custom library. Think of a package of essentials as a blueprint that allows you to work faster and not forget anything important.

Here is a practical example of this kind of kit, **Design System (Starter Kit)**, which you can easily find in the Figma Community:

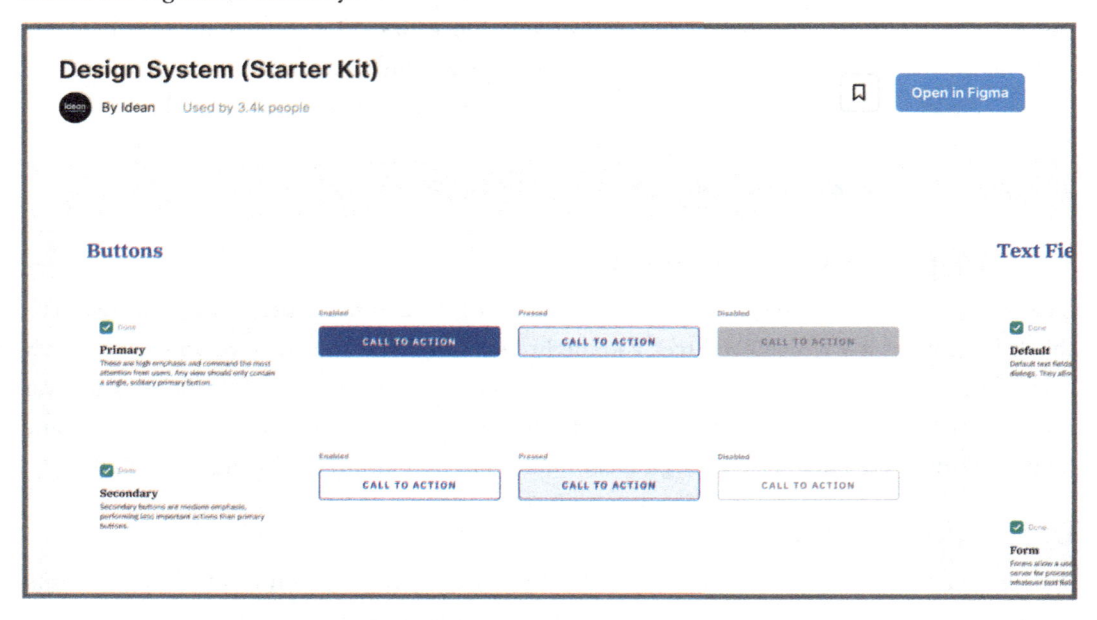

Figure 12.5 – Design System (Starter Kit) by Idean

The second approach involves using kits integrated into development frameworks. These kits not only provide a comprehensive design system that can be tailored to your needs but also come with pre-built code for each style and element. One of the more representative examples we mentioned earlier is Google's **Material Design**. You can find the official creator page in the Figma Community, which contains a whole series of open source files, including the latest version of their design kit:

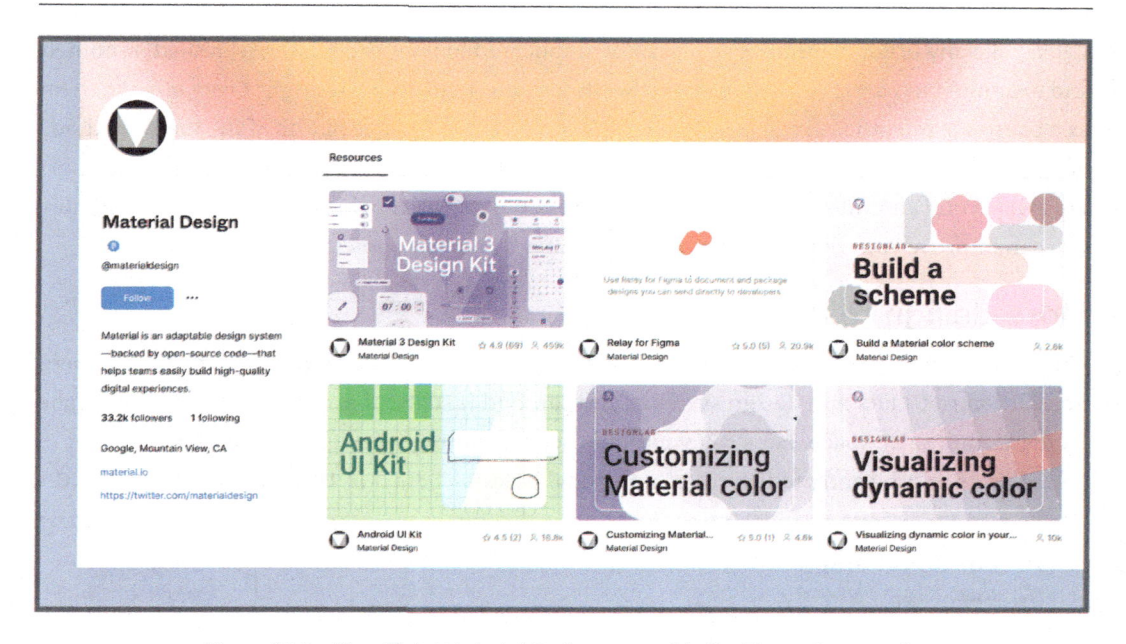

Figure 12.6 – The official Material Design account in the Figma Community

If you want to take a deeper look at this kit and its related design system, you can head over to the official `material.io` site to see the complete documentation on how to use it, as well as how to implement every design element and piece of code.

As you may know, Material Design is an Android-centric style, but what if you need iOS-styled components? Not a problem at all, since you can search for the Apple official creator page as well, and you'll find design kits for each Apple platform, such as iOS, macOS, and even Vision Pro.

Figure 12.7 – Apple's official creator page on Figma Community

Those, like any other community file, can be duplicated in your drafts, disassembled, modified, and examined in parts. You can just use the **Styles** and **Assets** libraries right away or have them as a complete reference for any complex work you want to do. In fact, one of the main methods of mastering every aspect of interface design is examining the source files of other professionals. This way, you can understand how everything is done, what is behind each decision, and how you can improve your design, or perhaps go further by adding something of your own.

More design resources

The Figma Community resources are limitless, and what you've seen is just the tip of the iceberg. In addition to UI kits and design systems, you can find just about anything for any need in the Figma Community space. Let's say you don't need a complete design system, but just a set of layout grids to copy and publish to your personal library – here it is, **UI Prep Layout Grids 4.0**:

Figure 12.8 – UI Prep Layout Grids by Molly Hellmuth

Alternatively, maybe you need a fresh gradient to test out some cool new combinations in your interface? No problem – you can find a lot of them, for example, **uigradients - Figma Style Library**:

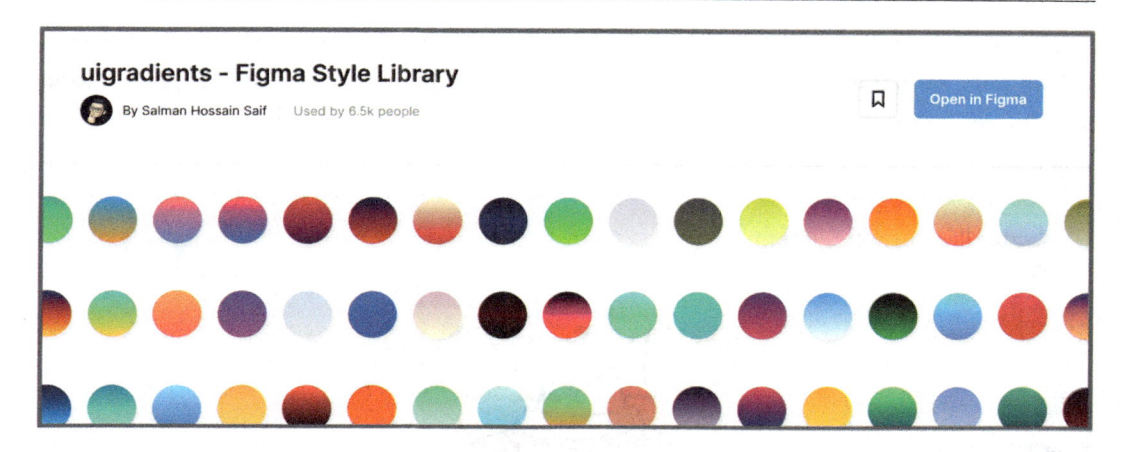

Figure 12.9 – uigradients - Figma Style Library by Salman Hossain Saif

Okay, we're done with styles, grids, and so on. Let's try something a little fancier and more specific, such as a set of cool travel illustrations, for instance, **[Orbit Design System] Illustrations**:

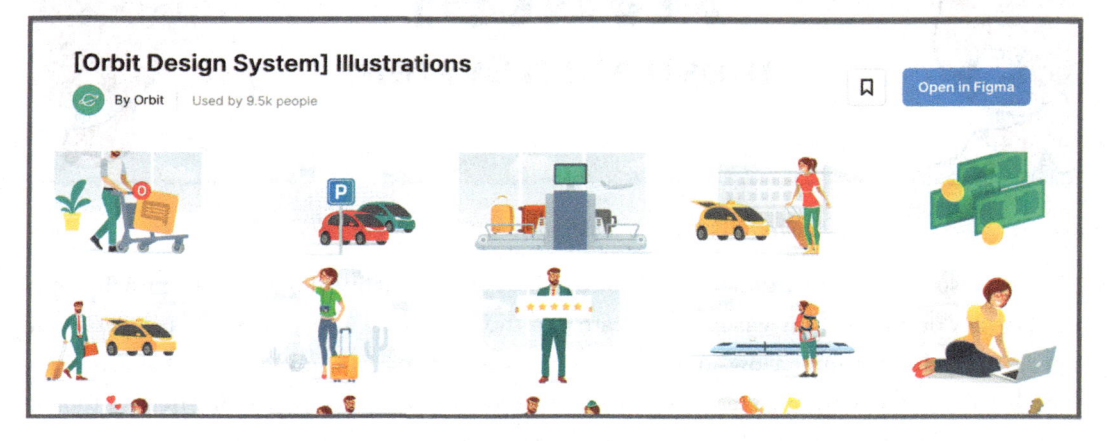

Figure 12.10 – [Orbit Design System] Illustrations by Orbit

As you can see, you just need to understand what you need, and then you can find it in the Figma Community, even if it's something really specific. This could be icon kits, project presentation slide kits, or even avatar generators that make use of components and variants to create dynamic assets, such as **Avatar Illustration System**:

Figure 12.11 – Avatar Illustration System by Micah Lanier

This is all useful, but as mentioned earlier, be cautious of low-quality files. Before using a file from the Figma Community, it's wise to duplicate and thoroughly review it to ensure it meets your needs. If you do encounter a low-quality file, simply discontinue its use and seek out alternatives with better reviews or more likes. The **Likes** and **Reviews** system in Figma is an effective tool to help you avoid resources that are poorly crafted, outdated, or not maintained.

As you can see, there are a lot of designers in the Figma Community who volunteer to share their masterpieces with their peers, and this is a really great opportunity for you to ease some aspects of your workflow and get some tips from these files. It's perfectly okay to get help from the Figma Community because that's what it was created for, but try not to overuse its resources, and find the right balance between using resources and creating projects with your own unique approach.

However, not all of the Figma Community's resources are related to design itself; there is a whole section dedicated to extending Figma functionality, namely **Plugins**. If you've ever installed some of these in your web browser, you probably know how plugins can add a little extra to your usual experience. Well, plugins in Figma work in a similar way, and in the next section, you'll learn everything you need to install and start using them!

Extending Figma with plugins

You've now explored all the tools and features in Figma, from the basic to the advanced, and they're all great without exception. However, while some of them can significantly improve the quality and speed of your workflow, you will still run into limitations in the case of even more specific personal requests, or if you need to further optimize some part of your work. Of course, this is a completely normal situation that many designers find themselves in, so in the Figma Community, you can find such solutions for specific tasks, and these are plugins. Plugins are extensions for Figma and/or FigJam created by third parties that further empower your tools, by providing extra features to speed up your workflow even more. So now you're going to explore these incredible plugins in the Figma Community space, then learn how to run and manage plugins in your Figma account, and finally, take a look at some of the ones that you might find useful in your design workflow.

Running and managing plugins

Getting and using new plugins in Figma is super easy. Unlike some other apps that can make your computer slow, Figma's web-based nature keeps things running smoothly. Plus, you won't even have to "install" plugins like you normally do with software.

It's more like copying files. Just follow these steps to do it:

1. To begin, head over to the Figma Community space. There, you can search for the plugin you need. To make sure you are looking for the right type of resource, there is a very useful filter that limits searches to plugins only, hiding anything else:

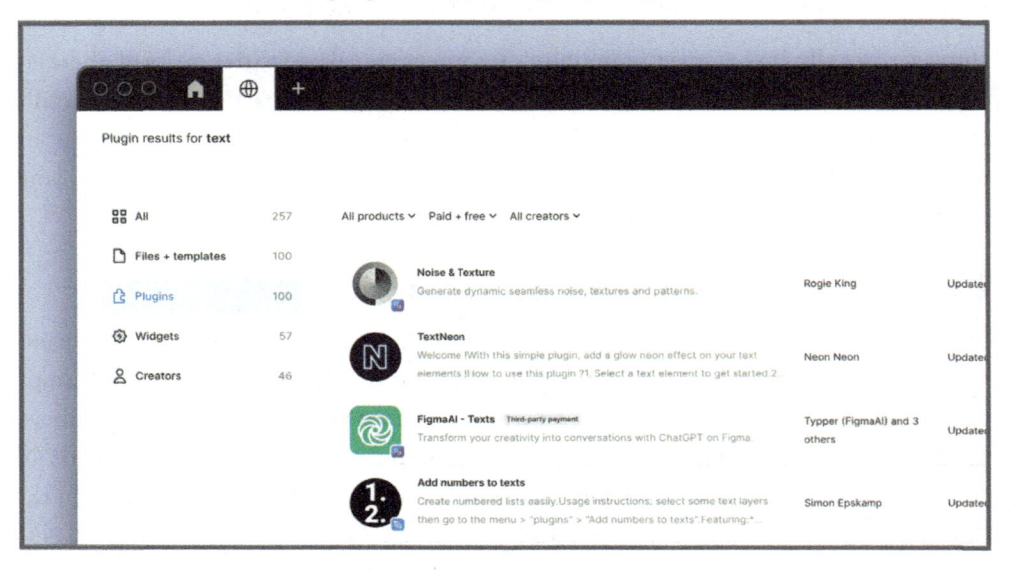

Figure 12.12 – Searching and filtering plugins

2. Once you find the one you are looking for, click on the **Try it out** button. This will automatically open a new playground file for you with the plugin running in it, enabling you to quickly test its functionalities.

To access and use the extra features from Figma plugins in your ongoing projects, simply right-click anywhere on the canvas or use the main menu in the upper-left corner. This action opens a menu where you can navigate to the **Plugins** section. Here, you'll find a list of all the plugins you've installed. This list also includes your recently used plugins, making it easy to quickly select and apply them to your current project. This streamlined access allows for the efficient utilization of plugins across any of your Figma files.

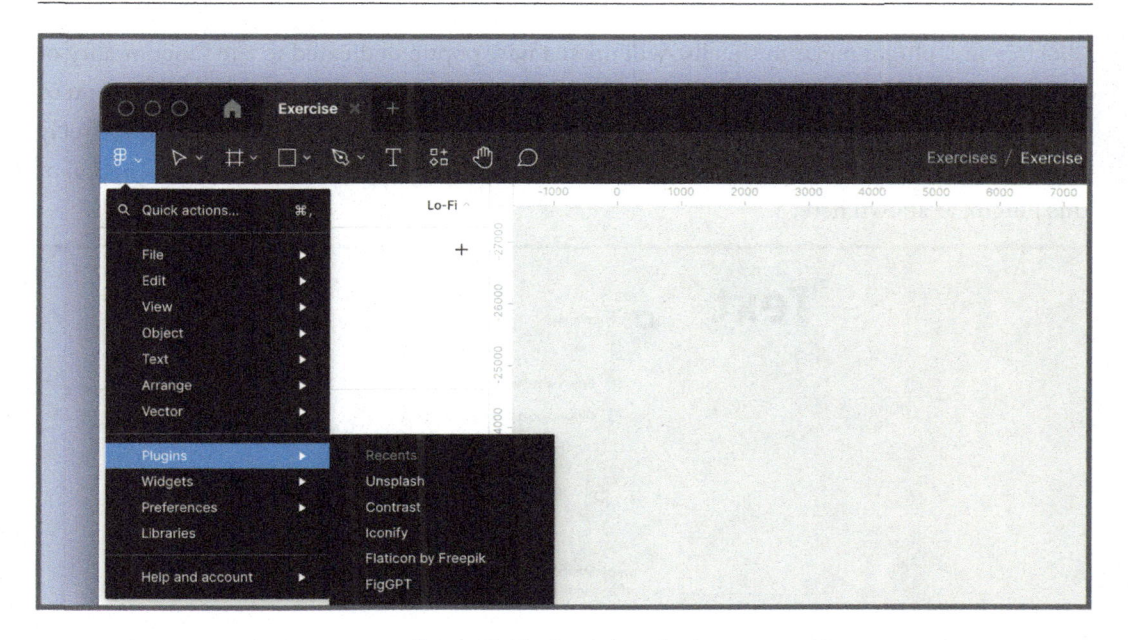

Figure 12.13 – Accessing plugins

For a more straightforward approach to accessing plugins in your Figma file, simply use the keyboard shortcut *Shift + I*. This command quickly opens the **Resources** drawer, a dedicated space within Figma where you can conveniently find and select from your available plugins and widgets, or search for more.

> **Note:**
> Many plugins in Figma are available for free, which is great. However, there might be instances where a plugin offers partial usage for free and requires in-app payments to access more features, or even requires complete payment. If a plugin involves in-app purchases, you'll find that information directly on the plugin's page.

Clicking on a plugin name in this list will open a new popup dedicated to the functionality of that particular plugin only. For example, if you open **Lorem ipsum**, a plugin that allows you to automatically fill selected text fields with placeholder content, you get a pop-up window (freely draggable around the interface) that allows you to configure all the parameters for the action of this plugin, as shown here:

Figure 12.14 – Setting up the Lorem ipsum plugin

As you can see, it's pretty easy to find and run installed plugins in Figma, but there is a way to do it even faster. What's more, this method can also be applied to quickly access many other basic functions, not just plugins. All you have to do is remember a shortcut that you can use in your daily life, that is, *Command + /* (macOS) or *Ctrl + /* (Windows). For non-US keyboards, the shortcut may not work, so you can use *Command + P* (macOS) or *Ctrl + P* (Windows) instead. This shortcut opens the **Quick Actions** window, a convenient tool for finding what you need efficiently. It gives you access to all the menu options under the Figma logo, like hiding/showing rulers, saving your file, and more. For instance, instead of manually opening a plugin like **Lorem Ipsum**, simply use the shortcut and start typing Lorem to activate it quickly:

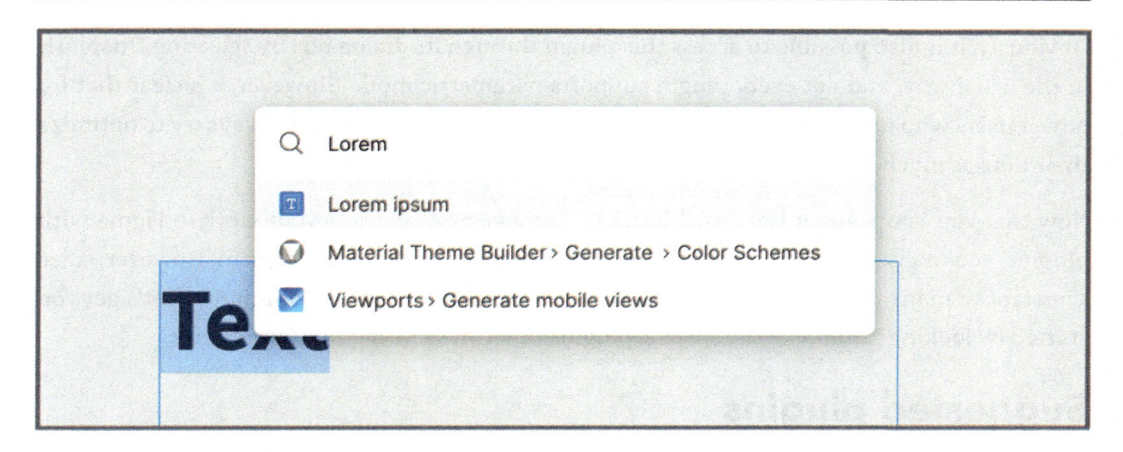

Figure 12.15 – Launching plugins with Quick Actions

Figma encourages designers to make the most of **Quick Actions** by providing even more functionality. Now, you can use plugins seamlessly without dealing with additional dialog boxes. Just rely on your keyboard for a faster workflow. But how do you use these plugins without opening their interfaces? It's quite simple – just use **Quick Actions** and specify the necessary parameters. Here's a practical example with **Unsplash**, another great plugin that lets you instantly select royalty-free images from `unsplash.com`, without ever leaving Figma. After running it, you can use the **Quick Actions** shortcut, find Unsplash, and instead of pressing *Enter* to launch it, press *Tab* to insert all of the following options, one by one:

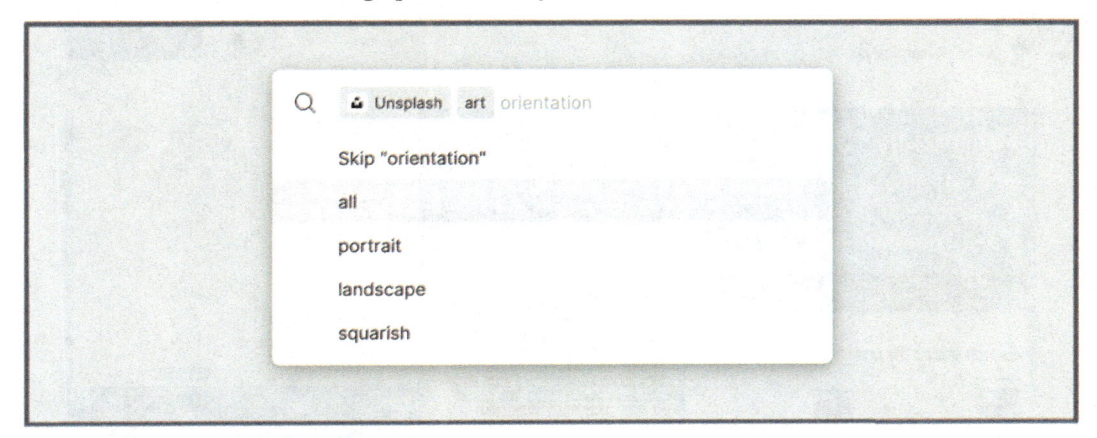

Figure 12.16 – Using the Unsplash plugin with parameters

Obviously, it is also possible to access this plugin through its dialog box by selecting **Unsplash** in the usual way, and not every plugin supports parametric mode. However, it's clear that for power users who use keyboard shortcuts and keyboards a great deal and always try to optimize their time as much as possible, this is a very important turning point.

Now that you know about the possibilities to improve and facilitate your work in Figma with plugins, you might be feeling quite excited and want to know more about them. However, since there are so many of them for all sorts of different uses in the Figma Community, let's get you started by looking at some of the specific plugins that can serve as your foundation.

Suggested plugins

Just like with file resources, the Figma Community is filled with numerous plugins. Initially, it can be quite challenging to distinguish which ones are genuinely useful and which ones you should steer clear of. In such situations, you can depend on reviews from other users and also check the last update date of the plugin. The last update date is a good indicator of whether there's a developer or team behind the plugin who is actively maintaining and improving it. However, if you are still feeling overwhelmed and unsure of where to start, there are a few suggestions for reliable plugins that can be very helpful in your day-to-day work.

Iconify

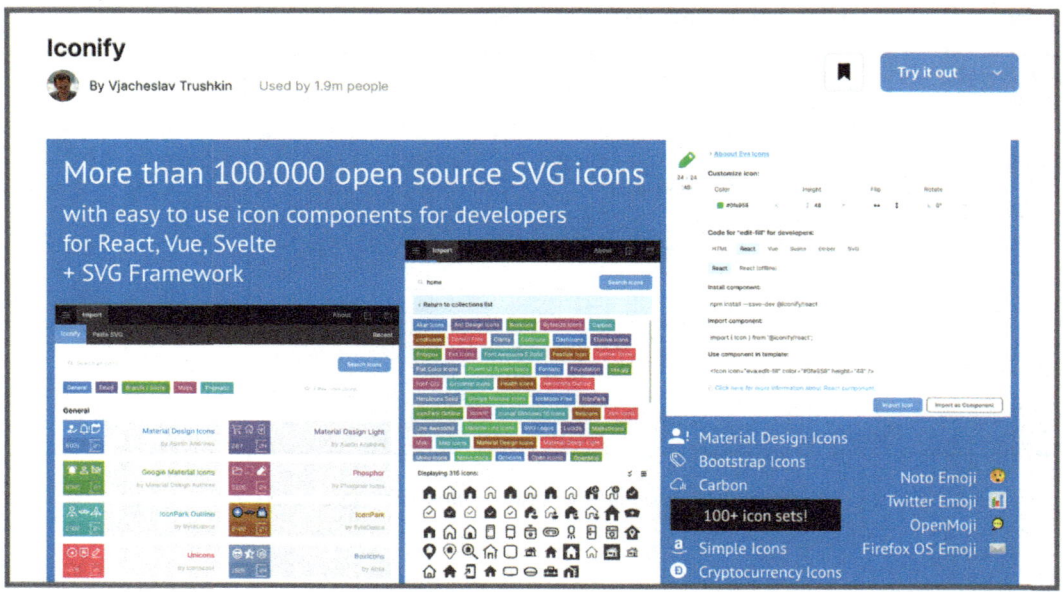

Figure 12.17 – Iconify by Vjacheslav Trushkin

Iconify offers a curated selection of the most renowned and freely accessible icon libraries, conveniently accessible with just a few clicks within Figma. Whether you're searching for a specific icon by entering keywords or exploring dedicated libraries, you can effortlessly import vector assets directly into your project, making them instantly usable. Leveraging entire library sets simplifies the task of maintaining design consistency throughout your work.

Content Reel

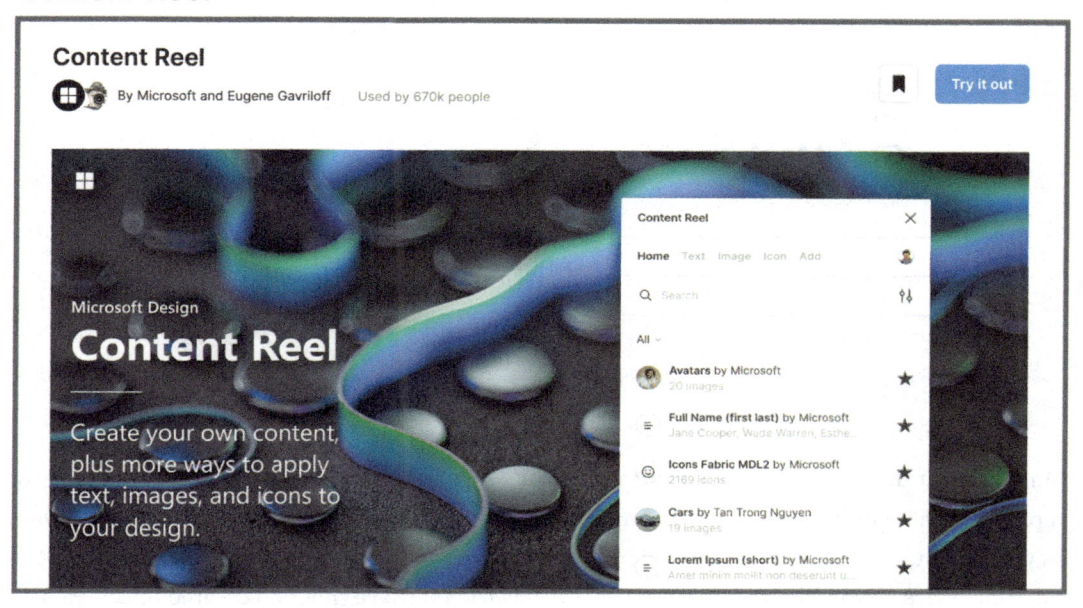

Figure 12.18 – Content Reel by Microsoft and Eugene Gavriloff

Content Reel is a plugin published by the Microsoft Design team that makes the process of filling placeholder content incredibly fast. Here you will find not only the classic *Lorem ipsum* but also entire collections of placeholder texts, useful icons, and various images. All of this you can start using with one click to simulate a more realistic interface, using libraries provided directly by the plugin (for example, addresses, phone numbers, or placeholder profile pictures). You can even upload your own personal content libraries from here.

Clay Mockups 3D

Figure 12.19 – Clay Mockups 3D by Hamish

Making great design projects is important, but it's just as important to know how to properly represent what you've been working on. This plugin will make this aspect much easier for you, as with it, you can easily create quick 3D mockups to represent the designs in your portfolio. Rotate the device as you like and, in one click, display the interface that you created onscreen. It's incredibly simple, fast, and impressive!

Contrast

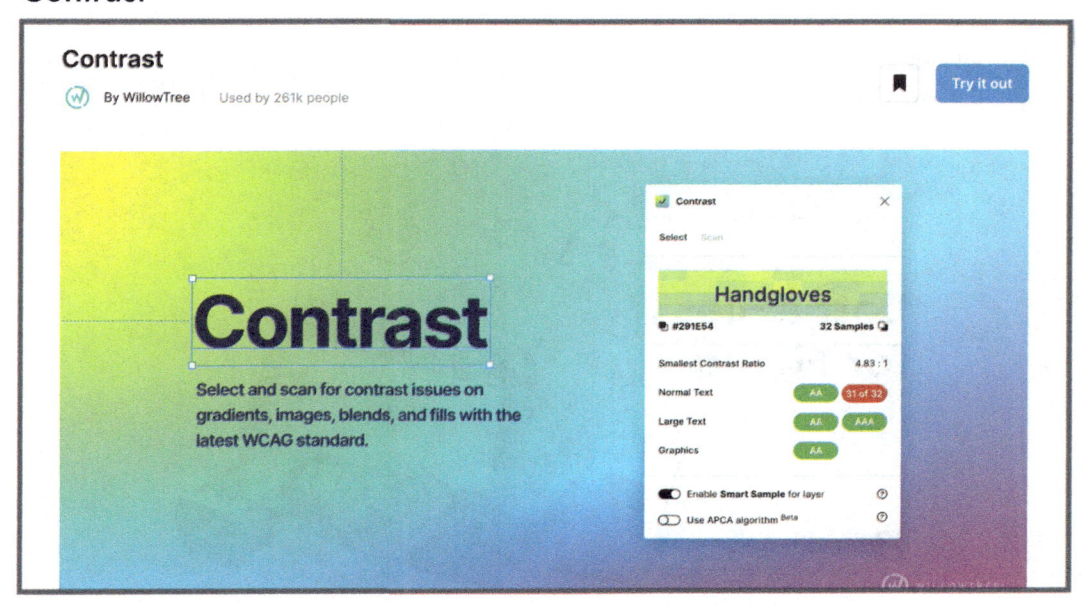

Figure 12.20 – Contrast by WillowTree

Accessibility makes a huge difference in design, but it happens that among the many things that need to be done, this aspect is often overlooked. Thanks to this plugin, you can make sure that there are no errors in the contrast and readability of text in your files. To do this, you just need to select individual levels or scan all pages to see reports related to errors in the interface, according to the **Web Content Accessibility Guidelines (WCAG)**.

LottieFiles

Figure 12.21 – LottieFiles by LottieFiles

LottieFiles for Figma is an innovative tool designed to enhance animation capabilities within Figma, streamlining the design workflow. This plugin allows you to create both single- and multiple-frame animations and export your Figma designs as production-ready Lottie animations for use across websites or apps. It offers access to an extensive library of over 80,000 free, ready-to-use animations, alongside the ability to bring in private and team-specific Lottie animations. While Figma does not natively support Lottie animations yet, the plugin enables the conversion of Lottie animations into GIFs, which can be easily incorporated into Figma designs. Additionally, it allows for the personalization of animations, using custom brand color palettes, and supports inserting animations as high-quality SVGs. This makes LottieFiles for Figma a comprehensive solution for adding dynamic and engaging animations to your Figma projects.

Plugins are amazing, aren't they? And the best part? There's even more magic in store – unlock the true power with a host of AI-powered features!

Speeding up your flow with AI

In the modern era, the integration of AI into major software platforms is revolutionizing our workflows. While the concept of AI can sometimes be seen as a marketing move, its strategic use can significantly enhance productivity.

For instance, in the realm of design, AI can assist in moving beyond the limitations of stock images. This collaboration with AI allows designers to generate unique, custom visuals that align more closely with their project's specific needs and vision. It enables the creation of tailored imagery that can't be found in standard stock libraries, fostering a more personalized and creative approach to design. In the field of copywriting, where immediate human assistance isn't always available, AI's role becomes invaluable, offering suggestions, generating content ideas, or even drafting initial versions of the copy. This support from AI empowers creators to maintain efficiency and spark innovation in their work.

FigJam introduced its first AI features in November 2023, revolutionizing collaborative work for both designers and non-designers. These features, developed using OpenAI technology, include click-and-go prompts that adapt to teams' previous usage patterns, enhancing efficiency. The AI also helps you create diagrams and templates (as shown below), groups sticky notes by theme automatically, aiding in organization, and includes a summarizing tool to condense information into easily digestible formats. These AI features in FigJam represent the beginning of more advanced, AI-integrated tools in Figma's ecosystem.

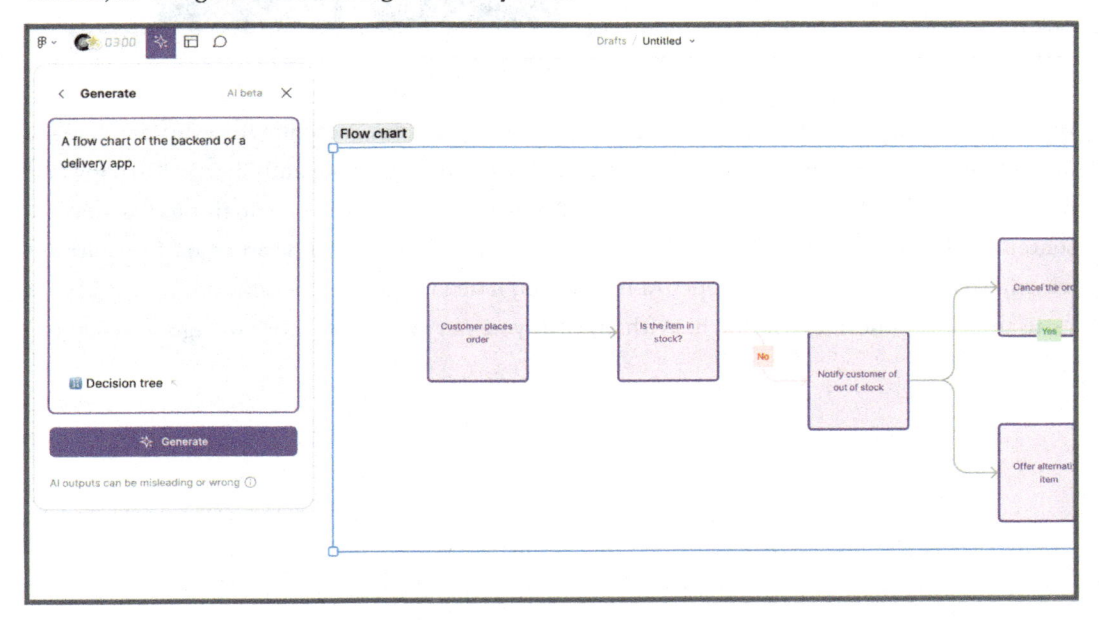

Figure 12.22 – FigJam AI for creating flow charts

While Figma itself may not yet have extensive built-in AI features, its acquisition of Diagram, a company known for AI-powered plugins and widgets, signifies a commitment to integrating AI into its platform. So in today's context, what's the best usage of AI in Figma? Here, you'll find a few suggestions:

FigGPT

Figure 12.23 – FigGPT by Alex

You probably know about ChatGPT, right? It's used by almost everyone for everyday tasks. I understand how annoying it can be to keep switching between Figma and ChatGPT to copy and paste paragraphs. But here's a solution: FigGPT. With this plugin, you can do things like making sentences shorter or longer, improving your writing, and picking the tone and mood, all without leaving your canvas. It uses the OpenAI API, so you'll need to set it up the first time and pay for its usage, but it doesn't cost much. With FigGPT, you can make your work in Figma easier and more efficient.

Figma Autoname

Figure 12.24 – Figma Autoname by Hugo DUPREZ

Renaming layers can be a bit of a challenge, but it's a necessary task. However, if we happen to miss renaming a few layers along the way in our project, we can give Figma Autoname a shot. This handy plugin employs AI to analyze your layer's content and swiftly suggests a suitable name for it. Still, it's essential to not solely depend on it – continue manual naming and use AI to assist with any necessary refinements.

Wireframe Designer

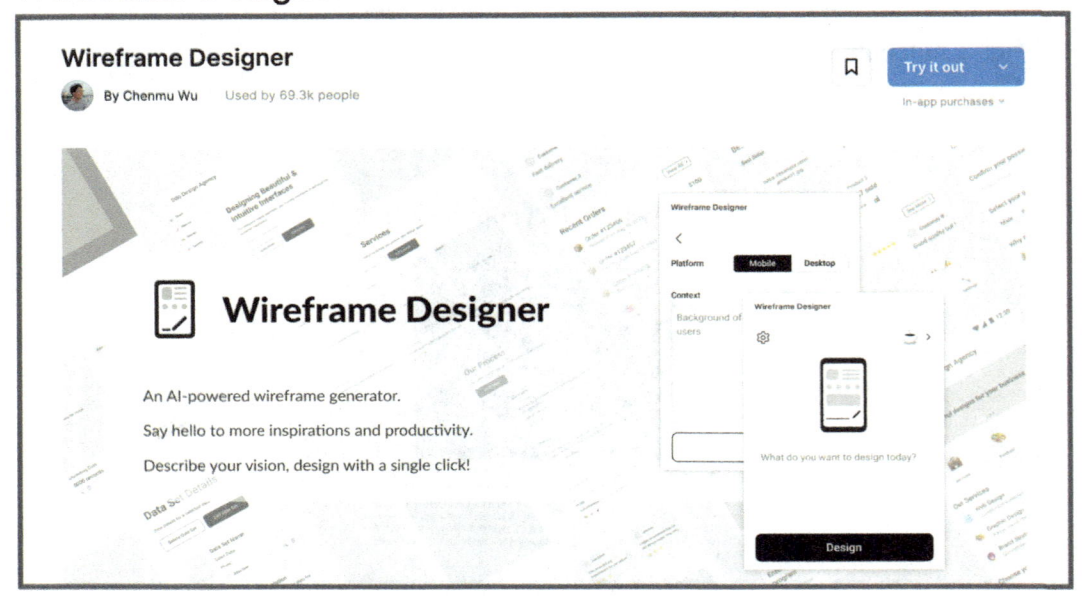

Figure 12.25 – Wireframe Designer by Chanmu Wu

If you need a fast way to convey your ideas and concepts to your client, your search is over. Wireframe Designer lets you simply describe your idea as a prompt, and you'll see it transform into a visual representation in just seconds. Again, it doesn't replace your creativity but enhances it, by speeding up the visual presentation process and sparking inspiration.

Magician

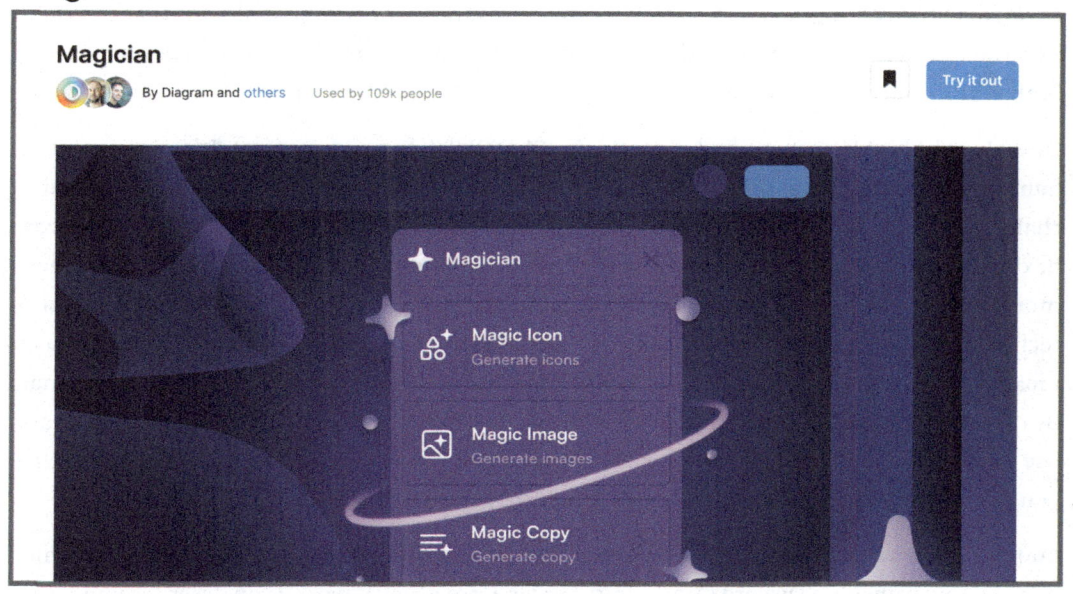

Figure 12.26 – Magician by Diagram and others

Magician for Figma is a versatile AI-powered plugin that enhances the design process with a range of innovative capabilities. Its **Text to Icon** feature allows designers to create unique icons from textual descriptions, while **Copywriting** assists in generating engaging text content for various design needs. Additionally, **Text to Image** empowers designers to transform written descriptions into visual images, further expanding the creative possibilities. These functionalities, **Magic Icon**, **Magic Copy**, and **Magic Image**, work in unison to foster creativity and imagination, providing designers with smarter tools to elevate their work in Figma. It's an incredibly versatile one, but what's most intriguing is its origin. Magician is actually a Diagram plugin, a company recently acquired by Figma. This makes it a plugin to keep a close eye on in the future!

The Figma Community is a goldmine of incredible plugins and opportunities waiting to be discovered. In the coming years, we can expect to see a surge in AI-powered plugins that can assist in various tasks. Here's a valuable tip: consider integrating AI into different stages of your projects, both within and beyond Figma.

One AI tool I highly recommend exploring is **ChatGPT** (chat.openai.com). It's not just for enhancing text; it can also assist in brainstorming ideas, analyzing data, and even solving technical challenges when they arise. Its free plan covers a wide range of text-based tasks, offering significant flexibility for integration into various workflows. Upgrading to the Premium plan unlocks even more capabilities, including web search and the ability to create stunning images with DALL-E technology. This expanded functionality of ChatGPT, from generating ideas to assisting in technical problem-solving, positions it as an invaluable tool for designers and creative professionals. By the way, if you want to give the web search feature a try, you can head to **Bing** (bing.com) and use its **Chat** feature, which is based on GPT. Also, if you want to create free images with DALL-E, you can visit **Microsoft's Image Creator** (`bing.com/images/create`).

Another remarkable tool to consider for image creation is **Midjourney** (midjourney.com), which is tucked away inside a Discord Community Server. Here's how it works: you describe your vision, whether it's a scene or anything else, and it magically generates high-quality images that align perfectly with your description. This is incredibly useful because it enables you to create unique visuals for your projects, avoiding the use of generic stock images. But that's not all – it can also be a fantastic companion to enhance your mood boards. You can use it to evoke emotions, convey abstract concepts, and breathe life into your mood boards, making them truly immersive. While it offers tremendous power, it does come with a monthly subscription fee and no free plans.

If you happen to have an Adobe Creative Cloud subscription, you might want to explore **Adobe Firefly** (`firefly.adobe.com`) or **Adobe Photoshop** with their new Generative AI integration. They now provide commercial licenses for the images they generate, offering even more versatility in your design work.

As we move forward, integrating AI tools like these will revolutionize our work processes, not only in design but in many other exciting fields as well, and embarking on this exploration is the next big thing.

Using widgets in Figma and FigJam

In the realm of collaborative design and creativity, Figma and FigJam offer an array of powerful tools to streamline workflows through its Community. Two of these tools, **Widgets** and **Plugins**, play strong roles in enhancing your design experience. To unleash their full potential, it's essential to grasp the key distinctions between them.

> **Note:**
> Developers in the Figma and FigJam ecosystem can create plugins and widgets specifically for each platform or under the "Universal" label, an official designation for tools compatible with both. This flexibility allows for a seamless user experience, enabling access to these tools in both Figma's design environment and FigJam's collaborative space.

Understanding the difference between widgets and plugins

We just learned how plugins are remarkable tools, offering specialized functionality tailored to your needs. However, it's important to note that plugins operate within the context of individual user accounts and typically require manual activation to perform their tasks. When you launch a plugin, it goes through its designated process and eventually closes, presenting you with the outcome. This process remains visible to you alone; those collaborating within the same file can only witness the final results of your plugin-driven actions.

Widgets, in contrast, introduce a new dimension to the collaborative design environment. Unlike plugins, widgets are not confined to individual user accounts; they transcend this limitation by allowing any participant within a file to seamlessly insert them onto the canvas. Once added to the canvas, widgets become readily available for interaction by all users present in the file. This intrinsic collaborative nature of widgets transforms the design experience, as everyone involved can see and engage with the same instance of a widget in real time.

Furthermore, widgets distinguish themselves by accommodating multiple instances within a file. There is no imposed limit on the number of widgets that can coexist within a file, each ready to serve its purpose and facilitate collaborative endeavors.

This versatility allows for a wide range of use cases, from collaborative activities like voting to single-player scenarios that require on-canvas interactions, such as diagramming complex concepts or using checklists:

Figure 12.27 – Checklist widget in the workspace

Widgets enrich the collaborative design landscape by providing a dynamic and interactive way for all participants in a file to engage with shared elements, fostering creativity, teamwork, and efficiency. While plugins excel in automating single-player tasks or streamlining file activities, widgets emerge as the go-to choice to enhance collaboration and facilitate on-canvas interactions.

Suggested widgets

If you're on the lookout for widget inspiration, here is a curated selection to spark your creativity. This collection showcases a range of innovative widgets, each offering unique functionalities.

Checklist (Figma/FigJam)

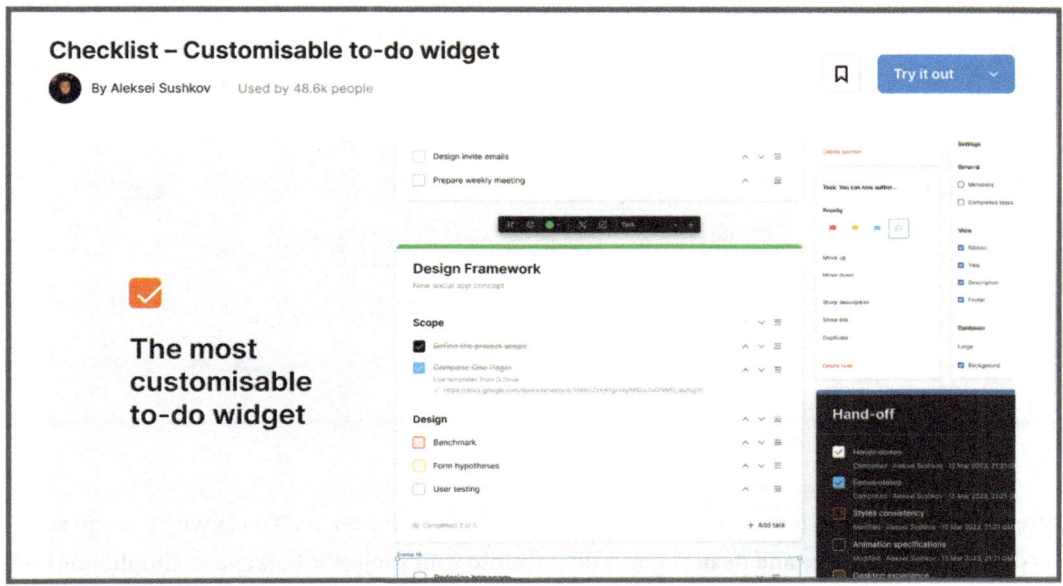

Figure 12.28 – Checklist by Aleksei Sushkov

With this simple yet essential checklist widget, you can efficiently manage your design tasks, helping you stay organized and on top of all necessary adjustments and improvements within your Figma project. Say goodbye to forgetting important edits, and say hello to a more streamlined and productive design process.

Jira/Asana (Figma/FigJam)

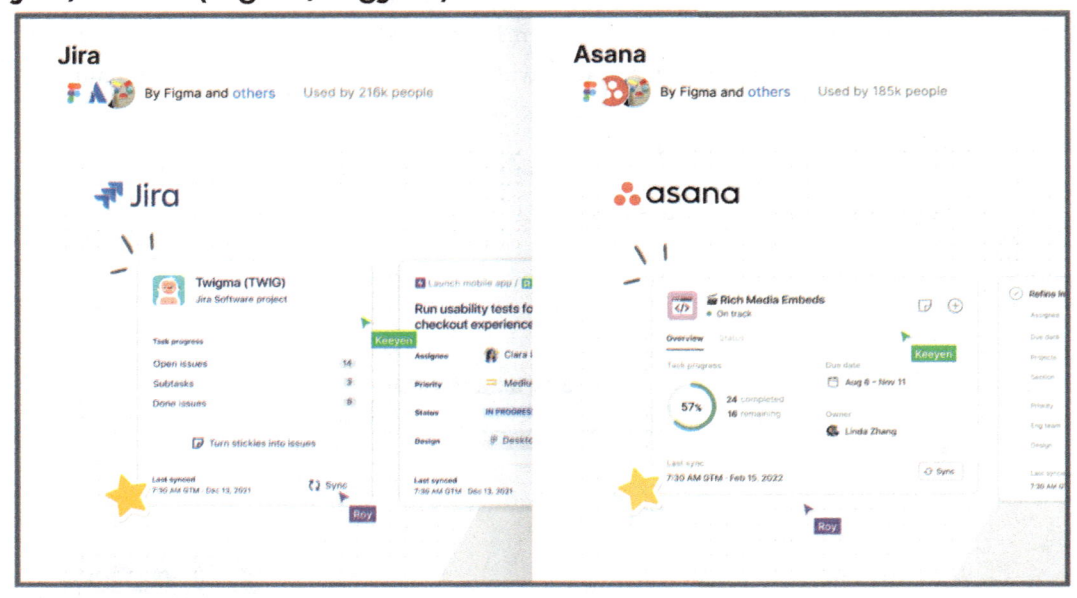

Figure 12.29 – Jira and Asana

Effective project management is a cornerstone for collaborative teams. That's why you can seamlessly integrate your Jira and Asana boards directly into your project's workspace, simplifying task management and ensuring a smoother workflow. This integration empowers you to oversee and coordinate all your tasks with ease, streamlining communication and collaboration across your team for more efficient project execution.

Giphy Stickers (Figma/FigJam)

Figure 12.30 – Giphy Stickers by Lichin

Work doesn't have to be dull. Adding a touch of joy to your canvas or boards can uplift your team's spirits. Dive into the world of Giphy Stickers to creatively express your emotions and share some light-hearted moments with your colleagues. It's a simple way to inject a bit of fun and enthusiasm into your work environment.

Jambot (FigJam)

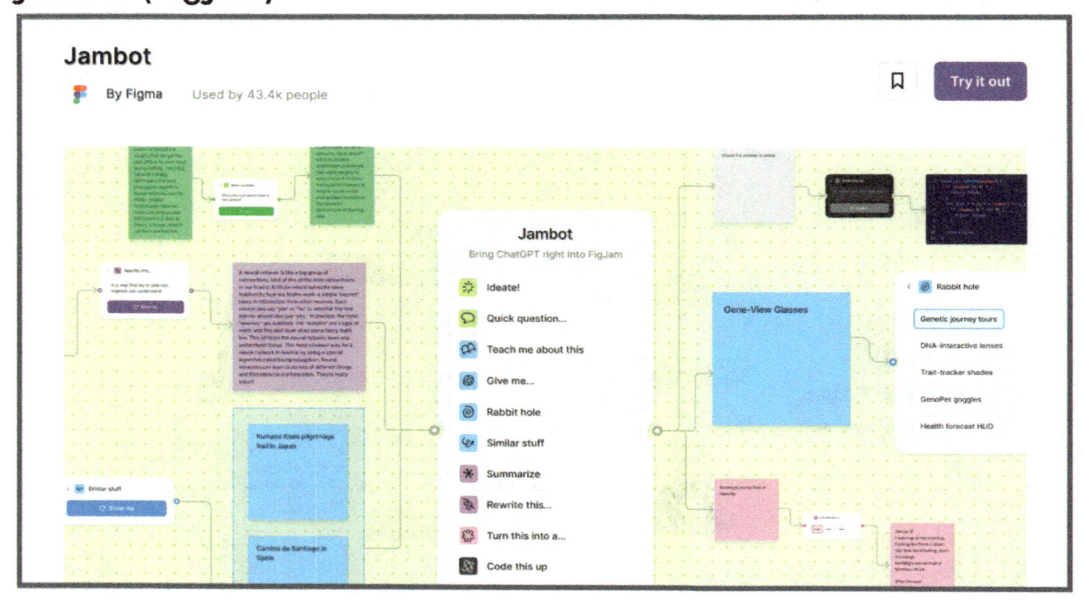

Figure 12.31 – Jambot by Figma

Seems like we weren't quite done with AI-powered features, after all. Elevate your FigJam experience with Jambot, a dynamic widget that seamlessly utilizes ChatGPT's AI capabilities within your boards. Jambot is more than just a widget; it's a versatile companion that can truly transform your collaborative efforts. Whether you're looking to spark creativity during team meetings, summarize discussions, craft captivating visual mind maps, or even access quick definitions, Jambot has you covered. The beauty of Jambot lies in its simplicity. It keeps staying on your board, ready to assist you. To put it to work, all you need to do is draw connectors from any text sticky to Jambot and initiate the desired action, just like in the following example:

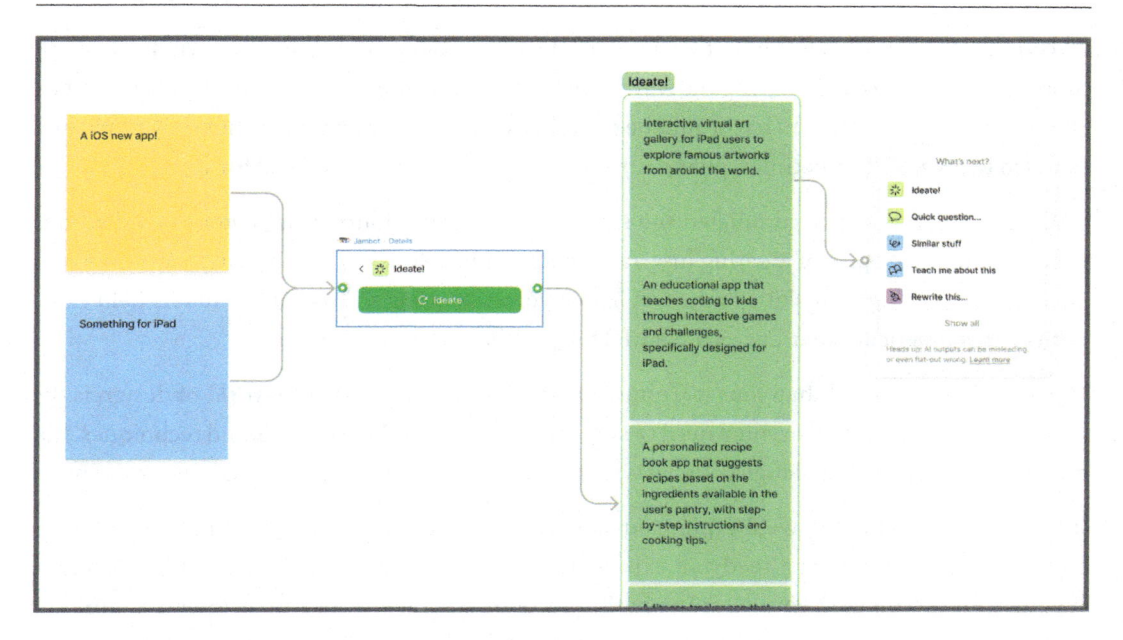

Figure 12.32 – Using Jambot for gathering new ideas

Jambot makes AI easy with its handy widget, but that's just the beginning of what you can explore in the Figma Community. Every day, new and exciting things pop up, so stay tuned for a continuous journey of discovery and creativity!

Summary

In this chapter, you have learned that Figma can be not only a cool design tool but also an equally cool place to connect with designers from all over the world, exchange resources, and get inspired, all with the help of the Figma Community, which can be accessed very easily directly from Figma! How amazing is that?

Now, you know what types of resources are represented in the Figma Community and how to search and filter them correctly. You have also learned about some examples of great files, widgets, and plugins that can be your basis for a collection of useful resources. By combining all of this with your knowledge of Figma tools and functions, you can now optimize your work as best you can. Keep in mind, however, that no matter how good the resource seems to you, it's always best to test the end result yourself to ensure that there are no inaccuracies.

Of course, there is still a lot more to explore in the Figma Community, and you will have many more incredible discoveries along the way. Who knows? Maybe, one day, you might even want to share your creations there! That would be great because it is very important not only to receive but also to give, and sometimes, giving turns out to be even more beneficial for you.

With this chapter, you've completed the starter phase of your journey, and you've learned the fundamental principles of creating interfaces with Figma. Now, it's time to embark on the real adventure – putting your skills to the test in everyday scenarios and gaining valuable field experience. This practical experience is essential for your growth as a designer.

However, keep in mind that your learning journey doesn't end here. The world of design is dynamic and ever-evolving, so you'll need to stay updated with the latest trends and techniques. It's crucial to continually challenge yourself with new and unfamiliar tasks to keep your skills sharp.

In the upcoming chapter, we'll explore advanced features and valuable tips to further enhance your proficiency. If you're already an experienced designer, feel free to dive right in. However, if you've just completed your learning path, I recommend taking your time. Spend additional months honing your understanding of the basic principles, create projects from scratch, and return to the advanced chapter when you genuinely feel ready and confident to tackle more complex challenges. Remember, the journey of a designer is a continuous process of growth and learning, and it's important not to rush.

Learn more on Discord

To join the Discord community for this book – where you can share feedback, ask questions to the author, and learn about new releases – follow the QR code below:

https://packt.link/figma

13
Going Advanced with Variables and Conditional Prototyping

This chapter unfolds the utility and application of **variables** and **conditional prototyping**, venturing into the advanced functionalities of Figma. Variables in Figma are your go-to for storing reusable values, aiding in managing huge design systems and creating complex products efficiently. Conditional prototyping, on the other hand, breathes logic into your prototypes, enabling actions based on user interactions or predefined conditions, thus elevating the interactivity and realism of your designs.

The synergy between variables and conditional logic not only streamlines the design process but also unlocks a higher level of fidelity in your prototypes, especially when building interactive dynamic products and responsive interfaces.

With this chapter, we mark a transition into more advanced territory within Figma. It's tailored for those who are ready to tackle complex design challenges. Variables and conditional prototyping are not requisites for every project; they come into play predominantly in larger, long-term projects with scalability in mind. If you're new to these concepts or find them challenging, it's advisable to revisit the previous chapters, practice, and return to this chapter when you're ready to step up to the next level. The knowledge and skills acquired here will be instrumental as you work on more demanding projects.

In this chapter, we are going to cover the following main topics:

- Understanding variables
- Exploring modes and collections
- Pushing further with conditional prototyping

Understanding variables

In the evolving landscape of digital design, our creativity grows with the features our platforms offer. Figma, with its variables, opens up a new world of flexibility and interaction, adding a fresh layer of sophistication to our projects. As we progress from static to more interactive and complex designs, the role of variables becomes increasingly prominent and clear, acting as the bridge between static design elements and dynamic user interactions. But before diving in with some practice, let's explore exactly when we should (and when we shouldn't) use variables.

When to use variables

The concept of variables might initially seem a bit intimidating, especially when compared to the straightforwardness of styles we've been accustomed to. Styles have been our reliable allies from the get-go, aiding in crafting beautiful, static designs proficiently. However, as our project complexity ramps up, the static nature of styles could start feeling limiting.

This is where variables step in, offering a dynamic and flexible approach to managing our design elements. Picture a scenario where your design needs to toggle between light and dark mode. With styles, you'd have to create both versions for each screen, doubling the workload. But with variables, you just need to define color schemes for both modes upfront, and, like magic, every screen can effortlessly switch between light and dark modes. The advantage of variables extends to responsive design as well. They empower us to create a single interface that auto-adjusts across different devices, saving us from the tedious chore of manually adjusting each page for various screen sizes, as we might have done in previous chapters. And there's more. Think of a multilingual site. Variables enable easy toggling between different languages, making the design both adaptable and user-friendly without much fuss.

The core difference between styles and variables boils down to their fundamental characteristics. Styles are powerful for managing properties that encompass a range of values, such as solid fills, gradients, images, videos, and blend modes. Additionally, they can even incorporate variables, enhancing their versatility. Variables, on the other hand, are specifically designed to handle individual raw color values through **tokenization** or, to reference other variables, a process known as **aliasing**. This distinction positions variables as a preferred choice for building complex design structures using Design Tokens. This approach mirrors the structural practices often employed during the development phase, making variables a bridge that aligns design with development practices.

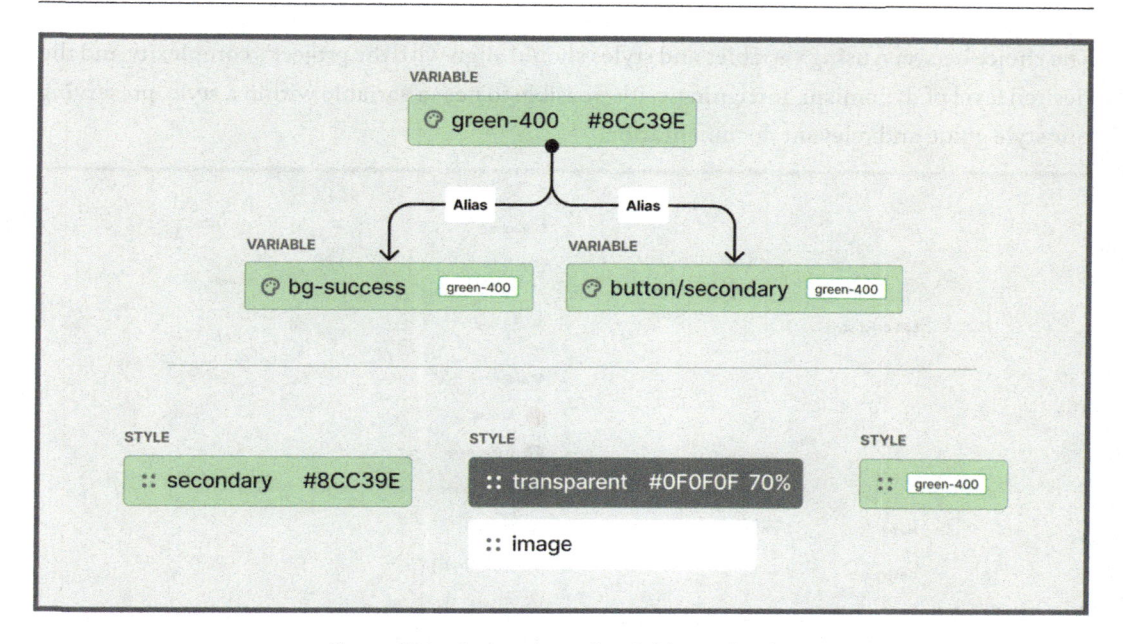

Figure 13.1 – Comparison of variables and styles

Furthermore, variables bring in a scoping feature, allowing designers to specify where a variable can be applied, boosting precision and reducing ambiguity during the design process. For example, you can restrict a **Color** variable solely to stroke color, ensuring it's not misused on other **Fill** properties.

Understanding the nuanced distinction between styles and variables is like leveling up in design management. Although the initial setup with variables may demand more time, the long-term benefits are significant, especially for projects requiring a higher degree of interactivity and scalability. Now, does this mean we abandon styles altogether? Not at all.

The choice between using variables and styles should align with the project's complexity and the desired level of dynamism. Intriguingly, it's possible to nest a variable within a style, preserving our style guide and relevant documentation.

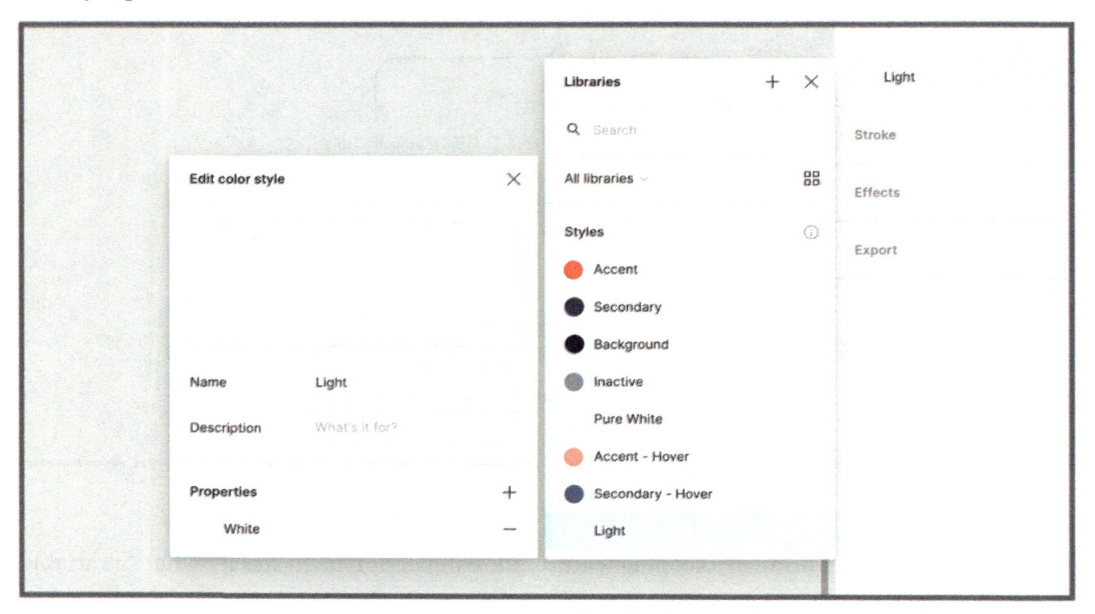

Figure 13.2 – Variables nested in styles

Mastering the use of both variables and styles will undoubtedly elevate the design process, carving the pathway for more captivating, user-focused, and forward-thinking designs. By harmoniously integrating both, you are not only retaining the foundational essence of your design but also augmenting its adaptability and future responsiveness.

Variables, collections, and modes

With the foundational understanding of styles and variables, it's time for you to explore all the types of variables, collections, and modes, and also to define the right terminology when employing these functionalities.

Let's start with the simple task of setting up a new variable, first and foremost. Crafting a **Color** type variable can be compared to shaping a new style, with the selection set to **Variable**. However, this approach often reveals its limitations, as it excludes other types of variables and notably lacks a comprehensive view of all the variables and modes. Therefore, the recommended route to create new variables – without an active selection on canvas among the complete list of styles in the file – is to click on **Local variables**, which will open a dedicated window.

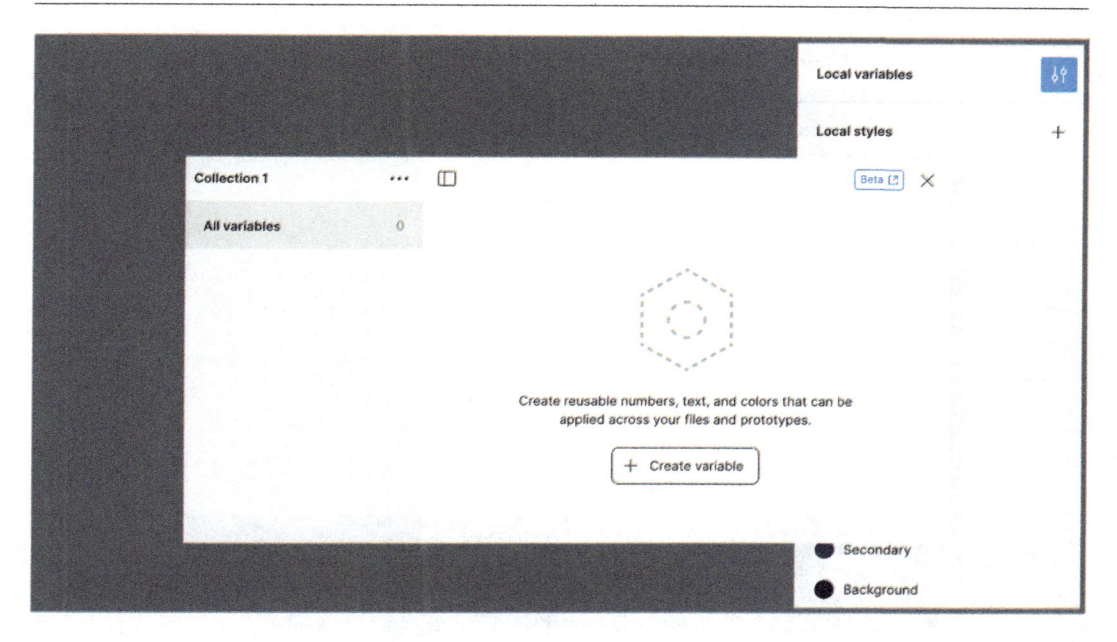

Figure 13.3 – Opening Local variables

From this dialog box, it's not only possible to create a new variable but also to choose its type, ensuring it becomes the most suitable container for the kind of data we require. Let's look at these in detail:

- **Color:** Stores solid color values, applicable to **Fill** and **Stroke** properties.
- **Number:** Holds numerical values, versatile for properties like **Padding**, **Gap**, and **Corner Radius**, and even in text boxes for specific design functionalities.
- **String:** Keeps text strings or variant names, suitable for use in text fields, variant instances, and aligning with component property names.
- **Boolean:** Represents `true` or `false` values, useful in managing variants with Booleans and controlling layer visibility.

These concepts may seem more intricate than they truly are. That's why, moving forward, we will embark on the practical endeavor of building a library of variables. This will serve as a real-world case study to facilitate the learning process and also lay a robust foundation for your forthcoming projects.

The first step in this hands-on journey – after creating a new **Design file** – is to enrich our list of variables with what we identify as base colors.

Click on **Create variable** and select the **Color** type. Name it `White` and assign the hex value `#FFFFFF`.

Figure 13.4 – Creating our first variable

However, a single variable on its own has limited capabilities. Let's proceed by adding a bunch of different colors, as in the following image:

Figure 13.5 – Structuring our base colors

Chapter 13

It's quite a mess, wouldn't you agree? Our list at the moment is a far cry from well organized, and we've just scratched the surface with a small base set of colors, not even delving into all the shades. So, how about embracing **Groups** to inject some order into this color chaos?

> **Note:**
>
> The unique numbering system used for color naming in large-scale projects follows a widely adopted convention. The "500" label represents the base color, with progressively darker shades marked as 600, 700, 800, and 900. Conversely, lighter shades are indicated by descending numbers: 400, 300, and 200, down to the lightest, 100. For smaller color schemes, a simpler naming convention like "normal," "medium," etc. can be used.

Select two contextual colors (e.g., **Red-500** and **Red-600**) simultaneously by holding down the *Shift* key, then with a right-click, you can choose **New group with selection**:

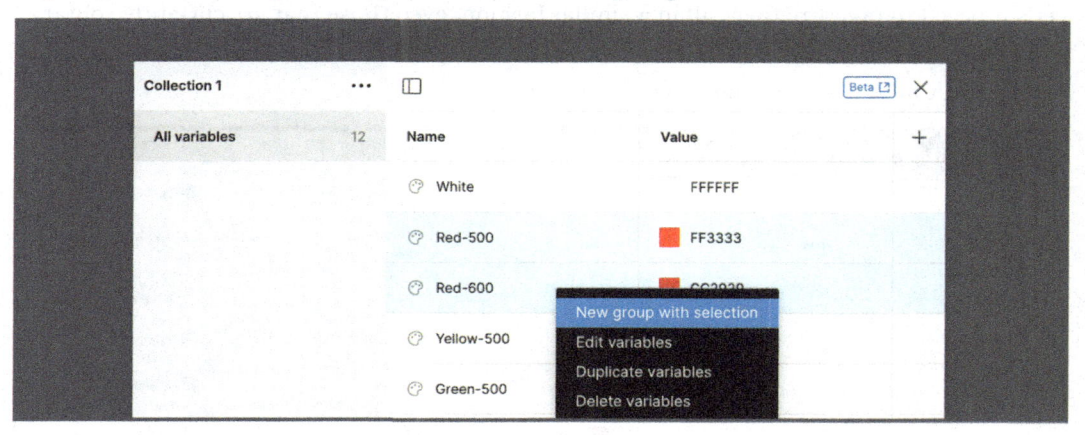

Figure 13.6 – Creating a group

Now, rename the newly formed group as Red by double-clicking the label, and eliminate the redundancy in their names by renaming each variable solely with its shade number, as you see below:

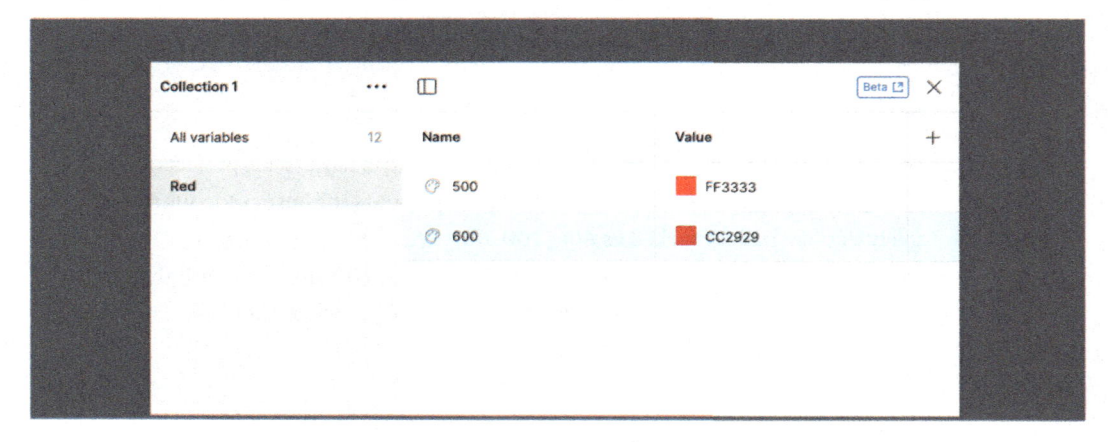

Figure 13.7 – Renaming the variables

Let's proceed to organize them all in a similar fashion, even those that are currently solitary – since more shades will be added later on – with the exception of white, which stands alone and remains so. Check the following image as a reference:

Figure 13.8 – Managing variables with groups

Quite better. Now everything is more readable and easier to navigate. With this, we've completed creating our first set of contextual variables, known as a **collection**. At the top left, we can see that, by default, this set is labeled as `Collection 1`. Let's make it more meaningful by clicking on the **Options** button and selecting **Rename Collection**. Let's name it `Primitives`.

The label `Primitives` here stands for basic, foundational colors that lay the groundwork for our design. Those are the raw colors yet to be tied to any particular function or element within the design. Following this, we'll establish a second collection with Semantic Tokens, housing colors with particular meanings in our design, like **Error** or **Success**. Such a distinction ensures a clear separation between the basic color palette and the meaningful, context-driven colors, leading to a robust and intuitive design system. We adopted a similar approach in the past with styles, using semantic names rather than specific color names.

To prevent accidental use of primitives in our actual design or by others accessing this library, we'll employ scoping to disable both usage and publishing, ensuring that primitives are utilized solely for aliasing:

1. Select all the primitives by using the usual *Shift* shortcut for multi-selection.
2. Right-click one of them, and go with **Edit variables.**
3. Deselect the checkbox for **Show in all supported properties** (which should toggle everything off) and turn **Hide from publishing** on.

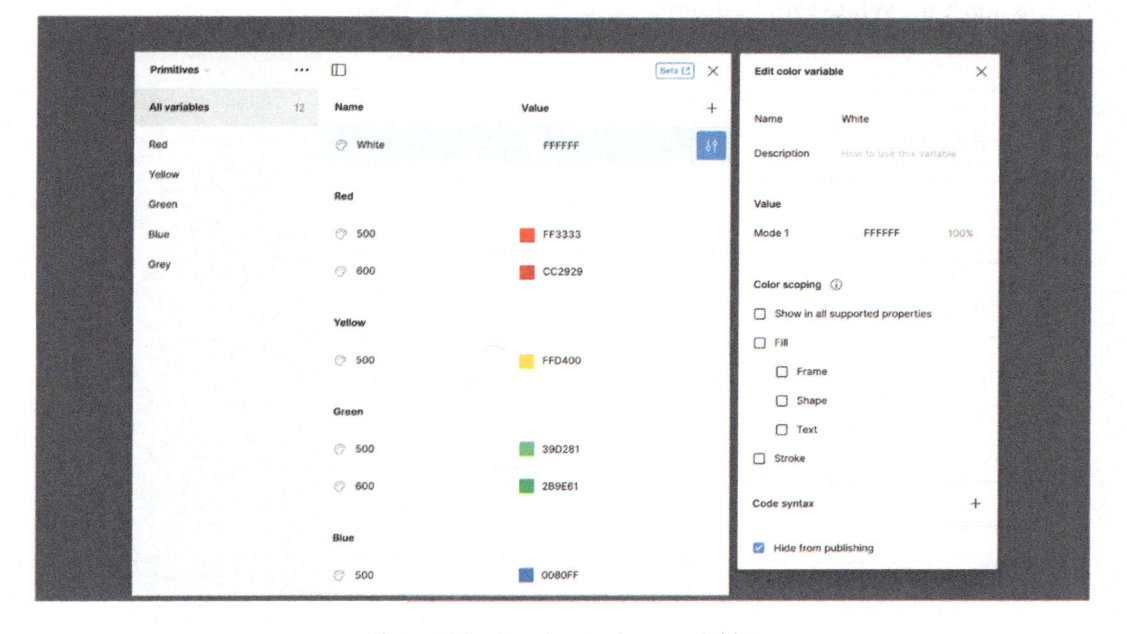

Figure 13.9 – Scoping our base variables

Now it's time to create a new **collection**:

1. Locate **Options** (indicated by three dots or "…") for the active collection and click on it.
2. From the drop-down menu that appears, choose **Create collection**.
3. Name this new collection Semantic Tokens. As mentioned earlier, we will mirror the approach we took with styles – focusing on creating colors based on their function, rather than their hue. We'll keep the setup simple, laying down the essential structures to understand its functioning. You are then free to expand this library independently, tailoring it to the needs of your ongoing or future projects. The categories we will structure within this collection are **Basics, Texts,** and **Buttons**.
4. Create a new **variable** within the new collection, naming it background. This belongs under **Basics**. Yet, there's no need to create a group each time in the old-fashioned way. Simply name the variable Basics/background and you've effortlessly created a new group for it. This nifty trick streamlines the process, keeping things organized right from the get-go.

This variable is designated to represent the color white, but instead of assigning a hex value directly, we'll link it to an alias from our library of primitive colors. In this semantic layer, our practice will be to exclusively use aliases that refer back to the color tokens we initially established in the preceding library. This ensures a direct linkage of our semantic elements to our foundational color palette. To do this, click on the **Value** field of the variable, select **Libraries** from the options, and then assign it the **White** variable from the list.

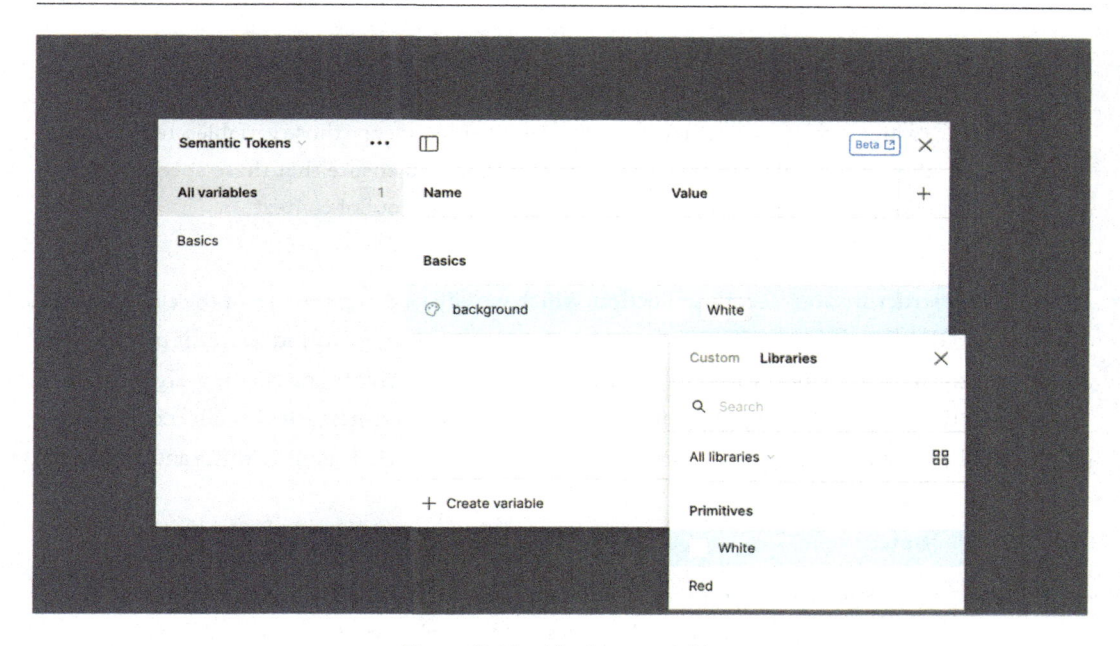

Figure 13.10 – Aliasing a variable

Proceed with organizing all the needed Semantic Tokens following the established scheme, as illustrated in the image below:

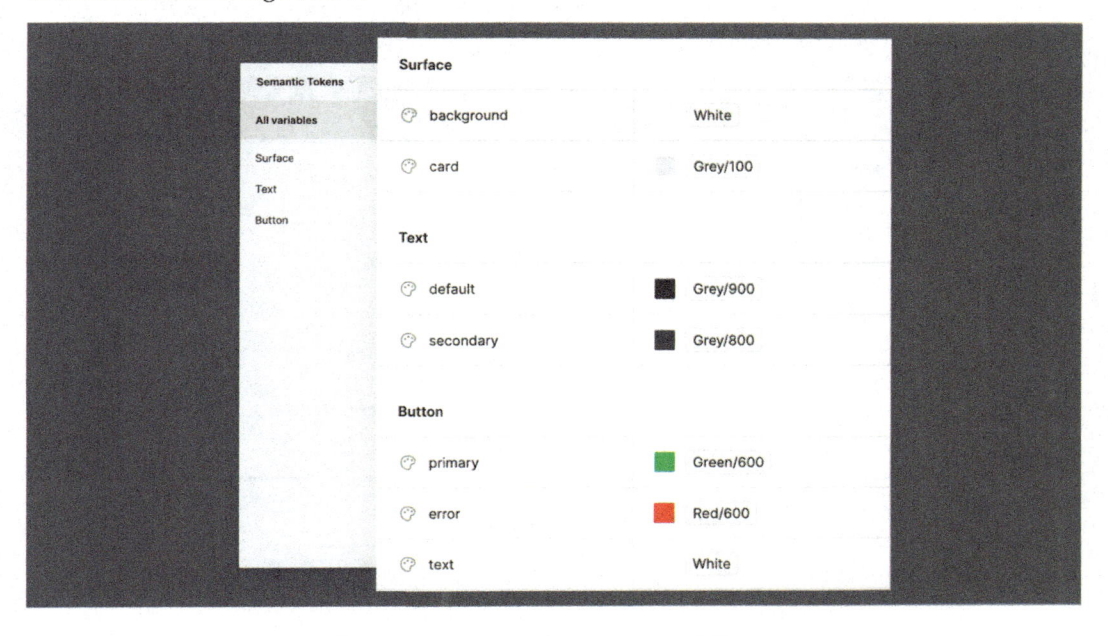

Figure 13.11 – Structuring our Semantic Tokens

> **Note:**
> To prevent the misuse of text colors, you may opt to scope those variables, restricting their usage solely to text elements. This way, you ensure that these specific color variables are employed accurately, and never used out of context.

We have now structured our second collection, which we will be using shortly. At the current stage, we have laid down a system akin to color styles, yet even with these foundations, it proves to be more versatile in many aspects. Mainly, because the same **primitive** token can be assigned to multiple Semantic Tokens, allowing us, in the future, to change all the interface elements connected to it in one fell swoop or – vice versa – changing individual Semantic Tokens to different primitives.

> **Note:**
> Developers can access Figma's Variables API to directly link design variables to the code base, enabling swift and seamless updates when variables are modified in Figma.

But the journey doesn't end here, as the true potential of this structure is unlocked by adding new **Modes** columns to our Semantic Tokens collection to set up light and dark color schemes. How? Click the + button near the last column.

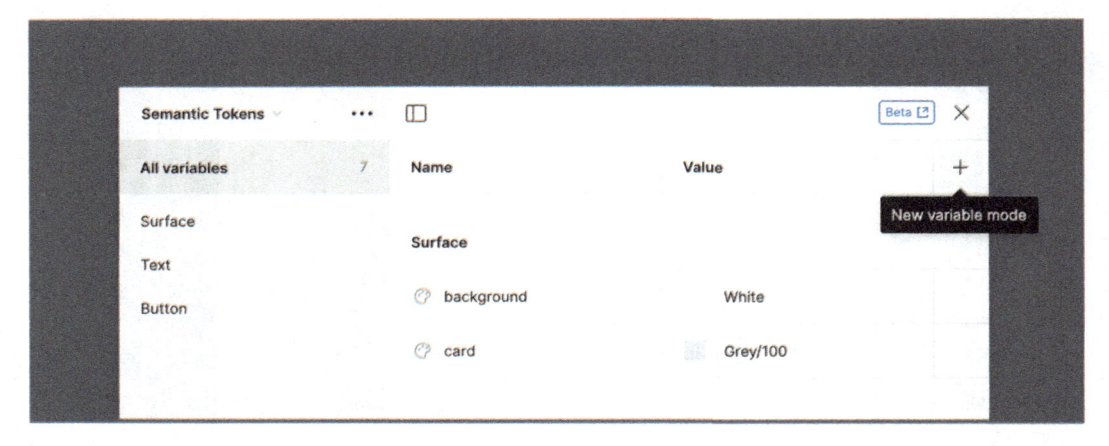

Figure 13.12 – Creating a new mode

Chapter 13

> **Note:**
>
> Creating additional **Modes** columns is a feature that requires a Professional account or higher. However, if you are a student and wish to learn about Figma's more advanced functionalities, remember that – provided you meet the requirements – you can access Pro features for free through an Education plan (`figma.com/education`).

We've introduced a new column of values, yet at a glance, both columns appear identical. What's the meaning of this second column? The initial setup we crafted represents the default interface color scheme, also known as **Light Mode**, while this second column reflects the color variations of each element in our product when toggled to **Dark Mode**. To reflect this distinction clearly, let's rename these columns based on their respective modes. Double-click on the label of the first **value** column and rename it `Light Mode`. Similarly, double-click on the label of the last column and rename it `Dark Mode`. By doing so, we effectively differentiate between the color schemes tailored for different display modes, thus laying a solid foundation for seamless toggling functionality between light/dark schemes in our design.

Next, adjust the aliases in the second column to correspond with the color variations we aim for in Dark Mode. Stick to the below scheme for reference:

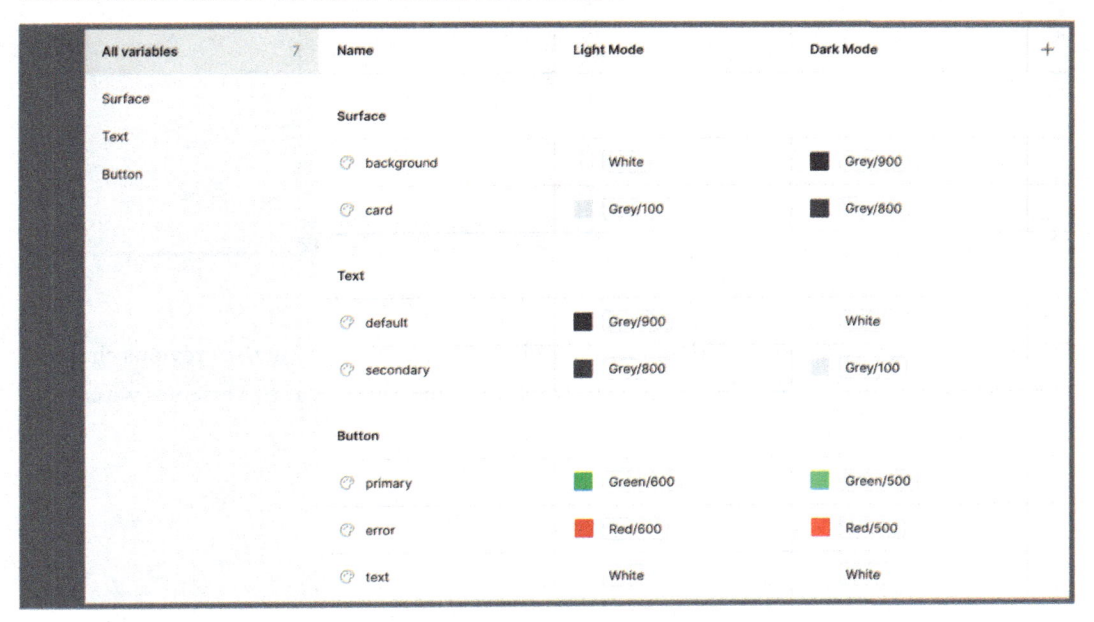

All variables	7	Name	Light Mode	Dark Mode
Surface		**Surface**		
Text		background	White	Grey/900
Button		card	Grey/100	Grey/800
		Text		
		default	Grey/900	White
		secondary	Grey/800	Grey/100
		Button		
		primary	Green/600	Green/500
		error	Red/600	Red/500
		text	White	White

Figure 13.13 – Setting up Light and Dark Mode

We will soon create additional collections to further harness the potential of variables, but now it's time to see them in action, to reap the benefits of what we've crafted thus far, and to understand in practical terms how this intricate setup can reward our efforts. Go back to your workspace and follow these steps:

1. Create a frame by selecting any device from the presets.
2. Rename this frame `Light Mode`.
3. From the **Fill** property, access the **Styles** library, and there you'll find the semantic variables we just created (the primitives won't be displayed thanks to scoping).
4. Apply the variable **Surface/background**.

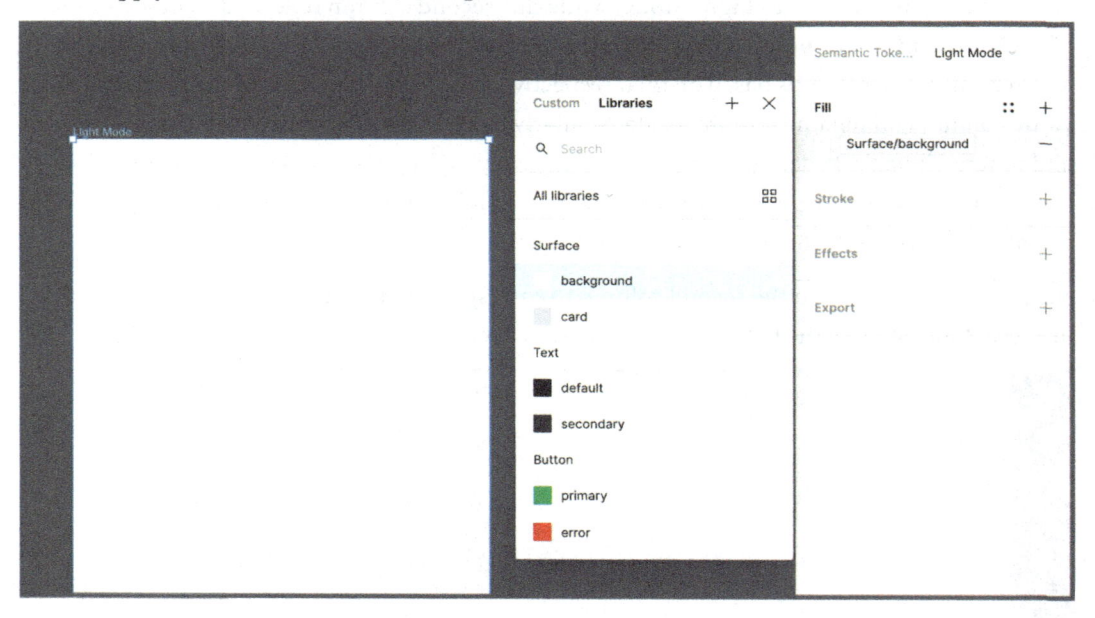

Figure 13.14: Using a variable for Fill properties

Following the same procedure, let's create a simple card, as we learned in the previous chapters, visually referring to the image below and applying the respective semantic variables we created for each of these elements.

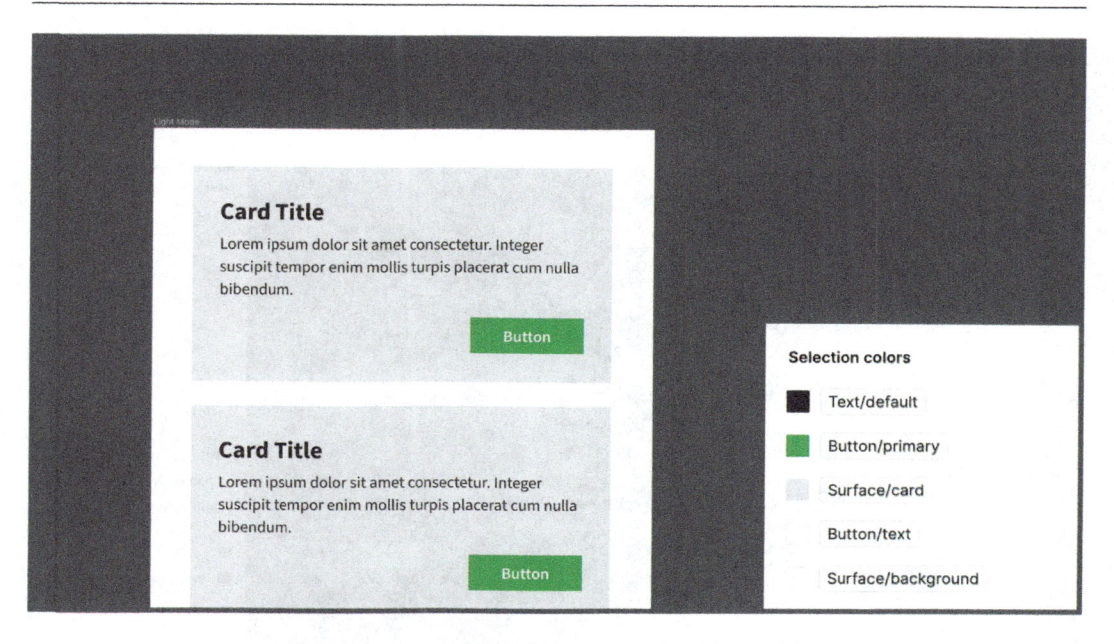

Figure 13.15: A simple card layout made with variables

In the **Layer** section of the right sidebar – while selecting the external **Light Mode** frame – you should now notice a new toggle icon appear. This occurs only when you initiate variables with multiple **modes** in the active frame. Also, the current mode should be displayed within a selector:

Figure 13.16: A simple card layout made with variables

Now comes the magical part. Duplicate your **Light Mode** frame and rename the new one Dark Mode. Select this new outer container, and simply switch the selector to **Dark Mode** (or use the toggle to navigate through the modes).

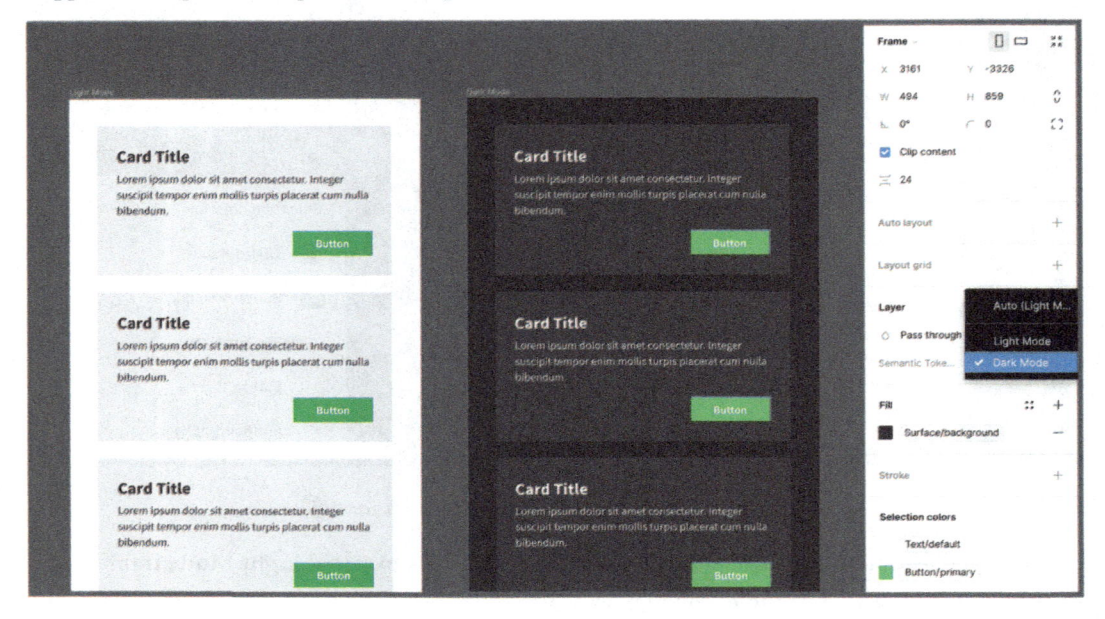

Figure 13.17 – Automatically displaying Dark Mode

This simple action unveils the dynamic nature of the variables setup, automatically transforming the appearance of the design to align with the color scheme we defined for **Dark Mode**. Also, try dragging a single card element from the **Dark Mode** frame to the **Light Mode** one, and you'll see that – again – it turns back to **Light**!

> **Note:**
>
> How you organize your collections really depends on you and the specific needs of your projects. You might find it helpful to add component tokens, or you might want to arrange your variables in a totally different way. That's completely fine, especially if it makes your work faster and helps you work more effectively with your development team.

What we've achieved so far is merely the tip of the iceberg when it comes to the potential of variables. In the next section, we'll uncover new possibilities, create additional collections to enhance our workflow, and delve deeper into token management.

Going responsive and multilingual with variables

Having explored **Color** type variables extensively, it's time to turn our attention to numerical variables. These variables come with an array of amazing capabilities and can be applied to a wide range of properties. They are not only great for maintaining consistency in spacing, padding, and corner radius but also for speeding up the creation of responsive interfaces.

As you might recall, in design, we aim to establish logical conventions to create consistency and harmony among elements, often adhering to basic rules such as the multiples of 8. However, as simplistic as it sounds, always remembering to maintain these proportions can be draining over time, and every now and then, some stray elements that don't adhere to the self-imposed rules pop up. So, why not create a new collection of numbers to help us keep track of those values?

Create a new collection by clicking **Create collection** and name it Number Tokens. Structure a set of new **Number** type variables, by following the scheme below:

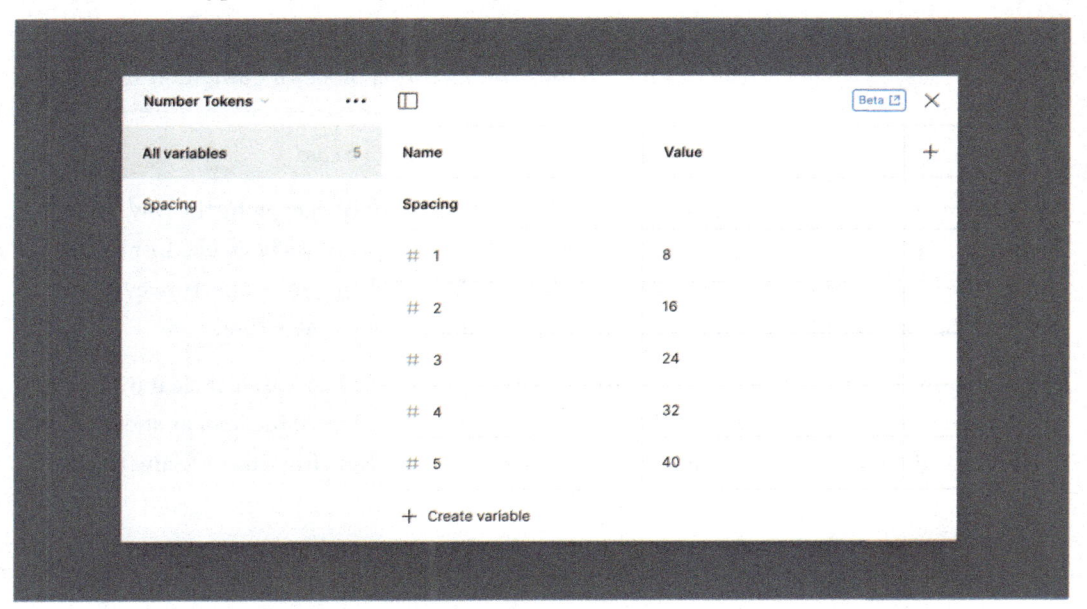

Figure 13.18 – Spacing variables

We have thus set up what we could call utility variables, which are a set of numerical variables that we can leverage to create consistency quickly and effectively. But how and where can we apply them? Imagine we want to create some new cards.

Ideally, we would follow the rule of multiples to achieve something like this:

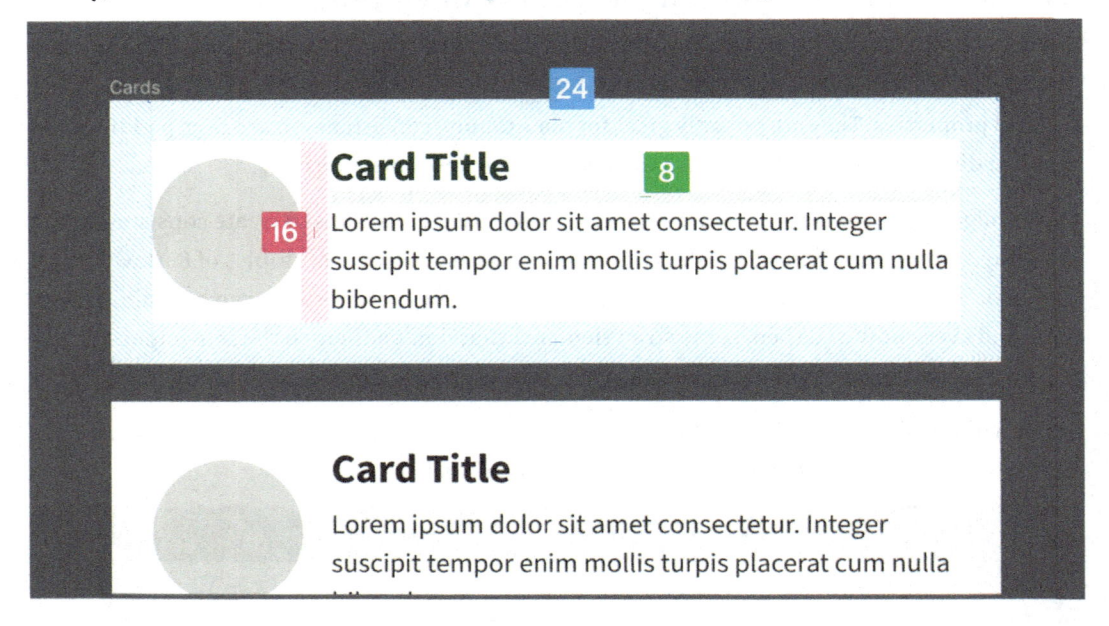

Figure 13.19 – Using the rule of multiples for a card

If we were to manually set these values, we could easily forget some pieces along the way. Moreover, if, one day, we decide to change the value of the spacing wherever it has been used, or maybe set it in a more compact way for mobile devices, we would have to do it one by one. However, we can enhance this process by using the handy spacing variables we created earlier.

Upon selecting the frame where we want to add padding or set the gap, we steer clear from typing the usual numerical value. Instead, click on the hexagon-shaped **Variable** icon as shown below (visible only if we have a proper collection set up) and pick the **Spacing** value we aim to apply.

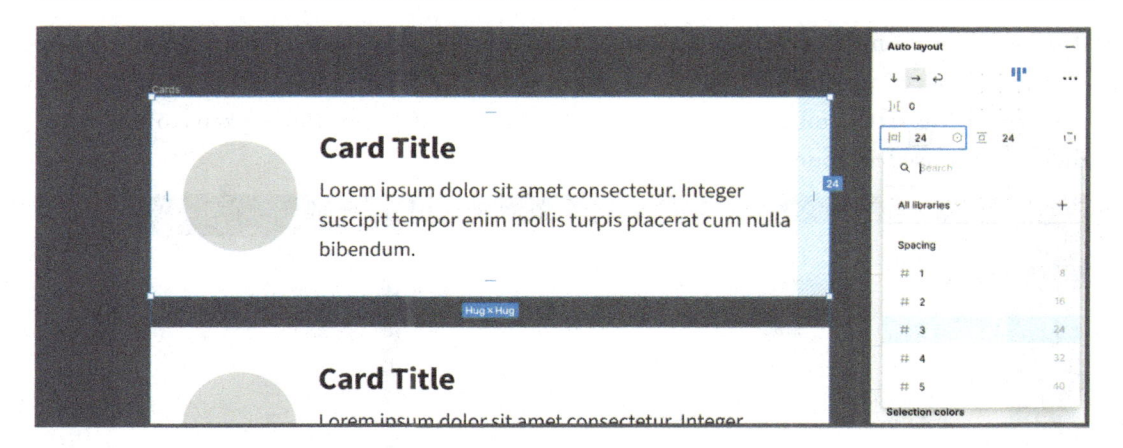

Figure 13.20 – Setting Spacing variables for padding

If streamlining your workflow isn't a compelling enough reason to start using utility variables, there are also substantial benefits this method brings to the development side. These values, in fact, not only get displayed in **Dev Mode** as visual labels on the design but are also automatically translated into CSS variables, significantly improving communication between designers and developers.

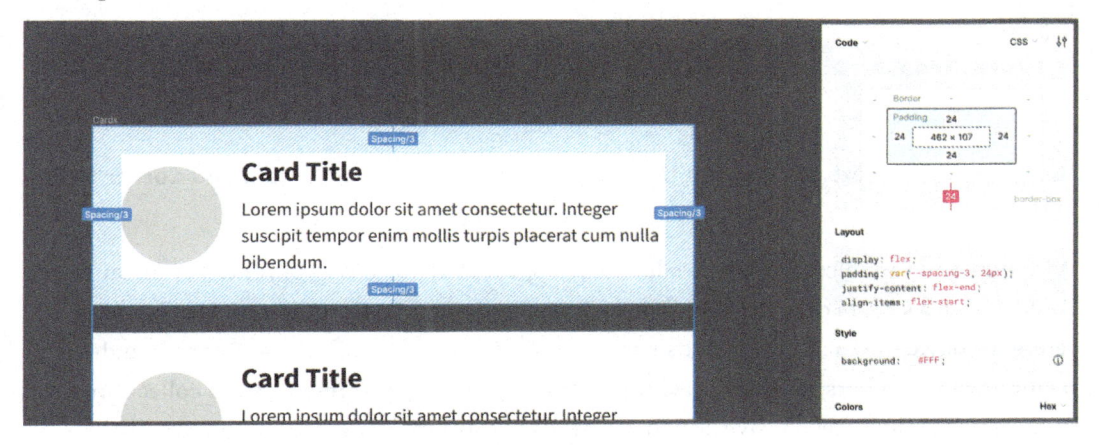

Figure 13.21 – CSS variables in Dev Mode

If we often use rounded corners in our design, adding a new set of number tokens for **Corner radius** to our collection could be helpful. This way, we can keep all the rounded corners consistent without having to remember the values each time. We can also scope these tokens to make sure they are only used for rounding edges.

Figure 13.22 – Creating radius variables

Using them is a breeze; just look for the usual **Variable** icon next to the standard **Corner radius** option.

With numeric variables, anyway, we have the opportunity to go way beyond. For instance, we could design a system of responsive frames that automatically adjust their content based on the reference device. To achieve this, it's suggested to create a new collection. Even though we're dealing with numbers, we won't use the previously created **Number Tokens** collection, for a very clear reason: for responsive design, we need to create specific modes for breakpoints. In our case, since the values for **Spacing** and **Radius** don't need adjustments based on various devices, using the existing **Number Tokens** collection would mean creating an unnecessary duplication of identical values across multiple columns.

In practice, we'll create a separate new collection named Breakpoints that will allow us to define and manage the modes for responsive design. Follow the below scheme, but remember that you can easily consult the preset frame sizes if you don't remember those **width** and **height** values.

Note:

Did you notice that your list of collections is automatically sorted alphabetically? There's no way to manually adjust this. However, there's a workaround: simply rename your collections with numbers upfront to establish your own order.

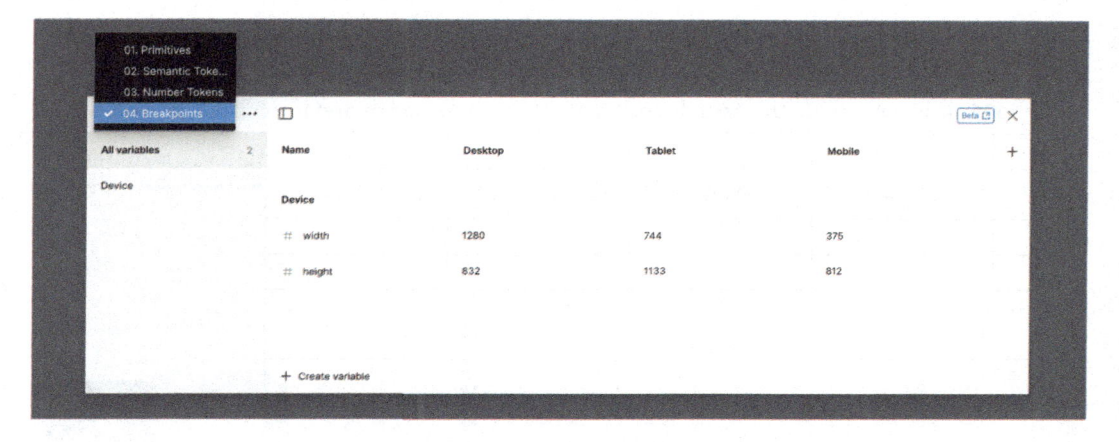

Figure 13.23 – Setting up a new collection for Breakpoints

Now, proceed as follows:

1. Create a frame of any size.
2. Set its **Width** and **Height** values using the respective variables, through the usual dedicated icon, without manually entering the numeric value in the field.
3. Turn **Auto layout** on, and make sure its **Horizontal** and **Vertical resizing** is set to **Fixed**.

Figure 13.24 – Using variables for Width and Height of the main frame

What we've just done is set our main frame in such a way that the variables indicate the reference device, and obviously, we now have access to the modes, which allow us to switch the dimensions of the frame based on the desired device. But it doesn't end here. If we set a mode to the outermost container – as we've already seen with the **Light/Dark Mode** – all the elements contained within it will by default inherit the affiliation to that mode.

Even this would be enough, perhaps in addition to **flex-wrap** on the outer frame and **Fill Container** for each of the inner elements, to ensure automatic responsiveness for anything we insert in this interface. By inserting some cards into the current frame, duplicating it, changing its mode to **Mobile**, and using the **Auto layout** feature as discussed in previous chapters, you would achieve this result:

Figure 13.25 – Switching to Mobile mode

Almost there. We're close to the desired outcome, but our columns currently lack width limits, which can trigger our breakpoints, ending up with elements being too narrow on **Mobile** and excessively wide when we stretch beyond the **Desktop** frame width. Yet again, variables come to our rescue.

We can create a set of variables – still within the **Breakpoints** collection – to define the minimum and maximum width values for our columns, for each of the breakpoints. Follow the example scheme below:

04. Breakpoints		Name	Desktop	Tablet	Mobile
All variables	4				
Device		Device			
Columns		# width	1280	744	375
		# height	832	1133	812
		Columns			
		# minWidth	340	300	200
		# maxWidth	430	400	400

Figure 13.26 – Defining minimum and maximum values for our columns

Let's proceed by assigning the newly created variables. You'll come across the **Min / Max** value field just beneath the standard **Width** selector. However, bear in mind that this field will only show up if **Fill Container** has been selected within an **Auto layout** frame. Select all the columns at once, then assign the minWidth variable to the **Min Width** field and similarly, maxWidth to the **Max Width** field, as shown below:

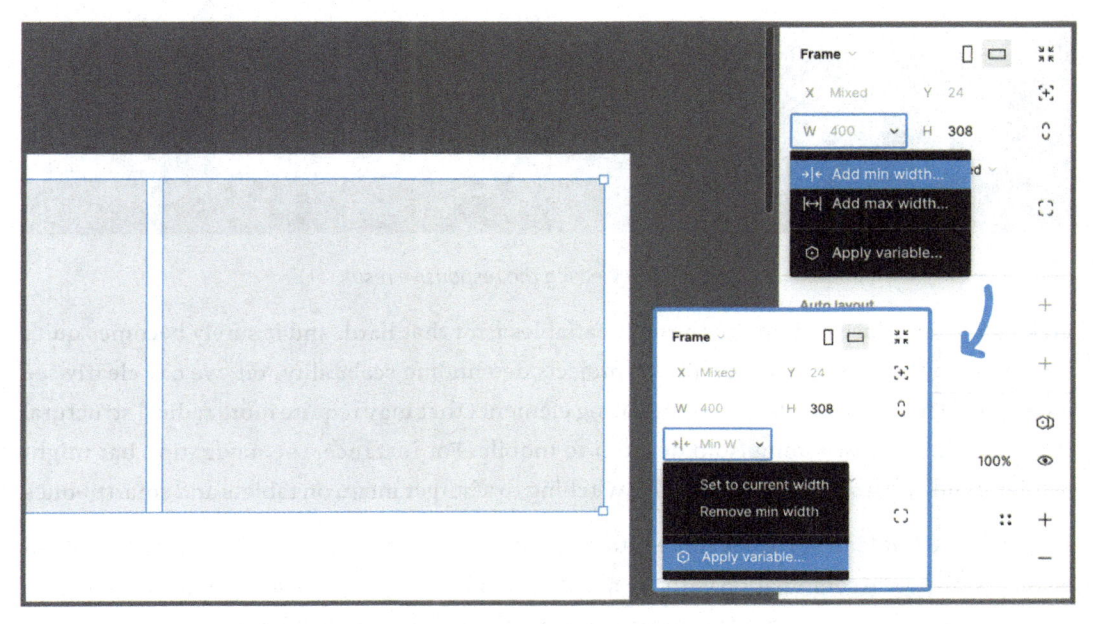

Figure 13.27 – Defining minimum and maximum values for our columns

With this swift and simple trick, your main structure is now fully responsive, adapting seamlessly based on the mode selected in the main external frame. Now, each column is bound by minimum and maximum width constraints, ensuring that the content remains readable and maintains a suitable size regardless of the device dimensions. This setup also preserves the layout integrity by allowing content to wrap to the next line when the columns reach their width constraints. Go ahead, give it a whirl – duplicate your frame once more and toggle the mode to **Tablet** and **Mobile**. You'll notice how effortlessly it reconfigures to fit the designated device dimensions while adhering to the established width bounds of each column.

Figure 13.28 – Viewing the responsive result

Making our interface responsive through variables isn't that hard, and it surely becomes quite intriguing in the long run, especially on projects demanding scalability. Yet, we can clearly see its technical limitations when contemplating elements that may require more radical structural changes when transitioning from desktop to mobile. For instance, the navigation bar might display plain entries on a desktop while switching to a burger menu on tablets and smartphones.

This is where **Boolean** variables come into play. With them, we can manage the visibility of our elements, always in combination with the modes. Initially, it might seem like a somewhat complex concept, but I assure you, with the upcoming example, you'll not only fully grasp the advantages that Boolean variables can offer but also how to use them in just a few minutes at most.

Let's set up a navigation bar, using **Auto layout** and **Auto gap between items**, which displays the navigation elements we need: both the desktop menu and the burger menu icon for mobile.

Figure 13.29 – Navbar with mobile and desktop navigation

Right from our **Breakpoints** collection, let's create new **Boolean** variables. These will determine the visibility of our elements, and we need to configure them so that an element is shown on tablets and smartphones, but not on desktops, and vice versa.

Figure 13.30 – Boolean variables for layer visibility

Then, head to the navbar element and select the burger menu element. In the **Layer** section of the right panel, right-click the eye icon, and a new menu will show up, letting you assign a Boolean variable for visibility.

Assign the `hasMobile` variable, so it gets hidden on mobile frames.

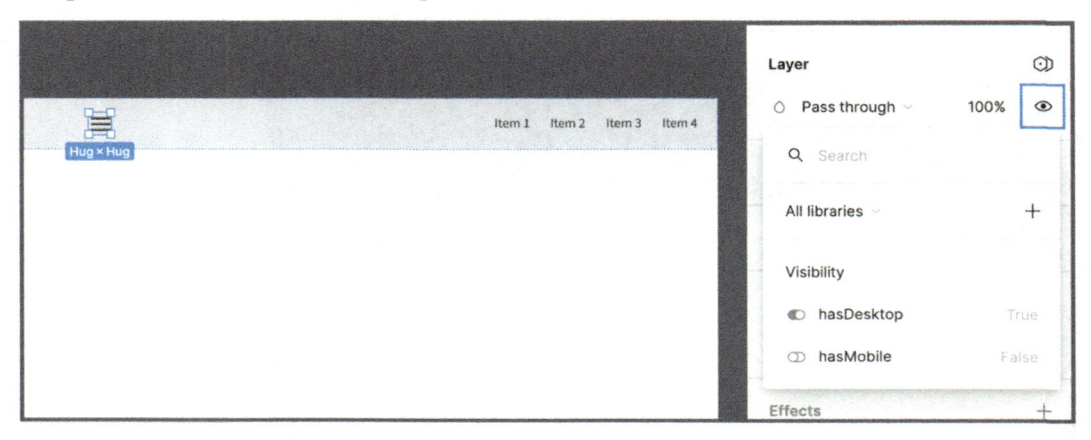

Figure 13.31 – Hiding the burger menu on Desktop

Do the same for the desktop menu, but this time, assign the `hasDesktop` variable, to make it appear only when your frame mode is on **Mobile**.

Using this variable, you can do the trick whenever you need it for any element of your interface, and if you try duplicating your main desktop frame and changing the mode to **Mobile**, your navbar will now re-adapt automatically, hiding the unnecessary.

Figure 13.32 – Navbar adapting to Mobile mode

> **Note:**
> If you create collections with different modes within them, it's possible to activate multiple modes simultaneously. This means we can retain the benefits of responsiveness without having to forego, for example, the automatic Light/Dark theme switching.

As we progress, we have unraveled the capabilities of **Color**, **Number**, and **Boolean** variables. Yet, our exploration wouldn't be complete without delving into **String** variables. While they might not have been pivotal in our journey thus far, they open up a new avenue, especially when it comes to simulating multilingual support in our design.

To understand how, let's create one more collection, which we'll name Copy (or **05. Copy** if we've decided to add the number upfront to maintain the order we determined), and structure it in a very straightforward manner as follows:

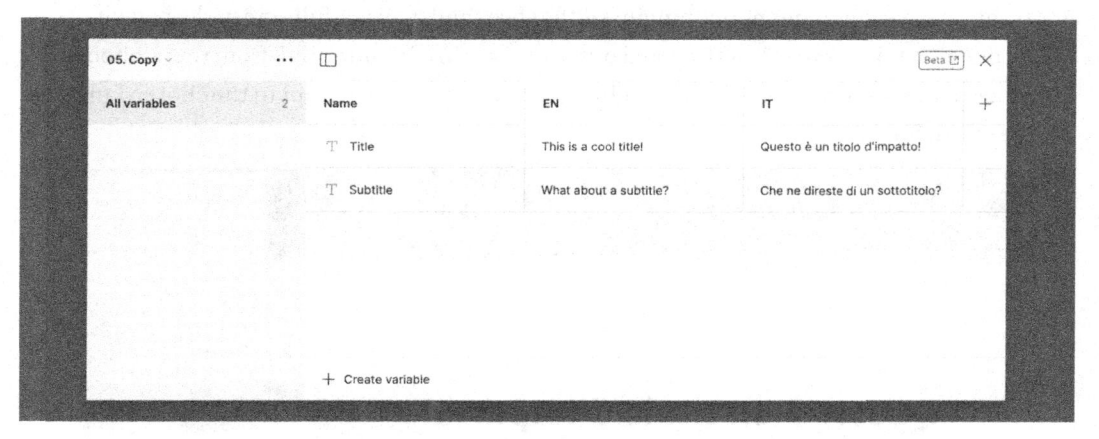

05. Copy		Name	EN	IT	
All variables	2	T Title	This is a cool title!	Questo è un titolo d'impatto!	
		T Subtitle	What about a subtitle?	Che ne direste di un sottotitolo?	
		+ Create variable			

Figure 13.33 – Creating a Copy collection for strings

Let's now actually create a text element anywhere in our frame by using the **Text** tool. It doesn't matter what you write here because it will be soon replaced by the variable's content.

In the **Text** section of the right panel, you'll find the usual variable icon popping up after a proper collection is available.

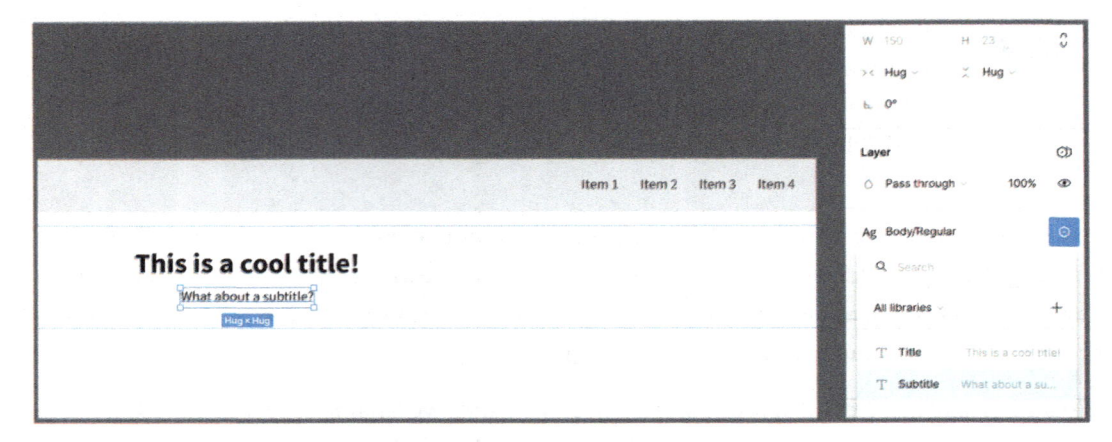

Figure 13.34 – Assigning text variables

At first glance, we might not notice tangible differences and may not fully grasp the benefit of this setup, but all it takes is to select the usual outermost main container and, from there, choose the language of our interface. Our title and subtitle will automatically adapt to the chosen language for the entire frame.

Figure 13.35 – Switching to another language with ease

Mastering variables, collections, and modes in Figma isn't straightforward and requires practice. Once familiar, like Auto Layout, they become indispensable due to their versatility. The framework we've outlined offers a solid base to explore these features across practical scenarios.

Additionally, new ways to use variables include applying them to effects like shadows, stroke weight, layer opacity, and binding them to layout grid fields such as count, width, and gutter. Significantly, string variables can now be used with nested instance variant properties. The true potential unfolds when you adapt and optimize these features for your workflow, enhancing developer collaboration with custom collections and modes.

> **Note:**
> Just like with styles, you may choose to publish variables as a standalone `Library` file. Then, by enabling the published library, you'll be able to see and use all of your (non-hidden) variables and collections in other projects.

Now, we'll shift our focus toward another engaging aspect of Figma – conditional prototyping. Although we are moving forward, we're not leaving variables behind as they will continue to serve as a cornerstone in navigating through this new topic!

Pushing further with conditional prototyping

As we journey deeper into the advanced capabilities of Figma, it's time to unfold the layers of conditional prototyping – a feature that not only enhances the interactive aspects of your designs but also elevates user experiences to a more realistic realm. Conditional prototyping is more than just a static representation; it's about mirroring real-world scenarios within your design framework, allowing for dynamic interactions based on user inputs or varying conditions.

This powerful feature can be a game-changer, enabling you to envision, test, and refine user flows in a more holistic manner. It's about adding a layer of logic to your prototypes, making them smarter and more aligned with real-world use cases. The conditional pathways you create can reflect a wide array of user interactions and responses, painting a more accurate picture of how users navigate through your design.

So, let's push further into the dynamic world of conditional prototyping, and see how this phenomenal feature can redefine – and simplify – the way you approach prototyping in Figma.

The logic behind conditional prototyping

Having reached this point, it's clear how remarkable the variables in Figma are. Much like what could be achieved with a Design Token system, they provide us with unparalleled modularity. However, the utility of variables extends beyond just this, forming the backbone of the conditional prototyping system as well.

Within the **Prototype** area, we will encounter two new options, **Set variable** and **Conditional**, which we'll explore together shortly:

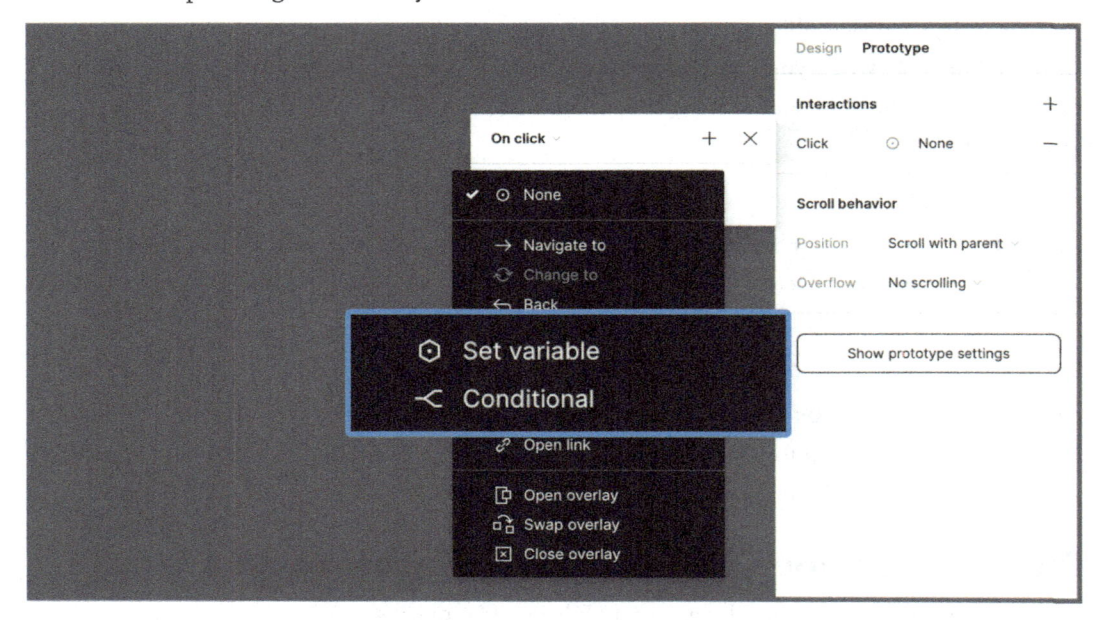

Figure 13.36 – New options in the Prototype tab

But let's start with some context. These additions aim to address a challenge that plagues more complex and detailed prototypes – the presence of numerous "spiderwebs" whenever a slightly more realistic interaction needs to be created. For instance, if I wanted to set up a simple interactive input stepper to act as a counter, this is roughly what I would need to put together:

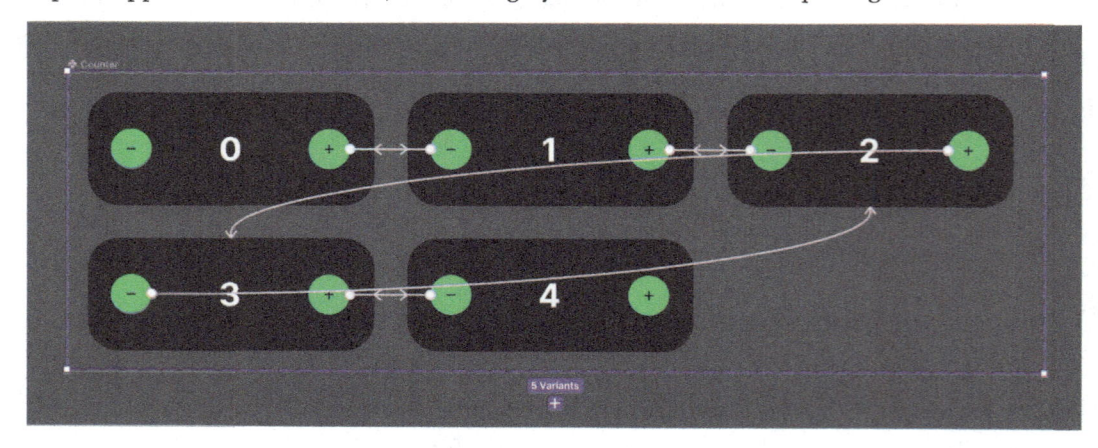

Figure 13.37 – An interactive input stepper

In simpler terms, frames are tasked with preserving every distinct state, which leads to an overly complex setup—so much so that typically, only a subset of possible states are simulated to avoid overloading the file. This approach, in turn, makes the file harder to manage and maintain over time.

By using variables and conditionals in Figma, we can simplify complex processes, such as creating an input stepper, down to a single frame. This method adds realism and efficiency to the prototype. Imagine replacing the stepper's displayed value with a variable, let's say, **X**. Then, assign the increment and decrement actions to this **X** value. Each button press adjusts **X**, either increasing or decreasing it. This setup mimics a real, programmatically controlled input stepper, offering a more intuitive and interactive prototype experience.

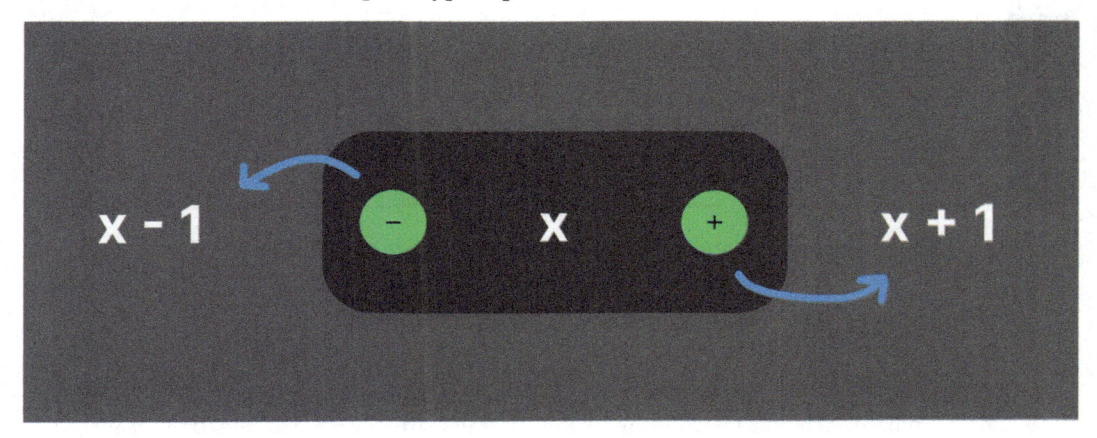

Figure 13.38 – Using variables to store dynamic data

Instead of altering the entire component with each click, the container will remain unchanged, and only the dynamic content of the variable will change upon triggering the action. This mirrors what would occur in the actual development of this element with any programming language.

With the logic now clearly laid out, we're ready to move from theory to practice, exploring how to create dynamic elements like these directly in Figma. This transition will allow us to bring interactive and responsive designs to life with ease.

Advanced prototyping with variables and conditionals

To best learn how to leverage variables with conditional logic, we'll start with the case outlined earlier – namely, the Input Stepper component – in order to grasp all the necessary basics before moving on to something different and more complex.

First of all, it would be great to create an extra collection, which we'll name Stored Values, to initialize all the variables that we'll use for dynamic components. The primary necessity for starting with our **stepper** component is a simple variable of the **Number** type, initialized to **0**. This initialization acts as a starting point for our stepper, ensuring that it begins counting from a neutral value.

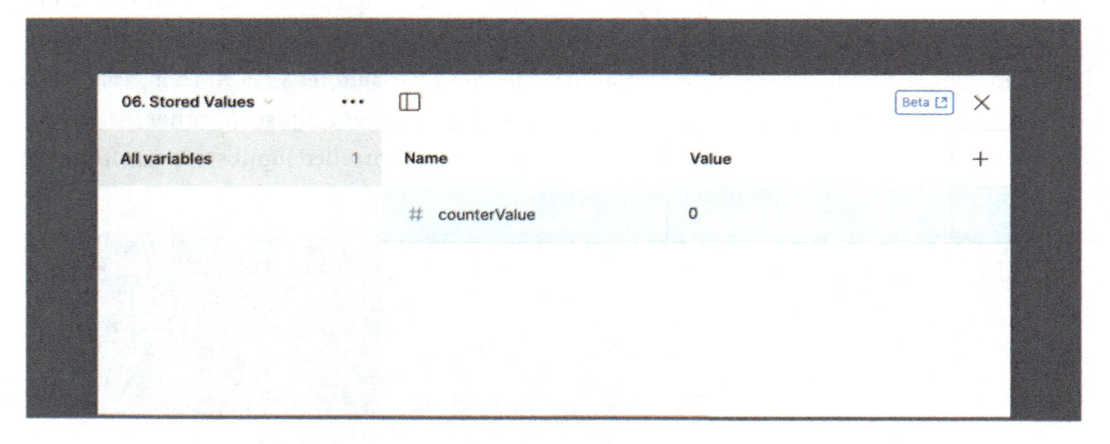

Figure 13.39 – Initializing a new variable to store Stepper data

> **Note:**
> When creating variables, you may choose to utilize camel case syntax, a convention where each word within the variable name starts with a capital letter except for the first word (e.g., myVariableName). This practice not only enhances readability, especially when your variable names are made with multiple words, but also fosters a developer-friendly environment.

Now that our variable with a starting value of zero is properly initialized, the next step is to replace the hardcoded text with the actual **String** variable. Select the **text** box and, using the **Variable** icon, apply counterValue to the string.

Chapter 13 413

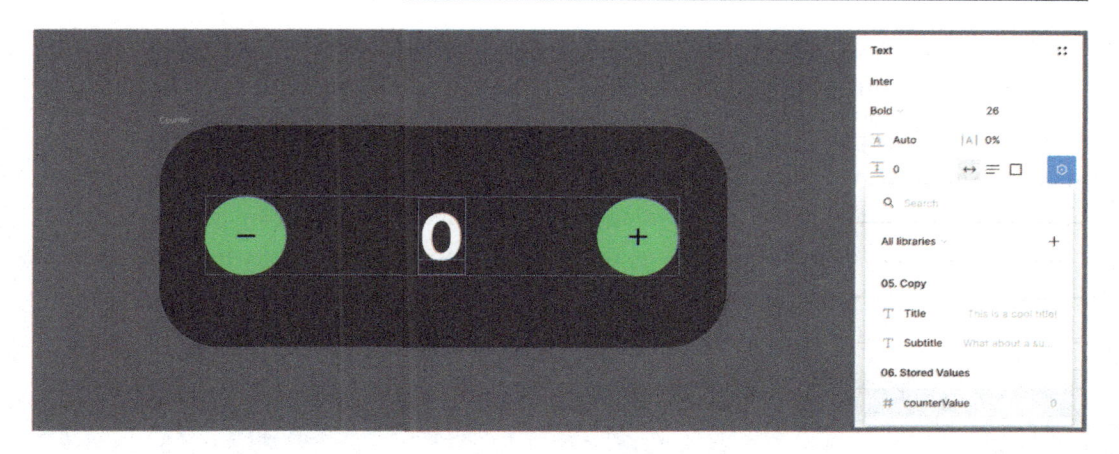

Figure 13.40 – Replacing text with a String variable

Initially, it might appear that nothing has altered. Yet, the truth of the matter is, the element now displaying **0** corresponds to an **X** value, tethered to a variable that can be modified dynamically through triggers. Let's apply those triggers to make our variable change:

1. Go to the **Prototype** tab.
2. Select the Stepper's **+** button.
3. Add a new interaction with the **On Click** trigger, and select **Set variable**.
4. In the from field, establish a base value for our action using counterValue.
5. In the to field, determine the output the base value will have after the click action. Instead of inserting a variable, manually enter the value **1**.

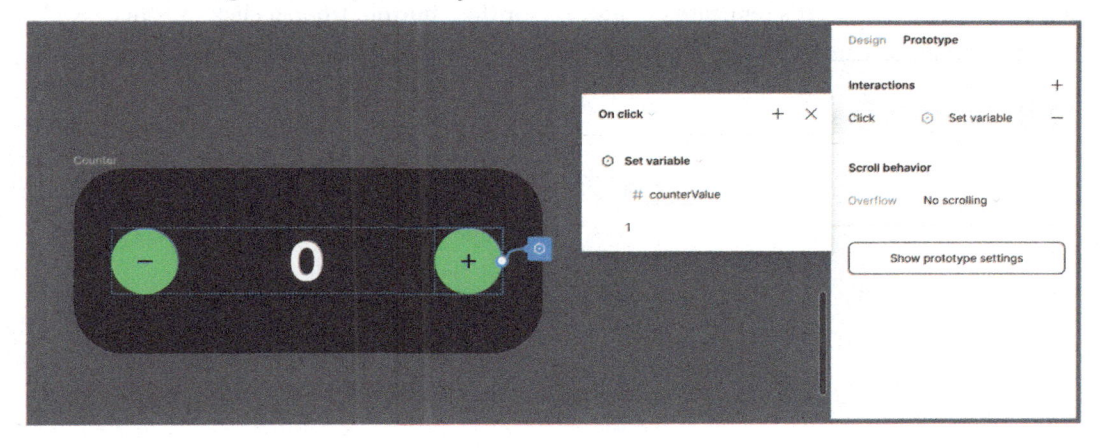

Figure 13.41 – Prototyping the + button

You can swiftly and effectively verify the functionality with the **Inline Preview**, by selecting the Stepper element and using the shortcut *Shift + Spacebar*.

Upon clicking the + button, our stepper updates to show the value of **1**. However, a small hiccup appears –subsequent clicks don't increase the value further; it remains at **1**. This issue shows up because our instruction only sets the value to a fixed value of **1** whenever we trigger the action, rather than adding 1 to the current value. To resolve this, we'll tweak our setting, ensuring that, with each click, the current value is retrieved from the variable and then incremented by 1, as shown below:

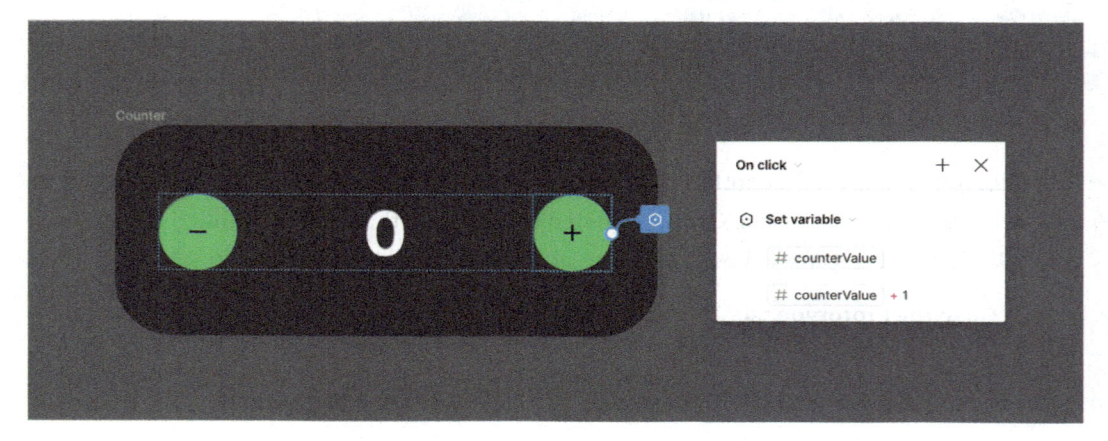

Figure 13.42 – Fixing the interaction

Through mathematical expressions, we can add, subtract, multiply, and divide variables to achieve complex interactions. Let's replicate the process for the - button. Upon a click (**onClick**), we'll change **Set variable** from counterValue to counterValue - 1, effectively decreasing the count by one with each click.

Chapter 13 415

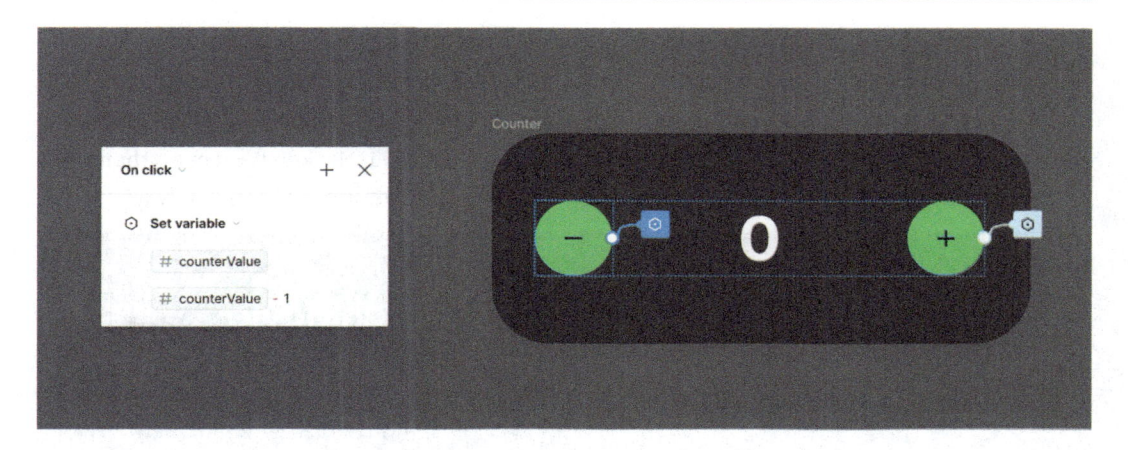

Figure 13.43 – Prototyping the - button

Great! Now our stepper operates for both increment and decrement, aligning closely with what we envisioned. However, there's still something unexpected. If we hit the - button when the value is **0** or less, the component will display negative numbers.

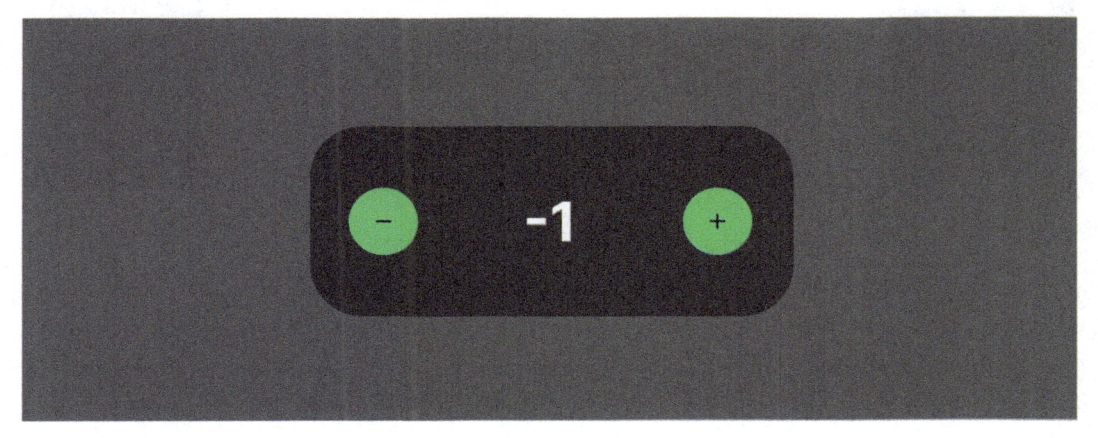

Figure 13.44 – Going into negatives

This behavior isn't what we anticipated and is definitely something we wish to correct for optimal results. This is precisely where **conditional prototyping** comes into play, which, in essence, embodies the concept of "if-else" logic.

In programming, the "if-else" cycle helps us decide what action to take based on certain conditions. For instance, "if" a particular condition is met, then a specific action will happen. On the other hand, "else," a different action will take place. To make this idea clearer, let's think about a Boolean variable named isWeekend. If this variable is true (if isWeekend = true), then we'll enjoy watching a movie; otherwise ("else"), we'll have to go to another boring meeting.

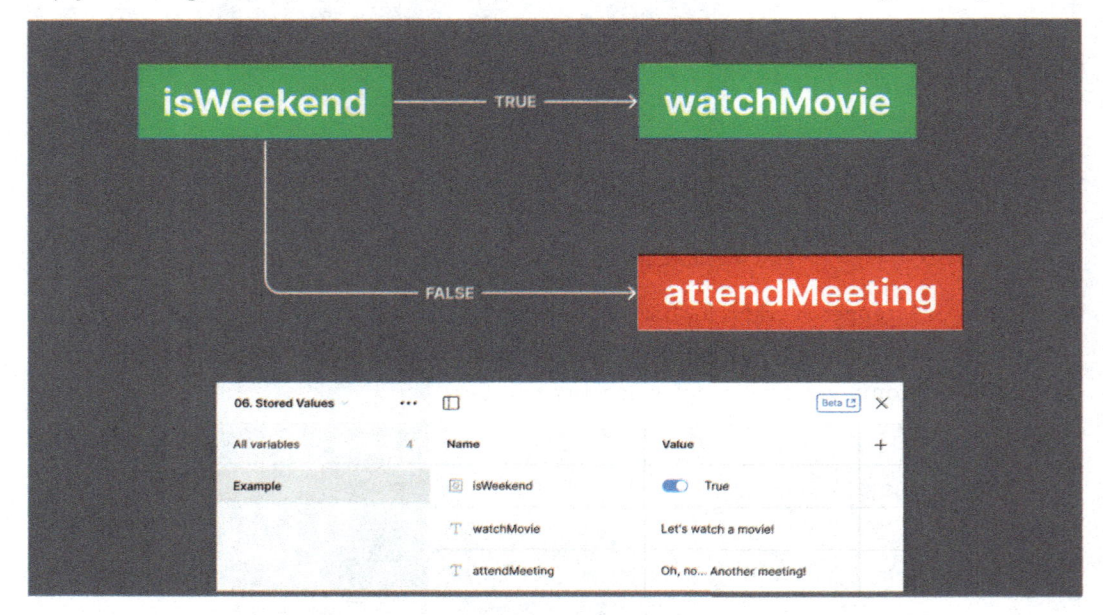

Figure 13.45 – If-else diagram

This straightforward concept will aid us in resolving the issue with our stepper. Before we get hands-on with the practical application, it's wise to think through our approach. It's essential, especially when dealing with conditionals, to have a clear plan in mind and to grasp the logic before diving in. In this scenario, we aim for the + button to function always, with no restrictions, while we want to apply a conditional solely to the - button. The idea is that "if" the counter isn't zero, then the - button works; else, it remains inactive. In practical terms:

1. Select the stepper's - button.
2. Remove any previously created interaction on it.
3. Add a new interaction, but this time, choose the **Conditional** type to access the **if-else** interface.
4. Specify the if condition by selecting that #counterValue should be **Not equal to** (a convenient list of comparatives is provided to ease this step) and set this value to **0**.

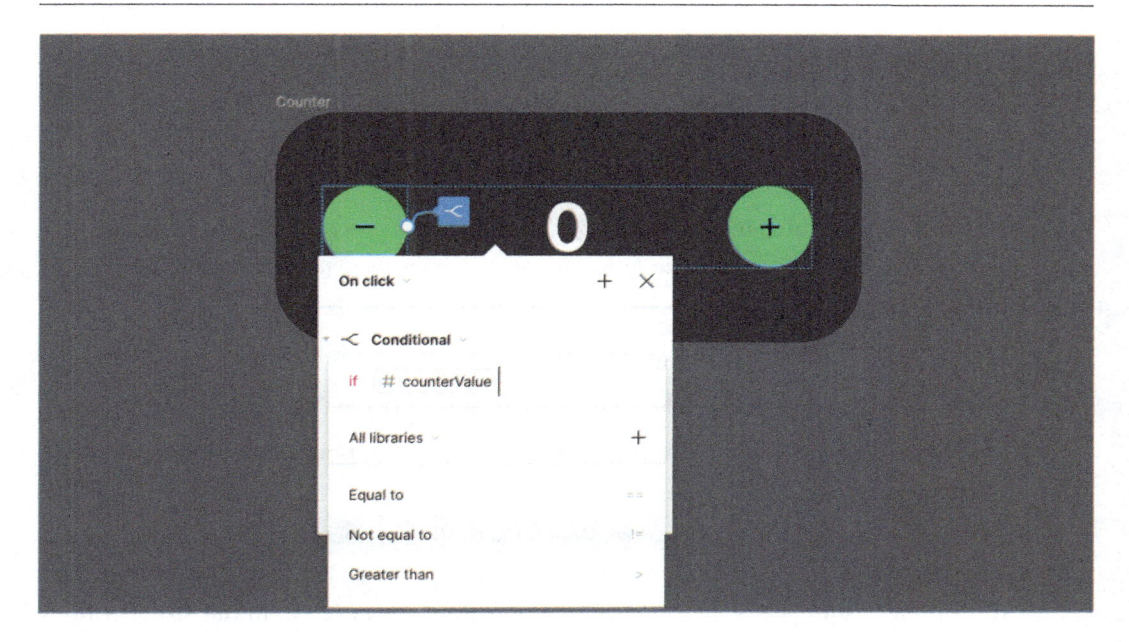

Figure 13.46 – A preset list of comparisons

If the condition mentioned above is satisfied, meaning if the value of the counter is different from zero, we want the button to be fully functional. In this case, we will insert a **Set variable** block, similar to the process we followed earlier. This part will instruct Figma on what action to execute when the condition is true – in this case, decrementing the counter value.

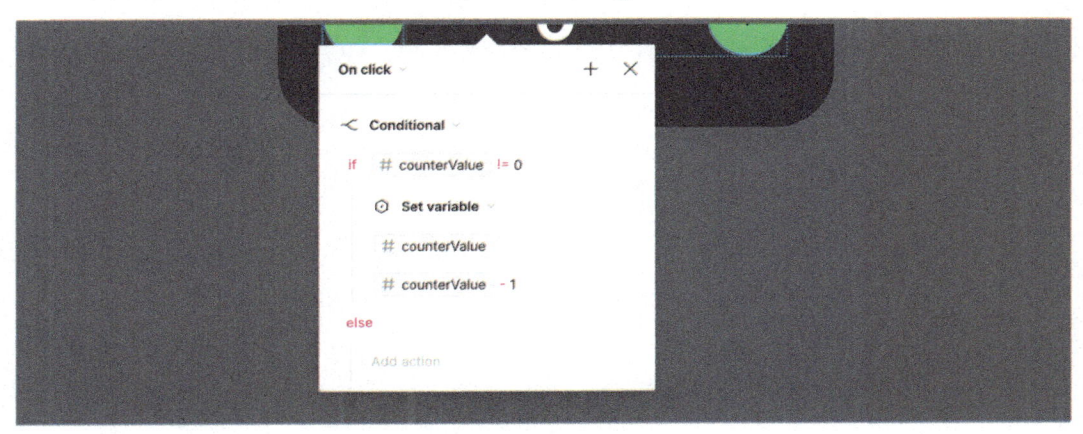

Figure 13.47 – Our first Conditional block

In this scenario, we'll leave the **else** block empty as we want the click to be ineffective when the counter value is at zero. Now, give the counter another try, and you'll see everything operates as anticipated – no negative values and all of it encapsulated within a single frame, streamlining our design while preserving the intended functionality.

Now, let's dive into something more complex. Although this is a specific case that you might not encounter often, understanding the underlying logic will empower you to tackle various challenges in your future projects. Our objective is to create a simple quiz app. To begin:

1. Design a basic interface skeleton for the app.
2. Create a component set named Selector with both active/inactive states.
3. Use instances of the **Selector** component within the app to represent the different answers to our question.
4. Here, we get to know a new feature. We can actually connect the variant's Booleans to Boolean variables. This means if we turn a variable to true, the variant can be switched to a different state. Let's then create three new **Boolean** variables in the **Stored Values** collection, one for each of the quiz's options (option1, option2, and option3), and set them to false.
5. Pick each **Selector** instance, then navigate to the component's properties and find the **Variable** icon. Assign each instance a unique **Boolean** variable (**option1**, **option2**, or **option3**) from the **Stored Values** collection.

Chapter 13

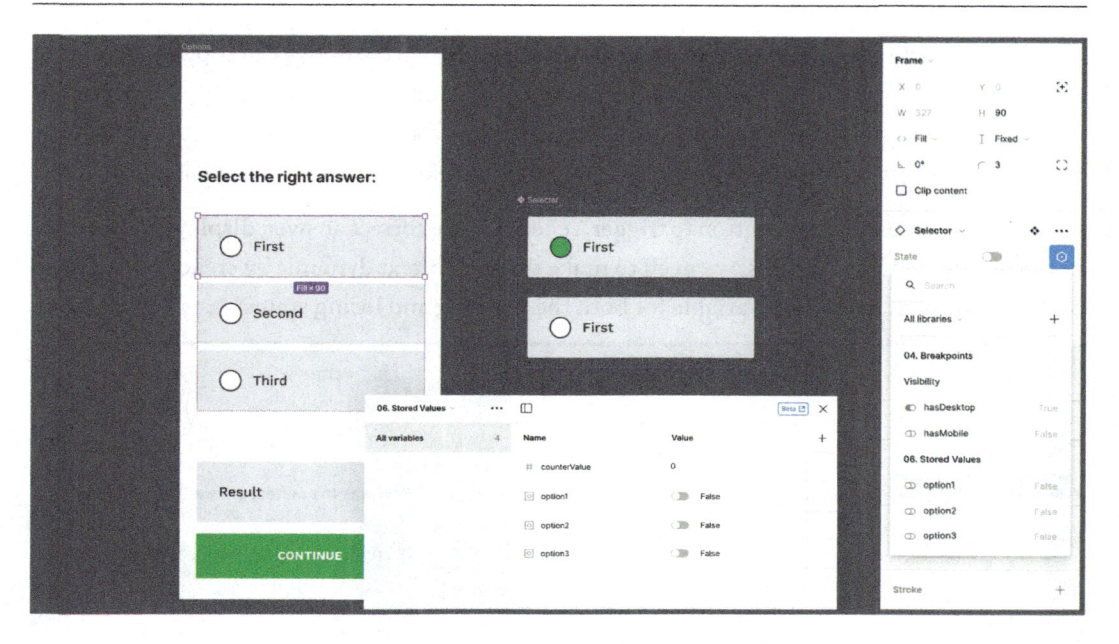

Figure 13.48 – Connecting variants to variables

Now we have the capability to track each answer, thanks to a variable bound to each one. The next step involves applying logic to these responses. What we aim for is to have a scenario where, upon clicking on a response, it gets activated, and if there were any other responses already selected, they get deactivated. We can achieve this by setting more than one output to a condition, as follows:

Figure 13.49 – Setting a conditional for the first selector

All that's left to do is to repeat the same steps with the other two boxes (we can copy the condition from the right panel, and paste it while selecting the second box, only changing the necessary values). Once this is done, if we launch the prototype, we should be able to select one and only one answer at a time, which will become active while deselecting the previous selection.

Next, we want the **Continue** button to trigger a check for the correct answer, displaying the result in the designated box. For this, we need to make the **Result** text dynamic by creating a variable with the dormant text, and a variable for both the winning and losing states:

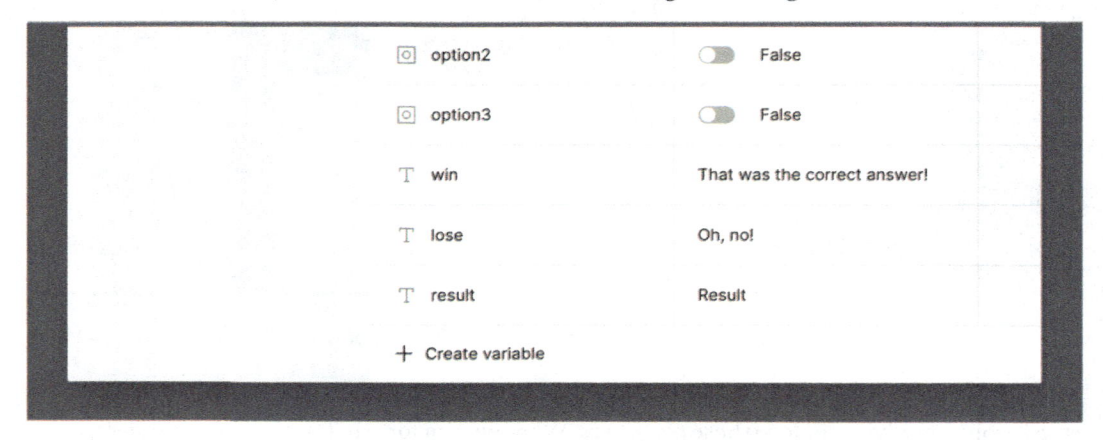

Figure 13.50 – Initializing new String variables

Apply the **Result** variable to the text field labeled `Result`, as shown in the following image:

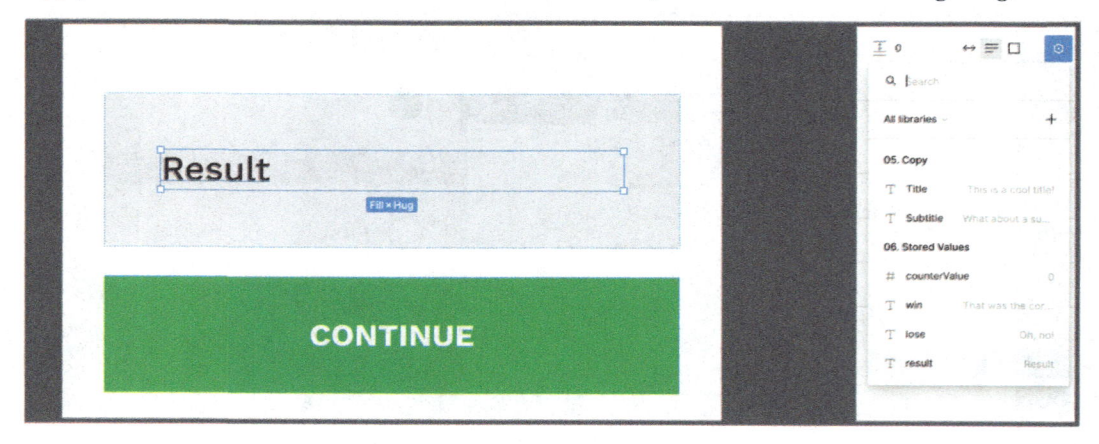

Figure 13.51 – Assigning the Result variable to the label

Then, proceed to assign an action to the **Continue** button upon clicking. We aim to simulate that the correct answer is the first one. The logic we'll use is as follows: upon clicking the button, we'll check if `option1` is set to **true**; if it is, then we'll update the **Result** text to display the **win** message. Otherwise, if `option1` is set to **false**, we'll display the **lose** message.

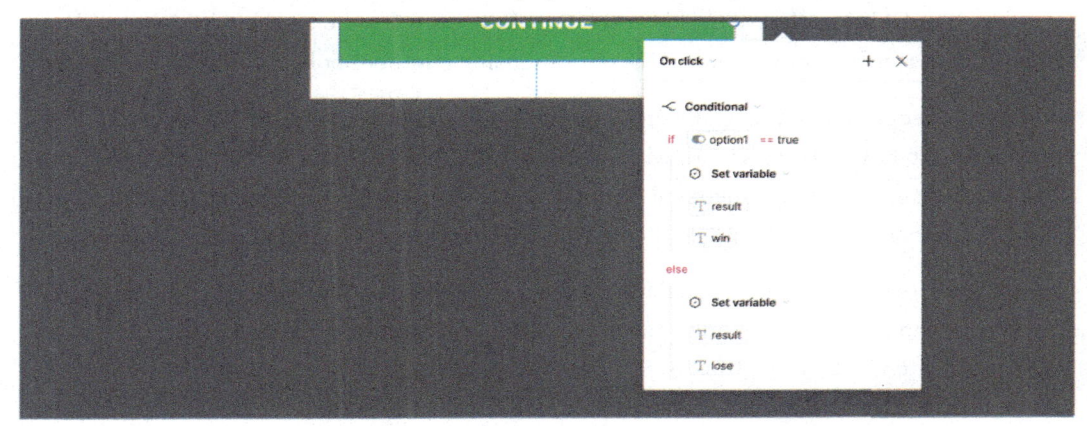

Figure 13.52 – The full logic behind our Continue button

Here we go. If the logic has been applied correctly in all aspects, you should now have a fully functional quiz product. And once again, all of this is accomplished within a single frame!

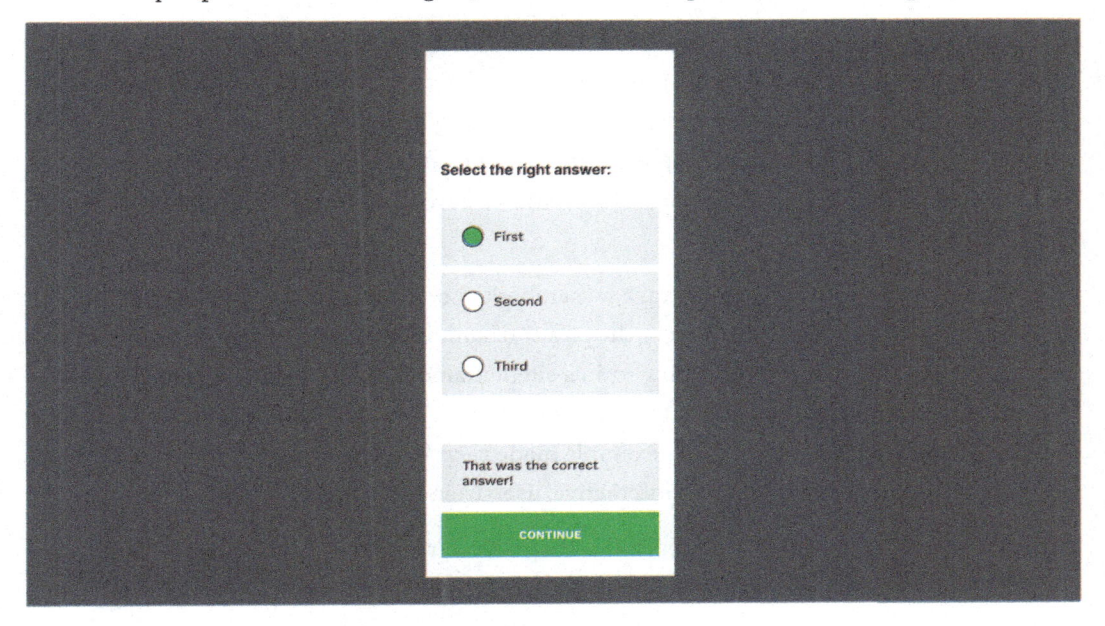

Figure 13.53 – Previewing the final prototype

With the structure in place, moving on to the aesthetic phase and enhancing the appeal of our design – especially given it's encapsulated within a single frame – becomes quite straightforward. There's room for creative exploration too. For instance, we can make the **Result** box change color based on the answer – green for correct and red for incorrect – by tweaking the assigned **Color** type variable. Additionally, we could set the **Continue** button to be disabled initially, and only enable it with the first click on one of the options, using another Boolean variable.

As you dive deeper into advanced conditional prototyping, you'll find many new possibilities. Understanding how variables work with conditions streamlines complex tasks and saves time. For instance, creating a fully functional e-commerce cart becomes less intimidating. Furthermore, blending smart animations and delays with variables can lead to even more engaging prototypes.

The more you explore, the more you'll realize that conditional prototyping significantly elevates your design capabilities. It not only makes complex designs manageable but also infuses a playful element into the creation process. Each new project transforms into an exciting playground where you can experiment, learn, and hone your skills. With variables and conditional prototyping, you're merely at the beginning of uncovering what's achievable in design. So, keep exploring, and enjoy the endless journey of discovery that lies ahead in your daily workflows!

Summary

In this last chapter, we ventured further into the powerful features of Figma, exploring the intricacies of variables and conditional prototyping. You discovered how these advanced tools can significantly streamline complex design tasks, making your design process more efficient and enjoyable. Starting with a simple input stepper component, we demonstrated how variables could be employed to manage dynamic values within a design, paving the way for more complex applications.

Transitioning to a more challenging task, we embarked on creating a basic quiz app. Through this exercise, you got a firsthand look at the power of conditional prototyping, enabling interactive and dynamic user experiences all within a single frame. You learned how to structure your components, use Boolean variables to track user interactions, and apply conditional logic to manage the flow of user actions. This example made clear how the integration of variables and conditionality could lead to creating interactive, user-friendly designs with ease.

With the knowledge and skills acquired in this chapter, you're now better equipped to tackle more complex design challenges. The exploration of variables and conditional prototyping has not only enriched your design toolkit but also expanded your horizon on what's possible within Figma.

As we close this chapter and the book, remember, the learning doesn't stop here – and it actually never does. The field of design is vast and ever-evolving. Continually challenge yourself with new projects, explore the endless possibilities with the tools at your disposal, and keep honing your skills. The real adventure lies in applying what you've learned in real-world scenarios, solving actual design problems, and creating delightful user experiences.

Your journey in mastering Figma has been remarkable and filled with learning, experimentation, and growth. Keep experimenting, keep learning, and most importantly, keep designing. The path you've traversed has equipped you with a robust set of skills, and the experiences gained will undoubtedly serve you well in all your future endeavors. Here's to many more creative and exciting projects ahead. Thank you for allowing this book to be a part of your design journey.

Learn more on Discord

To join the Discord community for this book – where you can share feedback, ask questions to the author, and learn about new releases – follow the QR code below:

`https://packt.link/figma`

‹packt›

packt.com

Subscribe to our online digital library for full access to over 7,000 books and videos, as well as industry leading tools to help you plan your personal development and advance your career. For more information, please visit our website.

Why subscribe?

- Spend less time learning and more time coding with practical eBooks and Videos from over 4,000 industry professionals
- Improve your learning with Skill Plans built especially for you
- Get a free eBook or video every month
- Fully searchable for easy access to vital information
- Copy and paste, print, and bookmark content

At www.packt.com, you can also read a collection of free technical articles, sign up for a range of free newsletters, and receive exclusive discounts and offers on Packt books and eBooks.

Other Books You May Enjoy

If you enjoyed this book, you may be interested in these other books by Packt:

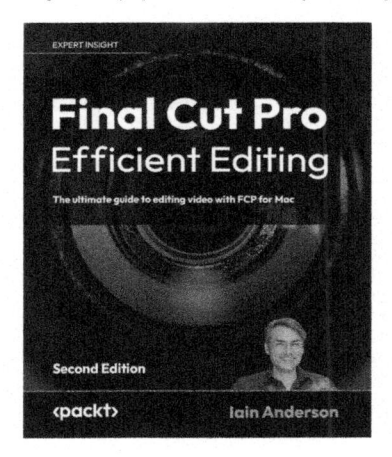

Final Cut Pro Efficient Editing, Second Edition

Iain Anderson

ISBN: 9781837631674

- Organize and manage media from multiple sources
- Edit and manipulate video with an intuitive interface and powerful tools
- Streamline your workflow with customizable workspaces and keyboard shortcuts
- Sync and edit multicam interviews with ease and learn advanced trimming techniques
- Use advanced audio and color grading tools to achieve a professional-quality finish
- Work with other editors using the built-in collaboration tools

- Create stunning visual effects and complex motion graphics titles
- Export video projects in a variety of formats for delivery to multiple platforms and user devices

The Music Producer's Ultimate Guide to FL Studio 21, Second Edition

Mr. Joshua Au-Yeung

ISBN: 9781837631650

- Get up and running with FL Studio 21
- Compose melodies and chord progressions on the piano roll
- Mix your music effectively with mixing techniques and plugins, such as compressors and equalizers
- Record into FL Studio, pitch-correct and retime samples, and follow advice for applying effects to vocals
- Create vocal harmonies and learn how to use vocoders to modulate your vocals with an instrument
- Create glitch effects, transform audio samples into playable instruments, and sound design with cutting-edge effects
- Develop your brand to promote your music effectively
- Publish your music online and collect royalty revenues

Learning C# by Developing Games with Unity, Second Edition

Mr. Harrison Ferrone

ISBN: 9781837636877

- Understanding programming fundamentals by breaking them down into their basic parts
- Comprehensive explanations with sample codes of object-oriented programming and how it applies to C#
- Follow simple steps and examples to create and implement C# scripts in Unity
- Divide your code into pluggable building blocks using interfaces, abstract classes, and class extensions
- Grasp the basics of a game design document and then move on to blocking out your level geometry, adding lighting and a simple object animation
- Create basic game mechanics such as player controllers and shooting projectiles using C#
- Become familiar with stacks, queues, exceptions, error handling, and other core C# concepts
- Learn how to handle text, XML, and JSON data to save and load your game data

Flutter Cookbook, Second Edition

Simone Alessandria

ISBN: 9781803245430

- Familiarize yourself with Dart fundamentals and set up your development environment
- Efficiently track and eliminate code errors with proper tools
- Create various screens using multiple widgets to effectively manage data
- Craft interactive and responsive apps by incorporating routing, page navigation, and input field text reading
- Design and implement a reusable architecture suitable for any app
- Maintain control of your codebase through automated testing and developer tooling
- Develop engaging animations using the necessary tools
- Enhance your apps with ML features using Firebase MLKit and TensorFlow Lite
- Successfully publish your app on the Google Play Store and the Apple App Store

Packt is searching for authors like you

If you're interested in becoming an author for Packt, please visit authors.packtpub.com and apply today. We have worked with thousands of developers and tech professionals, just like you, to help them share their insight with the global tech community. You can make a general application, apply for a specific hot topic that we are recruiting an author for, or submit your own idea.

Share your thoughts

Now you've finished *Designing and Prototyping Interfaces with Figma*, we'd love to hear your thoughts! Scan the QR code below to go straight to the Amazon review page for this book and share your feedback or leave a review on the site that you purchased it from.

https://packt.link/r/1835464602

Your review is important to us and the tech community and will help us make sure we're delivering excellent quality content.

Index

A

Adobe Illustrator (AI) 87
Adobe XD
　used, for transitioning Figma 9-12
advanced prototyping
　with conditionals 412-422
　with variables 411-422
advanced user testing 319, 320
advanced vectors
　with Pen tool 86
After delay trigger 274
AI flow 367
aliasing 382
Animation parameter 266
app structure
　developing 92
　interface, shaping 95-100
　skeleton flow, creating 93, 95
Asana 376, 377
Assets panel 66, 67
auto layout 142-144
　alignment 146, 147
　applying, to interface 156
　button, shaping 156-167

　direction 144
　element, adding 147, 148
　element, rearranging 147, 148
　element, removing 147-149
　gap 144
　nesting 149, 150
　padding 145
　view, completing 167-173

B

Background blur 123
blend modes 121
breakpoints 235, 236
　Content Detail view 242, 243
　Home view 239-242
　Login view 238, 239
　Sign Up view 239

C

Cascading Style Sheet (CSS) 52, 335
Clay Mockups 3D 364
collections 395, 396
color and effect styles
　creating 134-138
　managing 134-138

color model 122
color modes 119-121
color palette 122
  blend modes 121
  color model 122
  color modes 119-121
  color styles 122, 123
  eyedropper tool 122
  selecting 118, 119
colors
  working 112
color styles 122, 123
comments 314
components 178-181
  Content Detail view, setting up 199-203
  creating 178
  extending, with variants 198
  organizing 178
  used, for building view 182-184
conditional prototyping 381, 409
  logic 409-411
constraints 154, 155
Content Detail page
  overview 253-256
Content Detail view
  setting up 199
Content Reel 363
Contrast 365

D

Dark Mode 393
Design panel 67, 68
design systems 351-354

desktop app
  versus web app 8
desktop interface 244
  scaling up 245-253
development project
  documenting 340-342
  extending 338, 339
  improving 340-342
  reiterating 340-342
Dev Mode 331, 332
  exploring 329, 330
  extending 337, 338
digital product 339
Drop shadow 123

E

Ease parameters 269
effects
  creating 123, 124
  working 112
elements
  resizing 150-152
Encapsulated PostScript (EPS) 87
eyedropper tool 122

F

feedback
  working with 313
FigGPT 368
FigJam
  account and notifications 18, 19
  brainstorming 28-31
  exploring 22, 23

Index

files 17, 18
ideas and collaboration, exploring 22
ideas, defining 31, 32
marker tool 24
moodboards and personas, creating 33
sections 25
select and hand tool 23
shapes and connectors 25
stamps and reactions 26
stickers 27
sticky notes 24
table 26
templates 27
text 25
user flow, building 38-44
widgets 27

FigJam, moodboards and personas
competitive analysis, conducting 34
research phase 33, 34
streaming services sector 35
user personas, creating 36-38

FigJam template 350, 351

FigJam widgets
using 373

Figma 4, 5
account, creating 6
community 14
designs, transferring 13
drafts 14
exploring 13
exporting 324
files 17, 18
formats 324, 325
multiple-asset export 325-329
need for 5

plan, selecting 6, 7
plugins 357
plugins, managing 357-362
plugins, running 357-362
recents 14
reference link 7
single-asset export 325-329
teams and projects 14-16
transitioning, from Adobe XD 9
transitioning, from Sketch 9

Figma Autoname 369

Figma Community
accessing 347-349
exploring 346
FigJam template 350, 351
publishing 347-349

Figma design project 48
file types 48, 49
frames and groups 50, 51
interface overview 52, 53

Figma shapes 78
basic shape 78-81
combining shape 82-85

Figma tool sets
Help Center 72

Figma tool sets, left panel
Assets panel 66, 67
exploring 65
Layers and Pages panel 65, 66

Figma tool sets, right panel
Design panel 67, 68
exploring 67
Prototype panel 69, 70

Figma widgets
using 373

file

code design 334-336

overviewing 333, 334

flows

structuring 316-319

Font Installer

setting up 9

font pairing

reference link 114

font service

reference link 114

frames transitions

moving between 263-271

G

grids 106, 108

overview 106

grid styles

creating 126-129

managing 126-129

guides 108

working 108, 109

H

High-Fidelity (Hi-Fi) 125

hotspot 264

hue, saturation, brightness (HSB) 122

hue, saturation, luminance (HSL) 122

I

Inline Preview

using 305

Inner shadow 123

interactive components 280

creating 281-288

structuring 279

interactive overflows

creating 288

interactive overlays

creating 288

used, for making view scrollable 289-292

interactive prototype

Inline Preview, using 305

running, on desktop/web 298-304

running, on smartphone/tablet 305-308

viewing 298

interface overlays

creating 292-294

J

Jambot 378, 379

Jira 376, 377

K

Key/Gamepad trigger 273

L

Layer blur 123

Layers panel 65, 66

layout grids 108-111

libraries

managing 213-217

Light Mode 393

LottieFiles 366

Low-Fidelity (Lo-Fi) 125

M

Magician 371, 372
modes 393, 394
Mouse down trigger 273
Mouse enter trigger 273
Mouse leave trigger 273
Mouse up trigger 273
multiplayer features
   working with 211-213
multiple-asset export 325-329

O

On click/On tap trigger 271, 272
On drag trigger 272

P

padding 145
Pages panel 65, 66
Pen tool
   advanced vectors 86
   discovering 87-90
plugins 362
   AI flow 366, 367
   Asana 376, 377
   checklist widget 375
   FigGPT 368
   FigJam widgets, using 373
   Figma Autoname 369
   Figma widgets, using 373
   iconify 363
   Jambot 378, 379
   Jira 376, 377
   LottieFiles 366
   Magician 371, 372
   versus widgets 373, 374
   Wireframe Designer 370
plugins, iconify
   Clay Mockups 3D 364
   Content Reel 363
   Contrast 365
Portable Document Format (PDF) 87, 325
Presentation view 301
prototype
   embedding 311-313
   linking 309, 310
   permissions, managing 309, 310
   sharing 309
Prototype panel 69, 70
   frame or component, selecting 71, 72
   inactive state 70
Prototype tab 298

Q

quicker method 161

R

resources
   designing 354, 356
   design systems 351-354
   finding 351
   UI kits 351-354
responsive design
   code, with fluid layouts 224-226
   discovering 224
   mobile first 226-233
reviews
   working with 313

S

Scalable Vector Graphics (SVG) 87
Selection Colors 123
single-asset export 325-329
Sketch 9
  used, for transitioning Figma 9-11
smart animate 274-276
  animating with 274
  upgrading 276-279
Smart Animate 274
styles 125
  file, preparing 125, 126
Symbols 178

T

tablet interface 234
text styles
  creating 130-134
  managing 130-134
toolbar 54
  quick shortcuts 63, 64
toolbar, core tools 54
  Comment tool 60
  Frame tool 56
  Hand tool 59
  menu 54, 55
  Move tool 55
  Pencil tool 58
  Pen tool 58
  Place image/video tool 57
  Resources tool 59
  Scale tool 55
  Section/Slice tool 56
  Shapes tool 57
  Text tool 59
toolbar, settings 60
  active users 62
  Dev mode 62, 63
  file title 60, 61
  present 63
  share button 62
  zoom/view 63
transitions 262, 263
triggers 262, 263
  After delay trigger 274
  exploring 271, 272
  Key/Gamepad 273
  Mouse down 273
  Mouse enter 273
  Mouse leave 273
  Mouse up 273
  On click/On tap 272
  On drag 272
  While hovering 273
  While pressing 273
typography 112-118
  advantages 117
  working 112

U

UI kits 340, 351-354
UI Prep Layout Grids 4.0 354
User Experience (UX) 38

V

variables 381-392
  need for 382-384
  responsive and multilingual 397-408
variants 198
  implementing 203-210
  need for 199
  used, for extending components 198
vector graphics 86, 87
vector networks 90, 92
version history
  preserving 217-220
view
  building, with components 182-184
  content cards 191-193
  main carousel 187-190
  repeated rows 194-198
  top navigation menu 184-187
viewers 315, 316

W

web app
  versus desktop app 8
Web Content Accessibility Guidelines (WCAG) 365
web interface 244
  scaling up 245-253
While hovering trigger 273
While pressing trigger 273
widgets 375
  versus plugins 373, 374
wireframe 76, 77
  evolution 76
  mobile-first 77
Wireframe Designer 370

Download a free PDF copy of this book

Thanks for purchasing this book!

Do you like to read on the go but are unable to carry your print books everywhere? Is your eBook purchase not compatible with the device of your choice?

Don't worry, now with every Packt book you get a DRM-free PDF version of that book at no cost.

Read anywhere, any place, on any device. Search, copy, and paste code from your favorite technical books directly into your application.

The perks don't stop there, you can get exclusive access to discounts, newsletters, and great free content in your inbox daily

Follow these simple steps to get the benefits:

1. Scan the QR code or visit the link below

https://packt.link/free-ebook/9781835464601

2. Submit your proof of purchase
3. That's it! We'll send your free PDF and other benefits to your email directly

Made in the USA
Columbia, SC
31 August 2024